WE ARE ALL EQUAL

DATE DUE

DEMCO 38-296

WE ARE ALL EQUAL

Student Culture and Identity

at a Mexican Secondary School,

1988–1998 · *Bradley A. U. Levinson*

DUKE UNIVERSITY PRESS

Durham and London, 2001

Printed in the United States of America on acid-free paper ∞
Typeset in Adobe Minion by Keystone Typesetting, Inc.
Library of Congress Cataloging-in-Publication Data appear
on the last printed page of this book. Acknowledgments
for the use of copyrighted material appear on page 434
which constitutes an extension of the copyright page.

To Joan Pearl Levinson,

Arcadia Rangel, Ofelia Hernández,

and Debra Susan Unger Levinson—

strong and heartful women, across

cultures and generations

CONTENTS

ILLUSTRATIONS

PREFACE

My mother's hand has always moved with special grace when pointing or waving; she would have made a fine parade queen or even First Lady. Not long ago, I rediscovered this technique of hers while watching a video compilation of my family's early super-eight home movies. She was in her late teens, on vacation with her father and stepmother, strutting around a varied Mexican landscape: here she overlooks a broad bay (Acapulco? Puerto Vallarta?), pointing toward a large ship; there she stands in a Mexico City square, drawing attention to what seems to be an Aztec revival dance, Indians chanting and swaying; there again she stalks the great pyramids at Teotihuacán, her broad smile and motioning hand shadowed by the Temple of the Sun.

These images of my young mother came as something of a shock. Sure, she had occasionally mentioned her trip to Mexico. Sure, she had worked for several years as a bilingual teacher's aide at an elementary school, keeping her basic Spanish intact. And yes, a part of my *father's* extended family had lived briefly in northern Mexico—our cousins fluent in Spanish because of an unforeseen immigration detour. And yes, finally, I had my own fleeting history of contact with Mexico: quick family trips to Baja California, the somber Spanish cadences of our housecleaner's weekly visit, a few Mexican kids in my high school and baseball league with whom I made passing acquaintance. I had nevertheless persisted in my convenient self-image: the thirty-something cultural anthropologist whose specialization in Mexican studies served as a symbolic rupture with his suburban Jewish California roots.

My family emigrated from Eastern Europe, my grandmothers arriving from Ukraine as very young girls. Immigration officials at Ellis Island had bestowed my great-grandfather the last name of Gibbons because, so the story goes, he misunderstood when they asked for his last name and could only think to give the name of his cousin's street in Denver—his final destination. At home and in the synagogue, I adopted the tale of the Jews as a diasporic people destined to build a life from the ground up wherever we might land. In the histories of Europe and elsewhere, we were one of the great cultural "others," perennially condemned to a life on the persecuted margins or else a long struggle to "pass" into the center. Yet in the home video, I recognized another dimension of this history: an image of the Jew as triumphant, confident consumer of other cultural worlds. The filmed trip to Mexico was for me an important sign that my grandfather had made it to the center and thereby acquired a key privilege of U.S. citizenship: the right to consume the Other symbolically. And there was my mother, sweet charm aside, casting too this imperial gaze. To what extent was my own personal journey, then, the outcome rather than the antithesis of this historical-cultural trajectory? What was I trying to learn about myself, what awareness was I questioning or consolidating, as I set out to encounter the "otherness" of a Mexican school?

This book is the product of my long familiarity with a Mexican secondary school (*secundaria*) and its surrounding community. I first met some of the teachers and students at this school in 1985, and I have conducted ethnographic research there on and off since 1988, for a total of some two years of residence and observation. Yet rather than starting with the school itself, I've chosen to present personal vignettes that both provide the reader with a sense of the author and present emblematic issues in the book: self versus other, sameness versus difference, justice versus privilege, personal advancement versus collective solidarity, nationalism versus globalization. As I explore the ways such issues play themselves out in the lives of different Mexican secondary school students, I also examine my own relation to them.

I've often fancied myself an activist for progressive causes concerned with peace and social justice. In high school, I wrote anguished poetry and worried about the Bomb and world hunger. In college, I protested the 1982 invasion of Grenada and canvassed homes for the nuclear freeze movement. Between classes and Buddhist meditation sittings, I volunteered at the Resource Center for Nonviolence in Santa Cruz, California, and gathered signatures on behalf of Mexican farmworkers in the southern part of the county (victims of excessive work and pesticide poisoning). As a protest against the use of Central American beef, whose production is still responsible for the ongoing decimation of primary rain forest, I even helped launch a graphic form of guerrilla theater in front of a local Burger King: we mocked up a two-person beef steer that walked around eating leaves and crapping Whoppers. In all of this I expressed my political ideals, my horror at the shortsighted selfishness and crass individualism of U.S. society, and my hope for a more just world.

April 1995: I am teaching an upper-division anthropology of education course at Augustana College in Rock Island, Illinois. My students have read *Learning Capitalist Culture* by Douglas Foley and *Jocks and Burnouts* by Penelope Eckert. These books describe the painful factionalism of U.S. high school student culture, the class- and race-inflected divisions that often seal the fates of educational careers. Today, we are discussing a draft of my article that describes the "culture of equality" at a Mexican secondary school, with its emphasis on unity and solidarity (see chapter 4). The students surprise me by condemning the uniformity and, as they put it, "pressure to conform" in the school; they think the Mexican school has taken away students' freedom of choice and expression. In light of the prior readings, I had expected a more sympathetic reception to the Mexican teachers' and students' attempts to transcend their differences. Yet my students challenge my obviously admiring, perhaps romantic portrait of Mexican solidarity; they see it as an apology for heavy-handed limits on self-expression.

April 1998: I am a special visitor at an ethnically diverse, lower-income junior high school class in Chula Vista, California, near San Diego. The school has decided just this year to institute a uniform policy: dark blue pants with white tops and a dark sweater or jacket. To begin a conversation about Mexican schools and students, I ask these students what they think about the new rules at their own school. Most of them grumble about having to wear uniforms, and when I probe further, one girl says in tones of great exasperation, "They keep us from expressing ourselves." The students seem incredulous that their Mexican counterparts would want to wear uniforms in order to keep costs down and minimize the perception of differences among their classmates.

November 1996: I have been asked to participate as a discussant at a small Indianapolis conference on the effects of the North American Free Trade Agreement since its inception in 1993. My panel is on "national identity and cultural perceptions." I share some of the data I've collected on summer field trips in 1993 and 1995, especially those that reflect parents' and teachers' concerns over the influx of U.S. values through the media. Mexican youth in the region where I do my research have increasingly raised challenges to parental and school authority. Adults seem worried that youth have little allegiance to the Mexican nation, little interest in working for the common good. In the course of my presentation I must have made reference to the negative influence of "American individualism" because, at the break, an older man comes over to confront me. He asks if I'm a cultural anthropologist, and I confirm this. Then he wonders aloud how I can so easily sacrifice my "objectivity" about U.S. society and culture. He scolds me for abandoning the anthropological standard of cultural relativism for my own society, for making clear my critique of individualism. "Did it really come across that way?" I ask. "Your sympathies? Yes, loud and clear, loud and clear," he replies. I begin to consider what kind of personal and political drama I'm playing out through my Mexican research, why I so readily identify with Mexicans' emphasis on family and group loyalty, and their worries about U.S. individualism. I also reflect on whether my interlocutor is right: Have I conveniently abandoned the principle of cultural relativism, or have I merely suspended it in order to evaluate more critically my "own" culture and thereby take a stand in a contentious world of multiple differences? As the day wears on, however, I'm less inclined to lament my own contradictions. I surmise from his other comments that far from being "objective" himself, this man has an ideological ax to grind. His is a free enterprise dream that assumes the fittest cultural ideas will survive in the global marketplace. From this frankly neoliberal perspective, U.S. individualism represents the freedom all humanity desires; its diffusion will be the liberal linchpin sweeping away the archaic and authoritarian structures of the past.

When ordinary Mexicans hear about my research, they often solicit my assessment of their educational system: How are our schools doing? they inquire. Are we far behind the United States? I give varying responses, presenting myself as a sociologist interested in social relations, not quite qualified to pass judgment on curricular or pedagogical matters (anthropologists in Mexico, as elsewhere perhaps, are typically perceived as experts only on matters of folklore, and indigenous and prehistoric cultures). When they press me, I tell them it depends on the school, the subject, and the teacher, but in world history and geography, it seems, Mexicans are well beyond the United States. In mathematics and language, they may be equal; in the natural sciences, perhaps behind. These are all gross speculations. I suggest that the social and aesthetic components of education are much richer in Mexico. There is a greater concern with educating the whole person in the secundaria. Students learn more about the art of getting along and appreciating the world. In the United States, subject matter reigns supreme. Most Mexicans nod knowingly at this message, smiling and taking pride, but they still worry about the level of educational quality. They've been told that the global economy requires a higher-caliber education. They sense themselves now in a competitive system, and they want to know about their chances for survival in the new world order.

When U.S. citizens hear about my research, they tend to assert rather than ask: Things are kind of backward down there, huh?

Ethnography refers to the research process originally developed by anthropologists—long-term participant observation and interviewing designed to understand local social relations and cultural worlds. The kind of work represented in this book can best be called "critical ethnography," and one important component of any critical ethnography is a high degree of reflexivity about the process of doing research. In ethnographic work, specifically, reflexivity implies awareness of the ethnographer's self in the social order and in the construction of knowledge about that order (Shacklock and Smyth 1998). Some critics suggest that too much reflexivity threatens to occlude the real subject of our research, and I have thus sought a balance between self-disclosure and analytic description (see Foley 1998). Following the French sociologist Pierre Bourdieu, I am wary of overly personalistic forms of reflexivity that fail to examine the social *position* of the researcher, and the intellectual presuppositions that make possible certain forms of analysis and critique (Wacquant 1992, 36–41). Yet I also believe that field research calls forth rather more idiosyncratic attributes that are not entirely reducible to a social position. Thus, I have attempted to be honest about how my prior ideological and political commitments led me to "select" the field and might still lead me to favor certain interpretations of the data over others. I have also tried to allow the emerging relationships, insights, and dynamics of the fieldwork itself guide my interpretations (Levinson 1998c). Like the ethnographers I admire most, I have endeavored to let the field surprise me. Rather than provide a separate account of my "fieldwork journey" (Lareau and Schultz 1996), I write myself into the many surprises the field offered up.

What does it mean to do ethnography in a critical way? In the field of educational studies alone, this question has occasioned quite a discussion, a whole politics of "the critical."[1] Whatever definition they espouse, most scholars would agree that critical ethnography denotes a research method *informed* by a critical theory of some sort, *committed* to an analysis of domination and the search for an alternative project of social justice, and *enacted* through a constantly reflexive approach to the practice of gathering data and generating knowledge.[2] My own practice draws from a variety of theoretical sources. I eschew the rigid distinction between so-called emancipatory and hermeneutic knowledge, preferring instead to adopt an eclectic stance I call "critical interpretivism."[3]

The challenge of writing and reading such a text bears some mention. In any work of cultural interpretation, the author must remain faithful to the situated meanings of his/her subjects' lives, yet render those meanings intelligible, perhaps even sympathetic, to a broader audience. This act of translation carries numerous risks. It becomes especially problematic when the potential audience includes an enormous variety of readers (such as schoolteachers, university students, and professional academic colleagues) in several different countries (including Mexico). Even among my colleagues, I aspire to build conceptual bridges across disciplines and discursive fields that frequently do not meet—anthropology, sociology, comparative education, cultural studies, and Latin American studies. How to write a compelling, edifying account for these many readers? How to build "theory"—a way of conceptualizing the world—into the flow of the text? Here again I have sought to strike a balance. Some readers may resent the abundance of scholarly quotes and citations, but they are necessary to make conceptual connections. The level of discourse may shift at times, but generally I have sacrificed the subtler points of scholarly exposition for a more fluid, engaging narrative. Most of the explicit theoretical discussion has been set apart in the concluding chapter and a substantial appendix. The careful reader, of course, will note that theory is woven throughout the text. For instance, the regular mention of the "past" in an ethnographic study of the "present" advances an implicit theory of historical conditioning and cultural particularity. Such historical grounding is often absent in studies of U.S. or European student culture, where so many of the cultural assumptions historically sedimented in contemporary institutions are taken for granted (Varenne and McDermott 1998). Likewise, a theory about the relation between institutional structure and forms of subjectivity is exemplified, indeed made manifest, in the very titles of the chapters and the order of my historical-ethnographic narrative.

A mention may be necessary about a few other textual devices I've seen fit to employ. First, in order to protect my informants, I have given pseudonyms to the school, the city where it is located, and all the persons comprising my research. Such anonymity may seem unusual to some historians and anthropologists, though it is customary practice in most educational research. Many of my Mexican informants found it unusual as well. No doubt this strategy has required me to jettison a good deal of local historical and cultural detail in my account, a loss I do not take lightly. Still, this research was originally conducted under the supervision of the Institutional Review Board at the University of North Carolina–Chapel Hill, for whom I submitted a research design emphasizing confidentiality. During the fieldwork itself, I always assured participants that their responses would remain confidential. Few could imagine what harm might come to them should such a promise be breached, yet education is a politically and emotionally charged field in Mexico. Some of the statements and actions I report here can be controversial indeed, and might damage careers or reputations if they were to be associated with specific persons. Thus, I have chosen to maintain their anonymity.

I had also originally hoped to provide bilingual readers with much of the original Spanish from interviews and observations so they might independently assess my translations and interpretations. In the end, such a strategy made the manuscript too costly and cumbersome. Nonetheless, I have retained the original Spanish for a number of phrases and quotes, especially those given by students themselves, in cases where the use of language is either difficult to translate or significant for my analysis of discourse.

ACKNOWLEDGMENTS

There are many people to thank for helping bring this project to fruition, and I would like to make my social and intellectual indebtedness a matter of public record. First and foremost, I am extremely grateful to the people of San Pablo and Escuela Secundaria Federal. I could not have asked for more forthright cooperation from teachers, students, and their parents. Though I cannot acknowledge them by name, I am especially appreciative of the permission and support shown by the school's acting principal and vice principals. A very dear thanks also to those teachers, too numerous to mention, who generously allowed me into their classrooms and even their homes, offering their friendship and views of school life. Not all of them will agree with my analysis here, but I hope they find it educative in the best sense of the word.

My most profound gratitude must go to the students themselves, the main protagonists of this study. I wish I could reveal their names, for they deserve the honor. The students gave freely of their time, endured sometimes difficult and confusing interviews, and usually took the hint when I was fishing for an invitation to their extracurricular activities. Many of their parents went out of their way to contribute to my research or simply offer their hospitality. I remain deeply touched by the humble and selfless generosity of these families. To them I also give thanks.

For their assistance, solidarity, and friendship in San Pablo, I would like to acknowledge Marina Rodríguez and her family, Gustavo Nogués, Rubén Tapia and his family, Fidel Rodríguez, Fernando Ponce, Javier López and his family, and Alfredo Guzmán and Dalinda García. A very special thanks to the family of Atanasio Natividad and Arcadia Rangel for their emotional and material support. I am equally indebted to my dear friend and research assistant Ofelia Hernández, who shared with me the benefits of her keen mind and well-founded observations on local life. Thanks also to her sister, and my *comadre*, Lourdes Hernández. *Salud a todos!*

In Mexico City, many people provided support, advice, information, and constructive criticism. My institutional affiliate for a Fulbright grant in 1990–1991, the Departamento de Investigaciones Educativas (part of the CINVESTAV/IPN), graciously offered the use of computers and library resources for the completion of this work. In addition, many of the scholars, students, and support staff associated with the DIE gave me their time and friendship. Thanks, above all, to Elsie Rockwell for her thoughtful advice throughout this project. I also extend my appreciation to Ruth Mercado, Rafael Quiroz, Justa Ezpeleta, Eduardo Weiss, Rollin Kent, María de Ibarrola, Olac Fuentes, Lucila Galván, Teresa Romero, and Georgina Ramírez. Elsewhere in Mexico City, the family of José Antonio Martínez, as well as Daniela Spenser, Yael Bitrán, Eduardo Franco, and Siloé Amorim provided great friendship and comfort.

From 1988 to 1999, I benefited from my relationships with a number of other Mexican intellectuals and scholarly institutions. Among these institutions, I am particularly grateful to the personnel at the library of the Museo Nacional de Antropología, the Centro de Estudio Educativos, the Universidad Pedagógica Nacional, El Colegio de México, the now-defunct Centro de Investigaciones y Servicios Educativos of the Universidad Nacional Autónoma de México, the Instituto de Investigaciones Históricas of the Universidad Michoacana de San Nicolás de Hidalgo, the Instituto Michoacano de Ciencias de la Educación, El Colegio de Michoacán, and the Centro Regional de Educación Funcional para América Latina. Since 1992, I have also gained a great deal from my association with the scholars of the Interamerican Symposium on Ethnographic Educational Research. Thanks to Gary Anderson, Ann Nihlen, and Guillermina Engelbrecht for inviting me to join them in Albuquerque in 1992. My work has no doubt been enriched through presentations at the symposium, and through discussions with scholars like Beatriz Calvo, Margaret LeCompte, Etelvina Sandoval, Juan Fidel Zorrilla, Mario Rueda, Gabriela Delgado, Donna Deyhle, María Bertely, William Tierney, and David Bloome.

For financial and technical support, I am indebted to several institutions. During my graduate education, the Tinker Foundation, through the University of North Carolina's Institute for Latin American Studies, sponsored a predissertation trip to Mexico, while the International Institute for Education provided a Fulbright grant for my 1990–1991 year of dissertation research in Mexico. The Spencer Foundation provided a Dissertation-Year Fellowship to support a portion of the writing process, while the Graduate School of the University of North Carolina provided an On-Campus Dissertation Fellowship in 1992. The Department of Anthropology of the University of North Carolina hired me to teach courses between and after fieldwork stints, and this experience was both timely and useful. Ms. Suphronia Cheek deserves special mention for countless points of assistance and advice. Faculty and staff at the Institute for Latin American Studies—especially Sharon Mújica, Josie McNeill, and Lars Schoultz—were quite helpful.

Since moving on from the University of North Carolina, I first encountered the gracious support of colleagues and staff at Augustana College, particularly those in the Department of Sociology, Anthropology, and Social Welfare. In the School of Education at Indiana University, which I joined in 1996, I have been blessed with colleagues and students who are both decent and smart. Special thanks to Robert Arnove and Margaret Sutton for numerous favors and small kindnesses. Thanks also to Sandy Strain and the student assistants in the Department of Educational Leadership and Policy Studies. Finally, many thanks to Valerie Millholland, Patricia Mickelberry, and Cindy Milstein of Duke University Press for their fine work on the manuscript.

From 1996 to 1998, I held a National Academy of Education Spencer Postdoctoral Fellowship, which offered an unusual opportunity to return to Mexico for follow-up research and to engage in conversations with other NAE Spencer fellows. I am grateful to the NAE and the Spencer Foundation for this support, and especially thank Shirley Brice Heath and Catherine Lacey for their roles in bringing together a mentoring network for younger scholars.

A great number of students and scholars have heard or read various bits and pieces of this book over the years, and I hope to have learned from their comments. A special recognition must go to the members of my Ph.D. committee at the University of North Carolina, who played an important part in the book's earlier formulations: Donald Nonini, Judith Farquhar, Gilbert Joseph, Patricia Pessar, Craig Calhoun, and Dorothy

Holland. As my adviser, Dorothy Holland offered astute comments, timely advice, and unwavering support, and she has continued to be a key interlocutor for my subsequent work. I count myself as extremely lucky to have had such a mentor and friend. Others who have contributed intellectually to the project by reading chapters or responding to talks include Michèle Foster, Mark Ginsburg, Rolland Paulston, Margaret Gibson, Andrew Hargreaves, Frederick Erickson, Ruth Paradise, Ray McDermott, Richard Blot, George Noblit, Beatriz Schmukler, Debra Skinner, Julian Groves, Ana María Alonso, Elsie Rockwell, Margaret Eisenhart, Margaret Sutton, and Doyle Stevick. For their detailed and insightful readings of the book manuscript, I especially thank Jan Nespor, Amy Stambach, Nora Haenn, Ellen Brantlinger, Janise Hurtig, Mary Kay Vaughan, and Douglas Foley. Of course, none of these people bears any responsibility for the analysis and interpretation here, which is entirely my own.

This work would not have been possible without the primary support and constant love of my immediate family. No greater gratitude can go to my parents, David and Joan Levinson, and the grandparents I was privileged to know growing up: Meyer Gibbons, Ruth Gibbons, and Evelyn Levinson. Along with a precious circle of friends, too numerous to mention, my family has provided rock-steady confidence and support. Finally, my wife, Debra S. Unger Levinson, weathered most of the storms associated with this project, putting up with more than a little absence and irritability. Her love for Mexico and her unwavering belief in the value of this book have been a source of inspiration to me. I hope the final product can match such inspiration.

INTRODUCTION

Questions and Methods

for a Study of Student Culture

Todos somos iguales. We are all equal. How many times had the students spoken some version of this phrase to me, and in how many different contexts? In my early fieldwork at this secondary school, I dutifully noted it down, but not until about halfway through the research did I realize just how pervasive the phrase was.

How, when, and where did this phrase crop up? In many cases, students asserted *todos somos iguales* in response to some prompt of mine. They brought it up in discussions I initiated about group dynamics, teacher favoritism, or a number of other school-related topics. I was struck by the way the students unanimously and vehemently rejected my suggestions that teachers might discriminate against students by ethnicity, class, or gender. Sometimes the students smuggled the words in obliquely, to mask how certain students appeared to be rejected by their classmates or to justify wearing the same school uniform every day. Sometimes they used the expression spontaneously, in heated conversation with other students or in explaining something when I had not even broached the subject. In every case, students said it with a kind of insistence, an urgency, that always caught my attention. It was as if they were trying to convince themselves and their classmates, as well as me, that it were true. It was as if they were at once affirming and ordering their experience.

The rhetorical assertion of equality required me to rethink many of the expectations I had carried into the field. I would be forced to work things out, as my Mexican friends might say, *sobre la marcha*—as I went along. After all, I had come to this Mexican secondary school expecting to find deep class and racial divisions reflected in student talk and action. I was on the lookout for discourses of difference, and thought such discourses would privilege certain students. I was expecting student subcultures to be structured around these notions of difference and to channel some students' aspirations while squelching others. Instead, the assertion of equality gave me a figurative slap in the face. I looked more closely and found that students valued their similarities more than their differences. Even as some students formed exclusive friendship groups and made occasionally disparaging comments toward fellow students, the discourse of equality continued to undermine the dynamics of social division.

What I had discovered were some of the key symbolic resources for students to play what I call a cultural "game" of equality. Students appropriated teachers' discourses on equality, and organizational structures of solidarity, to produce their own strategic solidarity and identification, often directed toward specific material and ideological ends in the classroom. Students also took up these discourses in an effort to maneuver about in the sea of social differences among themselves. Mostly as individuals, but sometimes as members of informal friendship groups, students negotiated their positions in the game of equality, embracing, modifying, or even rejecting its rules along the way. The play of *todos somos iguales* probably acted to forestall or arrest the emergence of distinct and oppositional student subcultures. It provided students with an important common idiom through which to position their identities.[1]

How and why does this culture, this game of equality, arise at a provincial Mexican secondary school, and how and why does it help create common identifications among students across significant social differences? What are the organizational and discursive resources students appropriate to construct this culture? What is its power and influence relative to the moral forces of family, church, workplace, and other sites of adult authority? To what extent and in what manner does the school-based culture become part of students' broader identities and aspirations, playing a part in the trajectories their lives take? How, then, does the school as an institution participate in structuring students' life opportunities and positions? Such questions emerge most pointedly out of a body of scholarly literature known as social and cultural reproduction theory in education (see appendix A for details). Reproduction theory has sought to explain how schools in modern class societies contribute to the perpetuation—the "reproduction"—of structured inequalities between groups defined by class, race, gender, or other characteristics. Early studies in reproduction theory emphasized the work the school accomplishes in unjustly sorting students and preparing them differentially for their existing places in life. More recent research has shown the complexities and contradictions in how schools "work," and has highlighted the way students creatively respond to the contexts of school. Students make meaning out of their schooling experience; through interaction with parents, teachers, and other students, they construct aspirations and enduring identities. In addition to the subject matter, they learn to be certain kinds of persons, and this learning carries over into their subsequent lives.

Here, I pay particular attention to the dynamics of class, ethnicity, and gender in Mexico. I show how school practices in turn both differentiate and unify students according to such characteristics. The work of the school is indeed complex, and is perhaps poorly accounted for by reproduction theory. Yet more crucial still is the creative student response. Students draw on existing class, ethnic, and gender identities to make sense of school, but they also form new kinds of identities within, and sometimes against, school structures and discourses. The cultural game of equality becomes an important crucible for students to work out their position vis-à-vis school, hence their position in society more generally.

This book attempts to account for the sociocultural world in which the phrase *todos somos iguales* has great meaning. It is an account of how relations are structured at a Mexican secondary school such that equality is a major concern to its many participants. I aim to show not that *todos somos iguales* is necessarily true or false but that it circulates as a normative claim within a broad economy of meanings, and therefore enters into students' identities and aspirations. Equality becomes part of a strategic and serious "game" students play, a purposeful practice that draws together students' social backgrounds and personal goals in a field of power and identity.[2] Like the anthropologist Sherry Ortner (1996, 12–16), I view Escuela Secundaria Federal (ESF) students as historical actors involved in "serious games." In attempting to overcome the binarism of previous theories of structure and agency, Ortner coins this phrase to show

> that social life is culturally organized and constructed, in terms of defining categories of actors, rules and goals of the games, and so forth; that social life is precisely social, consisting of webs of relationship and

interaction between multiple, shiftingly interrelated subject positions, none of which can be extracted as autonomous "agents"; and yet at the same time there is "agency," that is, actors play with skill, intention, wit, knowledge, intelligence. The idea that the game is "serious" is meant to add into the equation the idea that power and inequality pervade the games of life in multiple ways, and that, while there may be playfulness and pleasure in the process, the stakes of these games are often very high. (12)

Theorists like Norbert Elias (in Goudsblom and Mennell 1998) and Pierre Bourdieu (1990; Bourdieu and Wacquant 1992) have also employed the metaphor of games to conceptualize practice.[3] The metaphor of playing a game is especially appropriate for the adolescent context of the Mexican secundaria, where highjinks and humor permeate daily life. Yet the game of equality is, in an important sense, also the game of life in the town of San Pablo—the intersubjective positioning of self in and around the local school, and the ensuing consequences for personal careers and socio-economic trajectories. The rules and resources of the game both enable and constrain (see Giddens 1979; Varenne and McDermott 1998), and the immediate play of identity in the contexts of school life is inexorably linked to the broader temporal and spatial structures of political economy.

In this ethnography of Mexican student culture and identity formation, the scene shifts quite frequently, ranging from microanalyses of classroom and street interactions to the national educational bureaucracy and global flows of popular culture. My primary concern is with students' forms of action and self-expression in the context of the school and the community where it is located, as well as later in the students' lives, in circumstances as disparate as law school or an agricultural field in the state of Oregon. Yet before I can focus my analysis squarely on the students, I must situate them geographically, historically, structurally, and institutionally.

Thus, in the first part of the book, I chart the broad historical, political, and institutional contexts for discourses of equality and solidarity. I try to account for the Mexican State's involvement in providing such symbolic resources for student culture. In chapter 1, I undertake a history of the Mexican secundaria in relation to Mexican political economy, educational philosophy, and state formation. The chapter charts the central importance of shifting concepts of adolescence, solidarity, and equality in the development of the secundaria, and ends with a brief historical sketch of the region of San Pablo and the school, ESF, where I did my fieldwork.

Chapter 2 tells the story of my own journey to San Pablo: my first visit in 1985, subsequent ones in 1988 and 1989—when I began formulating the research project—and my arrival in 1990 for a full year of fieldwork. I also discuss pertinent aspects of the history of the region around San Pablo, and describe the school, city, and region in terms of social class, economy, and population growth. Chapter 3 picks up from the historical account of ESF and continues the ethnographic journey through the beginning of the school year to see just what kind of institution the students encountered. What did teachers say and do, and how was the school week and year organized? What kinds of contexts made up the institutional structure—the concrete practices and discourses framing students' experience in the school? Among other things, I examine what the school looks and feels like to incoming students; how and why teachers form students into socially and academically diverse cohorts (*grupos escolares*) that stay together for most classes and activities through all three years of secondary study; the school's layout, and regular round of rituals and routines; the patterns of curriculum, evaluation, and pedagogical practice among teachers; and the components of the school's "gender regime" given by teacher example and expectation.

Having set the ethnographic scene, and rendered intelligible the historical and institutional contexts for student action, in chapter 4 I shift to the ethnographic account of such action. The narrative focuses on how and why students constructed a "cultural game of equality" in the grupo escolar. I describe what life was like in each of the four grupos I chose for intensive study. Then I demonstrate the means and effects of a grupo-based cultural game of equality, including a powerful "ethic of solidarity," and cultural forms like "passing homework" (*pasando la tarea*) and "goofing off" (*echando relajo*). In chapter 5, I provide a profile of socialization sites and patterns outside the school in order to give the reader a clearer sense of the range of social differences converging in the school. Then the discussion shifts back to the school, where I examine how the construction of grupo identity and solidarity complements a *school* identification, produced in relation to other local schools, as well as a *schooled* identity, produced in relation to the relatively unschooled. The remainder of the chapter presents ethnographic descriptions of how the schooled identity works to structure relationships, aspirations, and desires in and out of school. Chapter 6 highlights the tensions and contradictions in students' appropriations and uses of the meanings of solidarity and equality. The chapter opens with portraits of several students and their friendship groups, and moves on to analyze the way notions of equality and solidarity limit, but do not prohibit, the expression of class, ethnic, gender, and age differences in student culture. I present evidence of an emerging youth culture based on the consumption of cultural media, and show how this youth culture provides yet another arena for the structuring of equality and difference among students. Finally, I end the chapter with a specific focus on female students' orientations to school achievement and romantic attachment, and their correspondingly ambiguous strategies for social empowerment. Because structures of gender inequality continue to privilege men over women in Mexico, the analysis of gender relations must especially account for how and why young women struggle to carve out meaningful life options for themselves.

Chapter 7 shifts gears and extends the temporal range of the study. It opens with observations about the changes that San Pablo has undergone in the six years from 1991 to 1997, especially the deepening economic crisis. It then moves on to an update of the twenty-two focal students in the study, developing in-depth portraits of eight focal students, four males and four females. In chapter 8, I weave together a synopsis of my findings with prior work in the field, proposing new formulations of the relation between student subjectivity and school structure, and modifying cultural reproduction theory for the unique Mexican case. In so doing, I answer the questions posed earlier and provide an account of the contingencies that influenced students' trajectories after their secundaria years. Finally, I stress the comparative importance of the case, and the illumination it provides for questions of education and identity not only in Mexico but elsewhere, too.

AN INTRODUCTION TO THE METHODS AND SCHOOL SITE

I wanted to do a single study of difference in state schooling, so it was imperative that I find a school significantly heterogeneous in class, ethnic, and gender terms. This only seemed possible in a small city like San Pablo, since secundarias in both the larger metropolises and smaller towns tend to greater homogeneity. Because there was no high-quality private alternative in San Pablo, and because there were no geographic restrictions on enrollment, ESF had a rather heterogeneous student body. Students from the wealthiest and poorest families alike clamored to enroll at ESF, which boasted a regional prominence and longevity (since 1941) no other local secundaria could match.

Like most urban schools in Mexico, ESF was divided into morning and afternoon shifts (*turnos*) that shared the same principal and several of the same teachers, but that effectively functioned as two separate schools. I concentrated my efforts on the morning shift, whose class composition tended to be more heterogeneous than either the afternoon shift at ESF or the other two public secundarias in town, where the lower classes prevailed. The morning shift at ESF included children from San Pablo's monied, professional, skilled, and unskilled working classes, as well as some 13 percent who lived in outlying towns and villages, and so traveled daily to attend school. In addition, the morning shift had a higher proportion of girls to boys than any other public secundaria.

I chose to focus my research on the secundaria and not some other educational level for several reasons. The secundaria—or the level of schooling called *educación media básica* in Mexico—expanded drastically in the 1960s and 1970s, incorporating new social groups that had been previously excluded. Yet there has always been a high drop out rate between the first and third years of secundaria, and in recent years, overall enrollment has been declining in some areas, including the one where I did the study. Secundaria is also the last point in the Mexican "basic education" cycle.[4] After secundaria, students must choose between several different options, including college preparatories, vocational schools, "business" courses (comercio), and secretarial or cosmetological schools (see figure 1). Finally, most authors in the literature on student cultures have identified early adolescence as the period when strong subcultural identification often begins to develop. Social psychological processes of identity formation at this age encourage students to define themselves as members of distinct groups, over and against other groups (Woods 1990; Eckert 1989). This is crucial for understanding what students make of social difference in the school.

Of all the students in the school, I focused especially on the third graders, in their last year of secundaria (ninth grade in U.S. terms). I did this for two reasons. First, by their third year, students were likely to have gained a high degree of social competence in, and a high level of knowledge about, the rules and meanings of secondary schooling. Students were formed into grupos escolares that remained together in virtually every class period for all three years (see chapters 3 and 4). Thus, by their third and final year, students were likely to have developed well-defined strategies for negotiating the maze of requirements, expectations, and rules constituting the institutional structure of the school. They came to know

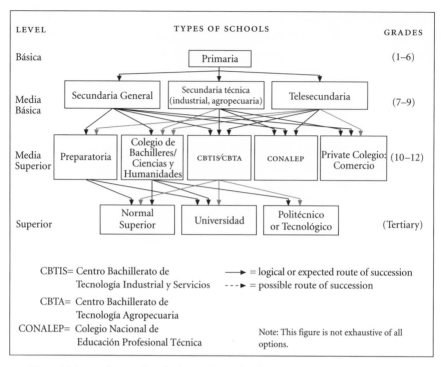

LEVEL	TYPES OF SCHOOLS	GRADES

Fig. 1. Major options and paths in Mexican schooling, 1991

individual teachers well, and had learned the limits of accepted behavior for each one of them, as well as for the school more generally. Perhaps most important of all, third-year students, organized into grupos escolares, had come to know their fellow classmates in some intimate detail.

The second reason I chose to concentrate on third-year students was the imminence of rather difficult and determining decisions. Because they had to soon decide whether to continue studying, and if so, at what type of school, the third year was pivotal for these students (Mir 1979, 107). I expected the dynamics of identity and cultural production to have a strong impact on the formation of educational and occupational aspirations.

After two previous brief research forays (a total of five weeks during June and July of 1988; another four weeks during September and October of 1989), I arrived in San Pablo in the early summer of 1990 and took up residence in the home of two teachers from ESF. During most of the summer, I sought to make contact with students I had met during the previous trips. In August, when all the teachers were returning for administrative tasks and students were coming to enroll, I began spending more time around the school, observing parent-teacher interactions, attending teacher meetings, and sitting in on special exams for the previous year's failed students. Because of my familiarity with the community and previous research clearance with school authorities, I was allowed virtually unconstrained access to all facets of school life, including classrooms, office dynamics, teacher union meetings, and parent-teacher conferences. I was also given access to all relevant school and student records, and collected a number of site documents, such as exams, informational flyers, memos, and political pamphlets. I also gathered what material I could about the school's social and institutional history, and interviewed several teachers about the same.

For most of the school year, from late August to late June, I was engaged in participant observation at the school. This chiefly involved classroom and playground observations, where I paid special attention to four of the six third-year grupos escolares (chapter 4). I also participated in extracurricular activities, attending parties, dances, church services, sports events, civic ceremonies, and study groups.

By early October, after more than a month of participant observation, I began choosing some twenty focal students for the study. I tried to select students I had met during previous trips, or who had shown some interest or confidence in me when I began my observations. In some cases, I sought to deliberately cultivate trust with those students I initially judged interesting or problematic. These twenty students ultimately represented a full range of backgrounds, dispositions, and academic records in the school. Ten were girls and ten were boys; some were judged by teachers and their peers to be "good" students, others "bad," still others "average"; some were clearly rebellious, constantly challenging teachers' authority, while others seemed more compliant; some were poor, others moderately comfortable, others part of a local elite. Moreover, the twenty were fairly evenly distributed across the four grupos escolares I had decided to study. Over the course of the year, I extensively interviewed each of these students at least twice, sometimes three times. I asked them questions about their personal and educational histories, and encouraged them to discuss their experiences since the last time we had spoken. My aim here was to fathom what events or experiences were salient to them in their young lives. Besides the interviews, I made particular note of these students during my observations. The observations provided an important angle on student concerns, and thus complemented the perspectives that emerged in interviews.

It must be said that as the year progressed, some of these relationships fared better than others. To be sure, a few students became more reticent during and after the first interview than I had anticipated. Perhaps it was not what they had expected (beyond the chance to skip part of a class for the interview) or perhaps the novelty soon wore off. (In some cases, I conducted the first interviews in the presence of a friend in order to lighten the atmosphere.) A few of these students successfully stonewalled my persistent attempts to visit their homes and interview their families. On the other hand, some students I had not initially expected to become focal subjects turned out to be rather insightful and forthcoming, and I found myself bringing them into the study anyway. I did visit the homes of most of the focal students and interviewed one or more of their parents in an extended, taped format. In a few instances, I developed an ongoing relationship with the families, visiting frequently throughout the year. I also interviewed all the teachers of these twenty focal students. In the end, the exact number of focal students fluctuated (I include twenty-two in the final analysis, chapters 4–7), and the group did not evenly represent the social class proportions in the school. Certainly I came to know best those students from more socially and economically stable families. Having said this, I don't believe my experience was unusually skewed, either. As will become clear, I did get to know students and families across the whole range.

At the beginning of the school year, I conducted a short socioeconomic survey of all registered students at the school (n = 667), and toward the end of the school year, I did a much more detailed survey of nearly all third graders in the morning shift (n = 190) as well as most of those in the afternoon shift (n = 92; see results in chapter 2). Beyond establishing a basic student body profile, my aim here was to provide a broader grounding for some of my initial analyses emerging from the qualitative data. To understand differences between schools in San Pablo, I administered the same survey to several groups of third-year students at both another public secundaria in town (n = 69) and a private secundaria (n = 42). I also visited every other secundaria and high school–level (*educación media superior*) school in town, speaking briefly with administrators and secretaries, and collecting information about programs, enrollment, and curricula. Aside from the surveys, I left San Pablo in July of 1991 with well over 3,000 single-spaced pages of field notes and interview transcripts. Chapters 3 through 6 present the better part of my analysis of that data.

In the summers of 1993 and 1995, and again in the spring of 1997, I returned to San Pablo for periods of three to six weeks. During that time, I visited with teachers and families, collected documents, and most important, sought out my focal students for chats and interviews. Chapter 7 depicts the story of San Pablo and those students between the years 1991 and 1998.

The cultural game that ESF students created—the meanings they produced—had both sources and repercussions well beyond the immediate ambit of school. In order to understand what happened inside the school in 1990, one must examine the historical antecedents of contemporary Mexican education as well as the biographical details students brought from their families and communities. Then, in order to grasp the subsequent impact of what happened inside the school in 1990, one must follow the students' lives and pay close attention to their words. This book tells their stories, in and out of school, from 1988 through 1998. Yet before we rejoin their stories we must better situate them amid the others that make theirs possible: stories of the nation, the city, the school, and the anthropologist who writes them.

1. Historical Contexts: The Adolescent, the Nation, and the Secundaria, 1923–1993

How does history inform the way persons and institutions act in the present? Ethnographers have become increasingly sensitive to this question, and have tried to develop theories, methods, and styles of writing to answer it.[1] In the field of Latin American studies, there has been an especially vital exchange between anthropologists and historians in recent years (Joseph and Nugent 1994; Levine 1993). Perhaps this is so in part because Latin American societies typically maintain such a keen historical awareness of themselves. After all, it is one thing to affirm the analytic importance of recognizing historical patterns and discourses in the structuring of everyday life; such affirmation should apply even to those most amnesiac of societies—like the United States—that fancy themselves reinvented on a regular basis. It is another thing, and perhaps therefore doubly significant, to recognize and theorize history in Latin America, where the past asserts itself vigorously and people frequently articulate everyday practice in terms of the past.

The field of Mexican education provides a rich case. Schools in Mexico are imbued with a strong sense of history. Civic ceremonies often invoke events and persons of the past, textbooks and teachers highlight the knowledge of history, and the federal State continues to articulate educational policy in terms of a revolutionary legacy that now covers nearly a century. The themes of equality and solidarity that are of concern in this book figure prominently in such historical trends. Conquests, revolutions, population movements, community cultures, economic shifts, and presidential regimes supply the broadest contexts for such themes. My aim in this chapter is to provide an account of those historical contexts that bear most forcefully on the concerns that animated student life at ESF in 1990, especially those involving equality and solidarity.

I must also explore the interconnected meanings of adolescence as they touch on themes of equality. From the outset of my research, I was struck by the frequent use of the word *adolescence* (*adolescencia*). Teachers and parents wielded the term in 1990 to explain the behavior of their charges or exhort students to a certain standard of conduct. A few brief examples will suffice to illustrate: A parent at one meeting referred to what the "doctors" say about the hormonally driven caprice of adolescence, while in another discussion, a parent expressed an oft-heard adult sentiment when she characterized adolescence as *una etapa siempre difícil* (always a difficult phase), because her daughter had become obsessively attuned to peer-based interaction and correspondingly truculent at home. Then, during one of our chats, the school's principal admitted he did not have sufficient resources (doctors, social workers, or vocational counselors) to deal with the "special problems" of adolescents, even though the secundaria had been specifically designed for such duty. Another teacher lamented the decrease in kids' respect for elders, saying:

> It's obvious, they're adolescents. . . . They show one side of themselves with you as teacher, another with you as friend, and another with you as parent. They utilize and wield their hypocrisy a lot. . . . The adolescent is waking up now but only for his [*sic*] own purposes (*para su propia conveniencia*). He doesn't respect the teacher or parent anymore, he only has his own goals and attitudes in mind.

Other teachers and parents often expressed a similar concern about adolescents' selfish impulses, wondering if they would continue to cooperate (*jalar*) with the best interests of the family or school group.

These meanings of *adolescencia* highlighted the problematic and contentious nature of the transition to adulthood, its emotional volatility and heightened sensitivity to generational difference. Such notions would probably be familiar to most U.S. or European parents and teachers (Finders 1997; Lesko 1996, 454; White 1993, 31). Not all was storm and stress, however. Coexisting with this rather dire portrait of adolescence was a praiseful one. Many teachers portrayed the adolescent years as the happiest and most carefree the students were likely to encounter, generally identifying this period exclusively with the secundaria. In one classroom session toward the end of the year, a teacher told his group of soon-to-graduate students:

> So I have seen how you all have changed, from childhood to adolescence, a very beautiful change. . . . [B]ut kids, when you enter the *preparatoria* [high school–level college preparatory] you're going to see that the secundaria was unique . . . because over there in the preparatoria things are very different; there's no longer the same togetherness (*convivencia*) in the group, and the students don't get to know each other as well.

This was only one of many occasions when I witnessed a teacher prompting this kind of future nostalgia. Teachers tended to extol the virtues of group solidarity and convivencia, suggesting that the adolescent years were relatively carefree. Adolescence was conceived of as a safe and insulated training ground for adult roles and responsibilities. Kids could still feel free to be kids, to have fun with abandon, and postpone the more serious decisions about life and career. All this would presumably end when they graduated from the secundaria. Of course, teachers spoke implicitly to those students, around 70 percent of the student body, who would probably continue some formal studies. According to their cultural logic, it was as if a summer of inevitable fate would suddenly transform these adolescents into youth (*jóvenes*).

Most striking of all were the ways the students took up the term *adolescencia* themselves. Familiar with U.S. adolescents' use of *kids* or *teenagers* to describe themselves (Danesi 1994), I expected Mexican students to employ some homologue, conceding *adolescente* to adult use only. Yet they frequently used it as a label for themselves, as a way to explain or justify their own behavior. The greater contact and permeability between youth and adult cultures in Mexico, and the occasional adult use of *adolescente* as a term of address, clearly encouraged this appropriation. My field notes record many instances: One time, Leticia and her friends, obviously bored with recess, asked me what I might do if I were an adolescente at school that day. Not long after, I discovered another girl, my introspective friend Rosita, actually reading a book on adolescentes when I stopped by her house to visit. She said she wanted to learn more from the "experts" about the emotional turmoil she was going through. Franco, a laconic boy with a seemingly permanent sheepish grin, once told me that the most important thing he had done in his short life was to serve as a Catholic altar boy and attend the priest's talks given especially for adolescentes. And students also equated adolescence with their years in the secundaria. For example, in a taped conversation toward the end of the school year, Iván and Héctor briefly suspended their jokester personae to confess that the transition they would soon make to the preparatoria was a momentous one:

> IVÁN: In the prepa one passes on from being an adolescent to a youth [*joven*] who should be responsible in his way of being, his way of doing things for himself. One has to be more responsible in studying, and to be serious with the girls, not just to be thinking about nothing but sex, but to seriously conduct a nice friendship.
> HÉCTOR: Because in the prepa it's already about having a little more responsibility. . . . [T]he federal (ESF) is like a, how should I say it? like a little review, something to teach yourself, but in the prepa it really depends on you. . . . Here (at ESF) one is still small and over there in the prepa one gets more savvy [*agarra más mentalidad*].

Frequently enough, students chatting with me would explain their laziness, indecision, or misconduct with reference to their adolescente nature. They clearly appropriated the term from parents, teachers, and the popular media, applying it to an understanding of their own educational experience.[2] One could even say, as Linda Christian-Smith (1997, ix) comments on the subjects of Margaret Finders's study, that "students stage[d] behaviors to meet assumptions about adolescence."

The foregoing illustrations demonstrate the importance of concepts of adolescence for understanding and regulating the social life of youth in contemporary Mexico. They also hint at the active traffic in meanings between adult and youth uses of the term. The complexity of local articulations of adolescencia, and their association with the secundaria, has its roots in Mexican educational philosophy and policy as these have evolved over the course of the twentieth century.

EDUCATING ADOLESCENTS: THE MEXICAN SECUNDARIA

In Mexico, the concept of adolescence has always been a key point of reference in programs for the secundaria. Periodic reforms have often been articulated around the interrelated needs of adolescents and national development. The Mexican secundaria was created in 1923, quickly evolving to accommodate the adolescent life stage as this was variously conceived. For nearly seventy years, the secundaria served as an optional continuation of "basic" primary studies and developed a strong vocational component. For fifty of those years, the overwhelming majority of Mexican students sought merely to complete the six years of primary education. Only those who envisioned a professional career typically continued beyond primary school, using the secundaria as a stepping-stone to further studies in urban areas at a college-linked preparatoria. By the 1970s, however, secundaria enrollments had increased exponentially, and it was not uncommon to find students terminating their studies after completing this level. The increased accessibility of these schools and a labor market grown accustomed to workers with a secondary-level education, among other things, contributed to the popularity of secondary studies.[3]

Still, it was not until 1993, in the context of broad administrative reforms, that the Mexican Constitution was amended to mandate compulsory secondary schooling. This was an unprecedented political move. Compulsory secondary education had long been the dream of some reformers,[4] and by 1990, the Secretariat of Public Education had made great strides in providing communities with various options for secondary schooling.[5] Few thought the provision of secondary schooling could be extended to the entire population of school-age youth though. Indeed, many primary schools were still overcrowded or, in some remote rural communities, nonexistent. Moreover, few resources could be dedicated to the enforcement of the compulsory rule, and after ten years of economic crisis, many families were in no condition to support their children's ongoing studies.[6] Most observers agreed, then, that the constitutional amendment was primarily a symbolic measure, meant to signal Mexico's commitment to an advanced, so-called "modern" education for the further economic development of the country. Ironically, the amendment coincided with the ongoing stagnation of teacher salaries and an increasingly combative movement for political change in relations between teachers and the State.[7] Many educational actors had become critical of the State's efforts at educational modernization, seeing in them a neoliberal program to dismantle the progressive social reforms of prior epochs.[8] The year 1993 thus marked a watershed in Mexican educational policy and statecraft.

My primary fieldwork period, from 1990 to 1991, witnessed the rumblings of such change, but they did not fundamentally alter the historical patterns in place at ESF. I concentrate, then, on the pre-1993 historical contexts, postponing a discussion of more recent transformations to the final chapters of the book.

DILEMMAS OF EDUCATIONAL PHILOSOPHY AND POLICY IN MEXICO

Carlos Ornelas (1995, 49) echoes the observations many contemporary educational scholars make of other nations in describing the fundamentally "paradoxical" character of the Mexican educational system: its two primary mandates are to form citizens and human capital. These mandates imply rather different kinds of educational priorities that have not been easily melded into a coherent educational policy.[9] Annette Santos del Real (1996a, 1) and Yolanda Navarro (1996) have noted, moreover, that the Mexican secundaria, adamantly opposed to differentiated academic tracking, still attempts to reconcile two related yet distinct goals: preparing youth for the immediate demands of the labor market and for professional studies. Insofar as secondary education is thus conceived of as both formative and vocational, both preparatory and terminal, it attempts to navigate a difficult middle course.

The dilemmas of Mexican education at its present level of development and differentiation are not unlike those encountered in many other parts of the world. Secondary structures and curricula around the globe attempt to address diverse educational goals. In former colonial nations, especially, the postprimary years are often utilized to accomplish both work training and advanced academic preparation. What makes Mexico different, perhaps unique? In Mexico, three distinct cultural formations, which have tugged and pulled at one another throughout the modern period, can be identified. Following Larissa Adler Lomnitz, Claudio Lomnitz-Adler, and Ilya Adler (1993), I would call one the "hierarchical holism" of the Mexican political body, traceable to the Spanish colonial state, but perhaps best represented by the "Conservative" political tradition of the early nineteenth century. Hierarchical holism describes a social system in which proper relations of authority, rooted ultimately in ecclesiastical and patriarchal imperatives, sustain the organic hierarchy of the "body" of God and his earthly appointments. While this formation typifies the Spanish colonial structure, it also draws from the hierarchical model of the largest indigenous pre-Hispanic polities.[10] Another cultural formation would be that which emerged from the "Liberal" political tradition, with its principles of private property, individual initiative, rational progress, and formal equality before the law (Hale 1972; Mallon 1995). The third, in effect a kind of uneasy synthesis of the other two, would be the tradition of revolutionary nationalism forged in the early part of the twentieth century, with its emphasis on collective solidarity and substantive equality.[11] Revolutionary nationalism, itself the product of ongoing negotiations between the postrevolutionary State and local forces (Joseph and Nugent 1994; Mallon 1995; Vaughan 1997), has in turn undergone numerous permutations. One place that the evolving expression of revolutionary nationalism can be charted is in the structure and philosophy of the national school system.

As in so many other modern national contexts, notions of equality have suffused educational practice in Mexico. Yet the complex articulation of Mexico's cultural formations gives these notions a distinct cast. On the one hand, Mexico has adapted from the Liberal tradition conceptions of equal opportunity, rationality, and mobility that accompanied the expansion of capitalist relations and growth of anticlericalism. These conceptions dictate that schooling should free people from superstition and vice, while giving them equal opportunities to improve their material lives and enter into the "productive" sphere of society. The Liberal model also designates schooling as a key instrument of meritocracy—a fair, equitable means of selecting the best people, based on their aptitude, for the best positions within a technical division of labor. Citizens are allegedly equal in that they share the same, basic qualities of humanity, such as the capacity for reflexive thought and moral action. Citizens are not, however, equal in the sense of having the same kind or level of aptitudes. As Liberal positivism at the turn of the twentieth century would have it, citizens compete as individuals within the same social space, on the same level playing field, allowing the supposedly natural hierarchy of ability to best serve the social interest.[12]

The rationalist, meritocratic model of education had become predominant by the end of the nineteenth century, when the Liberal hegemony in Mexico had been consolidated. It was not until after 1910, with the explosion of social revolution in Mexico, that new forms of educational ideology and practice were regrafted onto the Liberal base. A renewed stress on cooperation, solidarity, and the collective good, oriented toward the construction of a national identity and culture, took its place alongside the Liberal model of individualism (Vaughan 1997). The collectivist emphasis, coupled with a corporatist political structure, drew on already existing practices and discourses of solidarity in popular and indigenous cultures, attempting to articulate their local, community-oriented focus to a hegemonic national project (Lomnitz-Adler 1992; Alonso 1995; Nugent 1993).

Why is the secundaria important in this framework of State and nation formation? In modernizing and urbanizing Mexico, as elsewhere, the growth of industrialization and expansion of secondary education exerted reciprocal effects on one another, creating the conditions for the salience of adolescence as a sociocultural category (Neubauer 1992, 6). Moreover, the transitional stage known as adolescence has become a crucible for forging enduring identities and allegiances, and the secundaria corresponds to this phase. Children and youth now form an extremely high percentage of Mexico's population, and educational authorities must design a secundaria that accommodates and channels youth for productive places in society.[13] The nationalist ideology of equality is also likely to be expressed more urgently in the socially differentiated secundaria. Indeed, at least since 1944, the secundaria appears to have been explicitly invested with this homogenizing function (Santos del Real 1996a, 8). Finally, the secundaria seems to have crystallized in the very structure and rationale of its curriculum the tension between Liberal individualism and nationalist collectivism, between effort for personal advancement and technical mastery, on the one hand, and effort for group welfare and selfless citizenship, on the other. How did this come to be?

POLITICS, IDEOLOGY, AND CURRICULUM: A BRIEF HISTORY OF THE MEXICAN SECUNDARIA

Like so many contemporary Mexican institutions, the secundaria is a direct child of the Mexican Revolution (1910–1921), which was fought by many different factions, and for a variety of principles and causes. The great peasant uprisings, such as the one led by Emiliano Zapata south of Mexico City, sought to reinstate a more equitable distribution of land among a society of communal freeholders. Yet the northern military movements—associated with leaders like Venustiano Carranza, Álvaro Obregón, and Francisco Villa—pursued other agendas. They mostly represented a Liberal alliance of professionals, businesspeople, and small property holders. As they fought to break the stranglehold of the Porfirio Díaz dictatorship, they also channeled the grievances of a variety of disaffected groups, from ranch hands to poorly paid mineworkers. The northern factions ultimately triumphed in the revolution, and their bourgeois interests largely determined the development of the new State. Still, because the revolution had energized enormous popular hopes, the developing institutions of the State would have to respond to local forces and conditions. Although the State emerging from the Mexican Revolution reinstated most features of the capitalist model of development fostered by the Díaz dictatorship, it did so under radically changed social and ideological conditions (Meyer 1991; Brachet-Márquez 1994; Joseph and Nugent 1994). Now more than ever, it was necessary for the State to attend to the great range of class, ethnic, and regional differences that divided the nation, and schooling was an obvious choice for accomplishing this feat of national integration. With the revolution, the first material bases for a genuinely popular public schooling would be established, and the question of equality and social difference moved to the forefront.

Soon after the definitive triumph of the revolution in 1921, President Álvaro Obregón appointed José Vasconcelos to serve as founding head of a new federal Secretariat of Public Education. Vasconcelos articulated a vision of revolutionary cultural action that, for perhaps the first time in the country's independence, explicitly valorized the contributions of popular and indigenous cultures. Perhaps paradoxically, he also laid the groundwork for a system of schooling that would be oriented toward *homogenizing* the customs and values of all Mexicans in the service of two predominant statist imperatives: national unity, and the material and spiritual redemption, or so-called elevation, of popular classes.[14]

The development of federal schooling, especially in rural areas, had already begun during the Díaz years, but the revolution infused schooling with new energy and focus because it responded at least to a number of popular demands. The idea of rural schools as *casas del pueblo* (houses of the people), first conceived by Vasconcelos and then elaborated by the great educator Moisés Sáenz, was received enthusiastically in many villages. This rural school model had been influenced by the active, participatory pedagogy of John Dewey, with whom Sáenz had studied at Columbia University. Rural schoolteachers were much more than instructors of literacy and mathematics. Rather, teachers were conceived of as moral, social, and technical "apostles" of modernity, as it were, guiding their communities to practical and spiritual liberation—and integration into national life (Vaughan 1997). In addition to the schools themselves, "cultural missions" were created at strategic locations in rural parts of the country. These missions were intended to serve as resource centers for teachers and other interested citizens, who could consult with materials and master pedagogues in order to more effectively teach villagers the latest skills. The intense cultural action of the revolutionary State was thus double-edged. While education responded to rural needs and demands, it deepened the power of state rule as well.

As a result, many authors have called attention to the way postrevolutionary schools were charged with creating, or in some cases reinforcing, a unified national identity (Raby 1987; Taboada 1985; Vaughan 1997). The regional and local identifications that had inspired diverse revolutionary movements constantly threatened the integrity of the postrevolutionary State. In effect, the penetration of State-sponsored schooling into previously neglected local communities represented an attempt to link such communities to the State and thereby consolidate the rule of revolutionary elites (Raby 1987, 308; Córdova 1984; Taboada 1985, 54). What occurred during this period was also an attempt to identify the nation in cultural terms with the groups comprising the State (Monsiváis 1992, 448). The nationalist concept of equality as a collective good was especially highlighted during the so-called period of national unity (post-1940), which followed the contentious era of socialist agitation under President Lázaro Cárdenas (1934–1940). Even the language of a federal education law in 1941, which reflected the constitutional article regarding education that was revised in 1946, sketched the relationship between equality and national identity:

> [Education] should tend to create and affirm in students concepts and feelings of solidarity and the preeminence of collective interests over private or individual interests, with the goal of lessening social and economic inequalities. . . . Through instruction and school activities, [education] will contribute to the development and consolidation of national unity, thereby excluding all political, social, and sectarian influences contrary or inimical to the country, and affirming in students the love of country (*patria*) and national traditions. . . . Special attention will be given to the study of the country's economy, environment, and social conditions in order to achieve the most equitable use of its natural resources.[15]

Indeed, if a "new Mexican" was created in revolutionary discourses on equality, it was a cultural subject oriented toward the collective (read: national) good (Bartra 1987).

It was into this political and ideological environment that the Mexican secundaria was born. Though the public secundaria was officially created by law in 1915, it was not until 1923 that the secundaria received serious attention. Until that time, Mexico had followed the classical European tradition of combining secondary education with college preparatory studies. Secondary education was, in effect, part of a program of professional studies that emphasized specialization and encyclopedic knowledge. In 1923, Bernardo Gastélum, subsecretary of education, proposed a reorganization of college preparatory studies by clearly distinguishing a phase of secondary education as an extension of the primary school. In this manner, the secundaria would still retain some of the subject matter and specialization characteristic of preparatory studies, but would now continue the "basic" cultural and ideological functions of the *primaria*. To understand these developments, it is important to highlight the ongoing struggle between the Catholic Church and postrevolutionary State for the hearts and minds of local subjects. Following the Liberal imperative to wrest power from the church and assign the task of moral socialization to the State, the secundaria would now focus on a formative *education* of the character rather than the mere *instruction* of specialized knowledge.[16]

Donald Mabry (1985, 222) suggests that the idea of the secundaria was borrowed from the United States, and thus fiercely resisted by some traditionalists who wished to preserve a strict separation between primary and advanced education, and feared the incursion of "foreign" educational philosophies. Raúl Mejía Zuñiga (1981, 225) goes further in saying that the Secretaría de Educación Pública founded the secundaria with the "pedagogical mold of the German secondary school and the democratic postulates of the U.S. secondary school, both adjusted to the popular needs and aspirations of Mexico." Clearly, by 1923, some key components of the new plan for secondary education responded to the uniquely Mexican postrevolutionary ethos. The four central goals of the new secundaria were to:

> 1) carry forth the task of correcting defects and sponsoring the general development of students begun in the *primaria,* 2) strengthen in each student the sense of solidarity with others, 3) create habits of unity (*cohesión*) and social cooperation, and 4) offer all students a great variety of activities, exercises, and teachings so that each one might discover a vocation and be able to dedicate him/herself to cultivating it. (Meneses Morales 1986, 408)

The secundaria's goals of correcting "defects" (that is, superstition and blind faith) while fostering solidarity and cooperation were consonant

23   Historical Contexts

with the revolutionary ideology of rural primary schooling and the need to offset church power over local worldviews.

Unlike the primaria, however, the secundaria was still oriented toward urban and mostly professional classes.[17] Moreover, the secundaria continued to be administered by the National University as part of its preparatories until a presidential decree in 1925, after which Sáenz created a separate Office of Secondary Education in 1928. It was then that the secundaria became more explicitly guided by methods and principles appropriate to the adolescente life stage.[18] As such, the divide between childhood (niñez) and adolescencia became enshrined in the primaria and secundaria, respectively (cf. Ariés 1962, 177), with the latter conceived of as the ideal time and place for creating the revolutionary subject.

By the close of the 1920s, the secundaria began to offer more varied options, adding to the arts and sciences a number of technical or industrial "shops" (talleres) that students would choose for different possible avenues of future work or study. The goal was to balance the desire for a curriculum more specialized than the primaria—a curriculum that would offer students the chance to explore their vocational options—with the themes of integration and national unity. In other words, the goal was to accommodate students' "individual differences" while still subordinating them to the imperatives of "solidarity," "cooperation," and so-called social values. Sáenz reaffirmed the State's commitment to unity and equality by suggesting that the secundaria would continue to oblige Mexicans to "take the same educational path," even as it provided the opportunity for distinction and differentiation (Meneses Morales 1986, 480).

At the outset of the 1930s, the development of the secundaria took a distinct turn. Increasingly, secundarias were established to prepare workers and rural teachers. Students were drawn from the working classes, and occasionally the peasantry, rather than exclusively from the urban-based middle and upper classes. The architect of this emerging emphasis on technical knowledge was Education Secretary Narciso Bassols. Partly because of the onset of world recession in 1929, Bassols wished to counter the intellectual, moral, and spiritual thrust of Vasconcelos's policies with a more practical approach to development (Ornelas 1984). Bassols hoped to emphasize the teaching of better production methods for the satisfaction of local needs, integrating the already existing normal schools, agricultural centers, and cultural missions into unitary "regional peasant schools." The State, in Bassols's Marxist view, was above the conflict of social classes inherent to society, and so, should represent the true interests of the nation, especially against what he saw as the insidious influence of the church. To this end, the State had to achieve a certain uniformity of all Mexicans. This kind of national integration could be more easily achieved, however, through straightforward steps toward economic development than any specifically cultural action of the schools (Ornelas 1984, 44–45; 1995, 111).

Such logic henceforth pervaded the movement for "socialist education," which building on Bassols's philosophy, burst onto the national scene with the presidency of Lázaro Cárdenas in 1934. Cárdenas (1934–1940) oversaw a significant growth in secondary enrollments.[19] Now with an avowedly socialist educational program, workers' children were more strongly encouraged to continue their schooling as the secundaria turned more technical and the curriculum included more hours devoted to practical, productive activities. Socialist pedagogical philosophy sketched the desired qualities of the new adolescent secundaria graduate: "a young person with a firm concept of responsibility to and solidarity with laboring classes and an intimate conviction of social justice, so that, upon completing his/her studies, he/she will be oriented toward community service and not the desire for private gain" (Meneses Morales 1988, 113).[20] Thus, the secundaria was to inculcate a renewed kind of relational adolescent identity, in solidarity with class and community, while channeling the students' skills and activities into service for the greater good. It was at this time that vocational counseling (*orientación*) first appeared in the secundaria; as well, the teaching of history and civics was given new emphasis. In 1932, the curriculum added "civic culture" to the required courses of Spanish, a foreign language (French or English), mathematics, science (biology, chemistry, and physics), geography, and history for each of the three years. This course contributed an important element to the curriculum, as it focused on what the State defined as political, economic, and legal problems in Mexico. By 1937, the civic culture class had been changed to one on "socialist information and practice," and in 1939, official policy reaffirmed that the secundaria was "an institution fundamentally placed at the service of adolescents" (Meneses Morales 1988, 115–19, 122).[21] Students increasingly learned about class conflict and imperialism as a way of understanding Mexican history (Vaughan 1997; Raby 1974). They participated in student government and mutual aid societies to practice cooperative social work. Finally, students made frequent trips to shops and factories in order to gain a fuller appreciation of working-class life (Meneses Morales 1988, 116).

25 Historical Contexts

By 1940, Cárdenas's attempt to engineer a popular socialist State foundered on the contradictions and constraints that had marked it from the beginning (Córdova 1974; Hamilton 1982). Even as the corporatist structure of the State endured, the reins of power swung over to the more conservative Manuel Ávila Camacho. It didn't take long for the Ávila Camacho administration to begin reversing the socialist experiments of the Cardenista period. Under Ávila Camacho, the third constitutional article was once again amended, this time deleting all references to socialism and declaring primary schooling compulsory. Conservative Catholic interests, such as the Unión de Padres de Familia, were given greater voice, and private church schools expanded rapidly. If the school under Cárdenas had given preference to workers and become a site for struggle, under Ávila Camacho's first education secretary, Véjar Vázquez, schooling became a place for "love," and then under his second secretary, Torres Bodet, for "unity." Official educational discourse thus reinstated the primary importance of national unity and reconciliation above class struggle, and secondary education, especially, stressed the preparation for productive work and a harmonious civic life.[22]

To be sure, the secundaria expanded under Ávila Camacho at an even greater rate than under Cárdenas. Once again, the uniquely adolescent character of the institution was proclaimed, and reformers sought to protect the secundaria from the "threat of two contradictory invasions": the primaria and higher education (Meneses Morales 1988, 283). The secundaria was to have its own personality, its own agenda. Despite the fact that Cárdenas had sought to conceptualize the secundaria as an agent of social transformation and enfranchisement, and despite claims that the secundaria began to grow after 1940 as a response mainly to urban middle-class aspirations (Muñoz Izquierdo 1981, 112), in fact the secundaria continued to provide a crucial means of socioeconomic mobility for members of the working and peasant classes. What changed mostly was the rhetoric that framed such mobility. Before 1940, workers and peasants were encouraged to utilize the school as a tool for class empowerment and enfranchisement. After Cárdenas, however, the State entered into a period of more comfortable alliance with national and transnational capital. Secondary schooling became valued as a means of preparing workers for the new wave of industrialization. In the official discourse of this period, the interests of the nation, subordinated classes, and capital were considered convergent; each could win in the hegemonic formula for national development and a stable "revolutionary" regime.

This formula has provided the basic continuity in policy and practice around the secundaria throughout the years of the so-called economic miracle (1940–1980), perhaps even until 1993.[23] In the period from 1950 to 1970, there was a 1,000 percent increase in secundaria enrollments (Barkin 1975, 186), and growth, though reversing slightly in the late 1980s, has steadily continued since then (Fuentes 1996, 61).[24] Even current official discourse recognizes that until the mid-1970s, the State was primarily concerned with covering educational demand through quantitative expansion. Under some version of the rallying cry "*Educación Para Todos*" ("Education for All"), the State further sought to fulfill popular claims for equality, participation, and social justice through schooling. And several times again, in the 1950s and 1960s, official policy restated the primordial goal of the secundaria: an education designed specially for the "integral formation" of adolescents (Meneses Morales 1988, 411, 482).

The first federal secundarias *técnicas* were built in the early 1960s. When a new secundaria was established in a large rural community or small provincial city, it was likely to be a técnica rather than a "general" secundaria. The vocational specialties of the new técnicas were often tailored to the unique needs and demands of the local economy: carpentry, clerical work, auto mechanics, and even fishing or forestry. The técnica was said to offer its graduates these more appropriate skills for immediately entering regional labor forces or continuing on to more advanced vocational studies. General secundarias, on the other hand, tended to be built only in the larger cities (Reyes Rocha 1986, 57). In this fashion, the State could fulfill its obligation to the popular demand for schooling while attempting to steer students away from the more desirable track of liberal university studies (Fuentes 1978). Not only did this strategy promise to match more students with potential jobs; it also assuaged those in the national bourgeoisie who were desperate for more qualified technical labor. Ironically, the strategy was less successful than hoped. The status value of university professional studies, along with their promise of greater earning power, still discouraged many students from pursuing the route of technical studies.

With the onset of an economic crisis in 1982, and the shift to a neoliberal economic model of privatization and free trade, secondary enrollments began to level off. I noted a curious dilemma in many families' educational expectations and practices by 1990. The secundaria, seen by many as an intermediate stop on the path to university studies, had finally come to form a vital part of most families' livelihood strategies. Indeed, the expectation of at least some secundaria attendance had become woven into the local cultural fabric of all but the poorest or smallest communities and social classes (Levinson 1996; Martin 1994). Studying at a secundaria was for many a kind of adolescent rite of passage. Yet, by 1990, the possibility of full professional employment had also become increasingly unattainable for those who continued their schooling beyond the secundaria. The symbolic significance of secondary schooling thus entered into contradiction with economic realities, and this appears to have generated a great deal of ambivalence about continued secondary attendance. It was in this atmosphere that the curricular reforms and constitutional amendment of 1993 were announced. Secundaria attendance, in principle, was now a citizen's obligation to the State.[25]

In the space of seventy years, then, the Mexican secundaria passed through a number of projects and phases. In dialogue with both local popular desires (morality, social justice, technical expertise, economic opportunity) and national, even global imperatives (capital accumulation, political legitimacy and sovereignty), the State attempted to craft an institutional niche for adolescent education. Prevailing themes of spiritual elevation, class struggle, technical development, national unity, and modernization (see Latapí Sarre 1998) have accompanied the evolution of the secundaria as the postrevolutionary State has continued to negotiate a space for its own ongoing rule (Joseph and Nugent 1994). Beyond these diverse themes, however, one can discern the persistence of revolutionary nationalism in varying guises. Emphasizing at turns the imperative of centralized rule and collective conscience (that is, "hierarchical holism"), and the advancement of individual talent and enterprise ("Liberal individualism"), educational policy for the secundaria has shown remarkable consistency and faithfulness to the original goals laid out by its founder, Sáenz.

ESF IN REGIONAL AND LOCAL CONTEXTS

Where exactly does the local ESF of San Pablo fit into this national history of secondary schooling and adolescence? What regional and local idiosyncrasies put their stamp on its development? The historical record for the school itself is rather spotty, as it has kept no organized archive. Thus, in order to answer these questions, I present a brief synopsis of regional history along with snapshots of ESF history and oral accounts by some of the school's first students.

28   We Are All Equal

Typical rural landscape of the San Pablo region

The region around San Pablo exudes a rich agrarian-based culture and long history of struggle over the land. Before the Spanish Conquest, the region formed the political core of the only indigenous imperial state ever to successfully challenge and remain autonomous from the Aztec power based in the central valley of Mexico. Shortly after the Conquest, the Spanish targeted the region for pacification and religious conversion. As in many parts of Mexico, such conversion was ultimately successful, and the region is now known for both its strong indigenous presence and deeply rooted popular Catholicism. This popular Catholicism anchors communities' relationship to the land, providing a frame of reference for agricultural activities.[26] Largely because of this relationship, west-central Mexico has often posed a problem of control for the Mexican State. Regional and community traditions have provided the resources for rebelling against State attempts to impose an agenda from above.

In the aftermath of the revolution, then, the region presented a puzzle to the newly forming government, whose leaders had been drawn largely from the petty bourgeoisie of the northern states. Its supposed otherness—Indian, agrarian, devoutly Catholic—was a challenge to federal incorporation. As governor, native son, and revolutionary general, Francisco J. Mújica at first attempted major structural reforms using the schools as agents of change.[27] Yet soon he was ousted by federal President Álvaro Obregón for moving beyond the dictates of central power too soon and too fast. Cárdenas himself became governor in 1928, in the midst of the growing Cristero War between supporters of the Catholic Church and radical farmers emboldened by the anticlerical policies of President Calles. Cárdenas was of a modest rural background himself, but he was a committed Liberal—a Freemason, in fact, who abhorred what he viewed as religious fanaticism. He instinctively knew that the popular Catholic culture animating these conflicts could not be simply destroyed. Along with his supporters, known as *cardenistas,* he elaborated a strategy whereby the promise of land and further agrarian reform would be conditioned on an alliance with the State and a disavowal of the church. The cardenistas organized a peasant and worker confederation, thus fostering a militant minority of *agraristas* willing to agitate against the church in exchange for land. But the cardenistas also wished to undertake a more thorough reformation of rural culture; as Marjorie Becker (1989, 163; 1987) puts it, they wanted nothing less than to "bring the campesinos' mental worlds under the sway of the state" (for other parts of Mexico, see Vaughan 1997). The public school would, of course, play a major role in this endeavor.

The school became an indispensable tool of State action in the region. In the years following the revolution, the area had already constituted one of several important laboratories for educational experiments, including the aforementioned cultural missions (Raby 1974, 201) and Sáenz's doomed community school in Carapán (Sáenz [1936] 1992). Now the cardenistas invested new energy in the schools. In a symbolic move of great import, church buildings themselves often served as the first community classrooms. Federal teachers, moreover, fancied themselves taking over the "priestly" function of community organizing (Raby 1974; Rockwell 1996). They attempted to "dispel the intensity of Catholicism" by co-opting traditional, often indigenous, cultural symbols, much as the church itself had done some three centuries earlier (Becker 1989, 223; 1995). Part of this process involved the reinvention of the local Indian in school-based discourse. Attempting to associate the goals of the revolution with the most deeply felt aspects of local indigenous culture, teachers alternated traditional Indian dances and songs with propaganda for the State.

Yet the campesinos were not buying all of it. Many of the radical agraristas had become powerful and parasitic bosses (*caciques*) in their own right, though they were few in number compared to the church faithful (Friedrich 1970, 1986; Becker 1989). Most of the latter still sought a reinstatement of their rights to open churches and worship there. Appropriating the very nationalist secular idiom employed by the cardenistas, the religious peasants cleverly justified their demands for free worship in terms of respecting the enduring colonial monuments that their ancestors had built as part of the mythic popular past (Becker 1987, 1989).[28]

The conflicts between Christian campesinos and State-supported agraristas had already erupted into a full-scale war when the federal Calles regime passed a series of draconian limitations on church rights in 1926. The resulting Cristero War soon arrived in the San Pablo region and dominated the west-central Mexican landscape until 1929. When Cárdenas became the national president in 1934, the embers from this war were still smoldering, ready to be ignited by the new program of socialist education. David Raby's (1974) study of socialist rural schools in this region from 1920 to 1940 demonstrates how many of the federal teachers were radicalized by their experience. Many came to quickly identify themselves with the State, self-consciously acting as agents for the diffusion of a "nationalist, secular spirit" (201). State-sponsored rhetoric about revolution and social justice caused them to question the structures of inequality they discovered in the countryside. Yet in many cases, the teachers perceived the State to be actively promoting, or at the very least remaining indifferent to, these injustices. They took revolutionary rhetoric to heart and began using schools as "real spaces for transformative action" (243), organizing communities to defend their rights and press their claims against the State. In this fashion, they carried forth the project of revolutionary justice.

The struggles of the cardenista period, as well as the work that Cárdenas accomplished on the region's behalf after his presidency, left an indelible impression on the regional landscape and in the popular historical memory. By 1990, the local countryside was dotted with primary and secondary schools bearing the names and statues of Cárdenas and his most illustrious associates; schoolchildren were exhorted by teachers and townspeople alike to faithfully commemorate the anniversary of Cárdenas's birth and death. As if by a kind of ideological magic, the image of Cárdenas himself had emerged triumphant from the endemic struggles between State and community that his own regime had in some measure exacerbated. Because of the extent of his agrarian reform and socialist projects, Cárdenas had become known as the benevolent provider for Indians, peasants, and the popular classes. Since so many teachers had used the schools as tools of empowerment, Cárdenas's consistent educational sponsorship came to be seen as tangible evidence of his commitment to social welfare.

ESF was the first federal secundaria created in the San Pablo region.

Initially established in 1941 through the special intervention of Cárdenas, ESF actually moved to San Pablo in 1943 after a brief stint in a nearby city. Despite Cárdenas's personal benediction, the secundaria was really a child of the period of national unity and reconciliation inaugurated by the moderate president Ávila Camacho. It was created even as federal senators were still debating the need to delete references to socialist education in the third constitutional article. Yet ESF probably also had to confront a situation ripe with the conflicts engendered by the recent impact of socialist education in the nearby countryside. It is important to note that some of the students and teachers who first came to work at ESF were veterans of rural socialist schools in these areas.

The secundaria came to occupy a building adjacent to the local church dedicated to the Virgin of Guadalupe. Originally a rectory and social center for the church, the building was outfitted with basic classroom equipment, and two separate rooms were designated for use as "technological" shops: carpentry and clothing design (*corte y confección*) were the first two such shops to begin functioning at ESF. In 1944, the first year that a full three-year contingent comprised the school, nearly 150 students were evenly distributed across all three grades. Girls formed only one-quarter of the school population.

Oral accounts collected from some of the first students to attend ESF in the 1940s and 1950s fill in a picture of school life during these years.[29] Before the creation of double shifts in the 1960s, students attended basic academic classes from 8 A.M. to 1 or 2 P.M., took a two-hour meal break, and returned in the late afternoon for technical shop activities, physical education, or the arts. Many of the teachers at the time were professionals who supplemented their incomes with stints in the secundaria or gave themselves over entirely to teaching. Local doctors would teach courses in biology and anatomy; lawyers would provide instruction in civics or history. The teachers tended to present so-called pure theory (*pura teoría*), followed by monthly written exams. Class size varied quite a bit, and by the late 1940s and early 1950s, some classes reached nearly a hundred students, though only for a short time.

The school added a great deal of color and excitement to local life, and many of the former students fondly remembered poetry and volleyball competitions, civic festivals, and dramatic plays (*obras de teatro*). The school's second principal, who arrived in 1943, apparently gave special impetus to theater. He wrote his own scripts for the students to perform (one of them was titled *Social Cancer,* with ominous themes—*de temática fuerte*—as some former students recalled).

Contrary to my expectations, most of the former students emphasized the individual nature of most academic work. Teachers rarely encouraged group collaboration, and students only gathered together in free moments or afternoon library rendezvous to help each other complete assignments. Still, in other regards, the school clearly fostered collective orientations. A doctor who studied at ESF from 1946 to 1949 recounted the time that students worked with teachers to level out a soccer field using simple plows. With the earth displaced by the plowing, the students helped manufacture adobe bricks that were later sold to raise funds for other school improvements. Values that were stressed by teachers included punctuality, respect for elders, good hygiene, love of country, civic duty, and faith in hard study and work. As one sixty-five-year-old woman who entered ESF in 1945 put it,

> In those days there was a lot of respect for the flag, the national anthem, the heroes, because the effects of the socialist education that Lázaro Cárdenas had installed were still being felt. All of us [former students] still boil [*hervimos*] with patriotic fervor to this day—and this is what's been lost because it's no longer given the same importance. Now the only thing they do are the civic acts and the flag ceremony every Monday, and even then [they do it] without much interest because the teachers are talking the whole time and don't help the teenagers and children to develop love for their country.

Though time with acquaintances in school was obviously circumscribed by the demands of family and work, former students displayed a remarkable memory for their friends and classmates. Many recited the full names and subtle idiosyncrasies of several classmates, whom they continued to see around town. Teachers in the 1940s and 1950s were often on familiar terms with students and their families, not so "distanced" as they are today. At that time, most ESF students belonged to the established families in town, and a good percentage appeared to continue on to the state capital for preparatory studies. Only about 5 percent of the students arrived from outside San Pablo, and most of those came from some of the larger towns and villages in the region.

By 1960, after an illustrious educator was brought to the school from a nearby city to act as principal, school enrollment still stood at just 170 students, although girls now comprised about a third of the overall student body.[30] In 1968, when the school was celebrating its twenty-fifth anniversary, ESF enrollment had nearly tripled to over 500 students. Girls at that time had come to comprise 40 percent of the student body, and four new shops had been created: printing and binding, mechanics, radio, and typing. As well, discussions about further expanding the school and constructing a new building had begun.

By the mid-1960s, the first secundaria técnica was also opened in San Pablo, less than a kilometer away from the present ESF site. This does not appear to have reduced enrollments at ESF, which were already circumscribed by the limited classroom space available. Rather, the técnica allowed many students who had not been accepted at ESF the chance to begin secondary studies. Many of these students were children of peasants and laborers.

In the early 1970s, construction began on the new school building for ESF. Through tripartite contributions from the State, teachers, and parents, sufficient funds were raised to erect entirely modern facilities. Many parents and teachers also chipped in with their labor or special knowledge. The new facilities allowed for a significant expansion of enrollments. By the end of the 1970s, enrollments were continuing to increase, and 1980 marked the first year that ESF expanded to six classroom groups for each of the first two grades in the morning shift (the third grade was comprised of five groups because of the substantial attrition rate). Yet another secundaria técnica opened up in 1981 and joined the other técnica in culling most of its students from the peasant and working classes. Indeed, the new técnica, located on the outskirts of town near a major intersection of regional bus routes, became a particularly attractive option for students traveling from outlying peasant communities.

By the late 1980s, however, enrollments were beginning a downward swing at both técnicas. Especially at the newer one, fewer and fewer students from the villages were attending, thus giving it a correspondingly greater proportion of city students. Not only did the economic crisis impede more of the former from attending but the establishment of new secundarias in smaller regional towns, as well as *telesecundarias* in some of the villages themselves, kept students closer to home.[31]

Such were the historical dynamics and contexts impinging on institutional life at ESF in 1990. Many administrators, teachers, and families had grown up in the San Pablo region, and many teachers had been steeped in the ideological discourses of cardenismo and the secundaria. They promised a solid education for the adolescent and nation. Yet as the school year at ESF began in 1990, enrollment rates and student expectations fluctuated with the uncertain rhythms of a faltering economy. How would ESF's noble history and regional prestige measure up to the new challenges of the day? What kind of adolescents would the school be forming, and what kind of region and nation would await its future graduates?

2. Ethnographic Beginnings:

A City, a School, an Anthropologist

In the spring of 1985, I arrived by bus in the center of San Pablo with my backpack and the name of a local family I had never met. Before graduating from the University of California the previous summer, I had arranged to tap its Mexican foreign study program in order to find a place to live and do volunteer work. The program kept a listing of schools, farms, clinics, and other potential work sites. Its aim was to provide a month-long experience of rural Mexico for students who otherwise would spend nine months at the national university in Mexico City. I was given the names and addresses of several such work sites on the condition that I not overlap my stay with that of a current program participant. Eventually, I chose to work at a rural elementary school in a large village just a few kilometers down the main road from San Pablo. The only local contact given me besides the school address, however, was that of a San Pablo family. That is why, when I arrived on a Saturday afternoon, I had to begin asking directions to the house of Mr. Solana and Mrs. Ramírez.[1]

The University of California wished to expose its students to the rural and provincial life pulsing beyond Mexico City. For myself, a native of suburban Los Angeles, rural Mexico presented a tantalizing sense of difference, a vaguely authentic scene well south of Tijuana and the border culture I had occasionally seen growing up. After all, I had journeyed all this way to learn Spanish and Mexican culture (whatever that was). When

I finally arrived in San Pablo after four months of travel and language study, I was ready to settle in for a while. The Solana Ramírez family accepted me into their home. Even though I soon switched to a room with a peasant family in the village where the primary school was located, I didn't lose touch with the Solana Ramírez family. I visited on weekends and became friends with their two oldest sons. Eventually, I would return for extended visits and then take up residence with them for the entire school year of 1990–1991.

Back in 1985, my primary school service came to involve more than I had expected or desired. I had hoped mostly to observe, perhaps to assist in keeping order or supervising physical activities for the kids. Instead, I found myself thrust into classrooms as a substitute teacher. Nearly each day a different teacher—responsible for a different grade—declared a holiday, sickness, or business leave. With less than four months of language practice, I stood and spoke haltingly in front of nearly fifty unfamiliar students. Most of the time the students ran wild, and I felt sure my presence was an unmitigated disaster. Apparently, though, the principal was pleased. I learned to keep some semblance of order; I entertained the students with stories and information about life in the United States, and took them out frequently to play in the field. To be sure, after a month my language skills had improved dramatically. More important, I had already gained a deep appreciation of the power the students had to press their interests and negotiate their claims on classroom time. I simultaneously cursed and honored these students, who quickly learned how to exploit my linguistic inadequacies, feign incomprehension, and challenge or circumvent what limited classroom authority I had managed to construct.

Almost two years later, after a stint teaching in a San Diego middle school, I entered graduate school in anthropology with a commitment to conducting research in Mexico. As I reviewed anthropological and sociological accounts of schooling, I became fascinated by the question of cultural reproduction and intrigued by the possibility of exploring it in a Mexican context. Yet I also knew that for questions about cultural reproduction, a rural primary school—with its rather young and socially homogeneous student body—would not suffice. That is when I began to consider a study of the secundaria in San Pablo, where I knew a few of my primary school's graduates might attend.

On a subsequent trip to San Pablo in the winter of 1986, I queried Mr. Solana and Mrs. Ramírez, both teachers at ESF, about the possibilities for doing research there. They took me to the school, introducing me to other teachers and administrators, and in the summer of 1988 I began making preliminary observations. It didn't take me long to discover that ESF had many of the characteristics that would bring fruit to a critically informed study. The mix of social classes and regions, rural and urban origins, even ethnicity (a number of students were indigenous), was fairly atypical by Mexican standards. Moreover, many of the teachers expressed interest in the proposed study, and felt my presence in the school could be useful to them and their students. Through the research, they might see their school in a different light; through my presence, students might learn about life in a different country. After one more preliminary fieldwork trip in the fall of 1989, I arrived in San Pablo in June 1990 with plans to lay the groundwork for my study of the coming school year. I would have the better part of a summer to settle in.

SAN PABLO: CLASS, CULTURE, AND ECONOMY
IN REGIONAL AND HISTORICAL PERSPECTIVE

San Pablo is best known for its colonial architecture and open-air market, which dominates the central part of town. From the official municipal market building, food and merchandise stalls spread in all directions, taking over side streets, and on busy weekend days, sprawling onto the small plaza. As any visitor to a Mexican market knows, the smells, sounds, and sights render the scene vivid and memorable. Slightly rotting fish mingles with the sweet fermentation of overripe fruit; the earthy vapors of warm tortillas mix with the acrid smoke of a nearby key shop. The bustle and open air, the predominance of simple wheeled carts and wooden crates, at first suggests an earlier time. Yet the market is a microcosm of the changes and contradictions permeating San Pablo. There, next to the braid-haired ancient woman selling tamales from an enamel pot between her stooping haunches, two teenagers repeatedly blare the song "Pump up the Jam," a wildly popular import from the U.S. rap group Technotronics. They have a table laid out with "pirated" tapes, amateur copies that sell for about an eighth of the original price. Nearby, a young housewife negotiates a purchase of fresh mangoes from a fruit stall. She wears an oversized T-shirt with the phrase "SHIT HAPPENS" in bold letters across her chest; her three-year-old child, straining her tenuous grip, reaches for the cheap plastic toys on the table next door. They are stamped clearly "Made in China," an offering of the highway entrepreneurs (*fayuqueros*) tripping back from the northern border.

Typical San Pablo street scene; the secundaria, ESF, is located down the street to the right

Most residents still call San Pablo a town (pueblo), even if it is now a significant provincial city in its own right—a regional market city in the west-central highlands of Mexico.[2] The city dates back to the colonial epoch as an important religious, commercial, and administrative center for an extensive peasant and artisanal region. From the earliest times, San Pablo served a nodal function in the regional culture and economy. Originally developed by the Spanish in the mid-1500s as a religious and administrative hub to displace the power of indigenous rulers, San Pablo soon acquired significant economic functions. The great Mexican anthropologist Gonzalo Aguirre Beltrán (1967) identified it as one of the "señorial" cities that exercised minimal control over the so-called "regions of refuge" configured by the flight of indigenous peoples to the most remote and inaccessible domains of the colonial territory. Such cities served to coordinate the exaction of tribute from indigenous communities as well as the schedule of Christian proselytizing. They also kept the indigenous effectively isolated from wider political developments.

San Pablo sits well over a mile high in Mexico's western transvolcanic belt, a region where one of Mexico's largest indigenous groups is still concentrated. In the area around San Pablo, this group continues to engage especially in farming, fishing, and small crafts production.[3] As I discuss below, since the turn of the twentieth century, many of those

39   Ethnographic Beginnings

communities once identified with indigenous language and culture have gradually incorporated themselves into the Mexican mestizo mainstream, shedding most traces of indigenous custom and adopting Spanish as the language of everyday discourse. Claudio Lomnitz-Adler (1992, 37–39) calls this "*mestización*," a historical process that effectively "deculturates" indigenous groups (see also Friedlander 1975; Frye 1996; King 1994). In the region comprised by San Pablo, mestización has been pervasive but not complete. Several communities retain a distinctive indigenous identity, while others only marginally preserve elements of native "tradition."[4] Further to the west, in the most rugged and isolated section of the mountains well beyond San Pablo, most communities are still marked by a strong, even militant indigenous identity. They have contributed to something of an ethnic renaissance even in the relatively more mestizoized region of San Pablo.

The rugged terrain of the western highlands insulated San Pablo from much of the ebb and flow of national life until some thirty years ago, when the first major through highways were built in the region. Up until then, San Pablo had acquired a reputation as a rather conservative, religious town, timeless and picturesque. Mr. Álvarez, one of the teachers at ESF, invoked this image of timelessness on recounting his own move to San Pablo as a young teacher in the mid-1960s. What stood out in his memory was how local residents would freeze in the streets and bow their heads at the hourly tolling of the church bells. The first time he witnessed it, Mr. Álvarez was thoroughly perplexed. It took him a few days to grasp the meaning of this Catholic custom. Compared to the larger, more cosmopolitan city where Mr. Álvarez had grown up, San Pablo was still highly bound by what he called "tradition."

Today, though a local elite may try to conserve the image of tradition to booster a form of nostalgic tourism, San Pablo has changed irrevocably. It has been transformed by the combined effects of improved transportation, a long and sustained period of international migration, and an influx of new cultural and consumer commodities.

REGIONAL POLITICAL ECONOMY

When I first arrived in San Pablo, I was struck by the age of the buildings and colonial style of their architecture. Several churches from the colonial epoch dominate the town's landscape, while individual businesses and residences toward the downtown area must, by city ordinance, paint their buildings a traditional brick red and white, and maintain their adobe facades and tile roofs in good repair. Declared a national treasure, San Pablo inspires many of its residents to keep private and public property in good condition, and present a courteous demeanor to visitors.

In recent years, the development of a tourist industry by local elites has effectively postponed the promotion of significant manufacturing or extractive industry in the area. San Pablo could therefore be labeled a tourist town, though its tourism industry is modest, locally controlled, and oriented primarily toward the domestic, rather than international, market. Many of the hotels and restaurants are in the hands of just a few elite families.[5] Today, timbering, furniture production, and textile weaving constitute the most significant industries in the San Pablo region, and none of the independent enterprises employ more than some fifteen workers each. Many residents own or work for small commercial operations, or work in the public sectors of education and transport. The central marketplace is undoubtedly the single most important area of employment in San Pablo, providing a range of occupations from small store owner to clerk, driver, or *cargador* (manual carrier). Despite the paradoxically conservative effects of tourism, many of the families whose children attend ESF participate in the tourist economy as vendors, taxi drivers, hotel workers, and craftspeople.

The typical San Pablo tourist undoubtedly miscalculates its true size, as I did on my first visit. This is because the quaint center zone of the city still exudes a relatively prosperous small-town atmosphere. In 1990, it was not uncommon to find campesinos still negotiating their merchandise through these narrow streets on the backs of burros. And in a city that had some fifty to sixty thousand inhabitants, not a single traffic light existed: municipal police directed traffic at the four or five heaviest intersections. Few visitors ever confront the sprawling lower-class neighborhoods (*colonias populares*) where the bulk of San Pablo's population lives in varying degrees of poverty.

San Pablo has always been, and remains, a study in contrasts. At present, an increasingly small, landed elite owns orchards and ranches nearby, and continues to live mostly in the old, centrally located colonial houses. These families may trace their ancestry to the earliest colonial settlers or, perhaps more likely, to the political and military leaders who benefited from the upheavals of the Cárdenas years (1928–1940). They share power with an emergent upper class that has developed political connections and accumulated wealth through well-invested earnings from migrant stints in the United States; timely investment in lucrative enterprises such as hotels, timber operations, and soft drink distributorships; or as many allege, involvement in the drug trade.[6] This upper-class group has tended to construct new, American-style homes on larger lots toward the city's periphery. A small, professional "middle class" (lawyers, doctors, architects, engineers) and "lower middle class" (schoolteachers, shop owners, federal and state bureaucrats, and skilled tradespeople) are in many cases interspersed residentially with the poorest classes in San Pablo, which consist of small vendors, day laborers, housecleaners, construction workers, artisans, and the unemployed. The absence of large-scale capitalist operations, whether in agriculture or industry, has prevented the rise of a well-defined and stable working class.[7]

CLASS CULTURE, IDENTITY, AND CONSCIOUSNESS

Most everyone I came to know expressed some opinion about the class structure of San Pablo, both in the present and past. The Spanish cognate *clase* was actively used to describe this structure. Yet the perception of social class differences in San Pablo varied tremendously, and folk taxonomies correspondingly ran the gamut. On one end of the spectrum there was my artist friend, who pointedly divided local society into the rich, middle, and "screwed" (*jodidos*). Poorer city residents, for their part, tended to describe a group of *ricos* (rich), *pudientes* (wealthy), or *adinerados* (monied), while wealthier or professional residents would lament the plight of the *pobres* (poor), the *gente humilde* (humble folk). Between 1985 and 1995, I linked the emergent upper class to an observably growing pauperization. Yet San Pabloans typically downplayed such trends. They did acknowledge the gap between rich and poor, and several of my poorer friends drew attention to what they considered a crude and illegitimate display of wealth by some of the ricos. Still, most insisted that the vast majority of townspeople were "around the middle" (*en un término medio*).

I would soon learn that the majority of students at ESF also considered themselves "middle class" in the local terminology, regardless of their economic or cultural status, and despite their placement in what Claudio Lomnitz-Adler (1992) would call rather different class-ethnic "intimate cultures" of neighborhood and community.[8] ESF students thus articulated a hopeful portrait of the broad middle. This was the view of many young professionals as well, like the ESF teacher and his young female friend whom I engaged in conversation one day. Both argued that there were no longer any *gente acomodada* (privileged folk) in San Pablo, that the upper class had vanished with its fortune during the Cárdenas period or because of immoderate gambling and spending during the boom years of the 1940s and 1950s. Today, they said, most of the wealthier people in San Pablo had started out poor and worked hard to make something more of themselves (*superarse*). Though they might have made a lot of money, they remained modest and simple (*sencillos*) in their attitudes and customs, the two asserted. The cultural line between the upper and middle classes had been erased or blurred as the distinctive signs of wealth became less salient in everyday life.

Some of this was undoubtedly true, but the image of blurred class distinctions probably more accurately reflected a cultural ideal of solidarity and a large dose of wishful thinking. If the upper and middle classes were indeed blending together in some fashion, my own observations would suggest the line between the middle and low had never been stronger. The association between secondary schooling and so-called middle-class status had a lot to do with this. As I will show, school practices and discourses at ESF allowed some students to cross this line within school, especially to move symbolically from low to middle, from "country" to "city." Yet such practices, appropriated by students and their families, ironically served to reinforce class distinctions outside the school, in the reconstructed idiom of "schooled" and "unschooled" (see chapter 6).

Discourses of class identity issue from the social position and experience of the person (Bourdieu 1984), and they typically get expressed only in certain communicative contexts. My failure to detect a *persistent* sense of relationally defined class culture and identity in San Pablo may only reflect my limited perception as a foreign anthropologist or my limited ability to establish a relation of trust that might encourage such expressions. Nevertheless, something of a "hidden transcript" (Scott 1990) of subaltern discourse about dominant local groups would emerge from time to time. Less schooled informants, in particular, would comment on the injustices and indignities they suffered at the hands of more formally educated, powerful groups. They would valorize their more practical knowledge (of the land, automotive mechanics, or hunting, for instance) over and against the privileges of professional knowledge acquired and accredited through schools.

For instance, one Saturday afternoon in late January I was chatting with Ramón, a maintenance worker with the Fisheries Secretariat whom I had befriended during a bus ride a few months earlier. Ramón's five children had all studied for some years at secundarias, though most had never finished. His youngest was presently in his third and final year of the evening shift at ESF. In addition to his work at the fishery, Ramón trapped wild birds for sale and baked bread in an old-style adobe oven he had built in his backyard. He was a very resourceful man. When I asked him on this day when we might sit down at length to talk about his views on the school, "You know, what it's good for, all of that," he responded with a playful smile and effectively began the interview: "It's good for removing some of the foolishness from the kids" ("*Sirve para quitarles algo del pendejo de los muchachos*"). We chuckled together, but moments later he turned more serious, commenting:

> No, the school does work for us, it does us a lot of good, but it hurts us also, because there are people who know neither how to read nor to write, but who do know four or five trades. . . . So someone who ends up with many years of schooling, let's say he's a teacher or an engineer, but that's it, whereas I know people who can build houses and repair cars, they know how to farm and raise animals, that's right, they have many trades. . . . I think the professionals look down on us for being ignorant, they judge us for no good reason [*nos ven menos por ignorantes, nos juzgan, y no tienen por qué*].

In his remarks, Ramón clearly describes his "hidden injuries of class" (Sennett and Cobb 1972), the "symbolic violence" (Bourdieu and Passeron 1977) perpetrated by the school when it provides a socially recognized value to its graduates without honoring the knowledge of those who left school early. Though told in confidence to me, Ramón's is plainly a subversive discourse that aims to decenter dominant forms of knowledge and value.

Still, such utterances rarely articulated a sense of collective or class consciousness. While poorer San Pablo residents recognized many forms of hierarchy and power in the region, the absence of more deeply rooted class-based identifications around common occupation, residence, or social demands (unions or collective petitions for urban services, for instance) seemed to deny them the horizon within which to situate their experience collectively. Cross-cutting religious and kin affiliations, as well as stratification within occupations and neighborhoods, worked against class identification, too. Moreover, perhaps because in recent years the investments made by international migrants had created more fluidity in the local class structure, any sense of rigid, long-standing class distinctions had been blunted. The wealthy and professional seemed more avid to draw class lines, in part through the behavior they endorsed for their children. Most San Pablo residents smirked at those teenagers—called here and elsewhere in Mexico the *juniors*[9]—who ostentatiously drove their late-model cars around the main plaza and otherwise engaged in conspicuous displays of consumerism. As I learned, parents of these children were more apt to encourage their association with those similarly positioned in local society. Among the nonprofessional middle or lower classes, however, dispersed in different neighborhoods and workplaces, there was little feeling of class division. Fractured and isolated intimate cultures assured that amid plentiful signs of social class difference, there was nevertheless no well-defined class culture in San Pablo. Class identity and position was much more likely to be ascribed to others than assumed by individuals themselves.

POPULATION AND MIGRATION

Despite the lack of any significant industrial or manufacturing base, San Pablo's population has grown more rapidly than most cities in the state where it is located. Many attribute this to the deterioration of conditions for rural life in San Pablo's hinterland: on the one hand, high rates of erosion, deforestation, and drought; on the other, increasingly limited agricultural credit (Gledhill 1991, 1995; López Castro and Pardo Galván 1988). These natural and political-economic processes have forced more and more peasants into the precarious outlying shantytowns of San Pablo. Many longtime residents also emphasize the inflow of immigrants from Mexico City after the 1985 earthquake, as well as the increased popularity of San Pablo as a site for Mexico City's wealthy to construct their vacation homes. These observations are less than systematic, though, and I have reason to suspect them. The same residents were likely to lament the transformation of the town from a sleepy pueblo of some 15,000 people in the late 1960s to a midsize provincial city that, by 1990, had begun to take on the characteristics and problems of a larger metropolis. The population by then had been calculated at nearly 50,000 people, and the negative influence of Mexico City's *chilangos* (a pejorative term for natives of the national capital) was occasionally highlighted.[10]

Ironically, the very same conditions pushing rural peoples into San Pablo have also made the general region (the west-central highlands and Bajío) notorious as a launching pad for emigration to the United States and other states in Mexico as well. The state where San Pablo is located has always had among the highest rates of out-migration in Mexico (Fernández 1988, 116; Corona Vázquez 1988, 181–83). A sustained history of migration to the United States began around the turn of the twentieth century and received further impetus with the U.S. government–sponsored Bracero program of 1942–1964, which recruited Mexican farmworkers on a contract basis. From that time, migrants branched into other industries and formed more permanent settlements that acted as "daughter communities" to receive newly arriving migrants (Massey et al. 1987). By 1990, emigration was no longer restricted to rural communities. It was now common in San Pablo for unemployed professionals and sons of the urban working class to "go up North" (*ir para el Norte*), whether out of economic need, a sense of adventure, or both (see Chávez 1992) Remittances were being used to support families as well as to finance improvements and educational opportunities in Mexico. I knew ESF teachers and other skilled tradespeople who had spent a number of years in the United States, and by 1993, I was to discover that three of my twelve male focal students were residing illegally in California or Oregon (see chapter 7). Clearly, migration had become deeply incorporated into local repertoires of economic strategy and symbolic desire. Men were, for the most part, those who dreamed and traveled, but women, too, had begun participating in greater measure (Hondagneu-Sotelo 1994).

Like Mexico more generally, San Pablo's demographic structure is dominated by youth. Nearly 50 percent of the municipality's population is under eighteen years of age, and few means of adequate, full-time employment have been available to younger people since a long-term recession began in 1982. High school and college graduates rarely find work in San Pablo that corresponds to their training, so they are increasingly forced to look elsewhere. This, in turn, collides with a strong local sense of place and an equally strong parental imperative for children to stay somewhere nearby. Only in cases where families or communities have established migratory beachheads, *familiares* ready and willing to guide the arrival of migrants, do families typically endorse a child's move. Of course, young men and women do not entirely share the same options in this regard (see chapters 6 and 7).

SOCIAL CLASS AND SECONDARY SCHOOLING

Since the schools collect little socioeconomic data, I administered a basic survey in May 1991 to all students in the morning shift at ESF and several selected third-grade groups in each of three other local secundarias: the afternoon shift at ESF itself (ESF-TV, or Turno Vespertino, which I consider here as a separate school), one of the two public secundarias técnicas, and a *colegio* (religious private school). The survey didn't go quite as I had hoped, but the results were nonetheless instructive. Because students no doubt found it difficult to accommodate the complexity of their lives to a categorical instrument, the survey in fact turned out to be rather unreliable. Many students could not accurately describe what exactly their parents or guardians did, nor could they calculate approximate income levels, despite my guidance and explicit instructions throughout the process. In fact, in many cases, the descriptions they provided did not allow me to ascertain what their parents' economic activity might entail—especially considering numerous instances where parents performed several jobs at once. Some students listed their fathers as carpenters or ironworkers, without specifying whether they owned their businesses or worked for somebody else. What this exercise reinforced for me, above all, was the often unremarked crudity of survey instruments designed to gather "hard" data about stable and unitary families, jobs, and incomes. In San Pablo, in 1991, there were hardly any such animals, as they say.

The survey did enable me to confirm in a general fashion the class differences between the schools. The question of class in San Pablo, as I've already suggested, is rather complex, and the survey only allowed me to assign class location based on occupation, a rough indicator at best. I had broken down the occupational categories in such a way as to try to capture the overlapping differences of intimate cultures as well. Moreover, given the paucity of student mothers who worked full-time for monetary income, I tended to rely on the data for father's occupation to determine socioeconomic level. Most students listed their mothers as housewife (*ama de casa*), though many indicated their mothers engaged in some kind of small-scale commercial activity (between 15 and 20 percent for all four schools). In addition, some 10 percent of ESF mothers, in particular, were schoolteachers, with another 10 to 15 percent employed as secretaries, clerks, nurses, or maids. With the exception of the relatively high number of schoolteachers among ESF mothers, the figures for mothers were also similar at the other three schools.

What stood out most in the comparison across the four schools was the greater proportion of the student body with fathers in manual occupations at ESF-TV and the técnica, and a conversely high proportion of

Table 1. Fathers' Occupations, by School

	ESF (n = 190)	ESF-TV (n = 92)	EST (n = 69)	Colegio (n = 42)
Teacher	13%	1%	9%	6%
Merchant	25	22	7	60
Skilled Trade	9	25	25	2
Clerk/Employee	17	9	9	2
Peasant/Day Laborer	9	21	28	13
Artisan	2	1	0	0
Driver	7	9	9	2
Professional	7	3	1	10
Emigrated to United States	3	7	1	0
Municipal Worker	7	1	4	5
Other	1	1	7	0
Total Percentage	100%	100%	100%	100%

fathers as merchants and professionals (including schoolteachers) at ESF and the private colegio. Indeed, the concentration of merchants' children at the colegio was striking, though I suspect the reporting of occupational categories there may have been significantly skewed by a higher-status peer culture. On balance, and despite the high number of schoolteachers, the socioeconomic composition of ESF was nonetheless more similar to those of ESF-TV and the técnica than to the private colegio. Overall, ESF had the greatest balance and diversity in fathers' occupations and overall socioeconomic level.

Although it had not yet registered fully in the schools, an ongoing recession since 1982, which had hit San Pablo rather hard, threatened to alter the class configuration of school populations I have just documented. In fact, it appeared that ESF was suffering from an institutional crisis of underenrollment at the beginning of the school year in 1990. Fewer students than usual had taken the admissions exam, and class sizes had dropped dramatically, from over fifty in 1987 to between forty and forty-five in 1990. As I talked with teachers about this reduction, I noted a fascinating array of explanations for it. While the principal insisted it had most to do with his successful policies of selection and control, teachers proposed several alternatives. A number cited possible reductions in the overall birthrate after an intensive government family planning campaign during the 1970s, whose success would have translated into lower secundaria enrollments during the late 1980s. Other teachers suggested that the general population had continued growing, but that parents and students could either no longer afford secondary studies (the "voluntary" registration fee had risen at ESF more rapidly than at other schools; see below) or no longer saw the value of obtaining a secondary school certificate. Finally, a few acknowledged that the teacher mobilizations of the previous school year, which had forced ESF to close for weeks at a time, had shaken parents' confidence. They were said to be voting with their feet, and their choices now included two new private schools.

In point of fact, enrollments at the other two local public secundarias were also down in 1990, but not by as much. As the administrative head of secondary education in the state noted during a teachers' meeting later in the year, secundaria enrollments throughout the region had been declining and private schools were blossoming.[11] In San Pablo alone, two private schools began offering secondary studies in 1990, and as a result, ESF lost seventy-nine potential students. This did not threaten the viability of ESF or other public secundarias in San Pablo; certainly ESF did not stand to lose any teaching positions due to reduced enrollments.[12] Yet the trend toward privatization and greater numbers of dropouts—with a corresponding siphon of the wealthiest and poorest kids—did suggest that in the 1990s, ESF might experience even more of the class leveling that had slowly begun during the 1980s.

SETTING THE ETHNOGRAPHIC STAGE:
SUMMER 1990 AND THE NEW SCHOOL YEAR

Even at the beginning of the summer, it was clear from the teachers' point of view that the 1990 school year would not begin on a good note. The previous year had been filled with acrimonious exchanges between opposing factions of the official teachers' union. The *oficiales,* derisively named *charros* (cowboys) by their detractors because of their allegedly authoritarian style, supported the official State-sponsored union, the Sindicato Nacional de Trabajadores de Educación (SNTE). The self-named *democráticos,* scornfully referred to as *disidentes* (dissidents) or *faltistas* (absentees) by the oficiales for their tendency to call work stoppages and thus miss class, supported the breakaway Coordinadora Nacional de Trabajadores de Educación (CNTE).[13] As their name indicates, the democráticos were struggling for greater democracy in the selection of union representatives and job assignments within the corrupt and hierarchical union, as well as greater autonomy from the State. Not incidentally, they were also requesting a 100 percent increase in teachers' salaries, which in real terms had plummeted to their lowest point in over fifty years. Beginning primary and secondary schoolteachers were earning only between $150 and $250 per month, hardly sufficient in the inflationary economy that followed the 1982 crisis. The oficiales, for their part, clearly sympathized with some of the democráticos' demands, especially over salary, although most were either too indebted to the structure of union privilege or too committed to the authority of the State to press these demands. At least in rhetoric, they eschewed combative tactics, and promoted instead incremental change through union discipline and lobbying via official government channels.

ESF was thus racked by conflict. By my own estimate, approximately 65 percent of the regular teachers affiliated themselves with the democratic CNTE and its local organization, the Movimiento Democrático Magisterial (MDM, or Democratic Teachers' Movement), while the other 35 percent followed the official SNTE. Several teachers, of course, tried to remain neutral, including the principal and one vice principal, while others switched allegiances at various times during the year. The intentions and sympathies of the less visibly committed teachers were the subject of gossip and speculation on both sides, and sometimes the accusations grew ugly. Democráticos viewed the oficiales as corrupt and compromised employees of an equally corrupt State. The oficiales, according to them, tended to be lazy and poorly prepared. Many oficiales presumably were never trained as teachers, and had acquired their jobs through bribes or union "friendships." As the democráticos were fond of saying, numerous oficiales had been "made teachers out of thin air" ("*se hicieron maestros al vapor*"). Accordingly, the democráticos felt that to struggle for union democracy was also to improve the degraded professional image oficiales gave to teaching. The oficiales, for their part, saw the democráticos as a bunch of overpoliticized malcontents that had ruptured labor "unity." Their frequent work stoppages, which supposedly betrayed their own self-interest and laziness, would only serve to alienate parents and damage the professional image of teachers.

In July 1990, just after I had arrived, the democráticos' MDM began to remobilize its forces for the protests of the coming school year. They had already managed to shut down most schools in the state for a solid month the year before, and with classes scheduled for late August, they were threatening more of the same. This time, there was even more at stake. In addition to union democracy and higher salaries, their agenda now included a postponement of the national Plan for Educational Modernization (PME), scheduled to launch its first "test operation" in sample schools that fall. A set of curricular and administrative reforms proposed by the Salinas regime in 1989, the PME had apparently been developed with little input from teachers. For the rest of the summer, I listened to MDM's critical analysis of the PME in vociferous street protests, and read it in movement circulars and opposition newspaper articles. What struck me was the radical tone of the critique. The changes proposed in the plan were portrayed as veiled attempts by a bourgeois State to reverse the social gains of the Mexican Revolution—a U.S.-inspired program to provide cheap skilled labor for a ruling class at the expense of a more critical and socially progressive education. Indeed, the language and categories of analysis were remarkably similar to the neomarxist critique of the MDM capitalist education known as social reproduction theory (see appendix A).[14]

As I've said, the 1990 school year was not looking good, and to make matters worse, in early July, the general secretary of the democratic faction, Gerardo, fell mortally ill and died. I had arrived just the week before when one of my closest friends among the teachers asked me to accompany his family to the wake. On the way there, he mentioned that a number of democráticos placed the blame for Gerardo's death on the oficiales. Though he had ultimately died of liver failure, probably a result of excessive alcohol consumption, democráticos recounted the pressures and threats to which Gerardo had been subjected as general secretary. They even claimed that the oficiales had tried to run him over once with a car. Gerardo's health apparently began going downhill when the threats and accusations had intensified. The democráticos insisted that oficialista harassment, however indirectly, had precipitated Gerardo's death.

Most of the democráticos were sitting together at the wake. Several men tried to keep the mood light, and when I asked those present about the difficulties of pursuing a teaching career, the men regaled us with outlandish stories about their first teaching jobs in remote villages. These stories tended to exaggerate the backwardness and male dominance of Mexican peasant society. In one story, a man living with two wives, and thus morally compromised by prevailing Catholic beliefs, nevertheless threatened to kill the teacher just because he had become the object of the man's sister's attractions.[15] A while later, the mood turned more somber. The primary school inspector for the region, sitting next to me, began to lament the current state of the teaching profession. He was inclined to wait it out another two years, collect his thirty-year pension, and move on. The school year might not even begin on schedule if the union conflict continued, he said. Then he swept his hand around him so I would observe the modesty of our surroundings: a small, unfinished cinder block home in the poor part of town, and a muddy, unsheltered entryway, made gloomier by the afternoon drizzle. "This is what a teacher has after working for twenty-some-odd years," he commented. "Look around you. This tells you more than any words."

A month later, when the teachers first reported to school for duty, talk of strike was thick in the air.[16]

During the registration period of late August, I roved the school and observed exchanges between parents, teachers, and incoming students. I also witnessed meetings between teachers and administrators. Here was an opportunity to assess the school's interactional climate at the outset of the year. It soon became clear to me that some teachers were complaining about the task of checking registration "fees" from parents. These fees, in reality a donation called a *cooperación,* were established by the elected Parents' Association (*Sociedad de Padres de Familia,* or SPF), and used to improve and upgrade school facilities.[17] As a free and public institution, the school could not insist on such fees. In practice, however, the SPF, whose leadership was perennially dominated by wealthier parents, used various means to ensure collection. They set up a collection table in the central plaza and successfully enlisted most teachers to condition class registration on receipt of the cooperación. Arriving students and their parents would typically first pay their cooperación and then show the receipt to a teacher for enrollment. But many parents complained to the teachers about the fee, and others tried to enroll their children without paying. Some teachers effectively denied enrollment to those without a receipt, instructing them to pay first; most simply marked down the delinquencies and referred them to the SPF, which kept an accounting of payments in arrears. Payment could often be made over several months or in the form of labor and materials for minor construction projects.

On one of the last days of registration, I decided to spend a few hours at the SPF's collection table in the plaza. Behind the spare folding table and neat collection of receipt books sat a man and woman with rather stern demeanors. The woman, heavily made-up and dressed in elegant gray boots, a skirt, and a red wool sweater, barely acknowledged me when I gestured for permission to sit down and take some notes. A few parents were waiting to pay their fees. Some minutes later, just as I was about to introduce myself to the SPF representatives, the principal came by to greet us. He then directed himself to the man, a former ESF student and currently employed schoolteacher who functioned as the SPF treasurer. The principal told the treasurer that a number of parents had come to his office with rather vocal complaints about the high fees ("*Han llegado algunos muy groseros*"). In lighthearted fashion, the principal recounted a few interactions, and the treasurer nodded, smiling, and finally said, "If they can't pay, let them give us what they can now, and then the rest later, every two weeks, or whenever." The principal soon took leave and left us alone again to introduce ourselves.

Next, the woman, who I learned was a professional pharmacist and the SPF secretary, grilled me about the goals of my study, never cracking a smile. We were interrupted soon after by a man who took a rather aggressive stance in front of the table. Accompanied by his son, the unshaven man wore a stained white shirt only partially tucked into dirty blue work slacks. He told us that he would not get paid until Saturday and that his son had failed to warn him that the cooperación would be due at the time of enrollment. He glared at his son as if to direct the blame there. The treasurer assured him he could bring the fee on Monday and began registering his name in the notebook of delinquent payments. The *Doctora,* as the treasurer had been calling the secretary, then began to lecture the man about parenting, saying, "He's just a boy. You've got to make him learn responsibility" ("*Es chamaco. Hay que responsabilizarlo*"). She continued in this vein for another minute or so until the man cut her off with an irritated "*Está bien, señora*" ("Fine, ma'am"), and turned to the treasurer to confirm the information before brusquely striding off. As I would eventually learn, I had just witnessed a class-coded interaction in which the well-bred Doctora had assumed the prerogative to "educate" the poor man about proper child-rearing technique. The man had chosen not to confront her presumptuousness, but his exasperation was still palpable.

The students were due to arrive the following week for their first day of classes. What would the school look and feel like to them? How would they respond to the conflict among the teachers? Would they show the same sense of class status in relating to one another or would the trope of equality prevail? In the last chapter, we saw how and why the students, on starting their first year at the secundaria, would be discursively positioned as adolescents, striving in solidarity to serve the nation while still seeking their own personal advancement. The historical contexts of Mexican educational development, uniquely manifest at ESF, provided a set of symbolic resources that would both constrain and enable students' action in the school. In this chapter, I entwined my own ethnographic beginnings with a structural accounting of San Pablo and ESF. I offered yet another angle on the social world students would encounter and remake at ESF. Yet before the students are explored up close, it remains to describe the way history became present-day institutional structure and practice at ESF. This is the work of the next chapter.

3. Institutional Contexts:

The School Students Encountered

In this chapter, I continue the ethnographic journey through the beginning of the school year to see just what kind of institution the students encountered. What did teachers say and do, and how was the school week and year organized? What kinds of contexts made up the institutional structure—the concrete practices and discourses framing students' experience in the school? I cover such institutional elements in sequence, including the process of transition from primary school to the secundaria; the formation and discursive construction of the grupo escolar; the spatial configuration and ritualized routine of school life; the patterns of curriculum, evaluation, and pedagogical practice; even the gendered elements of teacher example and expectation. It was within and against such structural elements that students elaborated their own practice.

ENTERING ESF: THE STUDENTS' VIEW

The day before the first-year admission exam in mid-August, I was visiting some friends whose daughter, Irma, would be taking the test. They were both longtime schoolteachers—the father was principal of a nearby secundaria—and thus tried to reassure their daughter, who appeared quite nervous. In the past, it was true, the admissions exam at ESF had been used to select the best students. Long considered the most prestigious school in the region, ESF had always counted on a surplus of applicants that might be sent away to the other schools in town. Yet in recent years, the applicant pool had diminished, and there was reason to believe that most, if not all, applicants would be enrolled this year. Moreover, my friends' status as teachers would allow them to elicit reciprocal "favors" from ESF colleagues, virtually guaranteeing their daughter a place in the school. Irma was nevertheless fretting about her first day. The next morning, I saw Irma arrive at ESF with her mother. She was grasping her stomach, and her mother guided her quickly to the bathroom, where she promptly threw up.

Not all students respond so viscerally to their first days in the school, of course. Irma's jitters were in part due to the perceived pressure of the exam, but she told me later that she felt sick most of the first week of classes, too. Other students recounted similar experiences. These first-year students averaged eleven to thirteen years in age. Often, the admissions exam would provide their first occasion to enter the school, whose size and complexity could be daunting. During the enrollment period the following week, students would bring a parent or guardian to meet with teachers and fill out the enrollment forms. Among other things, students and their parents had to sign a form acknowledging their awareness of the school rules (*reglamento*), which included a variety of items, from attendance policy to personal appearance. Emphasis was placed on "respectful" and "orderly" conduct at all times.[1] The parents tried to concentrate their children on the forms as the students nervously eyed their new surroundings.

New students came from primarias, public and private, spread all over town. About 15 percent of the students had attended primaria in a small rural school or some distant city. For those who had gone to public primary schools, the change would not be so drastic. Many of the practices, even the physical design of the classrooms, remained the same. Students knew, for instance, that they would be expected to line up in the central civic plaza each Monday and render homage to the Mexican flag. The greatest change was in the size and complexity of the school. Some students had attended small rural schools with as few as two classrooms and a small dirt yard; others had attended the largest San Pablo primaria, with its twelve solid classrooms and cement walkways. Still, nothing prepared them for the multilevel secundaria, with its eighteen academic classrooms, two science laboratories, auditorium, administrative offices, "cooperative" store, and eight shop rooms (see figure 2). Nothing prepared

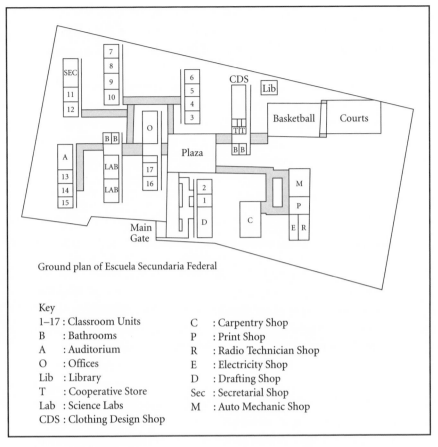

Fig. 2. Ground plan of ESF

them for the complex schedule they would have to follow or the adaptations they would have to make to the eight different teachers they'd face each week. In the primaria, students typically spent the entire day with the same teacher. At ESF, a manually operated central buzzer signaled the change between class and recess periods about seven times a day. Many students had also studied two or more years with the same teacher in the primaria. In the secundaria, they would be lucky to have the same teacher for a subject two years in a row.

For those switching from private schools, the change could be even more intimidating. The private colegios physically and emotionally cloistered their charges. Classroom groups were typically smaller, with the classrooms themselves physically and visually removed from city life. At colegios, teachers were often stricter, yet also more intimately aware of particular student qualities. Many students who had attended primary school at a colegio recounted their fear and apprehension on arriving at the secundaria. They had heard that students were "rougher" (*más groseros*) in the public schools, and for many, this expectation was later confirmed.

Third-year students told me that they had been most tentative during their first few months in the school. They would get lost on the way to a class, misinterpret the teachers' instructions, or misread a classmate's intentions. The familiar relationships of primaria had been superseded by a new set of classmates and organizational challenges. Most consequential of all was the structure and ethos of their incoming classroom cohort, the academic group, or grupo escolar.

THE GRUPO ESCOLAR: COMPETITION, SOLIDARITY, AND EQUALITY

Students got to know their classmates exceedingly well for they were placed in a structured cohort on enrollment that, with few exceptions, would remain together as a cohort for all three years. Within the secundaria, the grupo escolar weighed most heavily in the structuring of social relations. With the exception of technical shop courses (again, talleres), which were chosen independently by students when they first entered the school, grupos escolares stayed together for all classes and many extracurricular activities as well (for example, athletic contests, morning lineup, and school fairs). The social significance of the grupo escolar, however, transcended its organizational function. Teachers and students alike invested the grupo escolar with meanings rooted in discourses of equality, cooperation, and solidarity. (Indeed, because of this, I prefer to conserve the Spanish term *grupo escolar* and not gloss it with more familiar English terms, such as *class* or *homeroom*). Such meanings were only partly contradicted on occasion by cross-cutting emphases on individual progress and competition. As we shall see in the next chapter, students appropriated the social space and discursive resources provided by the grupo escolar to construct their relations to the school and each other. The grupo escolar became central to students' cultural game of equality.

Just how were the grupos formed? In August 1990, with only two weeks left before classes, teachers and administrators busily set out to form grupos escolares out of some five hundred newly enrolled students.[2] Those teachers designated to do the calculations had to average students' admissions exam scores with their overall grade average from primaria. Then, based on this composite score, teachers systematically distributed

Second-year students take a break from their lesson in a cold winter classroom

students among the six morning and six afternoon grupos escolares. The student receiving the highest composite score was placed in grupo 1A, the one who followed in 1B, and so on, until 1L was reached, after which the cycle was begun again. The logic of distribution was to create grupos as academically heterogeneous as possible, with little consideration given to ability, age, class, gender, or ethnicity. The effect was to create grupos equally heterogeneous in social terms.[3]

I became fascinated with the logic behind forming the heterogeneous grupo escolar and was determined to find out what the teachers thought. When I asked them during informal chats, many teachers cited the learning benefits in having a full range of abilities represented in the grupo. According to them, the smartest students would tend to bring the others along ("*jalar a los demás*").[4] Yet ESF teachers also articulated a distinct social logic for heterogeneous grouping: mixed grupos encouraged students of different genders, ages, social classes, and regions to learn about and adapt to one another. Top administrators, obviously self-conscious about representing the school's image to outsiders, expressed this point most clearly and consistently.[5] The vice principal, who had been at ESF since 1967, explained that at different times in the school's recent history, grupos had been formed by age, demonstrated academic ability, socio-economic level, or place of origin. Yet he was convinced that the homogeneous grupos had largely failed, both socially and pedagogically. Signs of discrimination had always surfaced, and this appears to have deeply offended many teachers' sensibilities. In our conversation, the vice principal himself recounted his experience with discrimination as a youngster. It is interesting to note how he constructs present school practices in light of that:

> VICE PRINCIPAL: I remember that in the school where I studied primaria there was one line for the studious [*aplicados*], another for the— what did they used to call them?—for the in-betweens [*medios*], and another for the dunces [*burros*].
>
> BRADLEY LEVINSON: And that's what the teachers called them?
>
> VP: Yes, that's what they called them.
>
> BL: Which line were you in?
>
> VP: In the last one I think [laughter]. . . . No, I was a genius as a child. As a *child,* I mean [more laughter]. When I got older I lost it. . . . Anyway, I was always one of the studious. I liked to study. But I remember that those in the dunce line, well, they looked pretty bad, and they felt bad. We even looked on them as sort of second class. So we don't want that sort of thing to be repeated here (at ESF). We don't want there to be that sort of discrimination, whether by intelligence or economic level.

Moments later in this same interview, the vice principal began to discuss the problems that emerged at ESF when students were formed into grupos according to their place of origin. It must be remembered here that some 10 to 15 percent of ESF's morning students normally resided in agricultural or fishing villages, many of which still preserved their indigenous language, dress, ritual, and subsistence activities. The vice principal revealed some of the more explicit principles underlying the school's rejection of difference and discrimination:

> BL: So how did it go when you had the grupos by place of origin?
>
> VP: OK, more or less. . . . They studied well, but the problem we began to see was that there wasn't any exchange of cultures, so to speak. Those from Cumbira kept on being from Cumbira, even though they might be living here [in San Pablo], and those from the city kept on being from the city, without any knowledge of another way of life.
>
> BL: And you teachers, on the other hand, want them to mix among themselves here in the school? [VP: Yes.] Are all the teachers definitely in agreement with that goal?

VP: Yes, in fact at that time, Mexican educational policy had that meaning . . . to homogenize the population. Mexico has a problem. We don't have a nationality. I mean, there are a lot of different ethnic groups, there are even a lot of different languages spoken, and it's not just the languages, it's the customs, the food, the dress, everything. So I imagine what the Mexican government was trying to create was a sense of nationality shared a little more between everybody, to create a Mexican culture, even if we were to become a mixture, but a culture that might be called Mexican.

In this exchange, the vice principal explicitly invoked the homogenizing, assimilationist logic behind State educational action in postrevolutionary Mexico. The discourse of homogenization endorsed a certain kind of equality—the equality of sameness in national identity, of commonality in a so-called Mexican culture.[6] At ESF, this discourse provided one of the key rationales for the present heterogeneity of school grouping. The vice principal, to be sure, had his story worked out with specific reference to official government policy. So, too, did the principal.[7] Yet even teachers less self-conscious about policy hoped to create common national identifications among students from disparate social backgrounds by subjecting them to the same educational messages and exhorting them to unified endeavor within the grupo escolar.[8] In this way, ESF teachers enacted an important "everyday form of state formation" (Joseph and Nugent 1994), linked to the historical project of creating and reinforcing national identity while encouraging participation in a national culture.

From the first day of classes, students learned through experience that their grupo escolar would become a basic reference for virtually all school activities. Teachers tended to foster identification with the grupo in a number of ways. Exhortations to maintain grupo solidarity constantly punctuated teachers' classroom lessons; basic or technical school knowledge became embedded in broader, directive statements about social conduct and responsibility. In a biology lesson, to give just one example, Mr. González turned a discussion of the human immune system—the dynamics of white blood cells uniting to attack infected red blood cells—into a moral illustration of the need for the grupo to stick together and discipline its own. As he said, "Here in the grupo, too, we must unite against those bad elements that might disrupt our healthy functioning and progress."

Students were told to help one another out in understanding class assignments or making the adjustment from primary school. Teachers emphasized grupo unity and the development of a healthy camaraderie (*compañerismo*). Importantly, teachers conditioned students' "rights" (*derechos*) to enjoy school activities on their "obligations" (*responsabilidades*) to their classmates (see Levinson 1998b). The principal himself used this language when admonishing a grupo to take care of its classroom:[9]

> Maybe there will be some students who don't want to put in their share, who don't have that sense of cooperation, of solidarity. Well, we'll just have to speak with them, we have to make them aware [*concientizarlos*], make them see that they belong to a grupo, and that grupo carries certain obligations also, so that they can then have certain rights.

Among the other obligations teachers stressed were trust and respect between and among students and teachers. Most teachers had harsh words for students who formed highly exclusive friendship groups within the grupo escolar. Especially in their official capacity as grupo advisers (*asesores*), they also emphasized grupo unity outside the classroom itself. They encouraged students to support their grupo's athletic team and sent student delegations, occasionally the entire grupo, to the home of a member who was ill or had lost a close family member.

Most teachers reinforced grupo allegiances and discouraged students from breaking ranks in other matters, too. Early in the year, grupos chose two student representatives to form part of a candidate slate (*planilla*) for student government positions. Only third-year students could run for president. As the candidates later recounted to me, some teachers apparently imposed the representatives they saw most fit. They then discouraged grupo members from voting for any candidate other than the one nominated by the grupo. Students by and large followed this command. Candidates themselves were often reluctant, but felt obliged to run if their teachers or classmates had chosen them (see chapter 4).

Comparisons were constantly being drawn between the grupos. Every morning, students lined up by grupos (and by sex) on the main plaza, and each week a different grupo was responsible for the Monday morning civic ceremony. Quarterly grade averages, failure rates, and punctuality records were also calculated and ranked by grupo, and then posted in conspicuous fashion. In one case, the Spanish teacher Mr. Cantú wagered a large cake that grupo 3A would not maintain its lead in the grade-average competition. If they slipped in rank, the students would have to provide

Third-year girls take a break from chatting in the classroom

the teacher—and the visiting anthropologist—with a cake to savor. More-over, schoolwide events such as special fairs, anniversaries, or sports com-petitions were always organized by grupo escolar.

From the teachers' point of view, heterogeneous grupos escolares helped constitute students as equals so that neither teachers nor students would discriminate against other students. Likewise at ESF, teachers espe-cially valued the wearing of common uniforms as a means of subverting tendencies to discriminate. They often enunciated the same phrase with great conviction at parent meetings: "Uniforms serve to erase [the percep-tion of] social and economic differences." The teachers were hoping that the wearing of uniforms would arrest a trend toward differentiation. Sev-eral mentioned the negative consequences that would likely ensue from students being allowed to wear normal street clothes. Poor kids, with their patched and unstylish clothing, would bear the brunt of wealthier kids' ridicule, while the latter would flaunt their designer wear.

Teachers made constant appeals to students to work for the collective good.[10] While this collectivity was located both in the grupo escolar and the school at large, the goals of student work also got identified with the nation, the transcendent collectivity. In ceremonial speeches and class-room discussions, administrators and teachers often invoked the nation as the defining context of their efforts. They exhorted students to work hard in order to "raise Mexico up" ("*para levantar a México*") or because "Mexico needs you." They even spoke more specifically of a need for better-educated scientists and technicians to contribute to Mexico's development. The discourse proliferated beyond the teachers' immediate words. At ESF, for instance, the phrase, "The Future of Our Fatherland Depends on What We Do Today" ("*De Lo Que Hagamos Hoy Depende El Mañana De Nuestra Patria*"), was painted in bold letters on the side of a building adjacent to the main plaza. Clearly, the dominant discourse on the nation was linked to the grupo escolar. Notions of equality and the collective good were meant to be a part of students' social learning, a historically resonant effort to create student-citizens, striving in "equal" solidarity, for a common national interest.

This emphasis issued from the historical project of nation and State formation, the hybrid cultural configuration of revolutionary nationalism that I discussed in chapter 1. Yet the tradition of liberal individualism also expressed itself forcefully in the school. The vice principal epitomized this hybrid discourse in one of his morning comments to the students: "We work for [the good of] society, for the country . . . but also for our own benefit" ("*Trabajamos por la sociedad, por la patria . . . pero también por nuestro propio beneficio*"). A focus on intragrupo competition and individual advancement occasionally irrupted into the theme of solidarity. In one morning lineup toward the beginning of the school year, the principal made a short speech encouraging students to "constantly improve, because we can't have mediocre students in the school." The principal noted how well the ESF contingent had marched in the weekend Independence Day parade, and suggested that "competition" (in this case, against other schools) was necessary to *superarse* (constantly improve). But this sense of competition was even more generalized throughout the school. Some teachers, to be sure, sponsored competition within classrooms more than others. Mrs. Rico frequently established competitions by row for solving math problems, and Mr. Carrizo gave prizes to the individual student with the best summary of current events for the day. The combination of modalities of cooperation and competition was striking in some cases. For instance, students sometimes complained about the trials of doing group projects, which were especially common in art education. Mr. Etilio gave a motivational talk inspired by such complaints, exhorting students to learn to work well in groups because studies at the level of the preparatoria and university would require even more cooperation. Moments later, he also encouraged a drive for constant self-improvement, noting that competition would be fiercer with each step up the educational ladder and only the most dedicated would survive. Here, even the goal of group cooperation was justified with reference to individual advancement rather than collective solidarity.[11]

BY DAY, WEEK, AND YEAR:
SCHOOL SPACES, RITUALS, AND ROUTINES

Most mornings I tried to leave the Solana Ramírez house by 7 A.M. in order to join the flow of students making their way to school. I took the most direct route, walking down one side of the small plaza and straight through the early bustle of the market on a street that eventually led to the main entrance of ESF. As I passed the plaza, I noticed students with different-colored uniforms climbing aboard buses and vans for the trip to nearby schools. I also saw ESF students disembarking with their own distinctive uniforms: an olive green military outfit for the males, and pink, sky blue, or burgundy jumpers with white blouses for first-, second-, and third-grade females, respectively. Students would turn onto the same street at different points along my trajectory. By 7:10 A.M., the trickle of students that initially accompanied me would form a busy torrent only a block from the school. I tried to use this time to engage different students in conversation. If the gates were locked when we arrived, I would join one of the many small groups of students formed outside the main entrance, chatting or horsing around. Sometimes we would stop to wave at the teachers bouncing by in the cars they used to navigate the rutted road. A tiny percentage of students received occasional automobile rides from a family member, but most would walk, despite the fact that the required hard-sole black shoes made traversing the city's many dirt and cobblestone roads difficult.

The morning lineup began at 7:20. Students were expected to join their grupos and begin forming lines toward the head of the civic plaza, facing the raised platform in front of the administrative offices. Starting with first-grade grupo 1A, students formed separate male and female lines by grupo from left to right, all the way up to grupo 3F. Within each grupo, lines then formed with the shortest students up front and the tallest in back. *Jefes de grupo* (group monitors) were supposed to help organize the lines, but they were seldom successful. After all, the students could be a rather intransigent lot. Most would mill around chatting and joking in the general vicinity of their grupo until the principal or vice principal emerged from the office building to take the microphone and bark, "Get in line, now!" ("*Fórmense, ya!*"). Usually there followed a short series of military-style movements, with students commanded to create more space between themselves ("*Tomen paso, ya!*"), make a half-turn ("*Media vuelta, ya!*"), and stand at stiff attention ("*Firmes, ya!*"). This ritual practice appeared to signal students' transition from a kind of "street state" to a "school state" (McLaren 1986). At least, that was the normative intent. In reality, students varied in the degree to which they altered their behavior to fit the school routine. Many quickly shifted back into a relaxed and bemused demeanor as soon as the administrative vigil ended with the call to start classes. There was, nevertheless, clearly a power in requiring students to identify with their grupos in this fashion every morning. Besides the discursive reinforcement of grupo solidarity, the morning lineup regularly produced a more tangible sense of membership.

On most mornings, students arriving after the first call to order would be obliged by a teacher to stand haplessly in a separate line off to the raised left side, their tardiness registered by that week's punctuality monitor. They would not be allowed to join their grupos until the first-period class. Sometimes, a teacher greeted students at the front gate and turned some of them back for long hair (boys) or excessive makeup (girls). Such students were not supposed to return until their appearance had been altered, though many simply waited for a more opportune moment to pass through unnoticed; they figured that other teachers were not likely to monitor their hygiene during the day. In any case, lineup began and ended with comments by one of the school's top administrators. The principal or vice principals informed students of school activities or accomplishments; they also admonished, cajoled, or exhorted students to high standards of behavior. Not infrequently, the administrators surveyed the lines and singled out certain students—typically males—for reproach. "*El compañero Talavera está faltando el respeto otra vez,*" the principal might say, equating Talavera's talking with a show of disrespect. The knowledge of a last name indicated a certain notoriety, a sign that this was not the student's first infraction. Another common warning was for students to remove their hands from their pockets if they were still in the "*firmes*" position.

Monday always brought the civic ceremony (*acto cívico*), usually lasting some twenty minutes and often wresting time from the first-period class, I witnessed the ritual for the first time during an early summer visit in 1988. For the acto, the student lines would form differently, with half

Second-year girls escort the flag at the Monday morning civic ceremony

the grupos placed on each side of the plaza, facing toward one another. The ragged blare of the school's all-boy drum and bugle corps (*banda de guerra*) piped up, then a teacher brought the flag from the principal's office and handed it to the six-member female color guard while those present raised their right hands over their heart in salute. Six girls in disciplined formation marched the flag around the plaza to the band's insistent beat, stopping in the front left corner. After a short silent pause, one of the art education teachers led the singing of the national anthem.

I was struck then, as I was almost always later on, by the distinct lack of student enthusiasm for the singing. The teacher stormed around the plaza, arms conducting and eyes glaring at students to raise their voices. The *prefectos* (student teachers who functioned as roving disciplinarians and substitutes) would aid the teacher in maintaining order and encouraging participation. When the lackluster anthem was finished, several members of the grupo escolar in charge of that week's ceremony read short anniversary notes (*efemérides*) recounting memorable world or national historical events that had occurred this same calendar week in another epoch. One of the grupo's best speakers then took the microphone for a short inspirational speech, followed by yet another student's dramatic poetry recitation.[12] After this, the bugle corps signaled the color guard to retire the flag. With the flag out of sight, another student announced the highest and lowest rankings for grupo punctuality, and handed the microphone to the principal. The principal, in turn, commented on the quality of the ceremony, announced some business for the week, and told students to work hard for the good of themselves and their country before dismissing them line by line to class. As I would learn later, the ceremony always followed a virtually identical pattern, both here and throughout Mexico.

I remember this first ceremony well because it presented me with a dilemma. I was standing on the platform above the plaza, well in view of teachers and students alike. When the flag salute began, I wondered whether to join in. If I complied, would they think me a hypocrite for saluting a flag, and thus declaring an allegiance, that could not possibly be my own? If I failed to salute, would they see it as an insult, a sign of disrespect? I imagine that I was visibly anguished, for I hesitantly raised my arm and then dropped it a few seconds later.

I didn't notice any reaction then, but later that day, Mr. Solana reproached me over lunch. Why hadn't I saluted the flag? he wanted to know. I related to him my confusion, and he shook his head in slight disgust. Nobody would have thought you a hypocrite, he asserted. "On the contrary, they would have applauded your solidarity [with Mexico]." So Mr. Solana had been disappointed by my apparent disregard for their patriotic sensibilities. The next day, however, I stopped in to see a vice principal with whom I'd developed a quite candid rapport. I again recounted my confusion during the flag ceremony, as well as Mr. Solana's scolding. He smiled and assured me that few besides Mr. Solana had probably even noticed. "Not all of us are quite so nationalistic," he concluded coyly.

By the autumn of 1990, I had learned much of the daily routine. I tried to get a sense of it from the students' embodied perspective, so I always took care to stand or sit with them, eschewing most adult authority. Most of the day required switching between classrooms for each of seven fifty-minute periods, with a twenty-minute recess break around 11 A.M. (though every day included at least one two- or three-period block in the social sciences, natural sciences, or talleres; see figure 3 below). The morning shift began at 7:30 A.M. and ended around 1:40 P.M. Students stayed with their grupos for all class periods except taller and recess.

What was it like to be a student in class? The physical environment differed little between classrooms, but teacher idiosyncrasies required some adaptation. Some teachers asked students to form neat single-sex lines along the outer wall of the classroom before allowing them to file in quietly to take their seats. If a classroom were unsupervised when a grupo escolar first entered it, students would take their seats or pass the time joking and chatting with friends. Some teachers required students to rise formally and greet them ("*Buenos días, maestra*") when they first arrived; others simply entered the classroom and went wordlessly to their desks. Teachers also had different classroom styles and personalities. A significant part of student practice involved learning and adapting to such differences (Sandoval 1998a, 1998b). There were those teachers who showed considerable tolerance for student conversation and game playing, even during periods they had specified for academic work. Others ran a much tighter ship, requiring total silence most of the time. Students knew their moods, too. Teachers like Mr. Solana, who upheld high standards for discipline and respect, sometimes relaxed into a humorous banter with students. "Today he's really in a good mood," his students noted to me on more than one occasion. Students also had to adapt to different sets of academic procedures and expectations. Teachers varied on such items as the use of homework, customs of verbal response (standing or sitting), encouragement of group versus "individual" work, and modalities of evaluation.

With the exception of shop classes, science labs, and physical education, most classrooms appeared virtually identical. Gray metal work seats (with a small writing surface) were arranged in neat rows facing the front chalkboard. The floor was smooth cement, and the modest teacher's desk, along with a small standing cupboard, occupied a slightly raised platform in front. Slatted windows extended the full length of the room on either side, admitting a good deal of light but also noise and distraction from the outside. Fluorescent lamps, many often broken or burned out, lined the steel ceiling. Between the side windows, front chalkboard, and back cement wall, there was little room for affixing notices or posters, though some teachers did manage to organize small bulletin boards and displays of student work. Often cold and dark, classrooms could seem bleak if not for the cheerful pulse of constant student activity.

Because of the classroom layout, teachers could effectively monitor student interactions whenever they wanted. I myself felt subject to the same scrutiny. Always mindful of the principal's gracious—but revocable—permission to study the school, I tried hard to follow the teachers' rules. Yet students often drew me into their communicative networks. On more than one occasion I was asked to pass a note or provide a test answer. I learned to employ the same surreptitious techniques that the students had developed: quick, furtive glances at the teacher, passing notes in "borrowed" books, and the like. Readers in the United States or Europe may find this regime similar to their own classroom experience (Everhart 1983; Foley 1990; Woods 1990). Perhaps because of the ever-present vigilance, most students seemed especially attached to their backpacks and book bags. On any given day, students would be expected to carry books for five or six different classes. In the absence of lockers or shelves, book bags became the only private space the students could claim. Though they often complained and grimaced about the weight, they invested the bags with distinctive personal meanings, and some filled them with music, magazines, toys, and other paraphernalia of popular culture. When they occasionally watched cinematic depictions of school life in the United States, students were most impressed with, and envious of, the pervasive use of personal hall lockers.

Recess punctuated the school day and provided a time for students to visit more freely with classmates or other friends in the school. Most would buy sandwiches or sweets and quickly wolf them down before starting up a game of basketball, volleyball, or soccer. Others would find a quiet spot with some friends and sit to eat, talk, or listen to music. Still others roamed the school grounds, looking to contact a number of different groups for gossip or horseplay. Recess seemed a swirling chaos until I discovered patterns of social affiliation and conduct. I learned how significant it was as a time for expressing and consolidating friendships. I also learned that the use of space signaled various types of student status. Students from the younger grades segregated most by gender. Many of the boys would play soccer while the girls stood in groups around the student store. Typically, the older and more popular students occupied the central areas around the main basketball court. Sometimes they set up a volleyball net on the lower court for a game that drew a crowd. Yet even third-grade girls and boys segregated by gender and sought their own social spaces. As I discuss in later chapters, especially those who were younger or from more socially conservative families occupied marginal school yard spaces, such as the walkways or grassy areas behind and between the main shop buildings.

Three class periods remained after recess, and students grew increasingly tired or restless with each one. Teachers sometimes conceded to this condition during the final periods by relaxing requirements or letting students out early.[13] As they poured out the school gates, most students would meet their friends and walk slowly back toward their homes. For many, this was one of the only times they might visit with friends outside the confines of school. Some would stop and buy more sweets or drinks, forming a small circle to chat. Others played tag games or shouted out to each other about upcoming work or play. Still others pulled out books and sat quietly copying or questioning a classmate's work. The school exit created quite a spectacle as uniformed students spread out in several directions, colonizing available sidewalks and streets.

This, then, was the daily routine of school, but there was also a set of regular yearly rituals and routines. First, the school year was punctuated by required academic functions. The Inicio del Ciclo Lectivo (Inauguration of the School Year) brought together prominent school officials, teachers, parents, and students to hear motivational speeches for the upcoming year. Then, quarterly grading periods each required a parent-teacher meeting for the *entrega de boleta* (delivery of report cards). On such days, classes ended around noon to allow for the students' parents or guardians to gather together with grupo advisers. These meetings provided one of the few opportunities for teachers to make general pronouncements about the grupo's performance. It also enabled parents to make special inquiries about their children or, in some cases, challenge the teacher's authority. Some parents regularly attended the meeting of the Mesa Directiva in their capacity as elected representatives;[14] others held office in the Sociedad de Padres de Familia (Parents' Association). The only other event that parents regularly attended was the Acto and Fiesta de Clausura (graduation ceremony and party), a year-end affair with great symbolic significance (see chapter 6; Levinson 1998b).

The graduation ceremony was one among several grand parties held throughout the school year. In her study of the cultural politics of Mexican schooling in the 1920s and 1930s, Mary Kay Vaughan (1997, 93–95) charts the way the postrevolutionary State strengthened and embellished existing school-based festivals and celebrations. Organized by local teachers as an expression of egalitarian principles in patriotic fervor, civic festivals served to mediate class conflicts in communities by "promot[ing] unity between factions" (94). Athletic competitions, especially basketball, allowed boys from across fractious communities to join in competition against a common adversary. At ESF in 1991, a busy schedule of civic holidays, both official and unofficial, still carried through the school year. Official or semiofficial holidays included celebrations of Independence Day, Revolution Day, Constitution Day, the birth of ex-President Benito Juárez, the birth and death of ex-President Lázaro Cárdenas, and the Cinco de Mayo. Most of these holidays required some form of student participation. For Independence Day, a sizable contingent from the school prepared itself to march in the city parade along with other schools. Several school days were shortened to enable practice and organization for this parade. For this and other holidays, students were to prepare speeches and presentations commemorating the figures or events inspiring the holiday. Open-air carnivals or basketball contests might accompany the ceremonies. In this fashion, students would bind themselves to the ritual forms of civic and national identity.

Yet another type of secular holiday provided relief from the everyday routine and enabled the school participants to renew their sense of unity. Most prominent among these were the Mothers' Day, Teachers' Day, Students' Day, and School Anniversary celebrations.[15] Each of these holidays was honored with a half- or full-day dismissal from regular classes. Traditionally, Mothers' Day was celebrated with a fair (*kermés*) and party in honor of the students' mothers, who visited the school en masse. Teachers' Day provided an opportunity for students to show their appreciation with gifts and the preparation of an entertainment program. Students' Day was celebrated most years with a dance at the school. Finally, because of its prestige and symbolic centrality, ESF each March celebrated its anniversary in grand style. The grounds were painted and spruced in anticipation of the day, when various dignitaries and school alumni took the podium of honor and presented speeches in praise of the school.

The historical separation of church and State in Mexico prevented the open celebration of Catholic holidays in the school, yet they were acknowledged and accommodated in various ways. Christmas and Easter were the most significant of these holidays, and the national school calendar provided two-week vacations around them. Día de los Muertos (Day of the Dead), celebrated on November 2, also required a day off from school. No other religious holidays received recognition in this fashion, though the forms and meanings of Catholic ritual did receive some mention. For instance, the annual graduation ceremony called forth the fascinating practice of ritual godparenthood (*compadrazgo*). Graduating students were expected to select a godparent to accompany them on their special day, much as godparents are chosen for other major events of the Catholic life cycle in Mexico: birth, first communion, confirmation, and marriage. The original meaning of compadrazgo was for religious Catholics to have spiritual guides and advisers for the difficult journey of life, yet anthropologists throughout Latin America have studied the rather more pragmatic use of compadrazgo relations to build networks of material exchange and security (Wolf 1956; Ingham 1986). It was thus not surprising to see this essentially religious practice refunctionalized in the context of school graduation. Relatedly, teachers and administrators arranged the starting time of the ceremony to accommodate family trips to church for a special mass giving thanks to God (*acción de dar gracias*).

Emerging historically through the interaction of State and local culture, school spaces, rituals, and routines at ESF wove together elements of civic, religious, and youth identity. They showed one way of history becoming structure and provided important cultural contexts for students to make their own meanings. The way school knowledge was packaged and presented, and the way teachers viewed the students, provided other key influences on student activity.

CURRICULUM, PEDAGOGY, AND TEACHERS' PRACTICE

As I noted in chapter 1, public education in Mexico is highly centralized. The federal Secretariat of Public Education in Mexico City establishes national guidelines for school policy, and some—like those regarding the formation of grupos escolares—are less directive than others. The Secretariat likewise sets curriculum and textbook content for the entire country. State goals of cultural unification are nowhere more transparent than in this structure of common knowledge.

In 1990, the curriculum at ESF still operated according to the "Chetumal Reforms" of 1974, which had rearranged some of the traditional subjects (*asignaturas*) into scientific areas (*áreas*). The national program of studies stipulated seven weekly hours each of natural sciences (previously taught separately as chemistry, physics, and biology) and social sciences (previously history, geography, and civics). These core areas were accompanied by four hours a week each of mathematics and *lengua nacional* (Spanish), three hours of *lengua extranjera* (English), two hours of physical education, two hours of artistic education, and six hours of *tecnología,* or taller (shop), for a total of thirty-five classroom hours each week.[16] The subject areas were distributed temporally in fairly random fashion, according to the availability of teachers and facilities: each day of the week, the grupo escolar encountered an entirely different schedule of classes. Natural and social science classes were each distributed in three two-hour blocks, with a single hour another day. One of the natural science blocks each week would be devoted to "laboratory" practice; students would meet in one of two laboratory rooms, but experiments were usually rather simple due to a lack of materials and instruments, and often a "normal" class (lecture, dictation, and group work) would take place instead. Technology classes—the only time students left their grupo escolar to mingle with other students in a formal school setting—were distributed in two three-hour blocks, while the other four subject areas (math, Spanish, physical education, and artistic education) were distributed in single-hour sections across the week. Physical education classes were convened on the basketball courts, with cancellation or room study in the event of bad weather.[17] Spanish classes typically met one hour a week in the library for reading activities. Thus, a typical student schedule might look like figure 3.

The practice of grading was another determining feature of school life. While grades were not considered for entrance into the next level of formal education, they were crucial for successfully graduating from the secundaria altogether. Three key features of grading deserve mention. First, students received subject grades on a scale of 5 to 10 for each of four quarterly grading periods. These four grades were then averaged at the end of the school year to determine the overall grade. Final scores of less than 5.5 did not permit a student to pass. Moreover, students receiving consecutive grades of 5 in the final two quarterly periods could not pass the course, regardless of how high their previous quarterly grades had been (in other words, students needed to show consistent or improving performance).

Second, students could not receive their school certificate without having passed *all* of their classes. There was no system of grade point averaging in existence. This gave teachers of the less central classes—English, physical education, and artistic education especially—both greater power and grief than otherwise might be the case. Power, because these teachers could effectively nullify a student's graduation if that student failed to pass their course; grief, because many parents complained that such classes were not as necessary, and so should not jeopardize a student's chances of graduating.

Third, all students were given opportunities to reinstate a passing grade through a system of "extraordinary exams." Twice a year, in February and August, students could come to school on a Saturday and take an exam—sometimes oral, sometimes written, or often both—that presumably covered the full previous year's course. Because students had to pay a small sum for the administrative cost of the exams, they were said to "owe" (*deber*) a subject until they "paid" (*pagar*) it off. Extraordinary exams thus provided some recourse to students who had failed the regular term.

	Monday	Tuesday	Wednesday	Thursday	Friday
Period 1	Educación Artística	Español	Ciencias Naturales	Ciencias Naturales	Taller
Period 2	Español	Matemáticas	Ciencias Naturales	Español	Taller
Period 3	Ciencias Sociales	Ciencias Sociales	Español	Ciencias Sociales	Taller
Period 4	Ciencias Sociales	Ciencias Sociales	Matemáticas	Ciencias Sociales	Ciencias Sociales
Recess					
Period 6	Ciencias Naturales	Ciencias Naturales	Taller	Matemáticas	Inglés
Period 7	Matemáticas	Inglés	Taller	Educación Física	Ciencias Naturales
Period 8	Educación Física	Educación Artística	Taller	Inglés	Ciencias Naturales

Figure 3. Weekly class schedule, grupo 3C, 1990–1991 school year

After their third and final year, students had three chances to pay off any subjects they still owed. Most schools at the next level would not let them continue their studies if they did not pay everything off and thus acquire a secundaria certificate by February of the following year (the second chance for extraordinary exams). Similarly, second- and third-year students at ESF who still owed subjects from previous years could not continue past February without a clean record. Otherwise, they would become *repetidores* (repeaters, sent back a grade).

The structure of the curriculum, distributive pattern of classrooms and subjects, and grading system, as well as the grupo escolar, provided important conditions for teacher and student strategies alike. Although teachers did not comprise the focus of my study, I did have occasion to observe and interview them in some depth. Here, then, I examine more closely teacher strategies and knowledge across the curriculum (Woods 1980; Mercado 1994) for classroom practice. The reader should note that my discussion presents pervasive and typical teacher practices, and is not meant to be an exhaustive catalog.

It became clear to me rather early in my study that virtually all the teachers shared a strong commitment to the integrative goals of the State and formation of a national identity. Regardless of explicit political ideology or class background—indeed, regardless of most elements of personal biography, including the route taken to a job in the secundaria—these teachers shared the nationalist sentiment that found one common form of expression in the dictum that all students be treated equally and work in solidarity. In chapter 1, I considered the special salience this sentiment might have due to the history of the region where I worked. I also believe that a form of professional and political socialization occurs in the school itself, where respect for patriotic symbols and the goal of creating a strong sense of citizenship obviously loom large. Even if students no longer "boil[ed] with patriotic fervor," as the old-time ESF graduate claimed in chapter 1, most teachers tried to impart a strong love of country.

Earlier critical studies of schooling had tried to show how the State, through its control of teacher training, imparted a dominant ideology that effectively transformed teachers into agents of the State and its allied ruling interests (Popkewitz 1987; for a similar approach in Mexico, see Calvo Pontón 1989). In Mexico, Elsie Rockwell and Ruth Mercado (1986; Rockwell 1987, 1991), Mary Kay Vaughan (1997), and others (Aguilar Hernández 1991) have demonstrated that in fact teachers are quite diverse in outlook and formation. These scholars suggest regionalizing and historicizing our conception of State hegemony, and nuancing our understanding of how teacher biographies intersect with structural projects of the State. Older teachers, especially, tend to identify their interests more closely with the communities where they immediately work than with the State bureaucracy, and most teachers still come from the peasant or working classes, as in the past. Teachers thus have their roots in various popular and intimate cultures before becoming employees of the State, hence workers in a school. Still, teachers also see themselves as professionals, with the prerogatives that correspond to their professional training. This complex set of histories, identities, and allegiances becomes apparent in teachers' daily practice.

Rafael Quiroz (1987, 1991, 1992, 1993), Etelvina Sandoval (1996, 1997), and Mónica Díaz Pontones (1998) have studied patterns of teacher practice in the Mexican secundaria most closely. Among their valuable findings have been the identification of teachers with their "specialized knowledge," the tendency to teach according to the "logic of evaluation," and the rote consequences of curricular time-space fragmentation. Quiroz (1987) argues that most secundaria teachers differ from primaria teachers in their devotion to a disciplinary base of knowledge. In theory, secundaria teachers must hold a degree from a Normal Superior, that is, a university-level program of teacher education with subject specialization. Since the early 1980s, newly hired teachers should have completed this degree. Many current secundaria teachers, however, began their careers in the primaria with the equivalent of a high school degree (*bachillerato pedagógico*). After 1983, on transferring to a secundaria, they were expected to update their degrees through summer or evening study at a Normal Superior. Still other secundaria teachers came to their positions through a less formal route, drawing on "friendships" in the SNTE for a job. Most of these teachers had little pedagogical training; they were mainly university-educated professionals unable or unwilling to exercise their training in some other context. Whatever their route to the secundaria, ESF teachers largely confirmed Quiroz's findings. They exhibited varying degrees of commitment to the general formative goals of the school, but all expected students to master their particular subject area.

Even more striking was the teachers' adherence to what Quiroz calls the "logic of evaluation" (1991). Time and again, I observed teachers exhorting their students to prepare themselves for an upcoming evaluation; in short, they were "teaching to the test." Students complained most bitterly about those few teachers who relied almost exclusively on exams to calculate their quarterly grade averages. Most teachers, by contrast, included homework, classwork, and other forms of "participation" in these grades. Thus, while exams were mentioned constantly, there was often quite a bit of negotiation between teachers and students around when and how the exams would be taken into account. Curiously, teachers were not compelled to use tests for the purpose of grading. No national exams or standards were in place. Quiroz suggests that various historical and institutional pressures nevertheless encourage teachers to emphasize the exam as a source of certainty, and teachers invest a great deal of their time and professional identity in the practice of grading.[18]

On a day-to-day basis, teachers made reference to grades and exams as a rather deliberate motivational tactic. Their aim was nothing less than to scare students into giving serious attention to their studies. In just one example of many I witnessed, the art teacher interrupted his roll call in early May in order to deliver the following remarks:

There are a few classmates in here who are at risk of not receiving their certificates because they haven't paid sufficient attention to their studies. Some of you look at your average and say, "Ah, well, I have nothing but '8s,' he has to pass me," but don't you believe it, you can still fail. Don't get too confident because it's no fun to lose all three years of work. . . . And then many of you are going to want to attend the graduation ceremony, which is very lovely and all, but they don't let anybody in who doesn't already have his [sic] certificate. . . . With me you only have eight or nine hours left to finish (in the school year), and you have to get a good grade.

Other teachers used similar methods of motivation and control to encourage student effort. Some teachers made frequent mention of what students would have to know in the prepa—the next educational level. If they didn't pay close attention and make an effort now, they would be lost at this time next year. Other teachers would try to scold or shame students into better school performance. Mrs. Rico, a third-grade math teacher, once berated her students for both failing to stand when answering a direct question and inventing simplistic word problems: "Now that you're almost graduating, you should know more than this." Shaming might make reference to the family as well: "Do you want your parents to make so many sacrifices so you can come here to fool around? Your parents think you come here to study, but I know otherwise." More drastic measures included asking the student jefe de grupo to "report" a student's frequent mischief to the grupo adviser or simply dismissing students from the room altogether.[19]

Thus, as much as teachers might appeal to the collective benefit of the nation, school, or grupo escolar, they often recurred to challenges and threats regarding personal academic performance. They might even mention the intrinsic value of school knowledge, but this too seemed to have little effect. The Spanish teacher Mr. Cantú, for instance, once despairingly chided his students for not demonstrating the desire to "prepare" themselves for the problems the country and world were facing. In yet another class, he was embarrassed when no student could say where Lázaro Cárdenas had been born or what an oil refinery was. "All of this is what you should know as Mexicans. . . . [I]t's a part of your culture," he said, lamenting the students' ignorance. In a science class, Mr. Díaz announced that for the following day, they should read the next unit—on the animal phylum of worms and mollusks—because it was "*un tema mucho muy importante*" ("a very important topic"). Beyond that, he didn't say. It was as if the sheer force of these teachers' suggestions might convince the students to make more of an effort.

Yet the social organization of the school and its predominant pedagogical traditions frequently failed to provide forms of knowledge that students might find "important." Together with the logic of evaluation came an emphasis on memorization and formula. Students spent much of their time taking dictation, answering *cuestionarios* (study questions), or copying passages from books. They had to learn formulas, dates, biographies, formal definitions, and the like. Teachers asked students to provide "correct" responses, and together they strove to "finish" the approved program of studies. The written word generally counted as the ultimate authority in questions of knowledge—students would often tell teachers when the book contradicted his or her words, and the teachers always begged gentle pardon for their error. There was, then, a highly reified quality to most school knowledge (compare Everhart 1983; Edwards 1985, 1995; Luykx 1999, 176 ff.). With the focus on product over process, on teacher-student collusion to meet curricular expectations, bits of transportable knowledge circulated rather freely among the students. They served as tokens of exchange, ossified data used to consolidate grupo solidarity and organize shifting friendship networks (see chapters 4 and 6).

Within this generalized encyclopedism, there was of course quite some variation (see Díaz Pontones 1998). Teachers differed in their use of group or individual work, their tendency to stand and lecture or allow students to research information on their own. For instance, echoing the theme of *auto-aprendizaje* (self-learning) endorsed in the latest plans for "modernization," one math teacher tried teaching students to "learn to learn." Enacting his interpretation of this principle, he asked students to resolve problems on their own before he gave any explanation. The Spanish teacher Ms. Hinojosa frequently had students check each others' work, by both asking the class if a student's board work was correct and having some of the better students go around checking their classmates' work. Other teachers, especially in social studies, occasionally invited opinion and debate about current or historical events. These were among the most animated classes I observed. Finally, some teachers did make regular attempts to bring school knowledge into the sphere of everyday life (what students knew experientially) or distant excitement (what they might want to know, given their current interests). For example, the natural science teacher Mr. Agosín tried to dramatize a plane taking off and train coming into a station to frame the problem of changing velocity—and pose the appropriate physics word problems. Mr. Alonso drew on a rather masculine interest to convey the importance of mathematical "coordinates" in war-making and naval technology. Yet despite these examples, there was little that truly engaged students, and they frequently complained of boredom. The constant lack of resources—videos, overheads, tape recorders, wall maps, and the like were not available in this or most other public secundarias—severely limited the teachers as well.

Then, too, because of institutional pressures and conditions, relatively few teachers took the time to explore student attitudes and feelings. In one of those rare moments that a teacher explicitly mentioned his or her training, Mrs. Ramírez told me that in the Normal, they had been taught that education be conceived of as a triangle between family, teacher, and student, with the family as the base. Teachers were also taught to make students their "friends" and to "pay attention to matters of emotion" ("*atender a la cuestión afectiva*"). Lamentably though, she continued, most teachers come to class and "go straight to nothing but [formal] knowledge" ("*van derechito a los puros conocimientos*"). Two other social studies teachers echoed Mrs. Ramírez's point, saying the packed curriculum left them no time to address "the crisis this phase—adolescence—produces for the kids." In my observations, these teachers were only partially correct. Though still a minority, a good many teachers did try to address their students' feelings and concerns, often through an acute sense of humor. They were, not surprisingly, among the most beloved by the students. Other teachers also used humor and parable to good effect, though there persisted a rather strict separation between the jokes and stories, on the one hand, and the subject matter (*conocimientos*) of the day.

Teachers at ESF clearly developed a set of situated concepts for interpreting student behavior and academic performance. Many of these were displayed spontaneously in practice, as teachers rebuked or praised students for their conduct. Others were highlighted or revealed to me through informal interviews that took place during the second half of the school year. Together, my data on teacher discourse suggests a surprisingly complex though coherent set of suppositions about students and their families. These suppositions sometimes acted to label and orient the treatment of students in ways that confirmed certain forms of class prejudice (compare Ezpeleta 1989; Finders 1997; Mehan, Hubbard, and Villanueva 1986; Rist 1970).

Students demonstrating low rates of academic achievement (*rendi-*

miento) were said to suffer from any number of problems. Many teachers, quite frankly, distinguished some students as not having much *capacidad*, or ability, for study. Some of these students might have an interest (*interés*) in studying and even exert a great deal of effort, but their achievement would remain low. Other teachers were fond of stressing every student's capacity to achieve; those students who did not or could not were seen as lazy (*flojo*), restless (*inquieto*), or having insufficient interés in their studies. They might be easily distracted or "absorbed" (*absorbido*) by their school friends. Perhaps most important, teachers tended to place the ultimate responsibility for students' conduct and achievement with the family. If students were not doing well, it was because there was some problem or lack in the family: students were spoiled (*consentidos*) by their parents and thus given insufficient motivation to study (*falta de interés*), or they were not adequately guided in keeping a focus on their studies, or the problems of family economy and communication led to restless and unfocused behavior in school. Since ESF regularly had high levels of enrollment, it could choose to expel so-called problem students and effectively send them along to another school. At the first teacher meeting of the year, one of the vice principals advised teachers to pay especially close attention to students repeating a grade: they would probably bring more problems to the school, and the administration was ready to give them the boot. On the other hand, students who kept high grades and exemplary conduct were rewarded with familial as well as personal praise.

Thus, teachers tended to interpret student behavior in terms of certain essential qualities (laziness, lack of intelligence, and so on) of person and family.[20] When they didn't have recourse to such qualities, they turned to the somewhat different explanation of falta de interés. The factor of "interest" in studying appeared to respond to a different logic than the other ones. In fact, it could be combined with the others in a variety of ways: a supposedly lazy or unable student might actually have strong interest in her studies, while a smart student might have little interest; a student with an absent father might have little interest, while a student with a pair of spoiling parents might have a great deal of interest, in spite of her alleged laziness or restlessness. Most important, the notion of interest appeared to index the influence of broader historical and structural fields. Teachers attributed students' degree of interest not only to family dynamics but also to students' perceptions of the value of schooling and adherence to traditional norms of authority. Waxing nostalgic for the sense of commitment and obedience students had manifest in the past, the teachers felt that today's students appreciated neither the intrinsic value of school knowledge nor the exchange value of a secundaria diploma. As recently as ten years ago, most students had behaved in class and studied hard because they respected the authority that came with the teachers' knowledge, and/or because they knew their studies would advance them in life. Nowadays, such students were rare, and in the teachers' view, most families fed the ambivalence that lay behind this lack of interest. According to the teachers, students had too many "distractions" from the television programs, videos, and magazines that had proliferated in the mid-1980s; they also wanted to carry their own money in search of immediate gratification. It had become near impossible to hold students' attention either through authoritarian gestures or that implicit promise of deferred gratification traditionally associated with schooling. Students demanded either that class be fun or the knowledge "practical." As I will discuss in chapter 7, by the late 1980s, student aspirations had apparently been adjusted to a greater variety and uncertainty of life options, including illegal migration, small-scale commerce, and the drug trade. The school was no longer a clear path to success or even pleasure as locally defined. To the teachers, this took shape in the form of falta de interés.

GENDER REGIMES

In the next few chapters, I describe patterns of gender relations in student culture at ESF; I also explore in greater detail the kinds of gender relations that students witnessed in their own households and communities. But what about gender relations in the institutional contexts teachers and administrators made available to students? What kinds of tasks did male and female teachers execute, and how did they treat male and female students? What kinds of gender models did they enact, and why? Linked in complex ways to historically evolving gender ideologies and processes of political-economic differentiation, school practices around gender provided crucial resources for and constraints on student action. Though gender encompasses relations between men and women, because women have been historically subordinated in Mexican society, and because they are relatively late entrants into the institution of schooling, here I focus my comments on the conditions they, especially, faced.

State discourses on equality and national unity in postrevolutionary Mexico have rarely made reference to women's rights. The revolution was, in many instances, fought by but not for women (Tuñon Pablos 1987;

Macías 1982), and the question of gender equality remained a largely silent issue on the male-dominated postrevolutionary agenda (O'Malley 1986). Mary Kay Vaughan (1990, 143) notes that women were "marginalized from industrial work, discriminated against in divorce cases, and told that domesticity and motherhood constituted their citizenship." Yet ironically, as Vaughan goes on to observe, the revolution "opened a field for creativity and self-realization for hundreds of Mexican women of humble, provincial background who became rural schoolteachers. They filled the ranks of the only profession open to women since the nineteenth century and took up a crusade for 'civilization'" (ibid.). Since education remained open to the participation of women throughout the postrevolutionary period, it came to constitute one of the primary arenas for the exercise of women's power and agency in the public sphere. Over the course of the twentieth century, women also came to provide an increased proportion of total educational enrollments, at both primary and secondary levels.[21]

I often asked ESF students if they thought their teachers discriminated according to their sex, and always their response was some version of the same: "They treat us equally here" ("*Aquí nos tratan iguales*"). Still skeptical, I ventured to focus my observations on teacher-student interactions in and out of the classroom. Based on numerous studies in the literature, both in Mexico and elsewhere, I had arrived expecting to find girls at some disadvantage for lacking the cultural capital—the style of reasoning and method of participation demanded in classes, for example—to fully succeed in school.[22] I had anticipated seeing teachers granting boys more time and attention. In fact, though, my field notes from this period record no instances of this kind of discrimination, and my journal reveals only disbelief at not finding it.

Were most teachers, then, "gender-blind"? Certainly not. Male and female teachers alike often commented that nowadays, women should get an education to fend for themselves. They recognized that at this age, anyway, girls were more obedient, disciplined, and motivated—not to mention smarter and more articulate—than male students. To be sure, this advantage was typically attributed to girls' faster physical and emotional development. Yet the acknowledgment of sexual difference did not appear to translate into differential treatment. A number of school practices did indeed attempt to erase gender differences, just as some were designed—through mixed-ability grouping, discourses on equality and solidarity, and common uniforms—to minimize the perception of class and ethnic differences. There also existed cross-cutting, clearly gendered practices and activities, however. Nothing better illustrates the fact that gender was a primordial category of social difference at ESF than the requirement of separate uniforms for boys and girls: while common uniforms among the same sex were supposed to inhibit perceptions of class and ethnicity as emblems of distinction, they served to accentuate the awareness of gender. If girls were supposedly "equal" to boys in the school, they were clearly not "the same." Gender remained a powerful source of distinction.

In the paragraphs below, I draw on Robert Connell's (1987) concept of the "gender regime" to discuss how it might be possible for ESF teachers to simultaneously and contradictorily empower and erase women's contributions to school life. Since Connell has worked a good deal in schools, he uses them to give one of his most compact examples of a gender regime. In his team research on Australian high schools, Connell says,

> We found an active though not always articulate politics of gender in every school. Among both students and staff there are practices that construct various kinds of femininity and masculinity: sport, dancing, choice of subject, classroom discipline, administration and others. Especially clearly among the students, some gender patterns are hegemonic . . . and others are subordinated. There is a distinct, though not absolute, sexual division of labor among staff, and sex differences in tastes and leisure activities among the students. There is an ideology, often more than one, about sexual behavior and sexual character. . . . The pattern formed by all this varies from school to school, though within limits that reflect the balances of sexual politics in Australian society generally. (120)

Connell calls this "not always articulate" pattern of institutional practice and ideology a gender regime. The gender regime describes a kind of "structural inventory" of local gender practice; such practice is, in turn, strongly constrained but not absolutely bound by conditions governing the broader societal "gender order."[23] In order to understand the formation and expression of students' gender subjectivities in the school, it is necessary to first identify the shifting structures of the school's gender regime.

GENDER AMONG TEACHERS

As Regina Cortina (1989) skillfully documents, the training of women as professional teachers is one of the few areas where the Mexican State has

Female teachers set a gendered example

articulated some semblance of a discourse on gender equality. In Mexico, as most everywhere else, the expansion of public education in the twentieth century opened up new opportunities for women's mobility and professional employment. Such expansion was accompanied by gender ideologies that essentialized yet valorized women's sensibilities, portraying them as ideal candidates for the instruction of children (Aguilar Hernández and Sandoval 1995; Sandoval 1992; Vaughan 1994). Perhaps for this reason, women today comprise a majority of primary schoolteachers in Mexico, but they do not have proportional representation in either secundarias or the upper echelons of educational policy and decision making. Socioeconomic, political, and ideological factors combine to assure that female teachers, who typically come from working- or middle-class families, do not get the same opportunities as men for the advanced educational degrees or political hobnobbing, which such higher levels often require.[24]

At ESF, in 1990, women comprised roughly a third of the professional teaching faculty.[25] They could be found in each of the core subject areas (natural sciences, social studies, math, Spanish, and English), as well as several of the talleres (secretarial, knitting, and clothing design). Nevertheless, there was a relatively clear sexual division of labor at ESF. Men occupied the three top administrative positions exclusively. The physical and artistic education teachers, along with those in charge of most talleres (carpentry, drafting, automotive, printing, electricity, and radio), were men as well. The secretarial staff, on the other hand, as well as the vocational counselor, social worker, and bookkeeper, were all women. Women, moreover, received a disproportionate number of special "commissions" around the school. For instance, they tended to mind the school's cooperative store, where drinks, sandwiches, and sweets were sold at lunch. They were also put in charge of organizing decorations and refreshments at special school events, such as dances, graduation ceremonies, and regional meetings. For their part, men would help maintain the school's physical plant, act as masters of ceremonies, and play a larger role in enforcing student discipline.

Thus, in terms of formal positions and tasks, there was a rather marked sexual division of labor according to prevailing conceptions of gendered activity. Socially, too, relations between male and female teachers tended to reproduce the divisions observable in the local community. It was rare for men and women to have free, extended verbal exchanges with one another. Rather, at faculty meetings and parties, men and women largely kept themselves separated. Except for the occasional pair dance or committee caucus, they tended to sit in same-sex groups, joking or chatting. On those rare occasions that a male and female teacher were seen speaking alone on school grounds, students took sufficient note of it to indulge in playful romantic speculation.

The tasks that female employees generally executed in the school were thus often associated with domestic gender practices common in provincial Mexico. Women at ESF did not overtly question these practices, although there was evidence that women negotiated, and at times even contested, their tasks and positions established in the school's gender regime. Especially among the democrático faction, women asserted equal rights and took on previously denied responsibilities. After the faction's general secretary died in the summer of 1990, the principal's personal secretary took over the job. She conducted herself with poise and determination, keeping the movement afloat during a difficult period with aggressive calls to action and an admirable perseverance. (Indeed, it was in the context of union-based politics that I witnessed the most genuine give-and-take between men and women, and most active interventions by women in questions of tactics and leadership.)[26] Another female teacher regularly and bravely challenged the principal's restrictive rules on student behavior.

At ESF, some student activities were plainly more gender marked than others. For the most part, however, the gender regime at ESF delineated few gender-specific practices. Across a range of positions and activities, teachers insisted that boys and girls were equally capable. Most contests among students—in sports, oratory, and the like—were open to both boys and girls, though some showed clearer gender separation than others. During recess period, impromptu games of basketball and soccer were the sole province of boys, while volleyball games usually involved equal numbers of boys and girls. In more organized contests, the games split along the same gender lines.

The public school system sponsored regional and national contests in two forms of public speaking: oratory (*oratorio*) and dramatic poetry reading (*declamación*). Boys and girls were similarly encouraged to enter these contests, but in my time at ESF, I noticed few boys participating. During the weekly civic ceremony, too, far more girls than boys performed poetry readings and served as master of ceremonies. This was in marked contrast to the pattern in national public life, where men dominated both forms of public speaking, but especially oratory, since they typically held the kinds of social and political positions that required it.

Both formally and informally, girls tended to serve as leaders of the grupos escolares. Girls and boys were elected by their classmates in roughly equal numbers to serve as jefe and *subjefe* (head and assistant head) of the grupo. The job of jefe entailed several different functions: coordinating group action on common projects or activities, helping teachers maintain order by straightening rows during morning lineup and quieting fellow students during speeches, and serving as liaison between the administration and grupo escolar. Male and female teachers alike seemed to nominate and endorse female candidates more often than male ones. Teachers insisted that jefes de grupo be orderly and disciplined to set an example for the rest of the group. More often than not, these were girls and not boys.

Less formally, girls also tended to take leadership roles in making group decisions or negotiating student rights with teachers and administrators. If a grupo wanted to request permission for an excursion or a party, or perhaps bring some grievance to the attention of a teacher or administrator, girls usually took the initiative. When I made this observation to teachers, they generally emphasized the girls' greater maturity. The girls, they said, could be trusted more than the boys. While some boys struck a superior pose, arguing that girls failed to understand the futility of such requests, others admitted that girls were more disciplined (*ordenadas*) and thus in a better position to argue the grupo's case. For their part, the girls argued that they were indeed more effective. As Leticia put it, "We don't have any men [boys] in our class who can express themselves well."[27]

In other areas, too, little heed was paid to whether girls or boys participated. The three active extracurricular clubs at ESF—music, dance, and journalism—were mostly attended by girls, though I was told that in times past boys had participated in far greater numbers. The journalism club produced a few issues of a simple newspaper, which consisted mostly of gossip (*chisme*), school news, and astrological forecasts. Many boys said they refused to get involved because chisme was mainly a girls' activity.

Finally, of the many talleres offered at ESF, only three could be considered gender neutral. Drafting (*dibujo técnico*), electricity, and printing had roughly equal numbers of boys and girls enrolled. In contrast to a couple of the gender-ambiguous talleres I will discuss shortly, these three did not provoke commentary about whether such activities were more appropriate for girls or boys. Students, teachers, and parents all agreed that electricity was a good introduction to the increasingly attractive field of computers. Drafting was seen as adequate preparation for a career in architecture (a field that in Mexico, was admitting increasing numbers of women), or more modest kinds of clerical or design jobs. Printing, on the other hand, was one of the least-popular choices among parents and students alike for it required the use of specialized and increasingly obsolete machinery. Boys and girls thus got placed in this undesirable taller in roughly equal numbers.[28]

There were, in fact, few strongly gender-marked activities in the school. One of these, however, was the school's bugle and drum corps (banda de guerra). I never knew a single girl who was even inclined to join the corps, and teachers suggested it was only meant for boys.[29] Likewise, most of the talleres were strongly segregated by gender. During my time at ESF, not a single boy enrolled in knitting (*tejidos y bordados*), nor did anyone remember a male student in this taller in times past. The fact that a single boy in the afternoon shift had enrolled in clothing design (corte y confección) was cause for surprise among several teachers. Then, too, no girls were enrolled in carpentry, automotive mechanics, or radio technology. There was little challenge to this gender segregation; some teachers and students even laughed when I asked if girls or boys had ever been in these classes. Work with cloth was seen as inappropriate for boys, while girls were not supposed to learn the skills associated with heavy machinery. Nevertheless, teachers generally affirmed that men and women could do any of the same jobs nowadays, especially in the professions. Their affirmations were only contradicted in school by the patterns of shop enrollment and the promotional presentations given to third graders by representatives of high school institutions in the region. In one notorious case, the vocational counselor from a new private technical school in the state capital described the study options in strictly gendered terms. After listing just a few general careers (tourist administration, drafting), he announced, "And for the young women, we have six courses available," and followed with titles like nurse's aide (*técnica de enfermería*), cosmetologist (*corte y belleza*), and fashion assistant (*ayudante de modista*).

GENDER-AMBIGUOUS ACTIVITIES

A number of school activities were characterized by what I call "gender ambiguity." While they appeared to be associated with one gender or another, such connections were in fact susceptible to challenge. In effect, gender-ambiguous activities signified the gaps and borders of the school's shifting gender regime.

For example, in the Monday morning civic ceremony described earlier, girls typically escorted the flag around the main plaza as the all-boy banda de guerra played a marching tune. The six girls who formed the color guard usually spent part of the previous week rehearsing the steps to perfection. By Monday morning, the color guard was snapping it out in perfect time, parading the plaza in tight formation while maintaining expressions of requisite solemnity. Teachers told me that girls had usually comprised the color guard in order to balance the boys' participation in the banda de guerra. Girls, as mentioned already, were also viewed as being more disciplined—a matter of some importance to the honor of the flag. Yet toward the middle of the school year, the principal proposed that boys take over the color guard for the remaining months (although he never suggested that girls join the banda de guerra). He issued a challenge to the boys, urging them to demonstrate that they could accomplish this exercise in patriotic duty just as professionally and responsibly as the girls had. And so it was that boys began practicing the same steps girls had performed for so many consecutive years at ESF.[30] It must be said that my own presence and persistent questions about gender differences may have prompted the principal to make the change. A proud man, the principal would never admit that a simple gringo student like myself could have motivated his action. Yet the announcement came rather soon after my questioning and seemed far from coincidental. Thus, my anthropological queries probably played a role in shifting slightly the school's gender regime.

As I've said, students set out to organize a schedule of activities to occupy much of Teachers' Day and Mothers' Day. While any student could potentially participate in organizing these activities, few boys ever did. For Teachers' Day, to give one example, students planned a program of entertainment. When the day arrived, teachers seated themselves comfortably on the steps overlooking the plaza, where the program would unfold. Some boys were involved in the official part of the program—that is, the music and dance club performances organized by a music teacher. Yet the better part of the program—and by far the more interesting, gauging by teachers' and students' responses—had been planned and executed by several girls from different friendship groups. Five of these groups presented modern dance numbers based on the latest musical hits (two separate dance pieces accompanied the music to Vanilla Ice's "Ice Ice Baby!"). Still another group performed a humorous skit: girls played all the parts, including the father, hold-up man, and bakery shop owner.

For Mothers' Day, to take another case, an open-air fair had been organized. Each grupo escolar was responsible for preparing an item of food or drink to sell. Again, girls took charge. With some input from the boys, they determined the item to be sold and then set about preparing it. On the day of the fair, the girls spent most of their time behind the booths and tables, dispensing the items they had made. The boys, however, would also chip in by carting the items to and from the tables, and even dispensing some of the items themselves. Thus, while the girls did most of the serving and organizing, the boys who participated were not stigmatized for crossing gender lines.

Finally, one taller—secretarial (*taquimecanografía*)—was dominated by girls, but had a few boys enrolled as well. Typing and secretarial work in Mexico have historically been associated with men as well as women, especially in bureaucratic or political positions. Yet more recently, secretarial skills have become the almost exclusive province of women. Virtually no boys were enrolled in any of the two quasi-professional secretarial schools in San Pablo designed for secundaria graduates. At ESF, though, a few boys were enrolled in the secretarial class, just as a few had enrolled in the past. The two boys in the morning shift both suggested their parents had encouraged them, judging the skills taught there to be "practical" in any future career. Alberto felt the typing skills would come in handy for presenting his own papers and reports as he proceeded through high school and college, on his way to becoming a doctor like his father. Though other boys might have been subject to ribbing from class-mates, Alberto's masculine identity was secured through his heterosexual and athletic displays in and out of school (see chapter 6). Thus, Alberto was able to cross a kind of gender line into secretarial shop precisely because his masculine gender identity was so clearly pronounced in other areas of school life.

In this chapter, I have discussed the discourses and practices comprising key institutional contexts at ESF. While the broader historical contexts for the development of the secundaria provided discourses of adolescence, equality, and national identity (chapter 1), such discourses took on a unique life, and were given unique inflections, in the situated practices of ESF teachers and administrators. Local institutional contexts mediated historical discourses, and such contexts provided an important set of constraints and resources for students to develop their own cultural game in school.

4. *Somos Muy Unidos:* The Production of

Student Culture in the Grupo Escolar

Students at ESF appropriated school spaces and discourses to construct a cultural game of equality. They played their cultural game through a strategic practice both constrained and enabled by historical and institutional contexts. For instance, as adolescents they were understood—perhaps even expected—to act irresponsibly. The secundaria was designed to cultivate responsibility, and to channel students' aspirations toward a strong national commitment and productive ethic of work for the collective good. Yet just as students applied concepts of adolescence to interpret their own behavior, they developed unique applications of equality and solidarity within the school. I tell that story here.

MY WAY INTO THE GRUPOS

At the beginning of the 1990 school year, I sent home a typed memo explaining the purpose of my study to the students and their parents, and clarifying their rights as subjects. I also took the microphone before the entire student body and introduced myself, saying that I had come from the United States to understand how a secundaria functioned. I stated my interest in writing a book that focused on students' views and experiences, and I invited the students to share their perspectives as long as they did not disrupt an official school activity in doing so. Later, I had to repeat some variant of this little speech several times when I first made visits to classrooms, as it is common to make introductory remarks at this time. Finally, those students and their families chosen for more thorough interviewing were presented with further written explanation through an informed consent sheet.

It was difficult to discern just how students interpreted my presence. My occasional query about their perceptions of me often met with embarrassment or hesitation. Many thought I was just fulfilling my *prácticas* (practicum), a kind of service internship required of all advanced degree candidates (high school and above) in Mexico. I was fortunate enough to be given great liberty by the teachers and school administrators, and participated in as many activities as my schedule permitted. I studiously avoided situations that might put me in authority, though occasionally I was asked to watch over a class while the teacher stepped out, and I helped organize a basketball tournament along with other activities. Most students probably didn't care much about what I was doing altogether. Several bothered to ask me, but they quickly showed disinterest if my response became drawn out (perhaps they perceived me as the *alargón,* the long-winded one). Gradually, most students normalized my presence in the school. Only a few—primarily girls—ever showed sustained interest in my project. They were unusually mature and thoughtful, and two of them—Rosita and Leticia—had initial interests in a social science career. They regularly queried me about what and how I was doing, and I brought them on as "key informants," inviting them to record their observations and reflections in a notebook I provided.

In my original research design, I had intended to focus my observations and interviews on just two third-year grupos escolares. I thought that such a strategy would afford me greater knowledge of particular student relations within the grupos while still allowing some comparison across them. During my brief research trip a year earlier, I had concentrated my time with second graders in 2B and 2C, knowing they would be entering their third year by the time of the full study. That first trip proved to be a good investment, as several of these students greeted me warmly when they arrived at the school in late August. It did not take long to confirm what I had already suspected: students generally formed strong emotional attachments to their grupos escolares. One way I felt this was through their insistent bids for me to spend classroom time with the grupo. If I went more than a day or two without visiting during the first couple of weeks, students from either 3B or 3C would come and ask in scolding tones, "Why haven't you come in [to class] with us lately?" Then students from 3A and 3F also began to reproach me. They wondered why I didn't find their grupos of sufficient interest to merit interviews and observation. Eventually I accommodated them as well. In the end, I had chosen four grupos for study, with approximately five focal students in each grupo. I probably still spent more time with 3B and 3C, in part because my familiarity with them had deeper roots. Students from 3D and 3E, the two grupos from the morning shift left out of my classroom schedule, only mildly rebuked me for ignoring them. They came to understand my reasons, and I got to know many of them anyway through at-large school activities.

Clearly, part of my attraction to students was the novelty posed by my presence in the classroom. Teachers would banter with me, and sometimes use my presence as a springboard for jokes and playful challenges. Students also incorporated me into their networks for sharing knowledge or playing practical jokes. I came to be seen as a rather good source of general knowledge as well as a trustworthy confidant for gossip or note passing. Moreover, my regular presence in a grupo's activities seemed to garner them a kind of status, as if the anthropologist's interest registered their relative superiority. This status was then circulated in the competitive, intergrupo symbolic economy at ESF.

Despite the power of the grupo escolar, it would be wrong to understate the interest students had in me as individuals and members of small friendship groups, too. I've already mentioned Rosita and Leticia's academic curiosity. They, like several other girls, also saw in me a kind of big brother, and sought me out for advice on school or family matters. They frequently confided some of their emotional problems with parents, boyfriends, and teachers. Even though I gave what I considered rather waffling responses, my status as an ambiguous adult earned me some respect. As a U.S. citizen—a foreigner—and an anthropologist, I was deemed to have an expertise in practical questions concerning school, family, and romance. Yet though I was perceived as an adult of sorts, I also became incorporated into students' friendship networks to varying degrees. I went to students' parties, sat with them in classrooms, and played with them at recess and after school. I occupied a limbo between adolescent and adult, able to draw on the authority of experience and U.S. citizenship while participating nonjudgmentally in students' informal activities. In sum, I was a safe bet, a young adult with no official authority and a clear sympathy for student concerns. Other students seemed more intrigued by my status as a citizen of the United States. They asked me questions about life in my country. Boys especially wanted to learn about sports and cars. Sometimes, the students asked me to translate lyrics from then-popular U.S. musicians like Madonna, Milli Vanilli, and New Kids on the Block. For many students, no doubt, I was a simple source of amusement, someone or something to break up the boring school routine. Finally, just as the grupos escolares appropriated me to bolster their prestige, small groups of friends within and across the grupos escolares apparently enjoyed the status of my association.

Anthropologists have reflected a great deal on the sexual tensions involved in the gendered relations of fieldwork (see Levinson 1998a). In retrospect, I should not have been so naive as to think I might be immune. As I've noted, girls played a prominent social role as leaders in both formal and informal activities. Since I made it clear from the outset that I wanted to comprehend the school from the students' point of view, they took it on themselves to help the anthropologist learn the ropes. While boys were often indifferent to my presence, many girls sought me out and invited me to spend time with their friendship groups during recess or after school. I cultivated the ambiguity so often necessary to successful fieldwork, and gradually the boys and teachers alike came to accept my unusual association with the girls' groups. Still, a few girls appeared to develop crushes on me. This was one of the most direct—and compromising—ways I participated in students' "grounded aesthetics" (Willis et al. 1990). The fact that I had become an object of attraction for several girls drew me into the world of romantic gender relations at ESF in a way I had not quite expected. I was twenty-seven years old at the time of my 1990 fieldwork, though I was often told I looked much younger. Since I was twice the age of most of the schoolgirls, it had not occurred to me that they might take me as a romantic object. Not only had I overlooked the fairly common phenomenon of schoolchild crushes on teachers, I had also failed to recognize that relationships and marriages across such age differences are not so unusual in Mexico. This was pressed on me toward the end of the school year when, on informing them that I was sad because I had broken up with my girlfriend in the United States, two girls offered to match me up with one of their classmates. I chuckled and said I was too old, but one of the girls said her own father had been twenty-five when he started dating her then-fourteen-year-old mother, and the other girl offered her aunt and uncle as a further example.

A few girls apparently desired me from afar, and one began a corre-

A third-year boy in a quiet moment of seatwork

spondence as my secret admirer. It was relatively easy to gently and congenially discourage these affections. More difficult were a couple of cases in which I formed close, confidential relationships with "informants." Leticia stands out here: in March, she came and handed me the notebook I had given her to record her thoughts and "investigations" of school life. We had exchanged the notebook several times already, but on this day, she took advantage of my involvement in a basketball game to slip the notebook into my bag and deliver a cryptic "adiós." She avoided me for several days, and then through the intervention of her friends, I learned that she had developed feelings for me that made mere "friendship" too painful. When she finally let me approach her, I appealed to Leticia's maturity by explaining why a more intimate relationship would not be possible or appropriate given our differences in age, culture, and experience. After another week, she came to me and said our friendship was too valuable, and she would try to work through her feelings. Now Leticia is twenty-three, and we maintain contact through letters and calls, just as I do with many of her former classmates. Yet in the process of extricating myself from such attachments as delicately as possible, I learned a lot about how girls' subjectivities were being formed in and out of school, and about just what kinds of expectations were in play (see chapter 6).[1]

As the teachers were fond of emphasizing, the secundaria was "forming" these students for an uncertain future. Students supposedly used their time in school to "define themselves" (*se están definiendo*) and "form good judgment" (*están formando su criterio*) during an inherently unstable adolescence. While I have reinforced this future orientation with my own theoretical interest in aspiration and identity formation, I strive to keep the immediacy of students' experiences at the forefront of the analysis.[2] Students did reflect on and worry about their grades and futures from time to time, but most of them relished school for its immediate challenges and pleasures. The secundaria provided a space for the experimental games of bodily desire, peer relation, and fun. Most situations were highly charged with varying emotions of love, friendship, animosity, solidarity, betrayal, and triumph.

HISTORIES AND CYCLES OF THE GRUPO ESCOLAR

It was not until around November of the 1990 school year that I became aware of students' and teachers' regular circulation of stories about different grupos escolares. These narratives portrayed grupo qualities and reputations (see Sandoval 1998b). As they circulated, they were contested or modified, acquiring new meanings or emphases. Stories were narrated differently by teachers and students, and given different inflection according to the narrator (Herrnstein-Smith 1981). Past events were reinterpreted in the light of current predicaments. For example, a dropout previously maligned by both teachers and students might later be lionized by students as a martyred defender of their rights. Each grupo escolar at ESF developed what could be called a kind of microhistory embedded within the larger historical narratives comprising school culture. These histories enabled students to construct an identification with the grupo, and contextualize the notions of solidarity and equality communicated by the teachers.

Since I worked primarily with third-year students, I was privy to fairly well developed stories about grupos. Students had been at the school for quite some time. Most knew their classmates well, and could recite each one's approximate address, grade point average, socioeconomic status, history of school friendships, and so forth. Moreover, each grupo seemed to have at least one or two students who acted as informal chroniclers. They displayed a more active interest in grupo affairs and took measures to join the friendship clusters into a more solidary social network. These students may or may not have been jefes de grupo, but they were always among my best informants. Their historical narratives were usually the best developed because they seemed to invest themselves most in the grupo and its ethic of solidarity.

For their part, teachers talked the most about third-year students as well. Many had taught the same grupos for at least one other year. They tended to contrast the grupo's current behavior and academic performance with that of previous years. Those teachers who hadn't taught their current third-year grupo before often solicited advice or anecdotes from teachers who had, seeking to place their experience with the grupo in some kind of comparative context. Some grupos had become so notorious that stories about them were told spontaneously among the teachers, without solicitation. This was how teachers constructed grupo reputations. Grupo 3A, for instance, was considered the most cantankerous and least united socially, but regularly earned the top spot in grade rankings. Grupo 3C was known for being extremely united yet only sporadically focused on academic tasks ("Somos muy unidos"—we are very united—was a common refrain in 3C), while 3F was both internally fractious and academically unsuccessful (see below).

Teachers employed these narratives to modify grupo behavior, and clearly students appropriated them to help construct their own narratives. Grupo histories were always dynamically circulating and inflected by the perspective of the teller. During the first week of classes, both Mr. Carrizo, a social studies teacher, and Mr. Agosín, a natural science teacher, announced to grupo 3A that they had been forewarned about 3A's bad behavior and even given the chance to request another teaching assignment. Mr. Carrizo, especially, outlined in some detail the reports he had heard about the grupo's mischievous (latoso) behavior, only to say that he wasn't intimidated and hoped to turn such energy into a good "working spirit" ("ánimo de trabajo"). Mr. Agosín tried a more authoritarian approach, asserting that he relished the challenge of disciplining wayward grupos. For their part, the students enjoyed the apparent contradictions of these reports about how their mischief combined with positive academic results. They cheered mockingly, almost pridefully, on being told that they were the worst-behaved grupo in school, and a few offered playful explanations: "It's because we're geniuses," one boy shouted out. Later, when I got to know the students better, I noted how they incorporated parts of these teachers' narratives into their own.

What was perhaps most intriguing about these narratives was the way they focused on the grupo rather than individual students. While everyone acknowledged that individual styles or behaviors could contradict or complicate a grupo's reputation, the stories remained at the group level. To illustrate: After the first grading period, I witnessed a meeting between the teachers and parents of 3F students. Mr. Alonso, the mathematics teacher for 3F, had convened the meeting because 3F had become practically uncontrollable and was failing its exams miserably. Shortly before the meeting, I met with Mr. Alonso and another teacher, and they took pains to qualify the charge against the grupo, noting that only a few students were really responsible for its current predicament. These unnamed (but generally known) students were tagged as "bad elements" who were dragging the rest of the grupo down with them. Their influence was made to appear almost irresistible. This is how the problem had become a grupo one, and why the meeting had to be convened for the whole grupo. Only once, briefly, were these alleged bad elements mentioned in the meeting with the parents. When a few parents suggested that the difficulty lay more in the teachers' inability to engage or control the students, the discussion shifted again from the depiction of a few so-called problem students to the grupo at large. No individual cases were openly discussed at this forum.

Student narratives of grupo history, on the other hand, tended to highlight a developmental pattern that largely escaped the main themes of teacher accounts. Virtually all the students spoke of first-year tentativeness. Students who came from different primary schools didn't know each other on entering the school. They arrived timid and unsure, generally concentrating on their classwork. An ethic of solidarity had not yet emerged, nor had any of the collectively produced strategies I describe later in this chapter. Rather, students went about their business in a largely individual manner. Soon, however, members of the grupo became more comfortable together. They learned to trust one another (*tenerse confianza*). They also discovered their classmates' strengths and weaknesses, their resources and limitations. By the middle of the first year, students were collaborating much more confidently on projects and assignments. They were forming emotional bonds through particular age- and gender-specific idioms, and were constructing a clear identification with the grupo escolar. This was abetted, no doubt, by teachers' exhortations to grupo equality and solidarity. Interestingly, both students and teachers commented that most first-year students, especially toward the beginning, demonstrated greater dedication to their studies and less of a penchant for classroom mischief. It was only after a few months' time together that students began to *echar relajo* (goof off) on a regular basis.

As they explained it to me in casual conversation, by the second year, students already felt themselves to be "masters" (*dueños*) of the school. According to teacher and student reports, this was the time during which grupo unity appeared to be strongest. Yet it was also the period when students most tended to skip or disrupt class. Teachers claimed it was the most difficult year to teach.[3] In a fascinating combination of explanatory devices, some teachers attributed such second-year misconduct to its co-incidence with the beginning of puberty (*"el mero inicio de la adolescencia,"* as one teacher put it) and rush of sexual hormones, while others saw it as part of the institutional cycle that encourages second graders to *agarrar más confianza* (develop more trust, in the sense of complacency). This notion of confianza, which teachers actually saw as a form of insolence working to the detriment of students' studies, resonated with students' sense of themselves as "masters" of the school.

Finally, in the third year of secundaria, grupo histories tended to diversify. The value and integrity of grupo unity became more fragile. Though virtually every third-year student claimed that his or her grupo had been most united in second grade, many insisted that the grupo continued just as united in the final year. Others admitted that fissures had developed, but they attributed this to different causes. Some said their classmates were thinking more of the future, putting more emphasis on good grades and less on the goofing off that was so essential to maintaining grupo cohesion. They had been scared by a poor second-year performance and worried that they might not receive their graduation certificate on time. Other students thought their concerns lay more with after-school jobs or boyfriends and girlfriends, effectively devaluing the kind of emotional and practical support that the grupo escolar offered. From most student accounts, the third year was the most bittersweet. Some talked about the complete breakdown of grupo unity, with each student going his or her own way. Most, however, described the flux and tensions within the grupo, as some pulled against grupo unity while others did everything in their power to keep the grupo together as a moral and social unit. Whatever the specific status of grupo unity, though, most agreed with Leticia, who wrote that she would never love her classmates more than she had in secundaria because later, "in the preparatoria, everyone looks out more for their own interests than for those of others" (*"en la preparatoria cada quien indaga más bien por sus propios intereses que por los demás"*).

Breaking with an alphabetic convention, I will present the grupos in the order and depth that I got to know them, providing brief synopses of the eight focal students I highlight in this book (appendix B offers even briefer synopses of the other focal students).[4] In presenting these portraits of focal students, I draw on teacher and student narratives as well as my own school and household observations. The portraits are thus a kind of composite etched from different angles. Teachers' characterizations of these students may seem to carry much weight, but they only reveal other dimensions of those situated teaching concepts I mentioned in the previous chapter. The reader should not privilege this perspective over others.

GRUPO 3C

Grupo 3C was perhaps my most solid social anchor in the school. Most of my preliminary interviews in 1989 had been with members of 3C, and several were quite welcoming when I returned in 1990. Moreover, 3C, along with 3B, contained several of the students with the highest social profiles in the school, especially Iván, who eventually won the campaign for student body president. Grupo 3C was also arguably the most united among third-year grupos. Virtually every student was proud to be a member of 3C, and students from other grupos occasionally mentioned its positive reputation. From the teachers' point of view, it could be a pleasure to work with 3C, but also a challenge. The students in 3C were seen as being lazy and goof-offs (*relajientos*), prone to using their unity for mischievous ends. Along with 3A, they were the most consistently maligned grupo in the school, only occasionally redeemed by responsible displays of unity and ánimo de trabajo (work spirit).

ROSITA

My guide, interpreter, and sometime guardian angel in 3C, Rosita was one of the few students I met in 1988 and initially interviewed in 1989. At that time, as a second-grade student at ESF, Rosita had expressed a strong work ethic and a desire to become a psychologist. She said that she liked to study a lot, especially read, adding, "I've seen on television that those who don't study have a lot of problems." Her desire to be a psychologist was rooted in her inclination to help others with their problems. She was like this with her friends, she explained, always giving advice. Besides,

Table 2. Male Focal Students at ESF

Name and Grupo	Age in September 1990	Location and Quality of Home	Parents' Occupation and Education	Siblings' Ages, Education, and Occupation	Expressed Aspirations in 1990	Average School Performance and Shop Course
Franco (3B)	14	City center; modest but sturdy, three bedrooms	F: Veterinarian, tortillería owner; university studies M: Tortilleria owner; primaria, plus two years of colegio	Three younger sisters (6, 8, 9), and one younger brother (4); all studying in public schools	Study computer science at technological university	Seven to eight; an occasional failed course; electricity
Iván (3c)	15	City center; modest, sturdy, several bedrooms, with print shop	F: Print shop manager and owner; primaria M: Housewife; primaria	Twelve older siblings; most completed prepa (CBTIS). One younger sister; ESF	Highway patrolman; army officer; computer technician; illegal worker in the United States	Six to seven; several failed courses; electricity
Abel (3B)	14	Outskirts; large three bedroom with nearby cabaña, store in front	F: Dentist; university degree M: Housewife, store operator; secundaria	Four older sisters; two with university degrees, one studying dentistry, one in prepa, will study law	Lawyer; computer programmer; pilot	Six to seven; several failed courses; auto mechanics

Isidro (3F)	14	Poor peripheral colonia; poor home, mostly dirt floors	F: Campesino, U.S. migrant; no school M: Housewife, campesina; no school	Four older brothers (18–30), two older sisters (19 and 21); one brother and one sister finished secundaria, others primaria only	Possibly work with animals; emigrate to the United States	Seven to eight; drafting
Alberto (3F)	14	City center; nicely appointed four bedroom with adjacent medical office	F: Medical doctor; university degree M: Housewife, boutique owner; primaria, plus two years adult secundaria, plus three years comercio	Three older brothers (18–25); one a medical doctor, one an architect, one studying law	Professional, probably a medical doctor	Around nine; secretarial
Fidencio (3A)	14	City center and middle colonia	F: Furniture maker, store owner; secundaria M: Housewife, store owner; secundaria	Two younger brothers; one (12) in first year at the técnica, another in primaria	N.A.	Six to seven; failed several classes; carpentry

Table 2. Continued

Name and Grupo	Age in September 1990	Location and Quality of Home	Parents' Occupation and Education	Siblings' Ages, Education, and Occupation	Expressed Aspirations in 1990	Average School Performance and Shop Course
Vicente (3C)	14	Middle colonia; modest house	F: Welder and iron-worker; some primaria M: N.A.	One older brother; one year secundaria. Younger brother and sister; in primaria	Auto body repair worker; possibly a government post	Around seven; failed an occasional class; auto mechanics
Enrique (3A)	14	Peripheral colonia; simple three-room cement home with dirt courtyard	F: Truck and bus driver, U.S. migrant; primaria M: Housewife; no formal education	Five younger brothers and sisters; one at técnica, others in primaria	N.A.	Eight to nine; drafting
Paco (3B)	14	Indigenous village; modest two-bedroom cement house with mostly dirt floors, no plumbing	F: N.A. M: Sells fish in San Pablo market; no schooling, illiterate	One older brother (20); bilingual teacher with one year of university study. One younger sister; in first grade at ESF	Doctor; lawyer	Seven to eight; failed an occasional class; radio technician

	Age	Residence	Parents	Siblings	Aspirations	School
Socorro (3F)	16	Peripheral colonia; modest two-bedroom cinder block home	F: Fights and bets on cocks, keeps small farm for raising cocks; three years of primaria. M: Housewife; two years of primaria	Two older brothers; pharmacy (both with secundaria). Older sister; in CBTIS. Younger brother; in técnica. Sister; in primaria	Raise and fight cocks; possibly a social studies teacher in secundaria	Above seven; failed a number of classes; drafting
Fidel (3B)	14	Mestizo village; poor, small cinder block house, no plumbing	F: Deceased, 1989. M: Housewife; three years of primaria	Two older brothers (16 and 18); one with secundaria, another dropped out of secundaria	Possibly a lawyer; wood carving in village	Seven to eight; failed an occasional class; carpentry
José (3A)	13	Peripheral colonia; modest cement home under construction	F: Van and truck driver; primaria. M: Housewife; primaria	Two younger brothers; one in primaria	Accountant; lawyer; highway patrolman	Around nine; carpentry

Table 3. Female Focal Students at ESF

Name and Grupo	Age in September 1990	Location and Quality of Home	Parents' Occupation and Education	Siblings' Ages, Education, and Occupation	Expressed Aspirations in 1990	Average School Performance and Shop Course
Rosita (3c)	13	Middle colonia; Ample house under construction	F: Truck driver, cloth factory owner; secundaria. M: Housewife, cloth finisher; comercio degree	One younger sister (10); in colegio	Journalist; psychologist; tourism worker	Around nine; clothing design
Antonia (3B)	14	City center; ample house, well appointed	F: Autobus owner and administrator; two years of secundaria. M: Housewife; full secundaria	Younger brother (9) and sister (4); in public primaria	Early childhood educator	Around eight; weaving and embroidery
Lidia (3F)	14	City center	F: Traveling salesman; secundaria. M: Housewife, nursery teacher; secundaria	Younger sister (11) and brother (8); in private colegio	Flight attendant; possibly a psychologist; tour guide	Around eight; clothing design
Dalia (3c)	13	Middle colonia; small cement home	F and M: Schoolteachers; university studies	No siblings	Teacher; nurse	Around eight; weaving and embroidery

Leticia (3B)	13	City center; ample house, modestly appointed	F: Owns and operates auto parts stores; completed secundaria. M: Housewife; almost completed comercio course after secundaria	Three older brothers; biologist (22); dropped out of agronomy program (20); starting medical degree (18). One younger brother (10)	Translator; pediatrician or veterinarian; social worker; teacher	Around nine; electricity
Nidia (3F)	16	Mestizo village; large but modest home, all cement floors and indoor plumbing	F: Runs a commercial grain trading business; three years of primaria. M: Housewife; four years of primaria	Older brother (25); helps father, primaria only. Older sister (20); four years of primaria. Older sister (18); dropped técnica. Five younger siblings; in primaria	Early childhood educator; possibly a secretary or store attendant	Around eight; secretarial
Andrea (3A)	13	Peripheral colonia; very modest house	F: Crafts maker and vendor; primaria. M: crafts maker and vendor, primary teacher; secundaria	Older sister (16); in prepa, wants to be educator. Younger sister; in primaria. Younger brother (3)	Early childhood educator	Between six and seven; failed courses often; secretarial

Table 3. *Continued*

Name and Grupo	Age in September 1990	Location and Quality of Home	Parents' Occupation and Education	Siblings' Ages, Education, and Occupation	Expressed Aspirations in 1990	Average School Performance and Shop Course
Ivonne (3B)	14/15	Middle colonia; rather modest house	F: Timber cutter, truck driver; three years of primaria. M: Housewife, domestic aide, and babysitter; completed primaria	Two older brothers (16 and 17); one in CBTIS, another graduated ESF. Two younger sisters (11 and 12); in primaria. Younger brother (4)	Nurse	Around eight; weaving and embroidery
Alejandra (3C)	16	Middle colonia	F: N.A.; perhaps secundaria. M: Union officer; secundaria	Two younger brothers (4 and 14); one in TV at ESF. One younger sister	Secretary or hotel worker	Around seven; an occasional failed class; electricity
Matilde (3B)	13/14	Peripheral colonia; modest, well-appointed home	F: Truck driver; finished secundaria. M: Ex-teacher, housewife; some university study	Three younger sisters (11, 7, and 6); all in public schools	Architect; bilingual secretary; elementary school teacher	Between eight and nine; drafting

a friend of her mom's was a psychologist, and they chatted from time to time about her work. In 1989, Rosita also reported that one of her best friends was from a "*buena familia . . . donde salen bien educados*" ("good family . . . where the children are all well educated"). Together they spent a lot of time talking about the faults and strengths of teachers. Both had gone to a private religious colegio for primary school, and both had transferred to ESF because local wisdom suggested that they would have a better chance to go on to prepa from there. After their first year at ESF, though, her best friend transferred again to a new private school in town.

Rosita was the oldest of two daughters in a family of modest means residing in an established working-class neighborhood. Her father owned and operated a small cargo truck while also supervising the production of colorful cotton napkins and tablecloths at a small shop he owned with his father and brothers. Rosita's mother, herself a graduate of a high school–level *comercio* course, supervised domestic chores, cut and measured cloth, and subcontracted embroidering and other detail work on the cloth to poorer neighborhood women. Rosita's sister had not yet graduated from the primary school of the colegio where Rosita had also attended. Throughout the time I knew them, Rosita's family seemed on the economic upswing. They were constantly improving and adding to their solid brick home with tile floors, appliances, and consumer electronics. Rosita's parents were also solidly behind their daughters' education. Her father insisted he would somehow acquire the money to support them through a university degree. Her mother agreed, but she also had another agenda. She claimed to have been snubbed by her husband's family, especially the mother-in-law, for her dark skin and eyes as well as her questionable family background. Apparently, Rosita had not received the same attention or affection as the other grandchildren, and Rosita's mother was determined she succeed in spite of this.

A short, pudgy girl with a coy smile, only thirteen at the start of the school year, Rosita was known as a serious student. Teachers uniformly described her as dedicated, responsible, and hardworking. Several noted that she spoke frequently and well, but that she also tended to sacrifice herself for the welfare of others. Rosita had developed a rich interior life and decided that I—as her *hermano postizo* (pretend brother)—should be privy to it. Deeply religious, she had a sense of calling, of special mystery. At the end of the school year in 1991, when I asked her what she'd be doing over the summer, Rosita said only half joking:

109   Somos Muy Unidos

"I'm going to mass every day because my soul is black. I've committed a lot of sins." Earlier, in the notebook we passed back and forth, Rosita encouraged me to scold and correct her: "I've always liked for people to correct me, because really I'm a pretty special case. I do, say, and think things that don't seem right to most people. They tell me I don't make sense" ("*Siempre me ha gustado que me llamen la atención, de veras que soy un caso especial. Hago, digo, pienso cosas que a muchos no les parece, según ellos no tienen sentido*"). By 1990, her career thoughts had turned toward journalism or tourism management. At one point, she had even considered joining a convent, so serious were her commitments to serve God and others. Yet she was also driven to prove herself to her skeptical grandmother and thought a university career would provide the best route.

IVÁN

I had remembered Iván from my previous trips because his subtle defiance in class had caught my attention. In fact, my earliest field notes singled him out. He was much taller and huskier than his classmates, and seemed to strike a balance between masculine bravado and bemused nonchalance. In 1989, when Mr. Solana asked him and a few schoolmates to stand in front of the class for not doing their homework, Iván showed little compunction. He stood and smiled, gesturing conspiratorially to his friends. Soon to turn fifteen years old, Iván came from a large family, in which he figured as the second to the youngest of fourteen children. His older siblings had all attended ESF, and most had already completed a technical career such as accounting at the local CBTIS (vocational high school). Several worked in local banks and shops. Iván said that none of his older siblings had ever attended university, but his next-older sister, then in the prepa, had plans to continue. He also had one younger sister then enrolled in ESF's first grade.

Iván's father had for many years managed the printing operations for a local educational institute. He also ran a print shop out of his home, where he currently produced one of the small local papers in town. Though he had worked in the shop alongside his brothers from time to time, Iván didn't like it much there. He preferred working with engines, and every weekday afternoon he apprenticed four hours in a small engine repair shop. Some of his earnings would be turned over to his mother, but some would go to buying treats and adventures for his buddies and girlfriend, who was one year older and two grades above him, and well on her way to becoming a nurse (Iván abjured alcohol, cigarettes, and drugs, claiming he didn't want to make his parents "suffer"). The seriousness of Iván's courtship was the subject of frequent commentary among his fellow students.

Like so many of his male classmates, Iván dreamed of becoming a highway patrolman (*federal de caminos*) or an officer in the army. He liked the idea of handling guns and wanted to be on the right side of the law. Yet he knew those jobs required more study, and he wasn't sure if he could do more time with books and homework. He had never completed much homework (*tarea*), and said that even if he didn't work afternoons, he doubted that he would do the assignments. He was more drawn to working with motors or computers. At one point, he claimed to be taking a computer class because it was the "career of the future." Toward the end of the school year, Iván was even talking about specializing in math and physics at the prepa since he'd done so poorly in math and felt he had something to prove. Iván also thought about going to work in the United States. His mother insisted that he complete his secundaria certificate. After that, he could do anything he wanted, though they'd support him at least through three more years of study if he so chose. To me, this didn't look likely. In August 1990, Iván was "paying" off four classes that he had failed, while in the meantime he had advanced beyond apprenticeship at the engine shop. He even tried to con his physical education teacher by presenting his girlfriend's nursing anatomy assignments as his own work for the extraordinary exam.

Iván claimed to have been even more belligerent in primary school, where he failed one year. He often got in fights and developed a reputation as a leader. In the secundaria, these energies were apparently channeled into more benign activities, but Iván still liked to see himself as the leader of his gang (*flota, palomilla*), and sometimes the 3c flota would join together with boys from other grupos to form a larger *banda* that fought a few times with students from other schools. At the same time, most of the teachers confirmed one point that rankled Iván: his older brothers had already established the family reputation as rebels (*rebeldes*). In fact, Iván's mother had had to visit the school so many times over the years that she'd come to blame most of her sons' problems on the teachers themselves. The teachers, in turn, complained that his mother's attitude shielded Iván from legitimate criticism.

Teachers and students across the school often recognized the unity and solidarity that grupo 3B displayed in and out of the classroom. Along with 3C, they were seen as the most united grupo in school. Their handling of the civic ceremony was always spotless, and they competed favorably against other grupos for top awards in grades and punctuality. They also displayed their unity in activities specifically proscribed by school authorities. On one occasion, their faculty sponsors for a planned field trip abandoned them at the last moment, even though their rented coach was waiting just outside the school gates. The grupo defied the principal's admonition, heading off for an unchaperoned excursion to the capital city and a local bathing spot. Grupo 3B celebrated the unity that permitted them to make this decision, even though they paid for it dearly with a three-day suspension and parental meeting with the principal. Five years after this event, several former 3B students remembered it fondly, especially for its show of grupo solidarity.

LETICIA

My first documented interaction with Leticia occurred in the middle of September when she approached me on the side of the basketball court during the recess period (I had already spent a few days going into classrooms with 3B). Before I knew it, Leticia was providing an informal interview. She told me about her three older brothers, especially the one who had studied biology at the university and spoke good English and French. Each of her parents had once owned and operated an auto parts store, but now her mother stayed home as a housewife (before the year was over, her father would reopen a second parts store). Sometimes, she commented spontaneously, they have had "economic difficulties," and even recently she'd had to make it through recess in order to wait for the main meal after school. As she put it, in terms that still seem ironic to me, "We just have the most basic things: the house, a car, and that's it." Then Leticia turned the interview around, asking me some about anthropology and proclaiming her own interest in the "social sciences." She inquired if I'd seen the movie *Mississippi Burning*, which had recently played in town. Mr. Carrizo, their social science teacher, had relayed to them my recommendation of the film for their unit on slavery and civil rights in U.S. history. Then Leticia asked if I was "racist," and when I explained why I thought I wasn't, she recounted her discussion with a black U.S. tourist she'd met the previous year. Leticia would eventually become a frequent and astute interlocutor of mine. I visited her house regularly to chat with her mother or play with her cocker spaniel, but I only met her father on one brief occasion.

Leticia's mother was clearly a dominant force in her life, and by the time we met, Leticia considered her mother a close friend. They often left the house together to run errands or visit relatives, and her mother offered a great deal of practical and moral support. Given to bouts of depression, Leticia's mother still wondered if she'd sold herself short by getting married at the age of seventeen before finishing a course in comercio she had chosen specifically to "prepare" herself for any economic necessity. Having dedicated herself completely to raising her children, she trumpeted the satisfactions of motherhood yet still seemed unhappy. Meanwhile, on more than one occasion, Leticia characterized her family, like her grupo, as rather "united"; her older brothers often helped with her studies. The results paid off. Mr. Carrizo called Leticia a "dedicated" student and conjectured that she got her smarts from her mother, whom Mr. Carrizo had known himself as a fellow student. Other teachers agreed. Leticia never had academic problems, though some teachers noted that she liked to "stand out" in the grupo, to call attention to herself, especially through her fine command of language. This made a striking contrast with the rather quiet and timid girl some teachers had remembered from her first year at ESF.

MATILDE

I came to know Matilde as a rather forthcoming and cheerful girl who sought me out to discuss her problems with boys. By the time we did a more formal interview in December, Matilde could hardly wait to inform me about her family and friends. She was the most eager participant I knew, and liked to fill the notebook I'd gifted her with her own poems and thoughts about love.

Matilde's family had just moved into a solid, modestly appointed new house in an outlying *colonia* (neighborhood). She was the oldest of four daughters, who were all studying in public schools. Her mother had been raised by grandparents, and worked briefly as a rural schoolteacher until marriage and children, when she devoted herself to the family and home. Her father had only finished secundaria when, as the oldest of twelve children, he was called on to help in the family business. He started making deliveries of candies and other groceries, and eventually came into his own as a long-distance truck driver. He earned good money, but the jobs were often sporadic. I got to know Matilde's parents fairly well, visiting for lunch on a few occasions and completing one long joint interview. They struck me as honest and genuinely concerned for their daughters' futures.

It was also obvious that Matilde honored her family a great deal. On discussing careers, Matilde confessed that a university architecture degree was really her heart's desire (*"lo que me llenaría"*). She also considered studying to be an elementary schoolteacher or a bilingual secretary. Yet Matilde also wanted to relieve her father of his more difficult work. He was already getting tired, she said, and the family had discussed converting their garage into a small dairy store. By the end of the school year, Matilde had decided to attend the CBTIS and take the specialty of secretarial skills in order to help the family economy. She insisted this was her decision alone, that her parents would support her if she decided instead to continue her schooling. But Matilde wondered about the risks of advanced study:

> Sometimes I tell myself like, "No, why study so much and up to such a high level if, say, the architects are working as masons or traveling salesmen?" I feel like so many years, what for? To throw them away, really, because I think it's as much a waste of money as a waste of my life, no?

Matilde then added a gender twist by telling the story of an older cousin who probably would not finish her university studies until well into her twenties. She worried that her cousin paid insufficient attention to her personal life, and would realize "too late" that she'd lost the chance for love and marriage.

Meanwhile, Matilde's grades slipped a lot during her final year. Her teachers had always known her to be "respectful," "disciplined," and a solid worker. Now, they speculated, her involvement with boys and more mature girls had distracted her from schoolwork. Mr. Carrizo suggested that Matilde's best friends, such as Gina, had more *cultura* (professional parents, lots of books in the home, and the like), more smarts, even more "liberal" ideas than her. They could suffer distraction and still do well enough in school, but Matilde couldn't keep up with them. Matilde's parents generally concurred with the teachers' judgments; they also worried about how much her friends, bringing a more "open" and "libertine" attitude from outside San Pablo, "knew" about life.

Like Rosita, Franco was one of the first students I got to know at ESF. He had approached me with a group of friends back in 1988, and since then I'd frequently seen him around town. Franco's father, already some fifty-three years old, had grown up in San Pablo helping his own father distribute newspapers and sell candy at the only movie theater in town. With great sacrifice, three of this man's four sons had studied at the university and two had completed their degrees. Franco's father largely supported himself to study veterinary medicine at the national university in Mexico City, and then worked for a number of years on a pig farm (where he met his wife) and as a livestock inspector. His mother, almost twenty years younger, originally came from a farming village bordering Texas in the easternmost state of Tamaulipas. Franco had been born there before his parents had returned to San Pablo when he was still a young boy. They had high aspirations for Franco as the oldest child, but he often disappointed them with what they saw as his aimless disposition; they thought perhaps my association with Franco would give him greater focus. Franco's mother, who had studied primaria and taken a two-year course in comercio to be a bilingual secretary, also wanted to send Franco back to Tamaulipas, "up there with my people," so he might pick up some different and better habits. She had been a good student at her small rural primaria and would have become a nun but for her parents' insistence that she marry young—at nineteen. Meanwhile, Franco's four younger siblings required more resources. Two younger daughters were soon to enter secundaria themselves, and another required special care for her severe learning disabilities. The youngest child, a boy, was only four years old. In early 1990, after struggling to find work locally, Franco's parents decided to launch a modest wheat tortilla shop in the center of town (most tortillas in Mexico are made with maize). They had bought an expensive press machine and hired an employee to help. Still, Franco often had to work in the business afternoons and weekends.

Franco was by most accounts an average student who dreamed of a career in computers. He liked math and English classes best, as well as his electricity shop, because he got his best grades there and fancied the subjects important for his future. In the afternoon, he took an occasional computer class to get a head start on his career. Franco claimed that he received a lot of guidance and prompting from his parents. His mother said on more than one occasion that she hoped Franco would never be a simple laborer (cargador), an employee of anyone. Though he said his own determination kept him in school, Franco also said his parents warned him that their support of his further study would be conditioned on receiving adequate grades. Outside of school, too, Franco received guidance from and observed the example of several cousins who were already studying in high school and college. He liked to attend church and listen to the priests' talks to the youth, where he also derived some motivation and formed a separate group of friends.

In school, Franco had just a few good friends. He often fell asleep in class and became the butt of classmates' jokes (they would call him *dormilón,* sleepyhead). It was not clear whether Franco's bout of infectious meningitis some four years earlier, which had required treatment with a soporific drug, made him more likely to doze. In any case, most teachers didn't know quite what to make of him. Mr. Carrizo thought Franco wanted to excel, but that something in his family (too much work? too much "family control"? he speculated) held him back. Mrs. Hinojosa called him "passive" and frankly of low ability. Franco's English teacher highlighted his "nervousness," while his science teacher wondered at the inexplicable alternation between solid, dedicated work and careless work done on the fly. The electricity teacher, on the other hand, claimed Franco was constant in his work and liked to study. He conjectured that Franco had always wanted to get ahead, to "leave the situation his family is in." Toward the end of the year, when his English teacher asked students to write about what they would be doing the following year ("*¿Qué va a ser de mí el próximo año escolar?*"), Franco responded:

> Above all, I think I'll try really hard because I'm the oldest in the family and I've learned that time is short, that maybe now I have extra time but later I won't have enough [*Más que todo pienso echarle muchas ganas porque soy el mayor y he aprendido que el tiempo es muy corto y que ahorita me sobra pero después me falta*]. I made a friend who would get up every day at 5 A.M. to work, then he would go to [classes at] the technological university, then he would come home to study and do homework, and weekends he would take a computer course, and that's just about what I'm thinking about doing and because I have a friend or teacher who'll help me in everything I do. That's why. I'm going to study prepa in the afternoons and in the mornings I'll study and look for a hobby.

According to most teachers, grupo 3F apparently had gone from being a grupo with mediocre grades and adequate conduct to one of the most notorious in all the school. It wasn't until their third year that 3F seemed to fall apart, and the students were at a loss to explain it themselves. Some thought their jefes de grupo were not functioning well, and others believed that a few transferred students had altered the successful balance from before. The grupo struck me as neither especially fractious (like 3A) nor unified. What unified them most their third year was a complaint against the name-calling and insults of one teacher (Levinson 1998b). Ironically, most members of 3F with whom I would speak later, in 1997, recalled that teacher as strict though good. His scoldings had been "for one's own good" ("*por el bién de uno*").

ALBERTO

I first met Alberto in 1989 when he led a small group of students over to where I was sitting during recess. He asked me questions about schooling in the United States and then revealed that an older brother was completing his final year of high school with an aunt in North Carolina. It was clear to me early on that Alberto was something of a leader in the school. In his own mind, he distinguished between his compañeros—fellow students with whom he might collaborate on school tasks or goof off—and amigos—friends whom he might have known from his childhood or the neighborhood. He was most likely to speak after school, go to parties, play sports, go hunting, and the like with his friends.

Alberto was well known by all the teachers, who tended to refer to him by his mother's last name because she came from one of the long-standing elite families in town. Alberto's father was a general doctor with his own practice adjacent to their nice four-bedroom home. His mother's family owned a number of businesses in town, and she had inherited a clothing and crafts boutique that she ran on a daily basis. Alberto's brothers were all interested in professional careers. His oldest brother, like his father, had studied medicine; the next brother had just finished his degree in architecture; and the third had just begun studying in Mexico City for his law degree. All three had attended a private preparatoria in the state capital, but Alberto said his parents would not let him do the same. He was the "baby" of the family, and his parents wanted him close at hand. Besides, a couple of his brothers had gotten into academic trouble in the capital. Though the San Pablo prepa was considered to be of lower quality, Alberto's parents thought its location would enable them to more effectively guide their son's activities. Alberto confessed to having an interest in medicine. As a child, he had often spent time in his father's office, thumbing through books and observing the instruments.

Earlier in his life, and through a practice still common in many San Pablo families, Alberto had been switched from one of the best private colegios to what was considered the best public primaria in San Pablo for his sixth and final year.[5] In my first taped interview with Alberto, I asked him what he remembered most about his time in the primaria:

> ALBERTO: The problem I had when I first got to [the primaria] is that I was coming from a colegio, and the way [the students] saw me, they would even call me "little rich kid" ["*riquillo*"], or they would just about say anything, expressions like that. . . . At the beginning, it took me a long time to become a part of things [*acoplarme*]. I suffered a lot when I first came, because everyone was looking for a fight with me. . . . I would go to school with fear, saying, "They're going to gang up and slug me, they're going to hit me."
>
> BL: And did you feel that your schoolmates were from, let's say, another social class?
>
> ALBERTO: I saw everybody the same, you know? I wasn't paying any attention to that, that didn't matter to me. I'll tell you, I would even say, "We're all equal" ("todos somos iguales") when they were calling me "you little rich kid."

Alberto claimed this period of verbal and physical harassment didn't last long, but he apparently learned his lessons well. By the middle of the year, he had managed to successfully incorporate himself into the social life of the school. Besides his average fighting ability, one of his key resources was obviously the rejoinder "todos somos iguales." It was not clear where Alberto had come up with this phrase, but the strategy of using it carried over and found reinforcement in the secundaria (see chapter 6).

By his third and final year in the secundaria, Alberto had firmed up his ambitions to study medicine, yet he had also become something of a rogue. He would be the first to admit that he was not a model student, by any means. Teachers complained that while he had a good deal of intelligence and all the support he needed from home, Alberto often failed to apply himself academically. He had a lot of charisma, but teachers felt he applied it to the wrong ends. The Spanish teacher Ms. Hinojosa attributed his recent carelessness (*descuido*) to the attractions of a girl in 3F, who "absorbed" his interest and required his help. Several other teachers associated Alberto's apparent complacency with his family's wealth. He would do the work, but with little desire. Mr. Solana thought he could be a much better student because of his brothers and his family's *medio cultural* (cultural environment). According to the physical education teacher, Alberto was a "classic case of those rich children" who had grown accustomed to getting what they wanted. The math teacher concurred, noting Alberto's poor performance in the early part of the year until his mother denied him certain privileges in order to get his grades up. This teacher also observed that even though Alberto was from a "very elevated social status," over the three years he had learned to value the contributions (conocimientos) of his poorer grupo mates, and this had helped integrate him into school life. It seemed to me, however, that Alberto didn't have to spend much time studying in order to pull good grades. He also knew how to effectively exploit classroom exchange networks to acquire the knowledge or assignments he needed at critical moments. Finally, Alberto's unusual choice of the secretarial shop provoked that teacher to comment on his gradual acceptance by the overwhelming majority of the girls. She said Alberto always did his work, and did it well, but that he was also a "spark" in the class, restless and talkative.

NIDIA

Although she was one of the quieter girls in 3F, I came to know Nidia better as the year wore on. We developed a special bond because she lived in the village just outside San Pablo where I'd first lived and volunteered at a primaria some five years earlier (see chapter 2); we often talked about life there. Her father had worked in California in the early 1970s in order to save money for a truck and start his own business in trading grains. Originally from a town about an hour from San Pablo, Nidia's father had decided to buy land and build a house in the village in order to facilitate his access to the grains he wanted to trade. Nidia was reserved in school, and kept a low profile with a small circle of friends. Her parents told her to keep away from the boys. When I asked her teachers to discuss Nidia, some couldn't even recall who she was. Those that did, agreed that she was "quiet" and "reserved," not an excellent student although diligent (*dedicada, cumplida*). Her math teacher, Mr. Alonso, even ventured that Nidia had arrived at ESF quite "timid" because she felt like a kid from the "*rancho.*" Since then, she had shed this "complex" and come to feel like "any normal girl from the city."

Nevertheless, Nidia was one of those girls who remained in school under a parental threat of removal if she failed to maintain good grades. Her oldest sister had been taken away to the distant border city of Mexicali by an aunt and never finished primaria. Another older sister had dropped out of the técnica before getting her certificate because she got "robbed" by her husband. The oldest brother, twenty-five, now helped the father with his business, and Nidia had five younger siblings in elementary school. When she first arrived at ESF, Nidia wanted to be a secretary. Now she dreamed of studying to be an early childhood educator, but her parents insisted she first complete the high school course in comercio at a San Pablo colegio. If she dropped out now or anywhere along the way, they reasoned, she would at least have the skills to help them run a small grocery store they were thinking of opening in the village. By the time we chatted in November, Nidia was worried because she'd gotten her lowest grades ever (below eight), and discussions about her fate had begun at home. In late May, not long before graduation, Nidia still expressed a strong desire to attend the prepa in order to prepare herself for a teaching career. Her mother still preferred the comercio course at the colegio for her, but with Nidia's father's assent, was willing to grant Nidia's wish. Meanwhile, Nidia's grades had slowly recovered. In the end-of-the-year questionnaire applied by their English teacher, Nidia responded to the question about what she would be doing next year with a touch of the religious fatalism that surfaced from time to time: "I can't say because only God knows what might happen in the future."

GRUPO 3A

As I mentioned above, 3A's prior history prompted two teachers to issue anticipatory warnings in September 1990. Their Spanish teacher, Mr. Cantú, had taught them all three years. He was struck by how much they had fallen apart after functioning so well for most of their first two years. In particular, he drew attention to three middle-class girls who, in spite of their good grades, had developed an increasingly "negative conduct." The 3A math teacher, Ms. Rico, who was sitting in on our conversation, agreed with Mr. Cantú's assessment of the girls as "very disdainful toward the others; they think they're so smart, beautiful, and rich." By the end of the year, one of the teachers who had first warned the students, Mr. Carrizo, was taking some credit for having reformed 3A. Still, he noted the infamous reputation he had inherited:

> It was a completely disorganized grupo, incredible; there was no longer any respect among them. At any moment, boom! there came an insult [*Era un grupo completamente desmadroso . . . tremendo . . . ya no había ningún respeto entre ellos mismos, en cualquier momento, pácatelas venía el insulto*]. The teacher who had been their adviser portrayed them as the worst.

Who were the students in this troublesome grupo? In appendix B, I introduce several of them, but here we meet only the popular Enrique.

ENRIQUE

By most accounts one of the brighter lights in 3A, Enrique was gregarious and thoughtful. Several teachers qualified him as "very smart" ("*muy listo*"), but they also said he could be disruptively restless (inquieto). Mrs. Garfias noted his tendency to look for solace and support among his classmates ("*Busca apoyo aquí en la escuela que no tiene en su casa*"). With his male friends in the grupo, he could be as boisterous as any other secundaria student, echando relajo and playing vigorous games of soccer down on the field. In other contexts, though, he showed a sophisticated intelligence and remarkable tenderness. During a chat with his parents, I watched Enrique clean up his three-year-old sister from the mango mess she'd made, change her clothes, and initiate a playful game.

Enrique had come a long way from his rural background. The oldest of what would eventually be seven children, he had spent his first few years in a small hamlet some twenty miles from San Pablo. Already his father had begun to spend most of his time outside the home, living and working as a lumber cutter in a large city two hours away. His mother ran a tiny store and watched over their rented lands. Enrique had attended his first year of primaria in a one-room village school, but when his godmother's family moved to San Pablo, he followed them there. He attended a San Pablo primaria and lived with this other family for nearly two years until his parents moved to San Pablo to "watch over" someone else's house. Enrique's father found work in a local sawmill and eventually earned enough money to buy a small lot with a two-room house. Shortly thereafter, he went off to work in the United States, returning once or twice to work delivering soft drinks to stores or driving a city bus in San Pablo.

Despite his obvious intelligence and good grades, Enrique waffled about further schooling. I was able to chat with Enrique's parents during one of his father's extended visits home in 1991. In an unusual switch of expected gender positions, Enrique's father urged him to continue to the prepa while his mother thought he should quit school to work. She saw the numerous examples of CBTIS or prepa graduates still delivering Pepsi around San Pablo, so she doubted the value of advanced degrees. Why should she and her husband sacrifice themselves and their younger children for a dubious educational investment? Enrique's mother also wanted him to stay in the region, and she knew a professional career would probably carry him far away. Enrique appeared most strongly swayed by his mother. His father, after all, had never been home that much, and besides, Enrique had already enjoyed some pocket money earned while helping out his dad on the truck. His parents told me that Enrique had expressed some interest in studying architecture or joining the air force, but I never heard this directly. By the end of the school year, what Enrique most desired in the short term was to be in the world of work. Indeed, in the absence of any clear career aspiration, this seemed his destiny.

Focal students and grupos escolares. Individuals and collectives. Each of these responded to one another; each of these animated the life of the school. In my attempt to account for the meanings of student practice at ESF, I problematize this dichotomy, and look instead at how the person and group constitute one another. Focal students provide a window into the particularities of the Mexican secondary experience. They permit an assessment of the way school gets differentially incorporated into particular life trajectories. Yet they also enable a better view of the cultural principles and consequences of the Mexican school.

THE PLAY OF CULTURE: STUDENT APPROPRIATIONS
OF EQUALITY AND SOLIDARITY

What, then, did students make of the prevalent school practices and discourses oriented toward inculcating a sense of equality and solidarity? Students appropriated the social space of the grupo escolar as well as teacher discourses of equality and solidarity to fashion a cultural game responding to their own practical logics (or "interests," as the teachers and students might say). The notion of appropriation in the domain of student culture only makes sense if a dynamic discursive relationship between teacher and student "communities" is conceptualized (Hanks 1996;

Bakhtin 1981; see also Corsaro 1997; Finders 1997, 18). Meanings and terms circulated back and forth between the mutually permeable cultures of teachers and students. Collectively, students produced their own cultural worlds out of the spaces and symbolic resources made available to them in school. They worked within the existing historical discourses of Mexican schooling, yet brought in resources from other contexts as well. Individually, students creatively worked out their own positions vis-à-vis both these existing historical discourses and the more emergent, locally produced culture that they were, paradoxically, helping to create. In the normatively structured domain of the grupo escolar, teacher discourse made a greater impact and provided important codes for the construction of self and grupo meanings. Later, in chapters 5 and 6, I show how the more distant informal domains of student culture, constituted primarily by friendship groups, provided alternative meanings that often challenged those of much of the teacher discourse.

THE ETHIC OF GRUPO SOLIDARITY

As I noted in the last chapter, teachers' discourse on the nation and the broader social collective frequently provided the anchoring rationale for academic effort and grupo solidarity, yet it didn't appear to have much effect as a motivational tactic. Students often mentioned their desire to work hard in order to please family or God, impress teachers, gain personal confidence, help out the grupo, or prepare themselves for future studies. Never did I hear a student say he or she was working hard for the good of Mexico. It was as if the discourse on the nation remained suspended, failing to penetrate the logic of the practical strategies that students embedded in more immediate family, teacher, and peer relations. Still, related discourses on solidarity and equality, and the exhortation to grupo unity, could be appropriated and applied in the concrete and socially intense context of the grupo escolar. Even if students generally ignored the cultural nation as a motivating force, their proximate goals and actions were nevertheless animated by the terms of solidarity and equality ultimately rooted in a nationalist project.

Students appropriated the language of grupo solidarity (*trabajar juntos, sacar al grupo adelante*, and so on) and elaborated their own practical uses. On the one hand, as mentioned earlier, they generally endorsed teachers' attempts to foster grupo unity by enthusiastically supporting grupo candidates for student government, rooting for grupo athletic teams, and the like. At times when teachers explicitly designated classroom activities as *trabajo de grupo* (group work), students also drew freely on networks of support that extended throughout the grupo. On the other hand, the meanings of solidarity and equality were given unique inflections by the students, often in ways completely unintended by the teachers. As one teacher griped, "If only they were as united in doing their work as they are in messing around!"[6]

Few actions brought more opprobrium on a student than breaking ranks with a decision that the grupo had made together. During one social studies class, Mr. Solana arrived a few minutes late after arguing tensely with some teachers near the main offices. He immediately asked the grupo who had been responsible for delivering a written denunciation (*escrito*) of another teacher directly to the principal's office. The *jefa de grupo* interrupted him to say that they had had no other recourse because the other teacher had resisted all attempts at open communication. But Mr. Solana kept on about who had actually written the letter, until another girl intervened to admit that she had done it (she was the one who literally drafted the letter). Because this girl was normally a diligent, rule-abiding student, Mr. Solana persisted, asking who else had put her up to it. By now, a chorus of "No, teacher, you don't understand, we all did it together," was rising to a crescendo as he singled out a couple of the more mischievous boys in the grupo, grilling them with an insinuating voice. Finally, the jefa de grupo stood again and reiterated what the grupo had been trying to say all along: that they had all mutually agreed, asked their classmate to write the letter, and took a unanimous vote before sending the letter along. She turned around at this point and asked her classmates in general, "We were all in agreement, right?" Here a small, serious girl stood and said matter-of-factly, "I didn't do it, teacher." At this, the class burst out with recriminating barbs, such as, "Ah, you also voted [to send the letter], you were with us, and now you say you weren't." The girl sat down with a sheepish face, hands in her lap. Mr. Solana just shook his head in disgust, and then dropped the matter for the time being. Meanwhile, the girl became the subject of ongoing negative commentary by her classmates for some time. Many refused to speak to her, saying she had gone back on her word (*se había rajado*) and had betrayed the grupo (*traicionó al grupo*). Only after several weeks did she become reincorporated into the informal life of the grupo, although some classmates continued to harbor resentment for quite a while longer.

This was one example of the "ethic of solidarity" in action; similar episodes were not uncommon. Students also prided themselves on being able to use grupo solidarity as leverage in disputes with teachers. In another incident—which I did not witness, but that was reported to me by several students and the teacher involved—students stood together for the right of a classmate to take an exam after he had been reprimanded by the teacher. As Rosita recounted it to me, when Mr. Carrizo was returning from retrieving the exams at the main office, he could see that some students were throwing each others' pens outside the classroom, shouting, and shifting seats around. He was not pleased with the grupo and demanded that somebody own up to having started the horseplay. The one boy who had indeed begun throwing the pens, Valentino, remained silent, and after more pressuring by Mr. Carrizo, this boy's best friend, Benito, took the blame. Rosita relates:

> So then the teacher wouldn't give the exam to [Benito], and everybody argued some more with the teacher . . . so I said, "Teacher, if Benito doesn't get an exam I'm going to give him mine," and he replied with, "Fine, go ahead and give it to him, you'll be the one to decide if you go without an exam, I won't give you another." . . . We all argued some more, then I told the teacher, "Teacher, if Benito doesn't do his exam then *nobody*'s going to do their exam," and everybody started in, "Yes, that's right, teacher," . . . and he told us, "Fine, whatever you want. . . . [W]hoever wants to answer their exam, answer it, and those that don't will see what happens," and then Angélica said, "I *am* going to answer it," as if to say, "I don't have any reason to cooperate with these guys," but the majority were in agreement about not doing the exam. So I was already going to give my exam to Benito, I had even gotten up, he got up too and I said to myself, "Ah, he's already coming over to get the exam," but instead he went over to talk to the teacher, and the teacher, on seeing the pressure we had on him, didn't have any choice but to give exams to those who still didn't have one. But all this helped me to see that not all our classmates are as united as I had thought. . . . [I]n grupo matters, everyone cooperates except Angélica.

Rosita's story was compelling on several counts. She related it to me spontaneously, during one of several interview sessions. I believe her to be a reliable narrator, and certainly most knowledgeable about grupo 3C. In addition to this one, her other stories were invariably corroborated by classmates and teachers. The day after Rosita told me this story, in fact, Benito also brought it up in the context of a chat with some male classmates. I had asked the boys what they thought of some of their classmates, and when I mentioned Rosita, Benito immediately told a brief version of the story, highlighting his admiration for Rosita and calling her "noble."[7]

An interview with Mr. Carrizo shortly thereafter revealed that Rosita had indeed been a pivotal figure in the conflict. Mr. Carrizo's unsolicited account otherwise differed significantly from the students' version, however. The teacher emphasized instead the grupo's general denunciation of Valentino and gave voice to those students who seemed perturbed by the episode:

> So finally at the end [of the exam] there were still about two or three students [left in the classroom], and they tell me, "Know what, teacher? If they were to get rid of just three students, the grupo would be another thing entirely, because they're the ones that have hurt us since our first year. But what can we do? We have to put up with them and we have to protect them at certain moments, even if it hurts us more." So I tell them, "Well, on the one hand, you're doing the right thing, to support [solidarizarse] a classmate is good, but on the other hand, not to condone his misbehavior."

Rosita and Mr. Carrizo obviously constructed the incident in rather different terms. Yet despite this, what stood out was the importance of grupo solidarity. Rosita structured her narrative around the positive value of solidarity, which provided a kind of moral telos for the story as it bolstered students' power against the authority of the teacher. Mr. Carrizo, in contrast, challenged this positive valuation, distinguishing between solidarity for good and bad ends. He even tried to claim that Rosita's was a minority view. For Mr. Carrizo, the grupo was composed of students like Angélica who acquiesced to the pressures of the thugs and their apologists. His re-presentation of several students' concerns at the end of the exam provided a vehicle to express his own position. The solidarity appropriated in the grupo, according to Mr. Carrizo, could acquire negative value and work against the school's pedagogical mission. Nevertheless, Mr. Carrizo shared with Rosita a concern about solidarity as a value and structuring dynamic within the grupo. Regardless of their positions, teachers and students both recognized and negotiated the meanings of solidarity.

Another case of solidarity in action involved Iván, the charismatic boy from 3C. In the campaign for president of the Students' Society (Sociedad de Alumnos), Iván actually received his grupo's nomination over the slight protests of the grupo's adviser. At first, Iván wanted nothing to do with student government. He had been expelled the previous year for fighting and had even failed a few subjects. He knew the teachers would raise a fuss about his candidacy, and anyway, he thought the whole thing a waste of time. Yet his classmates' enthusiasm eventually prevailed, and he began to appreciate the prospects for pressing a range of student grievances within the school. Importantly, he did not accept the nomination until he felt unanimous support. As he told me at recess one day:

> IVÁN: At first I didn't want to be president, but then [my classmates] urged me on.
> BL: And how did they encourage you? What did they tell you?
> IVÁN: Well, the whole bunch came together, those that were supporting me, and they urged me on some more, and when I saw they were all going to support me, well I gave it a little more effort. It was the only choice I had.

Iván was not only responding positively to grupo support; he may have also feared the negative repercussions from abjuring such support.

Similarly, Alberto of 3F reluctantly received his grupo's nomination. After the grupo nominations, there was a meeting to narrow the field and organize the candidate slates (planillas). At this meeting, orchestrated by the principal, Alberto managed to eliminate his name from any slate. Clearly his resistance to the campaign was even greater than Iván's. Unlike Iván, he harbored no illusions about the prospects for real democracy in the school. He felt the principal had manipulated the process and taken away its democratic element. In past years, said Alberto, "one could feel the heat of debate" ("*se sentía el calor del debate*"). When I asked why he had accepted the nomination in the first place, he just said, "I had to accept, necessarily" ("*a fuerzas*"). In other words, his grupo's decision had compelling force, at least until the organizational meeting.

Indeed, the political campaign and voting for the Students' Society displayed other dimensions of the ethic of solidarity. Each of three planillas were formed with a third-grade student as presidential candidate and five other students as vice president, treasurer, and three representatives (*vocales*), respectively. The planillas were identified by color: yellow, pink, or white. On the days before the vote, each planilla was allowed to tour the school and make campaign pitches in the classrooms. This typically consisted of the presidential candidate presenting a short list of promises followed by a random tossing of candies and toys around the room. The planilla would leave the room chanting its color (*Rosa! Rosa!*) as the students scrambled to collect the largesse left behind. As I asked around in the days before the vote, it became clear that students were expected to select the planilla in which their grupo's nominee had been placed. This was especially important for the third-year grupos whose nominees had been postulated for president. Still, there was an active subterranean effort to alter the balance of voting. For instance, Iván called on his younger sister, a first grader, to sway her classmates' votes in favor of Iván's planilla. Most strikingly, the vote took place in the open, thus begging an explicit display of solidarity. For the anthropologist raised in the liberal tradition of the secret ballot, this election at best served as simulation, at worst farce: students lined up with their grupos in the plaza, received a small paper ballot with the three planillas listed, and were instructed to mark and then fold their ballot privately. Then, in front of the gaze of the whole student body, and with the candidates themselves seated behind color-coded urns, students marched up to deposit their ballots in the appropriate urns. Under the rationale of faster and easier counting, students were effectively denied a secret vote. To me, it seemed they had received instead an education in the personalistic arts of Mexican political persuasion.

In the notebook she kept for me, Leticia responded to my request for a "history" of her grupo 3B during the first two grades of secundaria. She produced a narrative that spoke poignantly of the experience of grupo solidarity. Among other things, she described the sadness of seeing third-year students graduate at the end of her first year because she knew that "they would distance themselves from their friends in order to pursue their lives, and because after three years in the school one grows to love it; they remembered the joyful moments they had spent together but they also remembered the bad times and bitter periods that had made them unite together more firmly each time" ("*los malos ratos y temporadas amargas que los hizo unirse cada vez más*"). Leticia also stressed the pattern of emotional support among the members of her grupo, especially the girls. She described the tearful fits of students with family conflicts or losses, and the consolation that fellow students offered. As the months and years went by, the peer culture of the grupo clearly came to form for some a safe haven from the family, a space for socializing emotion. Leticia noted her own sadness for many of her fellow students who failed to return from year to year. Especially at the beginning of the third year, she lamented the absence of those students she knew had the desire and capacity to study, but whose families presumably could no longer support them. They had "wasted" two years of secundaria studies.

ESF students frequently asserted the behavioral norm of substantive equality. They cited the teachers as a crucial source for this norm, saying on occasion, as Victor did to me one day, that "the teachers tell us not to discriminate against one another, to treat each other equally, that that's why we have uniforms and grupos escolares" (*"los maestros nos dicen que no discriminemos, que nos tratemos iguales, que para eso son los uniformes y los grupos"*). This norm stood out when some girls from 3C, at my prompting, discussed the different jefes de grupo that they had had over the three years. They took exception to a previous jefa's favoritism, saying she had failed to discipline the grupo consistently and often let the same students off the hook. Reyna bolstered the assessment by offering that "in the grupo, we're all equal, right?" (*"en el grupo todos somos iguales, ¿verdad?"*). The ex-jefa, who had since transferred to a private school, thus lost her moral authority in the grupo. I spoke with some girls from grupo 3B the very next day, and when I asked them if any of their jefes de grupo had shown favoritism, Pati responded that the present one, Susana, was well respected, and then shifted to make a more general comment:

> PATI: I think we're a very unified grupo (*somos muy unidos*) because I've noticed that none of the other grupos get along together as well as us.
>
> GINA: For example, yesterday we had a gift exchange, and all those who wanted to enter into it did. There was none of that, "Oh no, not you," because there are students who are poor and [some say], "No, that one shouldn't be allowed in because then he won't give anything," but we [in 3B] aren't like that, if they want to enter.
>
> BL: In other words, you're saying that the other grupos behave like that, discriminating against the poorer members.
>
> GINA: Aha, and in our room [grupo] no, since we're all equal because we're human beings. That's what interests us most, it's not the [physical] beauty but each person's way of being (*"Ajá, y en nuestro salón no, pues todos somos iguales porque somos seres humanos. . . . Es lo que nos interesa más, no es la belleza sino la forma de ser de cada uno"*).

There was perhaps more than a bit of self-conscious praise in this account. Yet even if 3B was not quite as magnanimous as these girls expressed, it probably was among the most united. My observations attested that subtle gestures of class and race discrimination did surface more in 3A and 3F, though not as strongly as the 3B girls suggested. Thus, grupos varied in how strongly they appropriated and identified with the terms of solidarity and equality. Individuals within grupos varied in relation to the discourse as well. I would argue that it was also no coincidence that the girls and young women of ESF appeared most active in both constructing and challenging the ethic of solidarity, as well as the value of equality that informed it. The school's gender regime positioned students differently in the game of equality.

After all, girls had to contend with a number of special conditions in school, including greater familial pressure to succeed in order to justify further studies, and a patriarchal culture that portrayed women as embodying caprice and disloyalty (see chapter 6; Cf. Alonso 1995). As already seen in the person of Rosita, girls were among the most vociferous defenders of solidarity and equality. Yet they also found themselves at the heart of conflicting peer evaluations regarding proper conduct. As a result, they were often forced to negotiate the contradictions of equality: that, as women, they could in theory equally pursue academic achievement, but only if they paid the requisite homage to grupo norms of substantive equality. Girls more than boys had to prove themselves. They were most likely to suffer accusations—those negative attributions of character most at odds with norms of equal treatment. In the offstage commentary typical of my group interviews, students singled out other students who they thought most "conceited" or "stuck-up" (they drew on a rich vocabulary of closely related terms such as *presumido, fachoso, creído,* and *sangrón*). Female students were most often labeled in this manner, and those who tried to stand apart or who otherwise violated norms of equality came in for venomous gossip and sanctions.

I can best illustrate this process by looking closely at what happened in grupo 3A during the year. Most of the students concurred that one of the new girls in the grupo, Teresa, was fachosa—overly affected in her self-presentation. Teresa had arrived at the beginning of the school year from Mexico City. She spent her first week in 3E and was then transferred to 3A. Her first mistake was to continue maintaining close friendships with a few girls in 3E. She also became good friends with Patricia in 3C because they lived in the same neighborhood and walked home from school together. When she later announced her vote for Iván, 3C's candidate in the student president elections, her grupo loyalty became even more suspect. Most important, Teresa displayed her exemplary student skills without either feigning disinterest or attempting to share her skills with others in the grupo.

Teresa came under intense criticism. She was quickly rejected by most in the grupo, who spoke poorly of her. One group of girls in 3A said she wouldn't "*jalar con el grupo*" (hang or "pull" with the grupo). While the boys, for their part, mentioned Teresa's tendency to seek friendships outside the grupo, what they stressed most was her fastidious self-presentation. In one spontaneous group interview toward the beginning of the school year, in which I specifically asked the boys about Teresa, I received the following response, a kind of collective performance in which different boys interjected, modified, and added points to produce a rough consensus:

> BOYS: Well, let's just say we don't really like her, I mean, she's really, like, conceited [*presumida*] . . . when she's, um, what do you call it? presenting a lesson [*exponiendo la clase*], for example, when she goes to read or something, haven't you heard her?
>
> BL: Well, yes, that's why I'm asking.
>
> BOYS: She changes her tone of voice . . . like she says it in a really exaggerated way . . . and whenever she responds to the teacher, she goes, "Well, I think" [imitating a very clearly enunciating woman's voice]. . . . Yeah, or, "I believe this and that," . . . so that's why nobody talks to her, because that just doesn't seem right to us. . . . [T]he thing is that nobody, er, everybody starts off equal [*todos entramos iguales*] . . . and right now in [technical drawing] shop, we had to return an exam with our parents' signature, and just because the teacher realized she didn't bring hers, he didn't check anybody else's. . . . She's the teacher's pet [*la preferida*].

In this passage, the boys interpreted Teresa's actions and characteristics as violating the implicit rules of solidarity and equality that had been constructed in the grupo. The phrase "todos entramos iguales" entered the ongoing discussion explicitly. Thus, part of the language the boys used to articulate their complaint against Teresa reveals how the cultural game of equality provided a kind of interpretive grid, a "figured world" (Holland et al. 1998) for evaluating fellow students' conduct.

In a rather striking coincidence, after the Christmas vacation yet another recently arrived girl from Teresa's part of Mexico City, Vivian, was placed in 3A. The new girl experienced some of the same rejection as Teresa. Since she had no other contacts outside 3A, and since she lacked the polished academic skills of Teresa, Vivian's rejection was less severe, however. She stayed mostly with a group of about six to eight low-achieving, lower-class girls. In February, I interviewed Teresa and Vivian together, asking them about their perception of grupo 3A. Both confirmed my suspicion that they were having difficulties in the grupo. They emphasized its closed nature, but attributed this to the more conservative ethos of San Pablo as a whole. Teresa and Vivian had their own ideas about solidarity garnered from a similar secundaria experience in the nation's capital. They characterized most of the girls in grupo 3A as "hypocritical" and "discriminatory" because they formed exclusive friendship groups and talked behind one another's backs, thereby keeping the grupo from "moving forward" ("*salir adelante*"). Grupo 3A did indeed have a reputation for fractiousness, though many of its students worked hard to maintain solidarity.

By the time of our talk, Teresa had integrated herself more comfortably into 3A life as Vivian continued to struggle. Teresa insisted that she had not accommodated herself to the petty social demands of the grupo, yet I found it significant that her assertion about maintaining personal integrity came only after her story of sacrifice and collaboration:

TERESA: Through [two girls] I began to make it into the grupo . . . and in a friendly way we began to talk more, so I could start to earn their trust, and we started to form a friendship, and then on the basis of "Pass me this" and "Pass me the other" and, well you know what it's like, it's just standard practice but that's how you win friends over, and so on the basis of this, and the fact that I showed myself willing to offer them anything I had that they might ask for, according to what I could give and as long as it was within my powers, they've come to accept me more, and now I already feel like I form a part of the grupo.

BL: Do you think you've had to change to fit into the grupo, like have you had to limit yourself to answering only a certain part of what you might be able to answer of a teacher's question?

TERESA [INTERRUPTING]: No no no, no I mean, I've stayed the same. For example, in the matter of the planillas I had a problem, because . . . my grupo was with the yellow, but, I don't know, the white seemed better to me so I voted for the white, and then everyone said, "No, you're really stuck up" [sangrona], they even stooped to cursing at me. . . . But at least I've stayed with what I think, whether others approve of it or not, I always stick with what I think. If I can improve my character so they'll accept me without having to lose what I think, then I'll do it, but if it can't be done I stick with my way of thinking, with my beliefs.

I admired Teresa's determination and integrity, unusual among ESF students. Yet observations by teachers and classmates indicated that Teresa had indeed made important concessions to her classmates. Without sacrificing the quality of her classwork, she was learning to be "equal." Many commented that she had begun to engage avidly in the practice of passing her homework (*pasar la tarea;* see below) to classmates. While most students took part in this practice to assure themselves a reciprocal favor in times of need, Teresa, who always did her work, clearly developed it as a way to gain the affection and acceptance of her grupo.

José, always a fair-minded observer of life in 3A, contrasted Vivian with Teresa, highlighting the latter's changes:

BL: Why don't you tell me about the new girl [Vivian] that arrived? Why do you say she's stuck-up [*fachosa*]?

JOSÉ: Yeah, well, everyone says the same thing, that she talks with kind of a high pitch [*tiple*], kind of strange you know, like she thinks too much of herself [*se cree mucho*].

BL: But isn't it true that everyone was saying the same thing about Teresa when she got here, and now more or less they accept her? Or is Vivian worse than Teresa?

JOSÉ: Well, yeah, she's worse. Teresa, you see, now she's OK because she finally understood that nobody would take her being like that, and now she gets along with everybody, but with this one [Vivian], who knows if they'll accept her.

BL: How did Teresa change, or what did she do to make everyone accept her?

JOSÉ: Yeah, she's not the same anymore, like the way she thought so much of herself. On the contrary, now she's just like everybody else, she talks normal and everything . . . she expresses herself the same as us, more simple like [*sencillo*].

BL: Can you describe more how she used to talk? What did she do to make you all feel the way you did?

JOSÉ: Well . . . the thing is that we don't like anybody that wants to show off [*lucirse*], nobody in the grupo likes that, because then they [other grupo members] start in, "No, then the teacher's going to have a preference for [that student]," or something like that, and what we want is for everything to be even [*parejo*].

In this passage, José articulated the homogenizing component of grupo escolar culture. Students that showed off or stood out risked ostracism by their peers, who viewed such behavior as threatening the "evenness" of grupo equality. In the end, it was Teresa who negotiated the demands of her grupo, keeping her "beliefs" while learning to talk and act "like everybody else." Teresa's move was strategic. She had to balance family and school expectations that girls excel with the equally gendered script for girls to cooperate and build relational bridges. I knew of no similar cases among the boys. Yet even as Teresa experienced a kind of coercion to group norms, she also came to invest in those very same norms. Like the other students, she came to be an articulate spokesperson for the value of grupo solidarity. Even though most in 3A admitted that their solidarity was rather a fragile accomplishment, like José they continued to find the implicit rationale for it compelling. The historical and institutional discourses on educational solidarity and equality had been appropriated into the students' local cultural game.

EQUALITY AND CULTURAL FORMS IN THE GRUPO ESCOLAR

In the last chapter, I presented an outline of teacher concepts and strategies at ESF. I highlighted the "logic of evaluation" that guided most teachers' pedagogical practice. Teachers often lectured or assigned a textbook questionnaire. They invited interventions from the students only when a particular response was desired, and relied heavily on books to provide the final judgment. Students who offered innovative, unconventional responses to teacher prompts were rarely praised; often, they were quickly passed over until another student finally produced the expected answer. In responding to these practices and others, students drew on the evolving cultural game of equality and solidarity to create what I came to see as collective cultural forms. Such cultural forms (*passing homework, goofing off*) enabled students to meet the institutional demands of schoolwork while molding such work to their own ends, thereby making it more palatable or even enjoyable. In the case of goofing off, student innovation often ran counter to the teachers' rote methodologies. The cultural forms also encompassed a rhetoric of collective equality that encouraged, perhaps I should say enforced, student participation within the grupo.[8]

Rafael Quiroz (1991) suggests that secundaria students respond to the logic of evaluation by developing competencies in adapting to different teaching styles and classroom rules.[9] These competencies are usually conceived of as being located within the individual student. At ESF, though, students tended to draw on the ethic of grupo solidarity and implicit notions of equality in attending to the logic of evaluation. Developing interpretive competency seemed a more negotiated, collective enterprise. Students produced strategic practices that subordinated individual interest to the common interest of the grupo in the completion of required tasks and attainment of adequate grade averages. Among these practices the cultural forms of pasando la tarea and echando relajo evolved.

PASANDO LA TAREA

I have already mentioned the practice of passing homework (pasando la tarea) in the case of Teresa above. I call pasando la tarea a cultural form because it was a recurring and central practice imbued with important meanings for institutional life. This form had a shifting and contested normative structure within the broader culture that students produced in the school. Moreover, the form of pasando la tarea developed in relation to the logic of evaluation, which emphasized above all a finished product with supposedly correct answers.

Students knew that most teachers had neither the time nor inclination to carefully assess their work or the process by which it had been produced. In truth, teachers themselves expressed a range of opinions about the students' tendency to copy what had been assigned as "individual work." Such opinions, in turn, were generally linked to the teachers' subjects as well as the relative weight of such assignments in the teachers' periodic grading schemes. Several teachers appeared indifferent; even if the students copied, they averred, the subject would be learned. On the other end of the spectrum, a few, like the Spanish teacher Mr. Cantú, went out of their way in class to regularly denounce copying, check students' homework against one another, or assign work that did not lend itself to copying. By far, the great majority of teachers felt required to adopt a principled yet pragmatic stance. They would prefer students not to copy, but had neither the will nor resources to stop it. They might occasionally exhort students to do the work "for their own good," but also admitted that copying was better than nothing.

Not all students participated actively or evenly in the cultural form of pasar la tarea. In theory, the ethic of solidarity required a student to "protect" any member of the grupo by sharing the results of his or her work. The practice of passing and copying assignments was rhetorically subsumed by discourses of equalization and collective action geared toward "moving the grupo forward" ("salir adelante"). Yet the effectiveness of these discourses required a commitment of value and reciprocity by all

Collaborative seatwork is often encouraged—but is this an instance of pasando la tarea?

students in the grupo. Such reciprocity might not always take the form of balanced homework exchange. Some students would exchange other favors, material objects (food, toys), or even the promise of prestige or protection. For instance, Iván appeared to provide nothing but his charisma and valiant fighting reputation as tokens for the homework he regularly received. Girls of lower prestige might trade homework for the attention or affection of a boy, and less frequently, vice versa. Virtually anything of value could serve as currency in the symbolic economy of grupo interaction (see Douglas and Isherwood [1979] 1996). Yet many students did resist the call to pasar la tarea to classmates, especially to those who failed to reciprocate over the longer term. Others were more selective about their exchange network, challenging the principle of grupo solidarity. Still others activated networks of reciprocity only at certain times or under certain conditions. Whatever students' particular contributions to the cultural form, though, pasando la tarea was strongly circumscribed by normative discourses on equality and solidarity. Students felt compelled to modulate or justify their actions in relation to the welfare of the grupo.[10]

To briefly illustrate, I'll return again to the case of Teresa and 3A. The following is one comment from an interview with three 3A girls who were discussing their fellow classmates. When I eventually mentioned Teresa, all three girls nodded their heads in agreement at what Eva was saying:

> There was this time that she handed in a homework assignment all by herself. All the rest of us [in the grupo] had made an agreement that we weren't going to hand it in, to be all together on it, you know [*para hacernos mas solidarios, ¿verdad?*], and we didn't know about her until the last minute. But she did hand it in, and we all looked bad because the teacher saw that the homework could be done. . . . I don't know where this girl gets her homework from, must be from beneath a rock or something, but the thing is that sometimes we don't even know there's a homework assignment, so she goes and asks, *but on her own account* [*por su propia cuenta*]. (emphasis added)

Eva highlighted Teresa's selfishness in pursuing her own goals at the expense of the grupo's welfare. Presumably speaking for all her classmates, she condemned Teresa for her self-directed action, which threatened the tangible benefits that grupo solidarity might bring on this occasion. Moreover, because Teresa studied excessively according to the girls, she also threatened those implicit grupo norms of equality that governed student effort.

Nationalist discourses of equality and solidarity, mediated through "official" institutional voice and practice, thus converged with students' practical strategies in the secundaria to occasion the production of a cultural form of solidarity. The irony should be clear: the strategic practice induced by teachers' rote pedagogy, a solidarity in passing homework, arguably worked against one of the longer term constructive goals of the State—the formation of talented human capital. And there was another set of interests and historical determinations pushing in the opposite direction as well. Students, of course, were also motivated to pursue their own survival or advancement in the school. After all, when Iván regularly asked (*pidió*) for a passed piece of homework, he was not selflessly facilitating the enactment of grupo solidarity; darn it, he was trying to get his secundaria certificate! As individuals, students were motivated by parents and teachers alike to get good grades in school. Though parents might endorse the school's stress on equality, they cared less about the fate of the grupo than the progress of their own sons and daughters. Meanwhile, as we've seen, the teachers expressed the tension between collectivism and liberal individualism, between an emphasis on grupo solidarity and individual promotion.

Nevertheless, the grupo still retained a strong hold on students' practice in the school. What was at stake was students' ability to modulate their academic practice such that it did not violate the norms of equality constructed in the grupo. Interestingly, even students like Teresa acknowledged and valued this grupo construction. Earlier, I presented Teresa's critique of the social divisions in 3A for keeping the grupo from "moving forward." Ironically, her own tendency to pursue individual excellence at the expense of the grupo led to a coalescence of grupo sentiment against her.

How are we to understand these contradictions? A helpful line of work draws attention to the kinds of cross-cutting moral outlooks that can develop within any institutional culture. In his study of preadolescent male baseball players, the sociologist Gary Alan Fine (1987) describes the creation of an "idioculture" whereby the boys use their own "moral rhetoric" to rework the cultural codes of their adult male mentors. In effect, the boys socialize themselves into a "preadolescent social world . . . that both reflects and distorts adult male behaviors" (79). Moral judgments of proper or improper behavior must pass through the idiocultural framework of the boys' friendship groups. William Corsaro's (1997, 134) studies of preschool children suggest that such peer cultures within adult-structured contexts can develop morally tinged "communal values," and that "children begin to develop an awareness of how communal values can be used to address personal interests and goals." Anthropologist Richard Shweder (1996, 20; see also Shaw 1994) advances a notion of culture that highlights this moral dimension as well:

> Members of a culture are members of a moral community who work to coconstruct a shared reality and who act as though they were parties to an agreement to behave rationally within the terms of the realities they share.

While teachers and administrators at ESF attempted to construct a moral community within the grupo escolar and school at large, students created and defined their own moral communities. Sometimes these overlapped with the community proposed by the school, such as the grupo escolar; other times they didn't. Teresa appeared to modulate her practice in order to abide by the ethic of solidarity in the grupo escolar. Importantly, a student like Teresa might come to valorize, perhaps even help produce, the ethic of solidarity, even as she chafed against it. Teresa agreed to temper her actions and adjust her self-understandings according to the implicit norms of this moral community. She utilized cultural resources from other contexts, such as family and neighborhood, to elaborate her agency and pursue her individual goals, but she learned how not to do so in a way that might violate the moral codes of student culture. Through their creative practice, then, social agents appropriate (Rockwell 1996) existing cultural resources and orientations; in so doing, they may alter the very way such resources are reproduced.

ECHANDO RELAJO

Almost fifty years ago, Mexican philosopher Jorge Portilla ([1966] 1984) wrote a series of essays that were later collected into a book with the title *Fenomenología del relajo*. Portilla tried to give philosophical shape to the well-known Mexican practice of echando relajo. The phrase *echar relajo* is one of those culturally embedded terms notoriously difficult to translate. (A rather literal translation might be "to throw a commotion," "to create disorder." More colloquially and contextually, I like to translate it as "goofing off.") Portilla developed a curious species of philosophical sociology by attempting to "penetrate the spiritual structure of a people [pueblo]" (13) through a hermeneutics of recurring daily practices such as echar relajo. Like so much of the literature classified as studies of "*lo mexicano*" (Bartra 1987), Portilla's interpretive method reified Mexican national character by failing to consider the institutionally and regionally differentiated contexts of *relajo* (see Lomnitz-Adler 1992, 259). Still, his analyses are highly suggestive for understanding the cultural form of re-lajo that took shape at ESF.

The phrase *echar relajo* circulated a great deal at ESF. Except for the very serious students, it seemed to be what *most* students liked to do *most* of the time. As I describe elsewhere (Levinson 1998b), even the serious students appreciated teachers who sometimes allowed students to echar relajo, or perhaps engaged in the practice themselves. It served as a catch-all phrase, a way of describing what one liked or intended to do: "No, we're just going to goof off [*echar un relajo*] today in math class." Students also wielded a variety of adjectival forms to describe themselves or their grupos as relajos, *relajosos*, or relajientos. Occasionally, they took a per-verse pleasure in their group or individual reputations as relajosos.

In addition to this verbal indexing, students in fact frequently and spontaneously enacted relajo in the classroom. Throughout this book, I have used terms like horseplay or goofing off to describe the kind of relajo I regularly observed, especially in the time before and after teachers would

Echando relajo at the Teachers' Day festivities

arrive. Yet equally significant for the students were the clever, even coordinated forms of joking and bantering that punctuated classroom lessons themselves. It is this kind of classroom relajo I prefer to call a cultural form, for I believe students had developed implicit understandings of its structure and value. Like pasar la tarea, not all students actively and evenly participated in creating relajo in the classroom, but they did support its tendency to democratize grupo life and advance the cause of grupo camaraderie.

Portilla's work provides us with a fascinating frame for understanding relajo. For Portilla ([1966] 1984, 18), the primary function of relajo is to "suspend seriousness," that is, to "suspend the subject's adherence to a proposed value." Relajo "cancels the normal response to the [proposed] value" of an activity, it "dis-identifies" (*se desolidariza*) the subject from the value of the activity and abrogates responsibility for its completion (23). Crucially, Portilla finds that relajo can only occur in a "community" that enacts "an immediate communicative intention" (22). It must be sustained communally by at least three people and requires repeated action (22, 24). A single joke interrupting a speech cannot in itself comprise a relajo. Rather, the person who initiates "suspending the value" of an activity

> tries to commit others to it as well by repeated acts through which he/she expresses his/her rejection of the behavior required by the value. With this, the behavior regulated by the corresponding value is

substituted by an atmosphere of disorder in which the fulfillment of the value becomes impossible. (25)

What Portilla labels relajo was the bane of most teachers at ESF, for there the "proposed value" of an activity included learning the subject knowledge imparted in class, developing respect for the flag and adult authority in the morning civic ceremony, and showing discipline and obedience in carrying out school tasks. Students would undermine these values through various forms of echando relajo. Most teachers acknowledged the communal quality of relajo, for they identified those students who most often initiated and sustained it. To the teachers, such students were negative leaders who "absorbed," as it were, their classmates into counterproductive behavior. They attributed this behavior to poor parenting, a lack of academic motivation, immaturity, and the disturbances of adolescence. Because of their structurally opposed position in the school, what the teachers were less likely to perceive was the communicative value of relajo.[11] Portilla never closely considered relajo's institutional contexts, but ESF's classrooms—where students were being asked to acquire forms of knowledge and conduct that often made little sense to them—seemed ripe for it. Like the U.S. junior high school students that Robert Everhart (1983) studied, ESF students inserted the "regenerative" knowledge of relajo into the "dry institutional text" of the school.[12]

In her study of gender and student culture at a Mexican vocational high school, Claudia Saucedo Ramos (1995) discusses the importance of relajo. Echoing Portilla, she characterizes relajo as a "group practice in the classroom that attempts to break with the lesson's formality. . . . A lesson is punctuated over and over again with diverse acts that unleash laughter" (57). Almost all ESF students participated in classroom relajo in one form or another, though gender differences appeared here as well. Toward the end of the second grading period, Mr. Carrizo concluded a class with 3C by reminding the students that more than four absences in a period deprived them of their right to take the next exam. He started down the list to call out the names of those with four absences, but after just the second name, virtually all the boys pointed at the student and made a hissing sound with their tongues, creating obvious mirth. This occurred three more times until the teacher looked up from his grade book to glare at the boys. Like me, he could not identify the instigator since the relajo had become so generalized among the boys. One of the more adventuresome boys then called out, "Ay, read off some more teacher, so we can keep going like this," while he pointed at the girl next to him and made the same hiss. This brought out more laughter, and the teacher, who seemed poised to begin a short lecture, said that recess would start soon and instructed the students to begin organizing a booth for next week's fair. At that, students jumped up and moved all around the room, shouting out or talking in small groups to one another. In this instance, the boys took the lead in challenging the serious message of academic delinquency and making light of their classmates' standing.

On another occasion, the art teacher had finally gotten through some business regarding grades and assignments before moving on to an exposition of the major instruments in an orchestra. This was the last class of the day, toward the end of the year, and I could see the 3B students settling into their seats with sighs of anxious exasperation because the teacher, who only came for a couple of periods today, seemed ready for an energetic lesson. Yet just as he began to list the instruments, one of the best students in the class, Marina, called out to the maestro and asked him where he thought the graduation ceremony should be held. This was a loaded question since the principal's determination to hold the ceremony on school grounds had created quite a bit of resistance in recent weeks. Marina suggested that the municipal theater downtown would offer better acoustics for the musical accompaniment. A bit of irritation first flashed across the teacher's face, but then he warmed up to the question. Before he could respond, however, another girl chimed in: "Yes, in the theater, since one can hear and sit better" ("*Sí, en el teatro, pues se oye y se sienta mejor*"). Several students laughed at this comment, since it involved a subtle play on the verbs *sentar* (to sit) and *sentir* (to feel, to experience).[13] Finally, the teacher also expressed his preference for the theater, and went on to recall several previous graduation ceremonies. When he launched into these stories, several of the girls smiled knowingly at one another. They continued to punctuate the teacher's stories with funny comments or questions of their own. Before he knew it, the teacher had run out of time and the school day was over. The best female students in the class had effectively sabotaged his lesson and cajoled him into a relaxing relajo as a willing participant. They knew his propensity to tell stories about music and past school events, and successfully diverted him into this activity.[14]

Echando relajo is a cultural form comprised of classmates' tacit understandings about the best ways to sabotage or redirect the "seriousness" of the school activity at hand. It could be considered a kind of "genre" in popular culture (Fabian 1998).[15] By their third year in the school, ESF students knew each other and their teachers well enough to regularly orchestrate such relajo. While students varied in the manner and degree of their participation, virtually all of them shared the value of relajo as a way to lighten their school experience. Even the most serious students, who occasionally lamented the more disrespectful or disruptive forms, acknowledged relajo's importance for breaking up the school routine. Most relajo thus reinforced the communicative solidarity of grupo life. Portilla describes relajo as central to the Mexican "character," and my Mexican friends, many of them teachers and colleagues themselves, often noted in half-sardonic tones the Mexican penchant for blowing things off ("*echamos relajo,*" or "*nos vale madres*"—"We don't give a damn"), what they called the Mexican "disease" (*enfermedad*). Echando relajo, then, appeared to constitute a national instance of "cultural intimacy," a part of the "rueful self-recognition" that played local counterpoint to the official exaltations of national culture (Herzfeld 1997, 6). On the other hand, Saucedo Ramos (1995, 57) attributes much of relajo to the "inherent" informality and liveliness of youth, an age-specific trait. Perhaps the truth lies somewhere in between, with the institutional qualities of grupo solidarity and formulaic knowledge providing the specific contextual gravity. Certainly, the age segregation of the secundaria appeared to accentuate the playfulness of adolescent identity formation, which provides one form of fuel for echando relajo. In any case, the cultural form students produced at ESF contained elements of all this, but also took shape in the determinate institutional contexts of school knowledge, teacher practice, and grupo solidarity.

The cultural game of equality that the students produced in the grupo escolar was played in large part through appropriated discourses put in the service of resisting dominant logics of power in the school. In Michel de Certeau's (1984) terms, this cultural game represented a collectively constructed "tactic of consumption"—that is, a means by which students interpreted, inhabited, and effectively modified dominant "strategies" of discursive power (xvii–xxii, 36–43). Certeau's description of "popular tactics" used to disrupt the order of capitalist discourse and production could apply to student culture as well:

> Into the institution to be served are thus insinuated styles of social exchange, technical invention, and moral resistance, that is, an economy of the *gift,* an esthetics of *tricks,* and an ethics of *tenacity.* (26)

Within contradictory discourses on adolescence, solidarity, and national identity, ESF students reintroduced into the grupo escolar, as Certeau puts it, the "plural mobility of goals and desires" (xxii), making it a space somewhat their own. Cultural forms like pasando la tarea and echando relajo embodied the reciprocity, inventiveness, and persistence of student practice indicated by Certeau's statement above.

In this chapter, I have endeavored to show how the grupo escolar at ESF became a contradictory space for the production of cultural practices and forms around discourses of solidarity and equality. Most students orchestrated forms of solidarity in order to leverage their power against teachers' classroom demands. In this sense, they were little different than the kinds of worker solidarity noted in a host of shop-floor ethnographies.[16] Still, what particularizes this otherwise universal dynamic is the way ESF students appropriated the very institutional discourses on solidarity to this and other ends, as well as the way such practices bled over into other areas of student thought and action. In the examples I've provided here, students drew on the values of solidarity and equality to help structure specific kinds of responses to the work regime. Yet in doing so, they also produced and reproduced forms of relationship, of communicative work, within and across the myriad social differences at the school. Subjectivities rooted in grupo identification found ample expression throughout students' tenure at ESF. Official nationalist discourses of educational equality and solidarity endorsed such identification and communicative work, but how effectively did they work to join differences into more enduring forms of collective social identity? What impact did they have on student subjectivities outside the official ambit of the school?

5. Sites of Social Difference and

the Production of Schooled Identity

Each year, people form long lines and shove one another around in order to
enroll their children in a school. Each year new schools are constructed, and
each year, also, there are more children who remain without a school. People
that have never been to school live convinced that this is the only reason for
their failure. Those who have gone to school, on the other hand, believe they
failed because they didn't take sufficient advantage of the opportunity. The
point is that school is a fundamental element in everybody's frustrations.
—Jorge Ibargüengoitia, *Instrucciones para vivir en México*

These biting lines by the great Mexican writer Ibargüengoitia ([1969]
1990) are perhaps too global in their condemnation of the perennially
unfulfilled expectations of schooling. Some Mexicans do after all succeed
through schooling, at least in their own minds, while others, like Ramón
in chapter 2, never went beyond the first few grades and don't put much
stock in school knowledge at all. Then again, Ibargüengoitia's observations might have been more apposite in the 1960s, on the cusp of the great
1970s' expansion of Mexican schooling. In any case, they carry more than
a grain of truth. For as the social theorist Pierre Bourdieu (1984, 1989;
Bourdieu and Passeron 1977) argues, formal education has become a key
axis of symbolic distinction in virtually all modern societies. The "symbolic violence" of schooling, according to Bourdieu and Passeron (1977),

is precisely its ability to convert arbitrary forms of knowledge and skill into the justification for higher social standing. Schooling provides (or validates) privileged styles and tastes, what Mexicans might call cultura, thus enabling class distinctions to form and persist. Those who "fail" school are made to feel responsible for their own lowly standing. Yet after the boom years of the 1970s, many Mexicans were questioning or even rejecting the value of further schooling. Just when secundaria study had superseded the primaria to become recognized as the minimum measure of proper social standing, San Pabloans seemed increasingly unwilling or unable to keep their kids in secundaria. No longer could they expect to convert the cultural capital of advanced schooling into reliable economic capital. Secondary schooling had thus become relatively devalued, though it continued to have important currency in local relations and strategies. Obviously, this was especially true for those families trying at all costs to maintain their children in the secundaria.

In this chapter, I discuss the meanings and symbols of secondary schooling in the San Pablo region of 1990–1991. I examine the production of what I call school identification and schooled identity in and beyond ESF. I then look at the broader social consequences of these student identities, paying special attention to how they affected existing patterns of social difference and distinction. How successful, after all, was the school in promoting equality by producing an adolescent subject oriented toward a common identity and the collective good? What conceptions of equality did students put into practice? Before I can undertake such an analysis, I must present an overview of the varying sites of social difference and identity formation in and around San Pablo.

SITES OF DIFFERENCE AND SUBJECTIVITY:
SAN PABLO AND ENVIRONS

In chapter 2, I presented a profile of occupation and social class in San Pablo. There I offered Claudio Lomnitz-Adler's (1992) concept of intimate cultures as a way of understanding key social differences within regions. Lomnitz-Adler wishes to problematize conventional views of both class and ethnicity, and therefore conceives of intimate cultures as the "signs and meanings that are developed by a localized class . . . [and] are based on localized experiences of class within a power region" (33). Careful not to imply a "notion of specific, bounded identity groups," Lomnitz-Adler writes that intimate cultures "share a class experience [that] implies sharing a position in space and time as well as a set of cultural understandings about that position" (ibid.). In other words, intimate cultures form one important and immediate matrix for habitus and the formation of class subjectivities. Intimate cultures may not have well-developed "identities" as such, but they do have "localist ideologies" that must be perceived and reconstructed by the ethnographer. Such ideologies circulate in the public "culture of social relations," the interactional frames that permit intimate cultures to speak to and understand one another within so-called "power regions" (32–34).

San Pablo clearly formed a power region, articulated in turn to the Mexican nation-state. In chapters 1 and 2, I discussed some features of this region. Here, I concentrate on the sites and spaces that comprised the subjectivities, the "set of cultural understandings," of San Pablo's intimate cultures. I pay special attention to youth and the socialization of subjectivity within these cultures.

ETHNICITY, CLASS, AND THE URBAN/RURAL DIVIDE

Did ESF students think of themselves as belonging to an ethnic group or even a "race?" Did they arrive at the school with well-formed cultural identities other than being Mexican? In provincial Mexico, identities have long been articulated in relation to the category of *indigenous, indígena,* yet very few ESF students in fact considered themselves indigenous. In San Pablo, *indígena,* or the even more pejorative *indio,* were most often terms of attribution, not assumed identity. Even more common as terms of social reference were *del rancho* or *de los pueblitos* (from the countryside, small villages). Ironically, many city dwellers tended to think of rural residents exclusively as Indians. For them, the signs of rural residence mattered more than language or dark skin color in attributing Indian identity. Urban ESF students at times referred to all children of rural families as *indígenas,* regardless of whether the latter actually identified themselves as such.[1]

Most of the towns and villages in the San Pablo region have, in fact, undergone a process of steady mestización (Lomnitz-Adler 1992) in recent decades. It is not uncommon for present-day residents of these communities to represent the first generation to have ceased using an indigenous language or indigenous forms of dress on an everyday basis. Several communities that in the not too remote past had been bastions of indigenous identity have now been almost entirely transformed into mestizo (cultur-

147   Sites of Social Difference

ally and racially "mixed") villages (Brandes 1988; Zizumbo Villareal 1986; Friedrich 1986). Only a few towns and villages in the immediate region (within twenty kilometers of San Pablo) have preserved a distinctive indigenous identity. And even then, not everyone agrees on the designation of identity. While a few settlements are recognized by residents and non-residents alike as ethnically indigenous, and while still more are universally perceived as nonindigenous ("*No, pues ahí ya no se habla el idioma*"), there are still many caught in a zone of ambiguity. As the parenthetical quote suggests, language is the determining factor in designating identity, but few San Pabloans know just how many in each village still speak the indigenous language. Even if they did, what percentage would qualify the village as indigenous?

Not surprisingly, outside their rural settlements, the pressure can be strong for villagers to relinquish features associated with Indianness. Lourdes Arizpe (1978, cited in Hewitt de Alcántara 1988, 241) and Barbara Luise Margolies (1975) have insisted that all things being equal in terms of class, indigenous groups in Mexico experience a kind of institutionalized exclusion from wider opportunities for socioeconomic mobility. The state of interethnic relations in the San Pablo region did not appear to be that different from the situation described by Judith Friedlander (1975) and Margolies (1975) for other areas of Mexico. Though indigenous culture was rhetorically extolled as an essential component of national identity, indigenous people suffered rounds of insults at the hands of the mestizo majority in daily life.

Merchandise and cultural forms were constantly being exchanged between San Pablo and the surrounding countryside. For rural inhabitants, the city served as mediator and purveyor of global cultural commodities like music cassettes and toys. It sent out a constant flow of urban symbols of progress. By 1985, children in the village where I first lived in the region had begun to organize dances clearly patterned after those they had attended once in the city. Yet because of rural-urban migration and the ongoing ties most city dwellers have to the countryside, rural forms exercised their power in the city as well. On market days and important religious holidays, San Pablo's streets swelled with villagers who arrived to sell their goods and worship prominent regional saints. In San Pablo, I saw burros walking through the streets, heard *ranchera* (country) music blaring from apartment windows, and tasted locally grown corn and beans at the elegant homes of the elite.

In her well-known study of a booming provincial city, Lourdes Arizpe

(1989, 14) stresses the mutual permeability, indeed the ongoing homogenization, of city and country. Yet despite the material and cultural flows I observed, I also noted most San Pabloan's rhetorical emphasis on their urbanity. City residents would sometimes disparage rural visitors for their lack of manners or sophisticated cultural knowledge. They might even ridicule the music, dress, or eating habits of these people. Poorer or more recently arrived San Pabloans moderated such comments, but their children soon acquired the urban habitus as well. Thus, despite the continued exchange of rural and urban forms, most San Pabloans reinforced a demarcation. They were less and less likely to adopt rural cultural forms except as occasional consumers, knowingly and deliberately indulging their tastes for so-called traditional things. Their disparagement of rurality could be seen as an effort to specify the "other" in their construction of a modern urban identity.

As I mentioned earlier, nearly 15 percent of the students in ESF's morning shift came from the pueblitos surrounding San Pablo. Some rural families had achieved a good deal of wealth through the tourist trade, craft production, the acquisition of more land, or large remittances from migratory stints. They constituted a kind of emerging elite in these communities (see López Castro 1986; Reichert 1982) and tended to send their children to ESF. Because these rural communities were themselves hierarchical, some of these students might even be better-off than the poorer city residents. Still, most students arriving from the pueblitos were poorer than even the poorest city residents. Most had attended primary school in their own communities, so their arrival at ESF marked the first time they traveled to San Pablo on a regular basis. These students typically worked long hours at home. Children were expected to contribute to the household economy in some fashion, by tending animals and fields or learning the rudiments of tourist-oriented craft production. Few were given much dispensation for study time, and this posed a perennial conflict for those seriously devoted to school success.

Thus, students who arrived at ESF from the pueblitos had to contend with both material limitations and the dominant, city-based construction of them as rural dwellers, or Indians. Some students had been raised in families where parents still spoke the local indigenous language as well as continued to maintain ethnically distinct traditions of dress and comportment. For instance, women often wore special skirts and shawls, braided their hair, and walked with an unmistakable shuffle, while men wore distinctive hats and sandals. Many such families hoped their children might retain something of their ethnic identity even as they acquired the educational credentials for economic mobility. Other families—perhaps the majority—had already begun a strategic assimilation to mainstream urban society. Some had even sent their children to live with relatives in San Pablo. It was especially ironic that the students from such families, who often endeavored to speak and act like urbanites, nevertheless got typecast as rural dwellers because of their accent, skin color, style of dress, place of origin, or taste in music, among other things.

FAMILY AND RELIGION

The anthropological literature on Mexico has documented the centrality of kin relations across class and locality (Lomnitz and Pérez-Lizaur 1987; Lomnitz 1975; Nutini et al. 1976; Smith 1984), and of course Mexico is famous for the widespread practice of compadrazgo—the creation of fictive kin relations to widen or reinforce networks of social support. Some scholars have argued that the strength of Mexican kinship has allowed local social relations to remain relatively impervious to the alienating effects wrought by the introduction of complex bureaucratic forms and instrumental rationality to Mexican society (Arizpe 1989). In other words, capitalism has been adapted to the personalistic idiom of Mexican family relations. People in San Pablo likewise reinforced the importance of *familia*. Virtually everyone I met urged me to look closely at families if I "really wanted to understand Mexico." According to them, the strengths and weaknesses of modern life could be traced back to the family. It was no surprise, then, that criticisms of the United States voiced in my presence attributed its rampant licentiousness and hedonism (*libertinaje*) to the breakdown of the family and questioning of parental authority (see Rouse 1992).

In San Pablo, kinship continued to be the predominant form of social alliance and identification. Certainly no other type of social relation—political, religious, economic, or civic—had displaced the centrality of it. Political influence in the municipality was often brokered through kin relations, and jobs could be similarly procured. Overlapping kin networks, where cousins regularly played and worked together, often constituted neighborhoods in San Pablo. Where this was not the case, residents were more likely to look beyond their immediate neighborhood for social and material support, to other neighborhoods or neighboring towns and villages where kin still resided. Regardless of social class, San

Pabloans traveled frequently. Trips might be made to the next village over for fresh milk and produce, or to places as far away as Guadalajara, Mexico City, or Mexicali. In virtually every instance, San Pabloans were also traveling to visit kin.

While Larissa Adler Lomnitz and Marisol Pérez-Lizaur (1984) identify a range of family and household types across social classes in Mexico, I found the nuclear family pervasive in San Pablo.[2] Occasionally, households were composed of extended families, though these usually included only one three-generation unit of grandparents, parents, and children, rather than several consanguineous units residing jointly. In these few cases, grandparents had come to live with one of their children's families in old age or illness. Neolocality was still the rule of residence, and the house belonged to the middle-generation parents who had established a new home immediately after marriage or sometimes after a short stint in the home of the bride or groom's parents. A number of ESF students lived with mothers who had been widowed, abandoned, or temporarily left behind by their seasonally out-migrating husbands. These husbands might visit for periods of a week to six months, but then they would return to their migrant jobs. The extended and matricentric household/family units were nevertheless the exception in San Pablo and its environs. By and large, and across social classes, students lived with mother, father, and siblings.

For most Mexicans, the value of religion is closely tied to that of family. Again, many observers have commented on the pervasiveness of religious practice and ideology in Mexico. Over 90 percent of Mexicans confess the Catholic faith, and the region around San Pablo, as witnessed by the Cristero struggle of the 1920s (chapter 1), is reputed to be one of the most fervently and conservatively Catholic in all of Mexico. Today, the broader region still supports a number of seminaries, evangelical units (such as Catholic Action), and other conservative Catholic organizations. Neither liberation theology nor evangelical Protestantism have taken root here to the extent that they have elsewhere in Mexico or Latin America (Stephen and Dow 1990; Higgins 1990).

I have decided to consider religion and the family together because in San Pablo they are both typically thought to exercise a conservative influence over social life, oriented toward maintenance and reproduction rather than change, and because Catholic congregations draw on the idiom of kinship to promote solidarity. Not coincidentally, religion and the family are also strongly gendered; men occupy a kind of titular position (father, priest), but the church and home are both conventionally seen as women's special zones of interest and action. In everyday practice, it is the women who typically expend the most time and energy in these social domains. Lourdes Arizpe's (1989) study certainly confirmed that women across classes invest themselves in their children, and in a devotional practice to God, to a far greater degree than men.[3]

Superficially at least, the San Pablo churches I frequently attended seemed rather like the school in providing a space for egalitarian rhetoric and practice. The poorest residents might have their own humble chapels in the colonias, but wealthy and poor alike could be seen attending Sunday services at the city's oldest, largest, and most ornate cathedral. The ideology of Catholic "brotherhood" in faith seemed to have a leveling effect on class and ethnic distinctions, and of course all believers equally received the Holy Communion. Yet closer observation revealed the teaching of the church often to be distinctly hierarchical. Sermons and exegetical pronouncements exhorted San Pabloans to love their neighbors and practice Christian charity, but they also encouraged abnegation, not agitation, by those who had the least. Collaboration and influence between the local elite and the highest church authorities in town was notorious, and some members of the lower and middle classes commented on it acerbically. I began noticing that wealthier families sat in pews nearer the altar because their places had been reserved. Certainly, many ESF families challenged the political quiescence of the official church and sought a more socially redemptive religious practice, especially through their devotion to regional saints. Bypassing the central churches, *cofradías* and kin organizations in poorer villages and colonias organized processions for prominent religious saints. In February, I walked some thirty-five miles through the night with members of Rosita's family and neighborhood to deliver a wooden *santo* to its home in a sacred church of the hot lowlands. This occasion strengthened local solidarity and faith, as well as a regional identification with those members of other classes and communities that converged in the final procession. Still, even these popular religious practices followed a common gendered division of labor in the church. Women took active although often subordinate roles: they disseminated the priests' instructions to the community, organized baptisms and first communions, and chanted ritually at funerals, among other tasks. They were indeed the foot soldiers, not lieutenants, of God's army.

In my work with ESF students it became clear that girls developed stronger attachments to religious practice. While some male students previously had been altar boys or continued to participate in the carrying of the santos on long pilgrimages, female students made more frequent reference to ongoing religious activities. This was true across social classes, though children of the professional middle class seemed least likely to organize their lives around religion. Many of the secundaria girls were involved in organized religious instruction; they visited different neighborhoods and parishes on the weekends, delivering catechism to younger children. Those girls who did not give catechism—a majority still—nevertheless participated actively in family-based religious practice, such as the maintenance of household altars or organization of religious festivals. Boys were not expected to play an active role in these activities. Moreover, girls obviously drew on religious concepts more easily and frequently than boys. They used religious idioms in our interviews and chats, often prefacing remarks with qualifiers like, "God willing" ("*Si Diós me da licencia*"). They also tended to organize their actions according to that which God might find acceptable; I seldom noticed this among the boys.

GENDER RELATIONS, GENDER IDEOLOGIES, AND HOUSEHOLD PRACTICES

In chapter 3, I introduced Robert Connell's (1987, 119–42) framework for conceptualizing the relation between institutional patterns of gender and those of broader regional and national societies. He calls an institution's prevailing pattern of gender relations its gender regime; the "structural inventory" of all a society's gender regimes is its gender order. Connell provides a relational theory of gender practice. The relations between those gender regimes produced in distinct institutions together constitute the broader gender order (34). Likewise, specific gender regimes can only be understood in dialectical relation to the overarching gender order and the material conditions that underpin it. Thus, the gender regimes present at any given historical juncture within institutions such as households and schools both draw on and continually constitute the wider gender order of a society. Such a conception facilitates an appreciation of the actions and movements of people struggling for change within and across institutions.

I briefly presented a portrait of the gender regime at ESF in 1990 in chapter 3. In the next chapter, I discuss the play of gender in student culture. Here, I give a general sketch of gender regimes within San Pablo households. I did not carry out extensive observations within a wide variety of households, but my own residence experience in the Solana Ramírez household as well as numerous interviews and home visits did provide a fairly consistent glimpse into the kinds of gender relations constructed there. I know a great deal more about these relations in San Pablo than in the pueblitos. As such, I will concentrate here on the kinds of class-based gender relations in San Pablo families that socialized student subjectivities beyond the school. To bolster this account and help fill in the picture for rural residents, I first turn to the suggestive literature on gender in Mexico.

This literature can be grouped into roughly four main areas. Like so much anthropological work on Mexico, the study of peasant and indigenous groups in a comparative Mesoamerican ethnology has contributed perhaps the most empirical work on women and gender in Mexico.[4] There is also an abundant sociological and anthropological literature on women in Mexican cities and factories, which can be situated within the broader Latin American literature on women's participation in urban politics and popular social movements.[5] Increasingly, literary and popular culture studies have examined the construction of gender, and more specifically the representation of Mexican women, in literature, art, television, and film (Franco 1988; Steele 1992; Berg 1992). Finally, a burgeoning regional and social history of Mexico has yielded insightful portrayals of gender relations in specific contexts and epochs.[6] Not all this work helps explain gender in a town and region like San Pablo, where little industrialization has occurred. Moreover, the bulk of research on "gender" in Mexico has in fact been research on women's roles, actions, and identities. I follow the lead of current scholarship (Stern 1995; Gutmann 1996; Alonso 1995) that examines the practice of both men and women in the construction of hegemonic masculinities and femininities.

Still, a number of useful insights into patterns of gender relations and ideologies in Mexico can be extrapolated from this growing body of research. Perhaps the single most salient observation running through the literature concerns the strong identification of women with the family, household, and children—that is, the so-called domestic or private sphere (Alonso 1992b; Mathews 1987; Arizpe 1989). This social construction of women's domestic roles appears to extend across most social classes and groups in Mexico. For instance, both in her work with shantytown dwellers and an elite business family, Larissa Adler Lomnitz has emphasized the salient role of women in building and maintaining kin- and neighborhood-based networks of action and reciprocity (Lomnitz 1975;

Lomnitz and Pérez-Lizaur 1987). Women appear to have a great deal of power as controllers of family affairs. By extension, they have power in those social arenas that are fundamentally structured by the imperatives of family and kin—arenas such as education, religious ritual, and the marketing of products from family businesses (Sault 1985; Mathews 1985; Stephen 1992). Women draw on their power in the domestic arena to ensure the successful social reproduction of the ethnic-class group and household, but they also utilize some of that same power to advance their own interests and agendas as social actors.

Feminist scholars have increasingly highlighted the sources of women's power within patriarchal societies. For instance, women often maintain important control over household resources and decision making, especially when they are themselves contributing a significant portion of those resources. They confront limits to their autonomy, however, because of the gender ideologies embodied in marriage (Benería and Roldán 1987). On the other hand, women have drawn on culturally constructed gender ideologies to validate and articulate their specific modes of emergent political action (Chaney 1979; J. Martin 1990; Alonso 1992a). The creation of new, often more public forms of female organization (such as collective kitchens in poor shantytowns, or the Zapatista movement in Chiapas) has enabled women to forge a broader political identity out of the myriad skills and subjectivities they bring to the work. Nevertheless, even feminist revisionists admit that the evidence for female power and new forms of female political-economic participation fails to outweigh the continued practical and juridical dominance of men over women. This dominance continues, in large part, because new forms of women's participation have not successfully challenged the oppressive gender ideologies and practices that reinscribe women into structures of inequality.[7]

As I've noted, the family is arguably the most powerful institution in the reproduction of gender inequalities. It competes increasingly with the school and media as a key site for the socialization of gender subjectivity. The families of different San Pablo intimate cultures could be said to comprise their own gender regimes. Thus, the difference of social class in San Pablo often translated into varying gendered patterns of opportunity, mobility, leisure, and self-expression. This can be clearly seen, to take one case, in the assignment of responsibilities within the home. Boys and girls of secondary school age tended to have well-defined responsibilities within the home. In lower-class and peasant families this usually meant girls attended to cooking, housecleaning, and the care of younger siblings. Girls, like their mothers, were seldom allowed out of the house; if they did leave, it might be to run an errand or work, perhaps in the family business, yet seldom to play or join up with friends. Playtime might be allowed, but it usually took place within the immediate environs of the home, well supervised by neighbors and kin. In contrast, boys were generally not expected to assist in domestic functions. Sometimes they might be called on to supervise a younger sibling for a short time or take care of tasks associated with a specifically masculine competence, such as repairing household equipment. They might also be asked to help out in the family business. For the most part, though, boys (like their fathers) were given the freedom to enter and leave the house as they wished. Many of them worked in the afternoons and evenings, at sawmills, auto body shops, market stalls, and the like. When they were not working, they could often be found playing video games and sports (volleyball, basketball, or most likely, soccer) or just echando relajo with a few buddies.

Just how unique was San Pablo vis-à-vis other Mexican regions in its pattern of gender relations? San Pabloans generally agreed their town was more conservative than most. A visit to José's family confirmed this perception. I arrived to find José's father ironing clothes in the main living space. I sat down and made small talk with his wife until he finally came over, and I then applauded him for ironing his own clothes. He smiled and returned, "They're not just mine, they're the whole family's," and went on to explain that a generalized "machismo mexicano" still made it difficult for him sometimes. Even his own children would have to shut the front door sometimes so people passing by would not see him engaged in female labor. José's mother, obviously enjoying the turn of topic, chimed in, "Yeah, because if they see him they'll say he's henpecked (mandilón), that he gets knocked around, a lot of things." I asked him how and why he started helping out in the house, and he recounted the time he'd gone to work on the coast for a while and had to wash his own clothes. He realized then what hard work it was and vowed to assist in the home when he could. When I asked them to elaborate on the extent of machismo, José's parents insisted it was worse in San Pablo than most other places. The mother cited the example of the state capital, which by 1990, had grown into a rather cosmopolitan center of half a million. There, she had seen lots of men spraying down and sweeping the sidewalks in front of their homes and businesses. In San Pablo, she said, you would never see that. Men daring to do so would be taunted. Thus, male contributions to feminized household labor were instead driven indoors and out of view.[8]

It is reasonable to believe that, historically speaking, such gender differences in household tasks and opportunities had actually lessened with the influx of girls into the secundaria. As economic conditions and schooling opportunities improved in the period before 1982, girls from the poorer classes were sent to the secundaria in greater numbers.[9] Students' mothers suggested it was largely through their own initiative that this began to occur. It was around the 1970s that husbands and fathers found it increasingly difficult to justify, either economically or morally, the cloistering of their daughters in the home. Mothers pushed hard for their daughters' right to schooling. Many of them recounted how they had wanted to continue studying themselves but for their parents'—usually their fathers'—contrary will. In their childhood (the 1950s to 1960s), girls were seen as a kind of economic liability: from the parents' point of view, girls were better to marry than to school. Then, too, senior daughters were much less likely to have a chance at further schooling, since they were most expected to assume domestic duties and contribute to the care of younger siblings. In cases where one of the parents died, these duties became even more onerous. To be sure, many boys could not study for some of these very same reasons. Older sons and daughters alike in larger families might have been prevented from continued studies, while the youngest sons and daughters, born in a new epoch of possibilities and reconstrued responsibilities, were given the opportunity. Even in 1990, many ESF students had older siblings who could not or did not continue their secondary studies. These siblings tended to support, even admonish their younger counterparts to take advantage of the opportunities they themselves had been denied.

It was not uncommon in 1990 to find the sons of lower- and even professional-class families working a part-time afternoon job while they were enrolled at ESF. I visited these boys in market stalls, tortilla factories, auto body shops, chainsaw repair shops, and small lumber mills. While their work was generally difficult, they appreciated the freedom and extra spending money it afforded them. Except in those instances where they were tending a stand or market stall often watched over by women as well, they also associated their jobs with a specifically masculine form of competence. Even some of the wealthier boys at ESF might help in the family business in the afternoons by running errands or taking interim charge of the operation. All the boys noted without compunction that their female counterparts at ESF frequently had to spend most of their time in the home.

Among the intimate cultures of the professional middle class, new merchant class, and traditional merchant elite the story was somewhat different. In fact, in many ways the daughters of the wealthiest classes led more restricted lives than their professional counterparts. While domestic chores might not be so burdensome, upper-class girls were expected to pay detailed attention to religious and social concerns, serving as exemplars and upholders of a proper morality. This required a constant monitoring of behavior and the development of an adequate feminine form in conduct, such as dress and greeting. It required a greater restriction to realms of kin and church as well (see Fischer 1975). Sons of the traditional elite, on the other hand, were often socialized by circulating in wider social networks—by learning the ropes of the family business, for instance.

For children of professionals and the emergent upper class, rules of conduct were generally far more relaxed. Both boys and girls were given a good deal of freedom and spent many of their free hours outside the home. While girls still had to shoulder a disproportionate share of domestic responsibilities, the common practice of hiring household maids freed them for study and play. Further, professional parents seemed to encourage greater equality of opportunity among their offspring, regardless of gender or age. Thus, in most of these families there was a kind of collective practice oriented to procuring the best possible education for sons and daughters alike.

This admittedly superficial sketch gives some idea of the senses of self and life trajectory encouraged for boys and girls in the intimate cultures of San Pablo. To be sure, household-based gender regimes were constantly negotiated and contested, especially by the women whom they tended to disadvantage most. For instance, schoolgirls often engaged in a variety of strategies to wrest more freedom from the limited ambit that their parents—usually their fathers—had defined for them. One day at school, Rosita and her friend Norma were talking about the recent funeral of their friend Antonia's father. I asked Rosita if her parents were letting her leave the house in the afternoons these days, and she said only her mother was: "I go out in the afternoon and I tell her, 'Mom, I'm going to the library, I'll be right back,' and she tells me, 'Fine, but don't be late.'" On one occasion, she returned home after her father had arrived and had to admit she'd been "strolling around the plaza with some friends." Her mother had already covered for her, though, and Rosita's confession caused an argument between her parents. Rosita concluded, "The thing is my mom and I have to get our stories straight." When I asked her if her mother was the one who always "defended" her, Norma cut in, "The thing is that the mothers are the ones who defend [their daughters], they always get along better." When Rosita then told me how her father recently bought a whole set of encyclopedias so she wouldn't have an excuse to leave the house for the library, Norma responded that her father "did exactly the same thing," and the two girls laughed and pushed each other playfully in mutual recognition. Most Mexican fathers, regardless of their class position, were reputed to be *celosos* (jealous, guarding) of their daughters, wishing them to stay in the home and away from possible suitors. Their updated rationale for such possessiveness was the need to keep daughters away from potential "distractions" to their studies. Yet the differing dynamics of household gender regimes provided differing resources for women to contest such arrangements.

THE CULTURAL MEDIA: YOUTH AS FRIENDS AND CONSUMERS

The 1970s and 1980s saw the emergence of a new youth culture in San Pablo, fostered by the democratization of schooling opportunities and proliferation of cultural media made easily available to young people. Indeed, the social categories of *youth* (*juventud*) and *friends* (*amigos*) had risen to great prominence, supplanting or converging with prior categories such as *cousins* (*primos*) and *schoolmates* (*compañeros de la escuela*). The social spaces and cultural forms through which young people related to one another grew more complex, and came to challenge the family, church, and school as key sites for the socialization of subjectivities. Many elements of the cultural media, from music to magazines, constituted the category *youth* in much the same way that the school constituted the *student* and *Mexican,* or the church constituted the *Christian.* Of course, the actual contexts of youth culture were considerably more dispersed and heterogeneous than these other sites of identity formation. Young people—usually but not always in sex-segregated groups of friends—read magazines, listened to music, danced, watched videos and television, and played video games in a variety of locales. Some of these, such as the dance hall or video parlor, were devoted exclusively to the enjoyment of youth. Others, like the home or school itself, provided a context for the use of media culture within the routines and practices unique to that site. Yet this heterogeneity should not hinder the development of a sociological account of youth and the cultural media. Like school, neighborhood, family, and church, media culture purveyed meanings and implicit suggestions for how youth should understand themselves and the world around them. A set of commercial interests—a culture industry—provided the programs and artifacts that circulated among youth, encouraging certain forms of subjectivity. In the process of using the cultural media, ESF students were also *appropriating* them, thereby "producing" new cultural practices and meanings (Johnson 1986–1987; Kellner 1995).

In terms of student-identity formation, what were the new forms of youth culture and what kinds of subjectivities did the new cultural media encourage? Historically, the spaces for youth cultural production had been limited in San Pablo. For boys from most social classes, school, sport, and work provided the most opportunities for connecting with nonkin youth. For girls, opportunities were even more limited to school and church. What has characterized the growth of San Pablo youth culture above all in the past twenty years has been its increased reliance on the cultural media.

Youth in 1990 spent much of their time consuming ready-made cultural commodities—playing video games, renting video movies or watching satellite television, buying teen-oriented magazines such as *Eres* or *Quince a Veinte* (*Fifteen to Twenty*), and listening to pop, rock, and rap. Parents and teachers remarked that when they themselves were growing up school, work, family, and religion had more closely circumscribed their lives. Today, they observed, young people generally had more freedom. Boys still worked, but that work often gave them more disposable income with which to pursue leisure opportunities. Even in 1985, when I first arrived in San Pablo, most cultural media had a low profile. By 1991, there was a video rental store on nearly every block (one day I counted fourteen just on my walk to the bus station, about two miles), while by 1995, the introduction of cable television had closed most of these stores as quickly as they had opened. Rock or rap-based music blared from the most incongruous places. The majority of these videos and musical tapes were produced in (or pirated from) the United States. Music seemed to be the most vital new arena for youth culture. Kids were endlessly exchanging their latest musical discoveries, interpreting or translating lyrics, and learning the steps to break or hip-hop dancing. Portable boom boxes had become increasingly popular, and the hiring of musical disc jockeys and sound systems—*un sonido*—had become the standard for school dances, girls' fifteenth birthday parties (*quinceañera*), and other significant occasions. Virtually every weekend, a different sonido would fill one of the local music halls, and kids across a range of intimate cultures would flock

The local and the global: ESF schoolgirls perform a hip-hop dance routine in honor of Teachers' Day

to dance or simply to survey the scene. The most popular musical events were the duels (*debates*) between two or more sonidos in the same music hall. The musical scene was perhaps the most heterogeneous of all social settings. While boys tended to monopolize the electronic video games, and girls more avidly consumed the glossy magazines, each attended dances and debates in roughly equal numbers, despite the greater difficulty girls had in obtaining parental permission to attend such dances.

Some of the most popular songs in 1991 included rap tunes by U.S. artists like Technotronics and Vanilla Ice, whose stylized lyrics were nearly incomprehensible to the Spanish-speaking students. Obviously, the subjectivities suggested by the songs' lyrics bypassed the teenagers, whose lives were "not in complete synchrony with the referential world which first gave birth to these songs" (Appadurai 1990, 3). Rather, student interest was more visceral, captured by the flow of tantalizing sounds and pulsating beats. What appealed, too, was the status conferred by association with products from the United States. The effect of some cultural commodities, such as music, was produced not through language but the politics of consumption itself. Paul Willis's work (1990) on the "grounded aesthetics" of youth indicates that the kinds of interests constituted by the latest technologies and cultural commodities may occasion new alliances and identities cutting across traditional race, class, and gender divisions. These emerging communities represent new solidarities based on locally articulated passions or activities. Such communities, according to Willis (1990), may eventually eclipse, or reconfigure, current class, race, and gender relations. Similarly, Akhil Gupta and James Ferguson (1992) argue that the way transnational cultural flows "deterritorialize" identities has important implications for how anthropologists have often viewed differ-ence. For example, social divisions may be reconfigured according to whether or not youth in so-called underdeveloped countries are caught up in the "modern" imaginary provided by Euro-American cultural com-modities (cf. Stambach 2000).

The kind of solidarity posed by the common use of cultural media suggests a construction of equality quite different from what happens in schools. The secundaria provided one crucial place for a key segment of youth—those who continued to be schooled—to regularly meet and ex-change perspectives. On Mondays, students were likely to engage in heated discussion about who had won the weekend "debate" between two sonidos. At recess, several boom boxes played concurrently. The slick magazines students brought with them to school also supplied a constant source of diversion and amusement. Yet the school was a place where a very different kind of activity took place as well. Intentional instruction under adult authority was a far cry from the kind of freedom found in a weekend music hall. Teachers exhorted students to value a different kind of cultura. In one instance, the art teacher had launched into one of his emotional defenses of classical music, recounting his studies in a conservatory:

> I spent three years immersed in music, but a fine music, not like the kind you kids listen to [*esa que andan ustedes escuchando*], and a classmate of ours always asked the teacher for permission to play or broadcast just one of those songs that were in style, but no, he didn't permit us. He used to say *that* music wasn't worthy of the school.

The students seemed attentive, but several had been passing back and forth a nice pen drawing of the U.S. teen pop group New Kids on the Block. This juxtaposition was more than ironic. The teacher's defense of a classical aesthetic fell largely on deaf ears, for the cultural capital he en-dorsed and accrued to himself (he often mentioned his formal music studies) indexed a different historical and social field from the one that the students presently occupied. For most ESF students, the really interesting music was in the so-called modern sounds of global pop.

Students, then, grew up in a complex matrix of sites and contexts for the socialization of subjectivity. In families and neighborhoods, churches and workplaces, through relations and discourses of class, ethnicity, religion, kin, age, gender, and friendship, students learned what was important and who they should be in life. Yet how did the school figure into this learning?

CREATING A SCHOOL IDENTIFICATION

What's in a uniform? School-sanctioned clothing, after all, served important internal purposes: parents could economize their clothing purchases and students would hopefully apprehend their supposed equality with one another. Yet uniforms also served the projection of identity outside the school. The principal at ESF often admonished students that wearing the school uniform obliged them to abide by school rules of discipline and uphold school honor. Some teachers cited the advantage of uniforms in identifying ESF students who got involved in mischief outside the school. For example, students who fought outside ESF while still in uniform could be suspended or expelled as if the offense had occurred within school gates.

Thus, uniforms allowed for school identification on an everyday basis, wherever students might live, travel, or congregate before and after school. Yet other occasions encouraged students to identify themselves as members of ESF within a broader community of students. Perhaps most visibly, almost all students participated in civic events, especially the festive Independence Day parade held each year on September 16. At these events, students wore their uniforms and conducted themselves with appropriate dignity, effectively announcing their status as serious school members. They also participated as students in other regional celebrations and contests.

Yet another way that ESF fostered students' positive identification with the school was through the establishment of favorable contrasts with other area schools, public and private. I have already noted the principals' frequent remarks about maintaining school reputation in regional activities. They often invoked ESF's status (*categoría*) vis-à-vis poorer schools in the area. Most ESF students actively promoted school identification as well. As they constructed distinctions between themselves and students from other schools, they also reinforced an inclusive sense of equality and solidarity within the school. ESF students felt substantively equal to one another to the degree that they felt different from other secundaria students.

Teachers and parents alike were fond of highlighting ESF's regional, even national, prominence. This prominence had acquired an almost mythical quality, since the school had been sponsored by one of the greatest Mexican leaders of the twentieth century. This leader's local stature enabled him to make ESF one of the first federal secundarias established after the reorganization of basic education in the early 1940s (Solana, Reyes, and Martínez 1981, 309). Teachers exhorted the students to live up to the school's long-standing reputation of academic excellence. They demonstrated the numerous trophies that ESF had won in regional, state, and national competitions in oratory, dance, music, and athletics. Parents also emphasized ESF's local prominence. Many of them and their relatives had attended ESF themselves. Other regional secundarias had not opened until the 1960s.[10]

What did students make of this construction? Did they invest in the school with the same fervor as the teachers and many of their parents? Did they adopt it as their own, creating a set of identifications across difference within the school, while establishing distinctions between their school and others? I understand student subjectivities in this matter as situationally produced for local practices of distinction. With few exceptions, students did endorse a positive view of ESF. Teachers encouraged students to have a sense of ownership, to "love" their school, because only through the voluntary dedication and financial sacrifice of students and their parents could the school function effectively. Ironically, students manifested the strongest sense of proprietorship when they (often surreptitiously) denounced maintenance workers for not doing their job adequately, berated the principal for not allowing enough freedom, or chided teachers for being chronically absent from class (see Levinson 1998b).

There was probably more at stake here than in the typical "school spirit" campaigns known to those who have attended U.S. public schools. In the absence of any regular or direct competition—whether athletic, scholastic, or otherwise—school identification at ESF was still constructed against nearby schools. Less overt reference was made to the other two

public secundarias than the several private schools in the area. Nevertheless, there was some evidence that in the past, antagonisms between ESF
and the other two public secundarias (both técnicas) had been generated
by class and ethnic differences. After the técnicas were built in the 1960s
and 1970s, student gangs from each school fought one another and made
incursions into one another's schools. Because of the colors of their respective uniforms, students from one técnica, just a ten-minute walk from
ESF, were called buzzards (*zopilotes*), while ESF students were known as
grasshoppers (*chochos*). The técnica tended to enroll poorer students
from San Pablo's outlying colonias, as well as peasant children from
nearby villages. In 1990, class and ethnic differences between ESF and the
two técnicas were probably less marked than they had been in the past.
Students at ESF, accordingly, seemed more conscious of sharing an experience as students of public schools ("*escuelas de gobierno*") with kids at
other such schools. For instance, they might have had several friends from
the same neighborhood who attended one of the técnicas. By contrast,
ESF students were more likely in 1990 to perceive and articulate the distinction between public and private schools than to rekindle past conflicts
with other public schools.

ESF AND LOCAL PRIVATE SCHOOLS

The socioeconomic composition of San Pablo's three private institutions offering secundaria studies did not appear vastly different from that
of ESF itself (see table 1).[11] Why didn't students from the local elite attend
these private schools in greater numbers? Most teachers and parents acknowledged that local public schools had better prepared teachers and
therefore higher quality instruction. Thus, many of the wealthier families
in town, concerned increasingly about educational quality and preparation for further studies, continued to send their kids to ESF. In some cases,
these families sent their children to public and private schools in the state
capital or a still more distant city, but such cases were rare. On the other
hand, parents of more modest means who could still afford the extra
expense often sent their children to local church colegios for reasons of
discipline and morality over quality of instruction per se. They were more
interested in the "healthy environment" ("*medio sano*") or inculcation of
religious values such colegios presumably offered.[12]

The reasons parents gave for sending their children to ESF, and the
image they thereby constructed of private schools, sheds light on where
the students themselves began their particular school identification. De-

spite the growing social diversity in local private schools, many ESF parents condemned them as elitist or separatist. By contrast, they emphasized the relatively egalitarian ethos of public schools. Most parents recognized the value in ESF's broader socializing mission (*formación integral*). José's mother recounted his shyness during his primary years at the colegio, and attributed his newfound confidence and energy to the environment ("*ambiente*") at ESF:

> Kids at [ESF] understand more. . . . [I]t's like those at the colegio are more innocent, I don't know, maybe those things they learn in the secundaria environment are more useful, things more like, from the street, you know, like how all the parents speak in different ways.

Clearly valorizing ESF's social diversity, José's mother believed that the school's looser disciplinary code and greater social mixing made for a more challenging, stimulating education. ESF students, according to her, "understood" more because they were in closer daily contact with students (and their parents) from even more diverse backgrounds than they would likely encounter in the private colegio. Moreover, students were not subject to the hierarchical restrictions on behavior that in a colegio might prohibit them from having freer communication with one another.

Students had their own take on the distinctions between private and public schools. In a manner reminiscent of José's mother, 3C student Rosita also identified ways of speaking as a crucial difference between ESF and the colegios. Referring to her former fellow students, she said that one never heard bad words (*groserías*) in the colegios, nor were there any fights. At a public school, by contrast, expletives and physical harassment were quite common. Throughout the school year, Rosita maintained an ambivalent relation to the practice of using groserías. She coyly, even proudly, admitted using them in the proper context of schoolmate banter, but she could not shake the feeling that this was somehow morally wrong. Her parents, who had only reluctantly enrolled her in a public school, undoubtedly would have disapproved.

Regardless of the actual social composition of private schools, ESF students tended to depict them as elitist; these schools, and the privileged students they were said to enroll, served as foils for a positive ESF identification. It was not uncommon for ESF students who had attended a private primaria to later characterize it in negative terms. Rosita's younger sister was still in fifth grade at one of the colegios, and her parents, dismayed with teacher strikes at ESF, were planning on enrolling her in the colegio's next level of secundaria when she moved on from primary school. Nevertheless, Rosita joked derisively about how the private students were such "little angels" ("*santitos*") and how the teachers exaggerated the school's moral superiority. She said she liked the rougher flavor of life at ESF, where students would say and do things not possible at a colegio. Meanwhile, ESF boys tended to ascribe a feminine quality to the colegios. Most private students were required to bring portable typewriters to school on certain days of the week, since comercio was a prominent part of the curriculum. Boys from ESF often ridiculed this practice; they said their colegio counterparts looked like "little girls" with typewriters in hand. José's mother reported that he rejected his parents' suggestion to continue attending the colegio after completing primary school there. He couldn't put up with the nuns one year more, and said sarcastically, "Imagine me, carrying that typewriter around all the time."

Girls at ESF tended to condemn their counterparts in the colegios as stuck-up, putting on class airs. One poignant illustration of this occurred when Lidia's best friend, Karina, transferred to a colegio just after the start of their third year together at ESF. Karina's grades had dropped dramatically in the last year, and her parents attributed it to the loose environment at ESF, especially her friendship with Lidia. When Lidia tried to maintain contact with Karina after the transfer, she was brutally snubbed. Soon after, I was chatting with Lidia and Rosita during recess. These two had attended the same colegio for primary school, along with Karina. I asked how their old friend was doing:

> LIDIA: No, that girl doesn't even greet us, let alone talk to us.
>
> BL: Maybe her parents told her not to talk to you and to keep to herself.
>
> LIDIA: No, I don't think so, but anyway, two, almost three years that we spent together here in the school, they don't just get erased like that [*no se borran tan fácil*]. And anyway, [her parents] can't stop her. I see her in the street and she goes like this [Lidia makes a haughty face, turning her nose into the air], she's very different now.
>
> BL: Why? What made her like that?
>
> LIDIA: I don't know, I think she was always like that, because she also went to the colegio with us, and that's the way she was before we got to the secundaria. . . . The thing is that here we are really unpretentious [*aquí somos bien sencillos*], right? [Lidia looks at Rosita for confirmation, who nods her head in agreement], and she isn't, she doesn't want to talk to us anymore.

Lidia spoke one phrase with special conviction: "Aquí somos bien sencillos." I have translated sencillo somewhat awkwardly as "unpretentious" when in fact the term refers to a whole attitude, a stance of "simplicity." To be sencillo is to not stand out, not make distinctions. It is to be accepting and utterly ingenuous. Lidia and Rosita were suggesting by their talk that they themselves had traveled a road from the colegio to ESF; in effect, they had learned to be *sencillas*. Actually, Lidia was still ambiguous about the path that Karina herself had followed. This ambiguity suggested that somehow Karina's socialization at ESF had been incomplete. Though she had showed signs of becoming sencilla, her transfer back to the colegio revealed the arrogant subjectivity she had maintained. Lidia and Rosita, on the other hand, had successfully constructed a "simple" identification with their ESF schoolmates.

The private school that ESF students most often vilified was a newly opened secundaria/preparatoria touting a program of innovative and high-quality instruction. Students at this school sported colorful, expensive uniforms, and the school's name (starting with the term *institute,* not school or colegio) contributed to an impression of elite status. Since this new school had just opened in 1990, several ESF students had recently lost friends and grupo mates to transfer. Some were bitter about these ex-compañeros. For instance, one transfer had been jefa de grupo for 3C, and several grupo mates remarked that she had carried out her functions in an imperious fashion, barking orders and sometimes playing favorites. They said that she "belonged" better at the new school, because "here at ESF todos somos iguales." The institute was located adjacent to the main church of San Pablo's nearest neighboring village. While local bus service was available, most of the students received rides in their families' late-model automobiles. In February 1991, I had organized a basketball game between some students from ESF and the new institute. We arrived early at the institute's home court, taking the local bus. Just before scheduled game time, a few cars arrived and dispensed the home team. The spectacle did not go unnoticed by our team. They mocked the boys' higher-quality athletic gear, and one player said, "Look, the moneybags are here. Mommy's brought them just in time." The team busted up laughing. The student who made the derisive joke came from a family whose income was probably greater than many of the private students' families. Still, he called them moneybags (*ricachones*) on this occasion in an attempt to reinforce an important symbolic distinction.

By contrasting themselves with students who attended private schools,

ESF students accentuated the quality of *sencillez* that presumably characterized relations at their own school. When the basketball players taunted their opponents, they were drawing on this construction: only private students avoided the bus and flaunted their fancy, name-brand clothing. The embedded notion of sencillez, made explicit only at times such as these (and perhaps by the questioning of the anthropologist), formed a crucial part of student subjectivities and what I am calling here school identification. I turn now to look at how students folded school identification into a broader schooled identity. If school identification could be situationally activated to promote solidarity and pride, I argue that schooled identity could encompass such identifications within more lasting and consequential social distinctions.

CREATING AND CONTESTING A SCHOOLED IDENTITY

How did San Pabloans define the "educated person" (Levinson and Holland 1996)? I have already noted the varied meanings around the Spanish term *educación*. A long-standing usage indicated the formation of habits and values in the moral space of the home. San Pabloans still liked to call attention to an educated person's fine manners and morals. Regardless of their schooling, *una persona educada* showed proper decorum, respect for others, and a base of general cultural knowledge (cultura). Yet more recently, the practice of formal schooling had usurped many of these prior meanings of *educación*. Increasingly, una persona educada also displayed the knowledge and credentials of advanced schooling. Minimally, it seemed, a secundaria certificate could place one in the ranks of educated people.

Most students strongly endorsed this view of the educated person. They elaborated what I came to see as a relational schooled identity: a component of self as a secundaria-educated person, a social position contrasting with those relatively unschooled. Parents and teachers also endorsed this perspective. Like students, they circulated the symbolic value of secondary schooling, a specific kind of cultural capital, through the local social field (Bourdieu 1984; Calhoun 1993). In plainer terms, people associated with the secundaria tended to distinguish those with a secundaria education from those without one. Formal status as a secundaria student enabled a series of cultural distinctions that signified the incommensurable value of proper schooling. Thus, across the occasional gulf opened by school identification, students from different secundarias could still relate to one another through the meanings of being secundaria-schooled. Context-bound school identification would give way to a more deeply rooted schooled identity developed across the sites of home, school, and work. This identity, however, was never fully secure for all secundaria students. The seemingly automatic conferral of social value on the secundaria-schooled was, in fact, constantly produced and contested. As I will show here, subjectivities formed through other sites of socialization—in the home, community, or workplace—could push and pull against the pretensions of schooled identity, in effect forestalling its consolidation as a primary form of symbolic capital for all students.

THE ASSOCIATION OF SECONDARY SCHOOLING AND SOCIAL WORTH

In my earliest taped interviews with ESF students, I was struck by the unanimity of responses to my question about why they wanted to be in school. In retrospect, my interview strategy was naive. It was a frontal assault on a corpus of meanings best observed through everyday movement and talk. Virtually all students said that they were in school to learn, to prepare themselves for future studies and a career, and most important, "to be someone in life" ("*ser alguien en la vida*"). Alongside the desire "to be someone," of course, were the desires to be with friends, please parents, escape household chores, flirt with suitors (*pretendientes*), and so on. The immediate pleasures of school life were always balanced against the deferred pleasures of career aspiration. Still, no matter how formulaically presented, most ESF students clearly identified further schooling with "being someone"—that is, having a palpable and widely recognized social worth. In their minds, it was almost impossible to "be someone" without schooling, and this meant at least a secundaria certificate, probably more.

Teachers, parents, and other relatives played a prominent role in convincing students of the relation between schooling and social worth. Teachers often threatened and cajoled students to stay in school. According to them, school served as both a springboard for economic mobility and a source of greater cultura. The economic opportunities afforded by advanced study were almost self-evident to teachers, even if this supposition had been challenged in recent years by the well-known underemployment of university graduates. Moreover, the cultura (body of specialized knowledge) provided by the secundaria had intrinsic value: it would permit students to have a greater appreciation of the world around them and enable them to "defend" themselves socially. As the teachers would sometimes say, math skills helped students to avoid being cheated and to run an efficient household economy; speaking skills allowed them to make a timely point or convey a good impression to potential employers; and science skills enabled them to understand and utilize technological innovations more effectively.

In social spaces outside the school, students often heard the same messages about school and social success. Parents, older siblings, relatives, and adult friends alike haunted them with the prospect of educational and social failure. Typically, these messages made a sharp distinction between mental and manual labor. Among the lower social classes at ESF, schooling was seen as a way to break the family cycle of hard physical labor; among professional and merchant classes, schooling was seen as an important means of maintaining a status prerogative through the acquisition of more knowledge and cultura. In either case, there was an active construction of difference through schooling. Those students who finished school, at least through the secundaria, were said to possess the knowledge and skills for a productive life in society.

Franco's father expressed this common view when I went to interview him at their family's modest tortilla factory. Franco listened to much of the interview while working in the background. When I asked the father why he bothered to keep his son in school, he replied:

> Because one needs knowledge, he needs to be prepared in order to do well, so he'll be in a better [economic] situation than mine. And only through studying can one do this, you know? I've told him many times that you have to work hard with your head, right? It's better to work with your head than with your hands. I often tell my son that on those occasions when I'm really lazy, and I don't like to work, that's when I invent things, I cook things up all over the place [*me las ingenio*] in order not to exert myself too much. So it's better to use your head than your hands, right?

Throughout the interview, but particularly at this moment, Franco's father was looking over at his son, as if to stress the point. On another occasion later in the year, I listened as Franco's father berated his son for not having purchased a copy of his grupo's graduation photograph. He urged his son to get the photo and write down the names of all his classmates, especially the boys. As he explained, with such a photo Franco could more easily draw on his past social connections to get a job or favor in the future. This concern revealed Franco's father's awareness that schooling imparted a social status and set of social contacts that counted for as much as specific skills or credentials.

As I have already remarked, the local emphasis on the economic benefits of schooling was offset by a growing skepticism. After eight years of sustained economic crisis, some adults in 1990 were apt to applaud the entrepreneurial taco vendor in the town market who could, with little schooling, make more money than a trained engineer or doctor. The return on educational investment had long ceased to make rational economic sense, especially if parents wanted to see their children stay close to home.[13] Indeed, many wondered if school attendance was still worth the effort and expense. For example, Fidel of 3B traveled nearly fifteen miles each way to attend classes at ESF. His father had died the year before, and now his uncle had assumed a quasi-parental role. When I visited Fidel at his village, he took me to meet his uncle, who lived down the street and made wooden masks for the tourist trade. Apparently the mask business was doing well. Fidel was learning the techniques as his uncle's apprentice, and said he often felt like working at the shop rather than going to school. Significantly, his uncle did not actively encourage Fidel's pursuit of further studies. When I asked Fidel in his uncle's presence whether he would continue his studies, he hesitated, and the uncle intervened, "He sees that those who finish up their degrees a lot of times don't earn much and they can't find work in their own field" ("*No pueden ejercer su profesión*").

Most students and teachers at school valorized the prospect of gaining more cultura through additional studies, regardless of its immediate economic return. They realized the social value of schooling as a form of cultural capital, over and above its questionable economic worth. It was not coincidental that the most forthright questioning of this value came from people like Fidel's uncle, an artisan from a mestizo (but historically indigenous) village. It was here, outside most of the metropolitan circuits through which cultural capital flowed, that schooling meant less if it wasn't translated into tangible economic gain. Interestingly, Fidel's uncle had achieved some renown for his skills as an artisan precisely through his ability to exploit timely contacts. The previous year, he had been flown to Chicago to give a weeklong seminar on mask making at a major museum. This experience didn't lead him to valorize the cultural knowledge that advanced schooling could impart. If anything, his uncle's relative fame proved to Fidel that it was possible to "be someone" without further schooling. Franco's father, on the other hand, perceived the apparent disjuncture between schooling and economic gain in broader terms. He was more likely to see the present economic crisis as a temporary setback as well as a challenge to draw on the less immediately economic benefits of schooled cultural capital.

SCHOOLED IDENTITY AND OTHERNESS:
CLASS, GENDER, AND THE TWO PLAZAS

Most students seemed to take the words of their elders (*mayores*) seriously; indeed, they were powerfully influenced by what their parents and teachers told them. The creative elaboration of schooled identity, however, took place largely in and through the realm of student culture, the charged meanings informing student-organized activities. It was through these activities that students eventually came to accept, reject, or modify their understanding of being someone through further schooling. Significantly, the expressions of schooled identity did not play themselves out within the confines of the school alone. They often extended to areas of social affinity, even sexual attraction, well outside the purview of the school.

San Pablo is famous for its two central plazas, but few tourists appreciate how these spaces figure in local practice. On Sunday nights, both plazas became sites for courtship and a kind of ritual strolling (*dar la vuelta*) through which girls and boys, women and men, came out to see and be seen. Yet each plaza had a distinct style, an ambience. The bustling *plaza chica* near the city market was more crowded. Groups of boys and young men sat on benches and planters to get a good view of the few girls who would walk by in groups of three or more. The *plaza grande* was a large, spacious square bordered by the municipal government building as well as a number of the more expensive hotels and tourist shops in town. The greater size of the plaza grande gave the stroll less intensity, less of the quality of spectacle. There, it was more common to find already established couples and families mixing in with the more diffuse courtship ritual. ESF students clearly identified the differences between the plazas with social class, and in turn, ethnicity and level of schooling. Typically, these students saw those who frequented the plaza chica as "another class of people," invariably from the poorer, peripheral colonias or pueblitos outside San Pablo, and with little or no schooling. They associated themselves more with the "educated" people of the plaza grande.

During one recess period, I chatted with a group of girls from 3A. I had taken this week to approach different friendship groups that I had provisionally identified as class based (see chapter 6). This group, which included Andrea from 3A, was comprised of seven to nine girls who could almost always be found behind the shop building during recess time. The girls were all from poorer families. They were aware that other girls in 3A had more money and often felt themselves disparaged by them. As the group's informal leader, Gisela, put it, "The ones who think a lot of themselves [*se sienten*], I mean the ones who have a lot of money and stuff, you know, it's like they make less of us, like they put us off to the side for that reason [*nos ven menos, por eso nos hacen a un lado*]." Since I had already intuited the class distinctions between the two plazas, I wanted to find out what the different friendship groups thought about them. I rarely saw ESF students at the plaza chica. The one boy from 3A who consistently loitered there, Enrique, said he liked the "action" better. Significantly, he always arrived with friends from his distant neighborhood, not school-mates. He had also grown up in the countryside before moving to San Pablo to attend primary school. This is central in light of what the girls from 3A observed about the plaza chica:

> GIRL 1: In the plaza chica it's like—I mean, yeah, the ones that get together are more . . .
> GIRL 2: Boys from the country [*muchachos rancheros*].
> GIRL 3: And here [in the plaza grande] one can stroll around without anybody harassing us.
> GIRL 1: No, but they also say that it's because in the plaza chica nothing but poor Indian girls [*guarecitas*] go. [Several of the girls say "Aahhh" in a loud, mocking voice.]
> BL: What's that? Guarecitas?
> GIRL 1: Yeah, guar . . . you know, like Indian boys [*guachillos*], and over there in the plaza grande.
> BL: But what does guachillo mean? [Lots of nervous laughter from the girls; they all look at one another.] That's what you said, isn't it?
> GIRL 3: No, she said it.
> BL: Fine, you said guarecitas, right? And guachillo also. What do they mean?
> GIRL 3: No, she said it. [The girls ignore me momentarily and accuse each other of having said the words. Apparently, nobody wants to admit it. After a few seconds, another girl jumps in.]
> GIRL 4: It means they're from the country [ranchos].
> GIRL 1: No, I said from the villages [pueblitos]. . . . [W]ell OK, and they're from the country and stuff, and in the plaza grande . . .
> GIRL 5: Most of the ones who go are from here, San Pablo. [There is a

short flurry of comments that I can't make out, then one girl mentions the plaza chica again.]

GIRL 1: Some of the boys [in the plaza chica] are even much better looking [*más guapos*] than those from [San Pablo]. [Another flurry of indistinguishable comments, finger-pointing, laughter.]

GIRL 3: No, but really, seriously, the ones from the countryside are more handsome than those from around here.

GIRL 4: Well, some of them.

BL: But they dress in a different way and everything, right? [Several girls say, "Yes," emphatically, in loud voices.]

GIRL 1: Some of them, yes, are already well educated [*civilizados*], but others aren't.

GIRL 4: Some of them look like they're not that way anymore, they no longer dress like the ones from the countryside.

GIRL 2: But then there are those who come with their sandals [*huaraches*] and it's like, no way. [Gales of laughter.]

In this remarkable exchange, peppered with relajo, the girls revealed their ambivalence toward the "country boys" who frequented the plaza chica. At the time of the interview, I was not yet familiar with the local terms *guarecita* and *guachillo*, which I have translated as "Indian girl" and "Indian boy." My ignorance clearly provoked a lot of mirth and self-conscious impression management among the girls, who were unwilling to take responsibility for such unabashedly pejorative terms.[14] Yet toward the end of the raucous exchange, two of the girls suggested that many of these boys were more attractive than their counterparts who lived in San Pablo (and presumably attended local schools). One even admitted that many were civilizados, a reference to either their level of schooling or the general formation of good habits in the home. The topic was closed by another girl's final ironic humor, however, which declared that despite these positive qualities, some boys even came to the plaza in their huaraches. For the schooled San Pabloan, the huarache—a rough, homemade sandal—was the ultimate country signifier, a symbol of rurality, poverty, and little schooling. For these San Pablo girls, the huarache "was like, no way."

The girls from 3A were not the only ones who viewed the plaza chica in this light, though their own relatively low-class position and struggles with disdainful classmates made their commentary especially poignant. Virtually all the students with whom I chatted about the topic agreed.

Most boys felt that the few girls who frequented the plaza chica were from another *clase de gente* (class of people). This point of view emerged clearly in my conversation with three boys from grupo 3C, who formed part of a clique led by Iván. Iván was still at work when I laid my tape recorder out on the table of the plaza grande restaurant to which I had invited his friends. First I asked the boys what qualities they thought a girl should have, and when they had collaborated to produce a picture I had solicited of the "ideal" woman, I asked if this kind of girl could be found at ESF. After some hesitation and a comment by Valentino that several girls at school attracted him, Benito jumped in:

> At school there are some girls who even look good in their uniforms, they know how to move themselves well, and those in the street, no. When you find girls in the street they're already more used [*jugadas*], like they know more, whereas here in the school it's like they're still half children. The ones at school are better . . . and those that don't study anymore, it's like they're already much more grown up, they think very differently already, and here at school, well, they're still studying a lot. The ones at school are better.

After this statement, I asked the boys about the two plazas, and they came forward with perhaps the most explicit and revealing statement I ever received about the encoding of class differences in these public places:

> MATÍAS: We like the plaza grande better because—well, it's like social classes [*clases sociales*] because in the plaza grande there are the spoiled girls [*fresas*], the richer girls [*piruris*], it's like the ambience here is finer . . . and the plaza chica is where all the masses go [*todo el pueblo*], and it's like "ahhh" and "ehhh." [He makes guttural sounds, apparently imitating a rowdy, potentially violent atmosphere.]
>
> BENITO: The plaza grande appeals to me more because this is where the prettier girls come, the better ones, I mean, over there, there's nothing but girls from the lake [*de las orillas;* literally, lakeshore—a coded word for peasants or Indians], and the ones from [San Pablo] are much better.
>
> BL: What types of people go to the plaza chica, and why don't you guys like them?
>
> MATÍAS: I think that nothing but Indians [*indígenas*] go there. [Here, his two friends rib him about his use of the term *indígenas*: "*Ay, ¿cómo indígenas, hombre?!*"; "*No te claves.*"]

BENITO: In other words, this is where the people with a little more money come; it's like over there is where all the economically lower people are concentrated, and that's why we like to come over here more. It's not that we don't want to get mixed up with them or anything [*no es porque no nos queramos revolver en nada*], it's just that the ambience is better over here, and because there are also fewer people.

VALENTINO: And here the people are less vulgar than over there. If one uses bad words . . . over there they say them to you, and there are a lot of wild ones [*mucho salvaje*], wild ones who still don't have any knowledge toward certain human beings [*todavía no tiene ciertos conocimientos hacia ciertos humanos*]. . . . Because they think they're a little lower, they react.

MATÍAS: Roughnecks [*gandallas*].

VALENTINO: They always come out right away swinging and everything, and that also indicates something: that they still don't think very well, those folks. Here [in the plaza grande] we have people a little more *civilizada*, who know more, who know what's going on [*sabe que onda*]. I also don't like that when a woman passes by they're saying vulgarities [groserías] and all that, that's what I really can't stand. They think they're such men [*se sienten muy hombres*], but they should just talk to her, chat with her, stand up to chat, not just whistle at her or shout at her or something.

Like the girls from 3A, the 3C boys constructed a sharp opposition between the two plazas. This opposition similarly hinged on a definition of education and attractiveness that referenced class, gender, and ethnicity. According to Benito—and the other boys nodded in agreement—girls at school were "better" than those found in the "street." They "knew" less (that is, were relatively innocent) but studied more! Likewise, girls in the plaza grande were "finer" than those in the plaza chica, who tended to be from outside San Pablo and quite possibly were indígenas. The boys in the plaza chica, moreover, were seen as wild, uncivilized, and potentially violent. They did not know how to "think" properly; they had not been properly educated. Valentino brought this out with regard to their crass style of courtship. In his opinion, one sign of their low educational status was their inability to speak properly to a woman. Students like Valentino probably felt more comfortable chatting with young women because of their coed experience in secundaria. The majority of youth in the plaza chica had never gone beyond primaria, where gender separation was typically more pronounced. Finally, I noted that the boys from 3C were still ambivalent in some regards. Benito was cautious to hedge his comments about "economically lower" people by saying, "It's not that we don't want to get mixed up with them or anything." What's more, the boys gave Matías a hard time for the pejorative connotation that the term *indígenas* could have. Like the girls from 3A, these boys wavered in their condemnation of the "lower" folk of the plaza chica.

One Sunday night, Constantín gave me a lift in his father's pickup, and we made several rounds of the city center. Alberto was already riding shotgun, and as we rounded the small plaza, which was packed with strolling girls and watchful boys, I remarked that there appeared to be a lot of action that night. Constantín did not seem enthused, saying, "Yeah, but it's another class of people," while Alberto nodded in agreement. A few weeks later, when I was taping a chat with Alberto and two other friends, I brought up the topic of the plazas:

> ROBERTO: The small plaza has kind of a reputation . . . for being tough [*machina*], that there are a lot of tough guys [*machín*].
> ALBERTO: Gang types [*chavo banda*].
> ROBERTO: Yeah, gangs [*Sí, de banda*].
> ALBERTO: Yeah, I mean nothing but dudes [*puro cuate*], you know, rednecks [*ranchero*].
> ABEL: Little punks [*gandallita*].
> ALBERTO: Well, you know, it's not just that they're rednecks, because we're all from here, from the same place [*No es que sean rancheros pues que uno tambien es de aquí del pueblo*], but they're nothing but punks, nothing but, "Come here, dude, what's up?" ["*Acá cuate, qué onda?*" imitating a raspy, confrontational voice.]
> ABEL: Big hatters, big booters [*sombrerudos, botudos*].

The key term in this exchange was the word *pueblo*, which I have uneasily translated as "place," since in Mexican Spanish it can also refer to a village, town, country, nation, or people. Alberto first used the term *ranchero* (redneck, or country type) to condemn his counterparts in the plaza chica; then he modified its use, invoking the common space of the pueblo as a position or identity that linked them all together. Still, this fleeting identification was finally submerged in the continuing stream of pejorative denunciation. Alberto and company distanced themselves from the gangsters (chavo banda), punks (gandallita), and toughs (machínes) of the plaza chica. Yet even as he asserted his distinguishing schooled identity, Alberto must have realized that a straightforward condemnation of rancheros jeopardized his own self-construction as a simple man of the pueblo. He therefore paused momentarily to qualify the condemnation before proceeding. Such qualification, like Benito's above, was common among ESF students.

ANDREA'S CHALLENGE TO THE
PRESUMPTIONS OF SCHOOLED IDENTITY

As I've shown here briefly, ESF students typically did not find themselves attracted to youth who no longer attended school. Indeed, students appeared to be constructing and following a school-based cultural model that distinguished among possible objects of desire (Holland 1992). At one level, this may have been linked to the school identification I discussed in the previous section. It was, after all, extremely rare for students from two different secundarias, especially public and private, to court one another, even when they may have had regular contact in a neighborhood, church, or workplace.[15] The physical space of the school, and the intensity and regularity of the social relationships it accommodated, certainly contributed to this delimitation of courtship. Yet the disparagement of other schools that sometimes occurred through the process of school identification must have inhibited the impulse to court beyond the confines of the school as well. When it did occur, however, girls were most likely to develop romantic relationships with boys outside the school. Many third-year girls found the boys at ESF too immature, too absorbed in sports and other peer-based pleasures. The boys they sought for such relationships, however, were almost invariably students at one of the local high schools. Parents did not generally support the idea of courtship at such a young age, particularly for their daughters. Those who might reluctantly concede permission for such courtship at least tried to direct their daughters' interests toward more educated suitors. Most girls who dated unschooled boys found themselves resisting the model of educated attractiveness associated with schooled identity.

This was obviously the case for Andrea, who risked ostracism by peers and punishment by parents to pursue a clandestine relationship with a neighborhood boy. Andrea's clique from 3A, the girls whose exchange I analyzed above, admitted that they found some of the "uneducated" boys in the plaza chica attractive, yet they still mostly followed the school-based model of romance. They often talked about boys at ESF and other schools, and kidded each other about their present or future prospects. They also chided Andrea for her interest in a boy who worked and no longer studied. As Andrea told me once when she had been out of school for a few days, "I see they've been going around saying things about me, things that don't please me at all."

A couple of months earlier, during our first taped interview, Andrea had already confided her difficulties with the girls in this clique:

> I'm not getting along with them very well right now. Supposedly Concha doesn't like that guy who works in the tire shop, and he's my boyfriend. They say she calls him a dirtbag [*mugroso*] and a who knows what, but I could care less. I say, let them say what they want. And they say that he doesn't love me and who knows what else, so I say, "Me neither, I don't love him, I'm simply going with him because I'm of age, but when I'm older who knows." But who knows what [those girls] think. Supposedly Concha has her boyfriend here (at ESF, in the afternoon shift), he goes around all spruced up [*arregladito*], but what's she got if he is deceiving her with another girl? It doesn't make sense. I say it's better that the guy works, even if he goes around dirty and everything. If he just goes around with me, that's sufficient. That's what I think, but who knows about [those girls], they've got another way of thinking.

In this statement, Andrea strategically rejected the girls' construction of "educated" attractiveness. She valued her boyfriend's "dirty" faithfulness over the potential deceptions of a handsome schoolboy. Curiously, though, she expressed indifference toward the future of their relationship. This was in marked contrast to other conversations around the same time, when I would stop to chat at her family's crafts booth in front of the cathedral. When I asked her one day if she wanted to get married soon, she responded,

> No, right now no, but when I get to the right age, yes. Right now he's sixteen and I'm fourteen. My parents don't like him because he doesn't study . . . but we already decided that when I reach eighteen and he's twenty, he's going to come ask my parents, and if they don't agree, he'll "rob" me and we'll get married.

Throughout this period, Andrea asserted a lasting affection for her boyfriend, detailed future plans, and recounted the intensity of her struggles with friends and family over the possibility of seeing him. Yet in the first interview above, Andrea was eager to distance herself from her school-friends' "way of thinking." She was engaged in a kind of strategic communicative practice with me and her friends, and for this her "true" feelings toward the boy were beside the point. What she wanted most was to defend her choices, in this case to establish the value of a "working man" who knew how to be faithful. In this way, she actively contested prevailing definitions of educated attractiveness.

Thus, not all ESF students happily endorsed the presumptions of schooled identity. Indeed, many like Andrea maintained only tenuous connections with the school-based student culture. Even though her parents largely embraced the schooled identity, Andrea retained strong ties to the intimate culture of her neighborhood. Most significantly, Andrea challenged those elements of a schooled identity that might alienate her from the relatively unschooled, yet she also selectively drew on school discourses to make sense of her experience and assert her desires. I have already shown how she worked against definitions of attractiveness and desirability. Andrea also critiqued the egalitarian presumptions of ESF's student culture, marshaling the very language of that culture to formulate her critique.

At one point in our second interview, in January, Andrea had responded to my query about her older sister:

BL: And why don't you get along?
ANDREA: Because she has another way of thinking from me. . . . I like to get along with everybody, and she doesn't. I like to have male friends and female friends, and she doesn't, she doesn't get along with boys, only girls. But I say living like a nun and then later going off with some fool who doesn't know how to work, no. Better to get looking right now while I'm able to, if not, then when I'm older who knows? [*Pero pus yo digo viviendo de monja que luego me vaya con un menso que no sepa trabajar, mejor me busco ahorita que puedo, si no ya estando más grande ¿pus quién sabe?*]
BL: So would you say you're more comfortable now with your male friends outside the school than with those you have in the school?
ANDREA: Yes, because [the ones at ESF] are stuck-up [*sangrones*]; sometimes they come out and say things that I don't like. [Later in the same interview, she adds to these "things" the pornographic magazines that her male classmates pass to the girls.] Outside of school it's like

they respect me more, they respect me more because they know I study and so I don't just let them do whatever they please [*no me doy a llevar*]. They'll grab other girls because [those girls] don't ask for any respect [*no se dan a respetar*], but they know full well that I like to have respect, just like I too give them their rightful place.

Despite this account of having garnered respect for her schooled status, Andrea effectively rejected the status just a few minutes later:

I think I'll keep studying, but sometimes when I see how everyone turns out over there by my house, I just lose all interest. Now my mother, no, she thinks that one is better because one studies and others don't, but I don't like that. I like to get along with everybody even if I'm studying and they aren't. . . . [Some of my friends in the neighborhood] stopped talking to me because one day my mother shouted at me that I got together with good-for-nothings [*burros*], that I was hanging out with nothing but dropouts and that I was in another class [*categoría*], that I do study. That's when everyone stopped talking to me. . . . But I still speak with a few; they don't study either but I talk to them behind my mom's back because I like to get along with everybody. . . . I'm not like my sister who sometimes doesn't talk to anybody, because she says they're not in her categoría. I say, "What do I lose, even if they're not in my categoría?" They're the same as me [*igual que uno*], I mean, not poor, but not rich either.

Such seemingly contradictory statements led Andrea's parents to accentuate what they called her "disorientation." From their point of view, Andrea was totally confused about what she wanted. Ironically, by the end of the school year, Andrea's mother thought that Andrea had been too easily influenced by the higher-status girls in her grupo. She had wanted to go around dressed up and plan a special fifteenth birthday party like girls of this higher class (categoría); she would not accept her family's humble status as folk originally from the countryside. How, then, could Andrea portray her mother as the snob?

What fascinated me about Andrea was the way she positioned herself vis-à-vis the exclusions of schooled identity. On the one hand, she asserted a schooled status as a means of gaining "respect" among the boys in her neighborhood. If she didn't fully adopt a schooled identity as I have discussed it, she nonetheless strategically identified herself as a student. On the other hand, she rejected her mother and sister's demands that she associate only with fellow students who were in her categoría. While she recognized in her schoolmates' taunts the fragility and hypocrisy of the school-based cultural game of equality, she appropriated elements of student culture to construct a kind of equality between herself and her relatively unschooled barrio friends. Clearly, Andrea felt more comfortable with these neighborhood companions. She gravitated toward their friendship because they accepted and respected her like none of her schoolmates, even as she was still attracted to the styles and practices of her schoolmates (going to discos, wearing jeans, and so forth). Yet it was no accident that she insisted on getting along with "everybody" in her neighborhood because they were, despite differences in schooling, fundamentally "equal" (igual que uno). Her intimate culture may have had its own egalitarian norms, but it seemed to me that Andrea took the terms of equality normally circulating at ESF, and extended them outward to defend and articulate the solidarity of neighborhood friendship against the presumptions of an exclusive schooled identity. In other words, Andrea resignified the school-based discourse of equality. While this discourse was intended to erase or transcend difference among secundaria students, Andrea contested the very grounds of schooled identity by extending these resources to include all youth, especially the relatively unschooled.

SCHOOL, WORK, PLAY, OR MARRIAGE?

ESF students tended to contrast themselves with students who had dropped out of school to work, indulge bad habits (*entregarse al vicio*), or marry. Picking up the cue from parents and teachers, ESF students highlighted the risks and pitfalls of dropping out. In different situations, students missed few opportunities to denigrate dropouts or the relatively unschooled. They dispensed such moral judgment in an effort to convince themselves of their own propriety, and thus buttress the foundations of a growing schooled identity.

Boys were most prone to condemning those age-mates no longer in school. In their opinion, the distinction between work, play, and "loafing around" was a fine one indeed. While they acknowledged many age-mates who worked hard and honestly, they also accused them of squandering their earnings on frivolities like cigarettes, tape players, and weekend dances. Even if the ESF students themselves worked weekend or afternoon jobs, they still characterized their counterparts as having given up—too lazy or easily distracted to continue their studies. According to the logic of schooled identity, age-mates who no longer studied had failed to become someone in life. Saúl, an athletic fifteen year old who planned to enlist in a military officer program after completing secundaria, denounced his former buddy Ernesto:

> The thing is, that little freckle-face wants to be a rich guy [*se quiere hacer burgués*]. . . . He started up with some vices, like smoking and drinking, and now you can't even take the cigarette out of his mouth. . . . He wants to sell tacos, and the only thing that matters to him now is grabbing enough money to go to the dances.

Saúl had been close to Ernesto when they were still attending the same primaria and living just down the street from one another in one of the poorer colonias of San Pablo. Yet the luck of the draw had placed Saúl in the afternoon shift at ESF and Ernesto in the morning, thus making it difficult for them to play or work together. Then, Ernesto quit school after his second year in order to work full-time at a taco stand in the market. This was the move that Saúl so harshly judged. According to Saúl, Ernesto had too easily succumbed to the immediate pleasures of the emerging youth culture in San Pablo. He had forsaken the possibility of a higher social status in order to pursue the instant gratification of money and leisure.

I happened to know Ernesto quite well also. I had befriended him the previous year on a shorter visit to ESF and often chatted with him at his taco stand. What struck me was how similar he and Saúl really were. Both came from poor families now headed by an abandoned or widowed mother. Each had to work several hours a day in order to help provide for his younger siblings. Moreover, both seemed to strike the tough masculine pose so common among the poorer urban youth. Saúl had channeled his energies into basketball and schoolwork, hoping to join the army and learn how to handle advanced weaponry. He felt the army would grant him a social status commensurate with his secondary education. Ernesto, on the other hand, failed to see the benefits of continued schooling. In his first and second years at the secundaria he had been hired to open up a refreshment stand in the market at 6:30 A.M., and to return at 2 P.M. to work until around eight o'clock. He complained of not having any time to do his schoolwork; in fact, he had almost no time to spend what little money he retained after handing most of it over to his mother. After enduring numerous complaints from his teachers about tardiness, absence, and incomplete work, Ernesto simply dropped out. His mother urged him to continue, but she also knew that she couldn't survive without his economic contribution. Ernesto made a strategic choice. By opting out of school, he could contribute money to his family and still have some left over to spend on dances and excursions.

Because he now only saw Ernesto at a distance, Saúl deemed this strategic choice a cop-out, an abandonment of the promises of schooled identity. He accused Ernesto of "bourgeois" pretensions, claiming that Ernesto's overriding concern was to acquire money to support his many "vices." Saúl's use of the term *bourgeois* to describe Ernesto's motivations was ironic yet extremely significant. Even though continued schooling promised Saúl himself a higher, possibly bourgeois status, he attributed Ernesto's immediate interest in money to the impulse for greater wealth and distinction. In contrast to the supposedly simple students at ESF, who abjured common vices and excessive spending for the promises of a schooled identity, Saúl portrayed Ernesto as seeking his own gain at the expense of others. The term *bourgeois,* taken from textbooks and teachers with a socialist orientation, was applied to Ernesto in order to accentuate the distinction between the motivations of the schooled and unschooled. To be sure, Saúl's judgment of Ernesto was highly charged. They had been close childhood friends and shared the same intimate culture at home. Saúl himself aspired to a less bourgeois, but certainly more masculine route (military college) than most of his fellow schoolmates (university study). This sharpened his critique of Ernesto, and provided a unique twist to his own emerging schooled identity.

Perhaps since few secundaria-age girls worked in paid and publicly visible jobs, only the boys tended to contrast themselves with workers. Girls at ESF, on the other hand, often contrasted themselves with those who had married young. To take on a schooled identity was to abjure the prospects of an early marriage in order to focus on advanced schooling and a career. Here perhaps more than anywhere else the discourses of student culture mirrored parental imperatives. For among the vast majority of girls enrolled at ESF, parents issued strong warnings against serious involvement with boys. Parents had not invested in their child's development of a schooled identity only to watch it get squandered on a socially compromising marriage. As I mentioned earlier, many ESF mothers had themselves been obliged to marry young. But "times have changed," as San Pabloans often liked to note, and in 1990, mothers whose aspirations had been thwarted in this fashion emotionally invested in their daughters' schooling success. Fathers, too, encouraged their daughters to continue studying and avoid serious courtship with boys. The notorious possessiveness of Mexican fathers, which had traditionally kept girls from openly pursuing their romantic and sexual desires, now worked to favor their diligence in school. For the most part, fathers now would much rather see their daughters in a successful career than a successful marriage (see Levine 1993).

As I discuss in the next chapter, at ESF, the persistent allure of romance had been displaced from its exclusive association with engagement and marriage. Girls were increasingly out to have fun (*divertirse*) with their romantic interests. Accordingly, those girls who insisted on serious courtship or youthful marriage were often maligned by their female classmates. With the exception of some girls like Andrea, who clearly contested both their parents and classmates' construction of a schooled identity, female ESF students disparaged girls who had dropped out of school to marry. Thus, an important part of girls' schooled identity was elaborated in contradistinction to those who married young. Here I would like to give just one brief example from a joint interview with Paco's mother and sister.

I had gone to have lunch with Paco's family at their poor village home. After lunch, Paco left me alone to do a taped interview with his mother, but his sister Riki, a first grader at ESF, stayed on to listen. After twenty minutes of conversation, I decided to involve Riki as well. Her mother had just said that she doubted Riki would finish school and have a career, because no girls she had ever known in their village had successfully done so. She seemed ambivalent about the prospect: she wanted to support her daughter's efforts, and felt a career would be a definite social and economic improvement; yet she was quite sure Riki's career would only serve to enrich her eventual husband and might be a waste of time (Paco's mother had herself been abandoned by her husband a number of years earlier). Furthermore, Paco's mother did not believe that Riki could complete her schooling, although she noted Riki's own insistence that she would. At this point, I turned to Riki and asked her why she thought she could keep doing well in school. Her reply revealed how her own schooled identity was being constructed against the possibility of marriage:

RIKI: I don't know, I like studying . . . and I don't want to be like some [girls], like my friend who got married three days after we graduated from primaria. . . . Before she used to watch her appearance and go around nicely dressed, and now she wears *enaguas* [traditional petticoats], she looks really ugly. I don't want to look like her; I'd rather have a career.[16]

BL: So it doesn't seem right to you [*no te parece*] that the friends you had [in primaria] got married and don't study anymore?

RIKI: No, it doesn't seem fair to me [*no me parece justo*]. I don't want to end up like them. It looks really bad.

BL: Why?

RIKI: Because that way one begins to have a family and then with—I don't know, that's just what I don't want. I want to have a career in order to support myself and have my own money.

Riki's case was interesting because she was one of the few girls who actively adopted this kind of schooled identity in the absence of obvious parental support. She plainly rejected marriage as an option, even while her mother did not give her wholehearted approval to continued schooling. Significantly, Riki singled out the "ugly" enaguas worn by her former classmate, associating them with the bane of marriage. The enaguas signified traditional gendered lifeways in her home village, and they could be the objects of derision among the mainly urban mestizo ESF schoolgirls. Riki made a clear choice to eschew her village's traditional gender script. Her involvement in the ESF student culture undoubtedly distanced her from some indigenous cultural patterns and fueled her resolve to stay the career course.

From the varied sites of social difference in students' intimate cultures to the spaces and discourses of school life, ESF students negotiated a highly complex world of identity formation. In the family, neighborhood, and other community institutions, students received their primary socialization, the development of habitus as a set of gender, class, and "ethnic" predispositions to interpret and act on the social world. Such socialization was ongoing, dynamic, and reciprocal as students moved out of the home into the institutional spaces of the school, church, and workplace. Students were developing their own life projects within the constraints and resources provided by these sites, and out of the pervasive signs of global cultural media and international migration. By the time they reached their final year of secundaria studies, the stakes had grown quite high. By 1991, virtually all children were expected to complete primaria and, at least in San Pablo proper, secundaria as well. Beyond that was uncharted territory for most ESF students. How would they choose to "be someone" in life? How would their response to the relations and practices of school life condition the trajectory they eventually pursued?

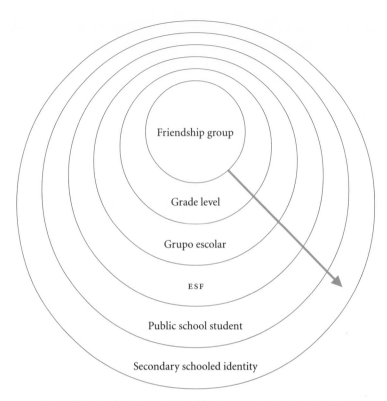

Fig. 4. "Nesting" of situated identifications and enduring identities

Over the last two chapters I have sketched out and illustrated the creative ways students appropriated the institutional discourses and practices of school life. Existing student subjectivities encountered these varied institutional dynamics, and took up accordingly varied and shifting positions in an extended cultural game of equality. Student identifications and identities were renewed or modified in the social dynamics constituting a variety of concrete or imagined collectivities: friendship groups, grupos escolares, the third grade of ESF, ESF as a whole school, public school membership, and those having status of secondary school enrollment. No doubt readers have wondered how it was possible that, for instance, a sense of solidarity constructed within a grupo escolar through competition with other grupos escolares could be transferred at another time to the school at large. Wouldn't a particular grupo allegiance prohibit identification with other grupos?

Yes and no, and only because contexts framed experience. I like to think of the collectivities mentioned above as sometimes nested, sometimes contradictory contexts for subjective identification and social identity (see figure 4). Different contexts situationally activated different identifications. Thus, friendship groups, as I show in the next chapter, brought forth and consolidated those differences rooted in students' intimate cultures, even as the ethic of solidarity in the grupo escolar encouraged the articulation of such differences for a common collective effort. Students varied in the degree of commitment they expressed to the friendship group or grupo escolar. Similarly, the grupo identification encouraged by teachers and wrought by competition between grupos escolares could be superseded by a broader school identification endorsed by the ESF administration for school pride or intermural competition. Finally, students' particular school identification could be subordinated to an even broader secondary schooled identity. I suggest that the other moments and spaces of subjective identification gave way to a more pervasive and enduring identity that began to organize student perceptions of self and others across a broader range of social contexts. Students in their final year of secundaria seemed to be either rejecting or consolidating such an identity. The positions they would assume vis-à-vis this schooled identity could have important consequences for their future lives.

6. Friendship Groups, Youth Culture,

and the Limits of Solidarity

The following is from an interview with two female social studies teachers about ESF students:

TEACHER 1: When I was in charge of 3C about three years ago, I remember a little problem we had, [although] it never got too bad [*no llegó a mayores*]. Some girls from the upper class never became part of the grupo [*nunca se integraron*], they always kept themselves separate, they wouldn't socialize with the grupo [*no convivían*]. When we made an excursion, the majority of the grupo participated . . . and these girls didn't, they kept themselves off to one side. If there was a disco or something, they always kept themselves apart, thinking they were better than the rest. I even remember that we had the election for the Sociedad de Alumnos, and two of these girls were in one of the planillas [candidate slates], and the majority of the students began to reject them. They even began to call it the planilla of the bourgeoisie, the bourgeois against the proletarians—yes, we were studying the class struggle in the third grade, the bourgeoisie and the proletariat, and they applied it very well [the teacher chuckles]. They said it was the planilla of the bourgeoisie, so these girls complained and distanced themselves even more, and another planilla won.

BL: Do the girls of that [upper] class tend to separate themselves more than the boys? Do the boys who come here from the upper classes blend in more than the girls?

TEACHER 1: Yes, I don't know why, but yes, I've observed that phenomenon.

TEACHER 2: I think it's because at home [the girls] are the ones who are most devoted to the family, I mean, the bourgeois families are the ones that stick closest to home, they're the families in which the fathers most emphasize the [class] differences. And the women are the ones who learn to emphasize the differences more than the men. I mean, the men always tend to mix more with people who have less money . . . while the women have a different educación, the families educate women in another way, they make them more bourgeois than the men. I've had some contact with bourgeois folks and I've always noticed that they educate their women more than the men for the bourgeoisie.

The social studies teacher who starts this discussion says they had a "little problem" that "never got too bad." The girls from wealthy families tried to maintain their distinction in the grupo escolar, so they were ostracized and called the "bourgeoisie." This event had taken place some three years prior to 1990. Because it did not occur frequently, it was apparently worthy of comment when I asked these two teachers if they ever saw the students maintaining class distinctions. The teachers forwarded a theory of class-gender habitus. The wealthier girls get "educated" for bourgeois life. Yet even more remarkable is the very exceptionality of the story. Sure, girls receive this kind of education in the home, but rarely does it get actively expressed in the school. Rather, school-based practices around equality and solidarity encourage a different sense of collective membership. Teachers hope and assume their educative action is successful in bridging class differences, but sometimes "little problems" emerge anyway. How often and how consequentially does this occur?

I have already explored some of the dynamics in the grupo escolar and the broader sites of community socialization. Yet what happened in students' freely chosen friendship groups as these intersected with the cultural game of equality produced at ESF? Did friendship groups nurture a sense of difference at odds with the school's project? Would such difference find freer expression in the informal domains of friendship affiliation—at recess, before and after school, during holidays and fiestas? Would the activities of friendship groups put the lie to the pretensions of solidarity? Were the former girls of 3C merely the most visible instance of ongoing distinction? In developing an answer to these questions, the prominence of the grupo escolar as a socializing space must not be forgotten. Students' sense of difference from one another was likely blunted by proscriptive teacher and student discourses in school-defined formal domains like the grupo escolar. I will show here the very real ambivalence in friendship groups, especially the way codes of equality appeared to penetrate them and make their work of differentiation less vigorous than it might otherwise have been.

Senses of difference, of relative superiority, existed, to be sure, and I will give evidence of it in abundance: the older belittling the younger, the rich belittling the poor, boys belittling girls, city residents belittling *pueblerinos,* and so on. Yet unlike the findings of educational ethnographers in Euro-American contexts, who studied the same or slightly older age groups (Foley 1990; Eckert 1989; Varenne 1982; Willis 1981b; Walker 1988; Canaan 1987), I did not find the development of clearly marked status groups or "situational identity groups" (Foley 1990, 77; see also Solomon 1992). Nothing comparable to "jocks," "burnouts," "greasers," or "freaks" existed at ESF. Friendship groups varied in size and durability, and tended to take their shape around common themes and interests that could be pursued together outside the school. These groups rarely developed subcultural styles or an oppositional ethos, nor did they join together in the configuration of "symbolic categories" (Eckert 1989). Insofar as ESF students formed friendship groups with symbolic status labels, they were rather more ephemeral and marked by a complex intersection of ethnicity, class, gender, and age. The affective and symbolic identifications that brought friendship groups together could just as easily pull them apart. Meanwhile, class, ethnic, and gender differences were not the only elements of friendship affiliation. Age, as well as key differences within students' intimate class-ethnic cultures, structured such affiliations, too. Most important, student subjectivities in friendship groups—as I inferred them through ethnographically palpable language, gesture, and affiliation—showed traces of the school's egalitarian codes. Wholehearted denigrations of social difference were tempered not only by the presence of the youthful anthropologist but also by an ongoing awareness—the presence of a "social voice" (Bakhtin 1981)—reminding students of their common ground.[1]

In chapters 4 and 5, I highlighted the social practices within and around ESF that enabled students to develop common identifications as grupo and school members, and a common identity as the secondary schooled. Even in these chapters, however, the reader could witness the persistence of distinctions. Identifications in one context would give way to distinctions in another, and the schooled identity was not fully embraced by all ESF students. In this chapter, I trace the logic of distinction in the opposite direction: from the friendship groups out. I look at the formation of friendship groups and the discursive construction of otherness across students' intimate cultures. Here, the reader may notice a related but contrary effect: the persistence of broadly egalitarian subjectivities even amid the distinctions enacted and produced in the friendship groups.

MUSIC, MEDIA, AND THE CULTURAL CENTER AT ESF

As I have already hinted, a shifting and amorphous group of ESF students constituted something like the "leading crowd" that James Coleman (1961) described at a U.S. high school nearly forty years ago. These were the students who tended to come from families of middle- to upper-level incomes; who all lived within the city of San Pablo, most toward the city center; and who frequently visited each others' homes, held study groups in the city's central library in the afternoons, and went to parties or discos together. They were also most likely to bring music cassettes, popular magazines, new fashions (on days when street clothes were allowed), and other cultural commodities into the school. This group of students had no label attributed to or assumed by it. It was, in fact, composed of numerous converging friendship groups and networks, and was facilitated by these students' residential proximity, available leisure time, and modest disposable consumer income. Still, because of the way they seemed to set standards of taste and conduct, I came to think of these students as forming ESF's "cultural center."[2]

Students of the cultural center moved most easily about the school, readily engaging in playful banter with teachers. Their demeanor across different school contexts suggested a sense of ownership, of belonging, that many other students lacked. They even tended to occupy the spatial center of classrooms, recess activities, and other school events. Surprisingly, there seemed to be little discernible relation between students' degree of participation in the cultural center and their level of academic success. Some were among the best students in the school, while others were close to failing out. Nor did teachers' treatment of the cultural center students differ noticeably from other students. While teachers might show more ease or familiarity with these students, they were just as likely to scold them or point out their faults in class. Indeed, because these students generally came from professional or merchant families, teachers were often less sympathetic to their academic and social lapses. It is also no coincidence that, in retrospect, many of my observations and perhaps close to half of my focal students came from the cultural center. After all, these students were both more articulate and forthcoming with invitations to visit their families or participate in their leisure activities (leisure [*diversión*] being a category of activity that hardly existed for some of the school's poorer students). Since I, too, lived toward the center of the city, I saw them more frequently around town, and I also provided a sort of cultural capital many were avid to acquire. Thus, my ethnographic data show an inevitable richness of experiences and discourses from the cultural center. I have tried to compensate for this by being especially attentive to how less privileged students, outside the center, viewed and felt life in the school.

Center students most actively introduced popular, mass-produced cultural commodities into the school, as I briefly mentioned above. They formed the cutting edge of an emerging public youth culture fomented by consumer capitalism and dominant trends in urban cultural style (compare Liechty 1995; Wulff 1988). The latest cultural commodities (*los que andan de moda*)—which in San Pablo in 1990 meant primarily U.S. and Mexican rap, hip-hop, and pop music, glossy teen magazines, and "action" videos—were avidly disseminated by ESF's cultural center. These students established a tangible hierarchy of forms, in which urban displaced rural and the "modern" (a term the students themselves frequently used) displaced the traditional. Though many ESF students still enjoyed these older, more traditional cultural forms (*música ranchera*, regional dance, "Tin Tan" movies, and the like), they clearly masked or modulated their preferences within the school environment. In a critical sense, accepting the modern was one condition of membership in the cultural center. Arguably, too, the modern imaginary came to constitute an important part of schooled identity altogether.[3]

A case in point is the consumption of music, primarily in the form of cassette tapes played on portable decks brought to school. Though many students confessed to me their taste for less modern styles of music, such styles were rarely heard at school or student parties. Some students recounted their prior attachment to these other musical styles, only to now profess a complete devotion to so-called modern music.[4] Still others, who perhaps felt more secure as leaders in the question of taste, could play and appreciate traditional music if the situation (*andando en ambiente*) were right. For instance, Abel and his buddies claimed that musicians such as Bronco or Vicente Fernández, who played more traditional ranchera music, provided a nice diversion from their otherwise steady diet of modern music. In fact, while most students were still scrambling to learn the beats and lyrics of the new music, students like Abel were going a step further by adopting a situational display of this more traditional music. They clearly thought it was cool (*de onda*) to play this kind of music from time to time, but only because they had already established their credentials as stalwart consumers and interpreters of modern music.

By the mid-1980s, the pastime of weekend dances with DJs and full sound and light systems had exploded onto the San Pablo youth scene. These discos became a regular part of school life at ESF as well. The traditional dance (*tardeada* or *baile*), which had employed a live group, was now displaced by the purely electronic sounds of the disco. Though a variety of music was played, including waltzes and other traditional dances, modern rock and rap music predominated, and was clearly preferred by virtually all the students in attendance. On special ceremonial days, students clamored for permission to sponsor a schoolwide disco. Over the years, teachers and school authorities had gradually conceded the students' right to sponsor such dances. Sometimes these were held in a private, rented banquet hall; sometimes on the school grounds themselves. In one notable case, the growing gap between adults' musical tastes and the electronic beats of the emerging youth culture became abundantly obvious. When students and parents were negotiating with school authorities about how best to hold a schoolwide graduation party, everyone agreed to hire a sonido (DJ and sound system) for the kids and a traditional band (*conjunto*) for the parents.

When I asked a number of students at year's end what new tastes or habits (*gustos* or *hábitos*) they felt they had acquired during their time at ESF, most cited disco music and dancing first (not the "taste" of school knowledge or the "habit" of study!). When they had entered ESF, most told me, they had felt awkward and reluctant to attend these dances. If they did go, they stayed on the margins, just watching. Now they had finally learned some of the rhythms and their corresponding steps. Many had become avid consumers of disco music and dancing, going to great lengths to buy recorders and cassette tapes in order to practice dance steps. Girls especially recounted their struggles with parents in wrangling a reluctant permission to attend a disco, if only for a short while. And girls, too, practiced long hours to present so-called modern dance numbers to the student body in celebration of Teachers' Day.

Not all students equally relished this kind of music and dancing. Many attended the school-sponsored discos in order to be with friends, but never went to those held independently on the weekends. Moreover, a significant number of students continued to listen regularly to the musical styles marginalized by the cultural center. They typically listened at home, however, well away from school. Revealed taste could be socially dangerous. For example, early on in the school year, I learned that Nidia of 3F liked more traditional groups such as Los Bukis, Bronco, and Los Temerarios, who played a style of romantic ballad, ranchera, or polka-influenced *norteña*. Soon after, I entered into a "secret" gift exchange with grupo 3F, and to my delight I pulled Nidia's name out of the hat. At this point in my fieldwork, I had not yet grasped the central position of modern music at ESF. It was to my chagrin, then, that Nidia faced a few jeers when a week later she opened my gift of Los Bukis's latest tape in front of her classmates. Because students remembered that I had been inquiring about musical tastes during the previous weeks, my choice of the gift became a tacit declaration of Nidia's maligned musical tastes.

FRIENDSHIP GROUPS AND SOCIAL DISTINCTIONS
WITHIN AND ACROSS THE GRUPO ESCOLAR

THE JUANITOS

Near the beginning of the school year, I became aware of a group of four boys who maintained a high visibility in most informal school activities. While they participated only halfheartedly in school-sanctioned events, they liked to garner attention by flirting with girls, playing practical jokes, and bringing scandalous items (such as a shock machine, live mouse, or whoopie cushion) to school. After school, they would often linger in nearby streets for nearly an hour, smoking cigarettes, making fun of passersby, bantering with fellow classmates, or secretly hitching a ride on the backs of passing trucks. Two of the four boys, Abel and Alberto, had befriended me from my earliest days in the school in 1990. Sons of a well-off dentist and doctor, respectively, they had strikingly different levels of academic achievement, and partly because of this contrast I chose them both as focal students. Alberto's best friend, Roberto, was also in 3F, while

Abel's best friend, Constantín, had been placed in 3B. The four would come together at recess, before and after school, and whenever else possible. Roberto and Constantín also came from wealthier families. Constantín's father, a former mayor of San Pablo, owned and operated the largest brick factory in the region while pursuing other commercial ventures. Roberto's father had originally started his own mechanic's shop and eventually came to own the largest auto parts store in town. As male members of a powerful intimate culture, these four boys clearly had opportunities not available to most other ESF students. While Alberto and Constantín did assist in the family businesses some afternoons, much of these boys' time was free to do as they pleased. They often played *frontón* (a type of squash), practiced hunting and shooting in the hills, or as I noted in the last chapter, cruised town in one of the family vehicles.

The four boys formed a strong friendship group that sutured two dyads across two different grupos escolares. They shared important elements of gender and intimate culture subjectivity. Yet even as these shared subjectivities distinguished them from most in their respective grupos, the boys identified themselves, first and foremost, as members of their grupos escolares, and they defended the egalitarian codes that occluded awareness of social distinctions. A look at these boys' contradictory practices around class, gender, and ethnicity sheds light on how school-based discourses and the cultural game of equality modified and challenged, but failed to fully displace, the dominant subjectivity inscribed in their habitus.

The contradictions were embodied in the very name that the boys had chosen for their informal friendship group. The previous year, they had called themselves the "Agapitos Lopis Casta," or Agapitos for short. An intended parody of an old-fashioned rural name, the term *Agapitos* also provided a sexual entendre (*Haga pitos* could be vulgarly translated as "Go do some dicks"). By the time I arrived in 1990, one of the Agapitos had graduated and their chosen name had thus changed. Now, as Alberto emphasized to me one day, "they call us the Juanitos, but it's only written like that, it's pronounced Jua-ne-tos, you know, the way they talk in the pueblitos." When I asked him what he meant, he said, "Yeah, haven't you noticed that's the way they talk in the pueblitos?" and he proceeded to speak a few random phrases off the top of his head, deliberately mispronouncing nouns and misconjugating verbs in singsong fashion. In Mexican literature and popular culture, Juanito might also refer to a poor, subservient (and often indigenous) rural male, not unlike the use of "boy" in the racist U.S. South. Its use thus enacted a linguistic condescension coded by class and ethnicity. To be sure, Alberto and his friends did not highlight this name. I rarely heard others call them Juanitos, nor did they use it much themselves. Most likely a closely related friendship group, or some members of 3B or 3F, had christened them this, acknowledging their penchant for mocking rural speech registers. Still, and however playfully rendered, the name positioned these boys above some of their schoolmates.

We can also see contradictions at work by examining what happened when another boy from 3F, Antonio, tried to become a member of the Juanitos. Through the first three months of the school year, I noticed Antonio tagging along with the Juanitos, following them around during recess and sometimes after school, and hooking up with Alberto and Roberto during 3F grupo activities. The Juanitos seemed to accept his presence, though Antonio rarely initiated interaction. Despite his persistence, he always appeared to me the odd man out.

Antonio was obviously from a different background than the other Juanitos. He was short and dark skinned, and lacked the kind of cultural capital acquired by the professional and merchant classes. Yet he was clearly making a bid for acceptance into the friendship group, and what made that bid desirable, even possible, was the fact that his family had recently struck it rich. Just two years earlier, his father had been struggling as a truck driver based out of a small, distant village. Antonio had lived his entire life in the countryside. Then, through astute investment (and some alleged, a good deal of illicit drug trafficking), Antonio's father had managed to first buy his own rig, then several others. By the time I got to know Antonio, his father owned and administered some seven transport trailers.

Antonio had thus moved into town and acquired some of the trappings of his new social position: a brand-new racing bike, snappy imported clothing, and the latest high-top shoes. Yet the marks of his rural past were still indelible, and the Juanitos were never remiss in pointing these out. On occasions when I asked if Antonio was really a Juanito, the boys' responses were coy and evasive; Alberto said, for instance, that Antonio could be considered *de reserva,* a benchwarmer or substitute. One day when I was chatting with three of the four Juanitos in Abel's family's kitchen, I finally insisted on knowing whether or not they considered Antonio a full-fledged member of the group. Here I reproduce part of that conversation, for my deliberately provocative interventions and the responses they evoked are equally significant:

198   We Are All Equal

BL: OK, so tell me if Antonio is a Juanito or not.

ROBERTO: Sometimes. The thing is sometimes he acts just fine, very in tune [*muy acá*], very . . .

ALBERTO: He definitely sticks with the guys [*jala con la banda*]. To go around with the guys means to stick with the guys, to hang with you, to do things with you, you know what I mean? that he sticks with you. Because there are times that he takes off and nobody even knows where he went.

BL: I see [Antonio] as very different from you guys, he's got another style.

ALBERTO: How do you see him?

BL: Let's see, how would I describe him? I don't know, like . . .

ABEL: Like from some other class [*otra sociedad*], you must think.

BL: Yeah, maybe that's it.

ROBERTO: Another kind of person.

BL: Like from another kind of family, or another type of . . .

ALBERTO [excitedly]: But that's, that's . . . you're referring to the school, and in the school it's another story entirely. In the school, you have friends that are all different kinds of students, from high and low society, but there are certain schoolfriends with whom you get together [here he lists the other three Juanitos] . . . then I also have friends from the secundaria that I won't see again after we leave school.

BL: Yeah, but that's why I'm saying, you guys may get along with everyone, from high society to low society, but even still, you best get along and most often get together with those who are more or less from the same economic standing [*situación*] as yourself, right?

ALBERTO: But I also get along well with all the rest!

In the original transcription, I noted that Alberto spoke this last phrase in a strong tone of protest, and the other two boys chimed in as well. I believe this reaction was consonant with the cultural premises of equality at ESF. Presumably, Antonio could never be more than a member of the group in school. Even though the boys acknowledged, in agreement with Alberto, that schoolfriends were different from after-school friends, they were not willing to endorse my final statement. They were not willing, in other words, to accept the sharper social distinction my observation suggested.

At this point, I diverted the conversation into the question of what constituted the rough urban machín style of dress and comportment. I asked with seemingly innocent provocation, again, which boys at ESF they might consider machín. The Juanitos together recounted Alberto's problems when first arriving at a public primary school, several years prior:

ALBERTO: Iván is machín. . . . I had a lot of problems before [at the nearby primaria] because of that, with Iván and with everyone else. . . . Because I came from a colegio, and they looked at me like I was a spoiled little kid [niño fresita], and I don't mean I was really well dressed, but more or less, you know what I mean? so they didn't like the way I looked, and all the time they were calling me little rich kid [riquillo].

ROBERTO: In other words, it made them mad.

ABEL: Envy [envidia].

ALBERTO: Envy, envy.

ROBERTO: They envied what [Alberto] had, how he was dressed, his way of acting, everything. He had a lot of problems because of that.

This short exchange reiterated what Alberto had already told me in another conversation (chapter 4), where he revealed his tendency to use tropes of equality to assuage class anger.

Then I returned the discussion to Antonio:

BL: So is Antonio machín?

ROBERTO: He's more Indian than machín [Es más indio que machín].

BL: OK, let's see, he just got done saying [Antonio's] more Indian than machín [loud nervous laughter from all three boys].

ALBERTO [breaking in]: The thing is that sometimes he talks with a little accent like, you know [Roberto and Abel are chuckling], "Yo tomí," and what else?

ABEL: "Yo saber."

ALBERTO: "Yo saber," and um . . .

ROBERTO: "Y que yo juí."

ALBERTO: "Y que yo juí," and "andábanos," and "comimos cominos" [more loud chuckles], and that's why we give him a hard time, and he is like half Apache, you know [está pues medio apache] . . . we don't like the way he looks [no le vemos bien] . . . and then he says, "We bought a Gol."

BL: A what?

ALBERTO: A Golf [a late-model Volkswagen sold in Mexico], but instead of saying Golf [with a hard "g"], he says Gol [with an aspirated "g"]. . . . Yeah, he says his brother-in-law's going to buy a Jetta [with an aspirated "j"—the correct pronunciation is a soft "j"] ... and with him a [Dodge] Phantom is a "Pantom," a [Nissan] Tsuru is a "Churu," ay no! [laughter].

Here the other two boys assisted Alberto, their most articulate and pungent spokesperson, in elaborating the distinctions that underlay their ambivalence toward Antonio and the whole cultural game of equality. Alternately, and in chauvinistic fashion, the Juanitos highlighted what they saw as Antonio's "Indian" appearance (apache in Mexico signifies savagism) and difficulties with standard Spanish. For the latter, they reenacted in some detail the kinds of errors—unconjugated or misconjugated verbs, misplaced accents, switched consonants—that Antonio supposedly committed while speaking. It was soon clear that the interview situation itself came to provide an occasion for relajo, hence outrageous exaggeration. I doubted, for instance, that Antonio had ever said something like "comimos cominos" (literally, "We ate cumin seeds"). Yet this discourse sequence still ended with a highly significant recounting of Antonio's alleged mispronunciation of late-model car names. While Antonio's newly acquired economic status permitted him to brag about his family's automobiles, the other Juanitos nevertheless made his lack of cultural capital painfully evident. They mocked his unfamiliarity with the cars' names and thereby sealed him off from full symbolic membership in the group.[5]

THE POTRILLOS

Although Iván considered himself its leader, the group known by some simply as *la banda de Iván* also dubbed itself the Potrillos ("little colts") after another key member, Benito, who was one of the swiftest runners in the school. As with the Juanitos, the Potrillos rarely used their own moniker, though they seemed gratified when others used it for them. In any case, with his size and charisma, Iván clearly formed the heart and soul of the Potrillos. Others supplied the brains, humor, or looks, as they themselves put it, but only Iván provided the protection.

Unlike the Juanitos, the boys comprising the Potrillos, all from 3C, came from more socioeconomically diverse backgrounds. Iván's family was solidly working class, and no member had ever studied beyond high school. Meanwhile, Matías's parents were both highly educated. His father, who had a Ph.D. in marine biology from a British university, and his mother, with a master's degree in chemistry, directed a local institute for fishing technology. Matías was an only child, and he had already developed a love for reading and discussing social issues. He was the most academically inclined of the Potrillos, and his clumsy frame offered amusement to the others, who were more athletically proficient. Yet Matías's often morbid sense of humor, his acknowledged role as the spark (*chispa*) for much of the group's antics, secured him the Potrillos's enduring affection. Andrés came from a local family of some means, near monopolists of the town's bicycle and moped trade. Benito's family maintained a modest trade in dried chilies and kept a large stall in the market. Finally, Valentino's parents both worked as schoolteachers.

While Andrés and Benito, like Iván, had several older and younger siblings, Valentino, rather more like Matías, had only recently acquired a newborn brother. Though their family's incomes and occupations placed them in a socioeconomic range from lower to upper middle, all the Potrillos but Valentino lived near the city center, and most expected to study at least to the university level. The Potrillos also ranged in age from thirteen to fifteen at the beginning of the 1990 school year. Teachers considered none of them a model student, but they all had different strengths. Matías, for example, could be found some afternoons in the public library, poring over old historical collections out of sheer interest. None of the other Potrillos would have been caught dead in the library, unless obligated. While teachers judged Andrés and Matías to be of exceptional intelligence, neither ever quite lived up to his academic potential.

These five boys formed the core of the Potrillos. What was it, then, that distinguished them from their classmates? The Juanitos had cited Iván and Benito as examples of machín students in the school, yet the Potrillos themselves, as mentioned in the last chapter, disparaged the so-called savage element in the small plaza. Though many acknowledged Iván's role as the group's protector, the Potrillos actually rejected some of the more rancorous kids who made bids for inclusion in their friendship group. The Potrillos shared many of the Juanitos's attitudes toward girls and youth from outside San Pablo. They, too, flaunted a double standard and made wisecracks about rural culture, though not nearly as frequently or viciously as the Juanitos. Importantly, the Potrillos did not share the same musical tastes. Iván and Matías expressed stronger preference for traditional music than the others, who had gone strictly modern. In the final analysis, what seemed to distinguish the Potrillos most from the other males in 3c was neither class, nor ethnicity, nor even age strictly speaking. Rather, the Potrillos stood out for their relative maturity, especially their propensity to flirt with girls.

I arrived at this conclusion after several months of observing a pretty clean split among the boys of 3C. During recess, the Potrillos roamed the school, seeking opportunities to flirt with girls from 3C and other grupos. Virtually all the other boys in 3C, with the exception of one or two, could be found regularly on a grassy knoll between two shop buildings, sitting quietly or occasionally wrestling and horsing around. I had thought at first that this split between 3C boys was due mostly to social class, until I realized the diversity among both the Potrillos and the group occupying the knoll. Then I had thought the split due mostly to age. Certainly, the boys on the knoll seemed younger on average. They tended to be smaller, less developed sexually, and less garrulous. Yet I discovered that their actual ages were just as diverse as among the Potrillos themselves.

It was then that I turned to asking them directly why they thought the split existed. The most resolute and illuminating response came from two boys, Gustavo and Fernando, whom I had already identified as emissaries between the two groups. In part because they also lived downtown, and in part because Iván's girlfriend was Fernando's older sister, these two boys obtained a kind of honorary status among the Potrillos. Still, they spent much of their time over on the knoll with the other 3C boys. Gustavo and Fernando attributed this distancing to the Potrillos's tendency to seek out romantically charged interactions with girls. As long as the Potrillos engaged in banter not directed toward sexual topics, Gustavo and Fernando were happy to join in. When the girls inevitably arrived to flirt with the Potrillos, throwing the kickball deliberately their way or sending out a coquettish salute, these temporary sidekicks retired. When I asked again why they thought this division existed in 3C, Gustavo and Fernando went straight to the heart of the matter:

GUSTAVO: The thing is that [the Potrillos] are older, and over here [on the knoll] we're younger and a little smaller . . . and they already play in a different way, while we still play like children.

BL: Like how do they play?

FERNANDO: I mean, they play basketball and we wrestle, or just a little something with a ball. And it's their way of thinking also, because if we say something to them, and they already think about things in a different way, they take it as a joke or a reason to laugh at us. . . . [T]hey're already more mature in terms of their thinking, and in terms of their bodies, too. They're just more mature, that's all.

GUSTAVO: More developed [*desarrollados*].

At this point, I suggested the split might also have something to do with social class, but like most other boys at ESF, Gustavo and Fernando vigorously rejected the idea. They admitted that Andrés could occasionally be sangrón (conceited) and that others in 3C, such as Javier, would sometimes make fun of their classmates who came from indigenous communities. Even so, they affirmed that most in the grupo were sencillos, that "we don't distinguish" ("*no hacemos discriminaciones*"). For these boys, as for the others in 3C that I interviewed, the perception of sexual maturity and serious interest in girls constituted an age-based division in the grupo. Fernando was actually older in age than either Andrés or Matías, yet he still perceived them as older, more mature. In this way, age and the display of heterosexual masculinity acted together to structure social attachments and provide one challenge to the ethic of grupo solidarity.

GENDERED SOCIAL DISTINCTIONS IN GRUPO 3B

Shifting friendship networks and ongoing tensions within grupo 3B illustrated a whole variety of ways in which student subjectivities might challenge the ethic of grupo solidarity and the cultural codes of equality in grupo identification. Here I highlight the way a few 3B girls from the cultural center managed potential conflicts through an ambivalent discursive practice.

Members of ESF's cultural center in 3B constantly pressed for parties, dances, and excursions, even knowing these might exclude those students who could not afford the expense or secure parental permission for such activities. Teachers often reminded the center students to take their poorer classmates into account when proposing activities, and they usually but reluctantly conceded. Some of the grupo's more magnanimous souls, like Leticia, would endorse such considerations, yet out of the teachers' earshot, many grumbled about their obligations to the less fortunate. It would be easy to attribute these and other tensions to a simple question of social class differences in the grupo escolar. Within 3B, however, there appeared to develop a kind of social and academic hierarchy structured by complex gender, class, and ethnic inflections of taste and so-called maturity. As among the Potrillos, age and perceived sexual maturity tended to divide the boys, though ethnicity, which I will demonstrate shortly, played more of a role here as well. Among the girls, meanwhile, class-ethnic differences in parenting and levels of sexual permissiveness seemed most determining of friendship networks and conflicts. The parents of many girls at ESF prohibited them from courtship, instructing their daughters to avoid all unnecessary contact with boys during the school day. This produced friction or, at best, indifference between the daughters of such "traditional" families (who tended to be of rural or lower-class origin), and those of more "liberal" or "modern" parents, who allowed—if not encouraged—their daughters to actively seek out "friendship" with boys at school.[6]

Girls of the cultural center, invariably daughters of more "modern" parents, manifested the greatest ambivalence about the presence of social difference in the grupo escolar. One day in mid-November, I ran into four of these girls walking home from school and invited them to an impromptu taped interview. Over the course of the next half hour, they clarified a great deal of what I had intuited about grupo dynamics until that point. I began by asking them about how they had seen their grupo change over the course of the three years they had been in the secundaria, and we eventually got around to how and why they considered 3B a unified grupo. I thought I understood them to be lamenting the divisions in their grupo, but they rallied to reject my interpretation:

MARINA: A lot of teachers have told us that ours is the most unified grupo, but also the most deficient [she gives the names of three teachers who have told them this].

GERTRUDIS: The truth is that we really are a very unified grupo. We all get along really well.

BL: But if you just got done telling me that [some don't get along well at all] . . .

GERTRUDIS [interrupting]: There are times when someone comes to school in a bad mood, and they take it out on everyone else [remata con todos]. That's when I'd say we don't get along. But when everyone is, you know, on their best behavior [todos están así en buen carácter], we work together really well [convivimos bien]. But the truth is that we have some problem in class almost every day. Every day.

LETICIA: No, but it's not exactly because they come in a bad mood; what happens is that some [grupo members] goof off too much, others are too serious, and so they clash. That's when the conflicts begin.

BL: Like which are those who are too serious, and those . . .

LETICIA: For example, the ones that are too serious, for example Roger, or a lot of the ones that are from the pueblitos, they feel inhibited, like really embarrassed [se sienten cohibidos, con mucha pena]. And Antonia, on the other hand, since she comes from a very, let's say, open family environment [*vive en un ambiente muy abierto*], she goofs off a lot, she tries to have some fun with the serious ones, and they clash.

I asked them here to mention a few more of the classmates that they considered most serious and most relaxed. Leticia began listing the names of three boys besides Roger, including Paco, and when Gertrudis realized what these boys had in common, she broke in:

GERTRUDIS: It's like they feel inferior to us [*se sienten menos*] just because they're from the pueblitos.

LETICIA: No, I don't think that's exactly it.

GERTRUDIS: Yes, because if you've noticed, when we're planning some gift exchange they just sit there staring at us, that's all, and it's like, yeah, we do feel bad not inviting them, you know? 'cause we don't want to make them feel below us [*para no hacerlos menos*]. But there are times, for example, when the whole group is having fun and they're sitting *over there*, and it's almost always the ones from outside San Pablo [whining tone of complaint].

Now I asked if there were any students from San Pablo proper who still felt like they weren't a part of the grupo, who didn't echar relajo with the rest of them. They discussed one girl who lived in San Pablo, but whose strict parents would only rarely let her out for some fun. Yet their solidarity with this girl, their attempts to include her in grupo activities, could be contrasted with the ambivalence expressed by Gertrudis and her friends just moments later in the interview:

GERTRUDIS: Look, the thing is that those who come from the pueblitos, the majority don't have the same tastes [gustos] as us. I mean, for example, they're very different from us in musical tastes, and in their clothing . . . in a lot of things, because we arrive at school in the morning squeaky clean [*llegamos hasta en la mañana rechinando de limpio*] . . . [nervous laughter] . . . yeah, with the soap coming out of us [*así nos sale jabón*] . . . [more laughter].

MARINA: And among themselves the ones from the pueblitos do get along really well, they get together a lot [*conviven mucho*].

FAVIOLA: But who knows why they don't want to talk much to us.

GERTRUDIS: It's like they think that if they say something, we're going to make fun of them because they're from outside [the city] [*nos vamos a burlar por ser de fuera*], and that we're going to feel superior to them.

But I think that in our grupo those differences don't exist; we treat everyone equally [*a todos los tomamos igual*].

In this section of the interview, Gertrudis finally and fully admitted some of the significant differences in gustos (tastes) that existed within 3B. The other three girls agreed with her, supporting her statements. Yet despite this cheery admission, a veiled insult immediately followed: Gertrudis's comment about her own group's "squeaky" cleanliness was meant to obliquely reference the contrasting dirtiness of those who came from the pueblitos. Gertrudis could thus indirectly express a common urban taunt. The girls then "managed" the implications of this assertion by first confirming and rationalizing the division of students in 3B (Marina says that the rural students hang out together a lot); then ascribing the division to the other students and not themselves (Faviola wonders innocently why the rural students won't initiate conversations with them); and finally accusing the rural students of unwarrantedly suspecting these girls of discrimination (Gertrudis wraps up the sequence by attributing to the rural students a misperception, and reaffirming the ethos of equality in the grupo). The discursive path that the girls jointly traced here—from an admission or even celebration of difference, to its denial or concealment—would be indecipherable were it not for an understanding of how school-based codes of equality exerted ideological force. Gertrudis's negative appraisal of village kids, rooted in her own urban subjectivity, required more oblique expression precisely because discourses on equality and solidarity sanctioned common identifications in the grupo. It is true that the 3B girls were busily constructing another view of otherness, and thereby contesting the premises of the cultural game of equality, yet the social voice of the school still exercised some influence here. The girls seemed genuinely disbelieving of their own complicity in cultural discrimination. Why did the rural students, after all, stand apart? Maybe it was because, at some level, they smelled a squeaky-clean lie.

The interview continued with a couple of the girls explaining why some of their urban female classmates formed their own insulated friendship groups and shied away from interaction with them. They carefully identified two or three occasionally shifting friendship groups among the girls, and these accorded with my own observations over the previous months. I had provisionally attributed the formation of these friendship groups to differences of social class and/or urban location (thinking the girls lived in poor outlying colonias, thus effectively barring them from participation in the cultural center), but when I suggested this in the interview, Leticia soundly rejected the notion:

LETICIA: They mostly live downtown; in fact, they live on some of the best streets downtown [*viven en un muy buen centro*]. . . . More than anything, I think [they stay apart] because their parents have ideas that are a little conservative, or maybe even very conservative [*muy conservadoras*], that for example they won't even let them out of the house.

The other girls fleshed this out:

FAVIOLA: The majority of them get scolded if they're talking with a boy, but I say it shouldn't matter at all that we're talking to a boy if he's our friend. But a lot of people do tend to think the worst; they think the boys are going to do something to their daughters. . . . I've noticed that because we like to have fun with the boys, and [those girls] move away from us when we do it [*nos gusta hacer relajo con los hombres y ellas se apartan de nosotras cuando platicamos con ellos*].

MARINA: They don't like the fact that some of us goof off in a way that's not too healthy, or natural [*les cae mal que hagan un tipo de relajo que ya no sea tan sano, tan natural*]. For example, they don't like it when Antonia and Silvia go off the deep end [*hacen un relajo demasiado fuerte*], like when they make comments that according to them shouldn't be brought up at our age [*no deberían surgir a nuestra edad*]. That's what they don't like. It even bothers us sometimes because it does go overboard [*A veces nos cae mal porque también como que rebasa*].

BL: Like what kinds of things do they say?

MARINA: For example, Antonia jokes around about sex. Sometimes she tells dirty jokes that are just too strong [*cuenta chistes de demasiado sexo, pero puros así fuertísimos*] . . . and everyone else cracks up, but those girls don't like it. We think sometimes maybe it's out of ignorance that they don't like it, but most likely it's because their parents are conservative and the girls have almost the same customs [as their parents], something like that. That's why sometimes they're a little distant from us.

Much like the Potrillos of 3C, the girls in this interview belonged to a wider group that included coed friendship and flirtation as a key dynamic. The fact that some 3B girls' parents prevented their involvement in this game, or that the girls themselves felt uncomfortable participating, created yet another social division, highlighted yet another difference, that challenged the cultural codes of equality. Most tellingly, the meanings of equality were projected in this case from the cultural center outward. The girls of the center could only wonder why other girls remained distant from them, whey they "moved away" from certain interactions. From their vantage point, equality required the so-called conservative girls to meet them in the center. They could not see how another view of equality might require their own travel out to the margins.

NEGOTIATING ETHNICITY AND THE RURAL DIVIDE: PACO AND FIDEL

Students from outside San Pablo, especially those from indigenous communities where the native language was still frequently spoken, developed different strategies for negotiating the social world at ESF. I learned that many of the students from pueblitos would stick together when they first arrived at the school. Often, these students would form a friendship network that cut across the organization of grupos escolares. The students might be from different villages, but they frequently took the same buses, using these occasions to have fun and talk. When one of these students would drop out, moreover, it was not uncommon for others in his or her clique to soon follow suit. The attrition rate was certainly higher for students living outside San Pablo.

One first-year boy who lived down my street had moved to San Pablo only recently, but his fellow students still thought he was indigenous, mentioning his physical appearance and lilting accent. Braulio clearly wanted to downplay his heritage. When I asked him if he spoke the local indigenous language, he paused for a moment and then said no. Several weeks later, I passed him on the sidewalk and overheard him speaking the language with his grandmother. Even though they had constructed an ample home in a middle colonia of San Pablo, Braulio's family continued to rely heavily on rural forms of subsistence. As I learned early in my stay, they kept numerous pigs on their small urban plot (breezy days carried the odor to my otherwise sheltered rooftop dwelling). Braulio would go to the local marketplace in the afternoons as they were breaking down the stalls, and then haul back bags and wheelbarrows full of vegetable waste to be used as feed for the pigs. I would often cross paths with him as he was making his daily run, and his demeanor would noticeably change. Rather than giving his usually friendly, though diffident, greeting, he would hurry past with a serious face, as if trying to remain invisible.

In school, it was a different story. Braulio seemed to take an active role in appropriating and promoting some of the latest trends in youth cultural commodities. Several days, I saw him toting a portable tape player that emitted loud music from some of the most recent U.S. and Mexican rock and rap bands. Several of his classmates would usually tag along as Braulio roamed the school yard, drawing attention to himself through the music. I must say the spectacle seemed rather incongruous. At recess time, I had grown accustomed to observing the first-year indigenous students huddled together in small groups toward the margins of the school grounds, chatting quietly or timidly observing the scene around them. Braulio, on the other hand, had managed to acquire and utilize one of the principal resources for acceptance in the cultural center: so-called modern music. He carried the tape player as though it were a badge of identity, an unequivocal statement about where and how he had decided to position himself within the social structure of the school.

I never spoke much with Braulio, so admittedly my interpretation here may be overly conjectural. However, I did get to know two other rural boys quite well: Paco and Fidel, both in 3B. During his first two years at ESF, Paco had remained mostly marginal to the life of his grupo. Paco, along with Fidel, skipped classes a lot and joined with other boys from outside San Pablo. Both boys said they had felt uncomfortable (*incómodos*) from their first days in school. Despite the proximity of their home villages to one another, however, Paco and Fidel did not become close friends within 3B. Fidel had arrived at ESF with five classmates from his village primaria, yet each had been placed in distinct grupos escolares. Nevertheless, the six boys reunited at every possible free moment, even cutting classes to do so. Paco formed a friendship group with several students from his own and other nearby villages, but not with Fidel's group. Then, when most of the other pueblito students had dropped out or switched schools, Paco and Fidel finally came together at the outset of their third year, in 1990. Observing them together much of the time, I naturally assumed that they had been close friends from the outset. It is significant that they first sought each other out in 1990 rather than develop closer ties to other San Pablo boys in 3B.

By their third year, most village-based students that remained in school made a more concerted effort to incorporate themselves into the social life of their respective grupos. This is what appears to have happened in the case of Paco, but not Fidel. Perhaps because his mother and older brother urged him to continue on to the preparatoria, Paco gradually reduced his commitments to Fidel and sought to strengthen other friendships within

3B. When I conducted a joint interview with them in November, the boys' fledgling friendship had already begun to weaken. Fidel, for his part, had become increasingly disaffected from the grupo and school. His father had died the previous year, and Fidel confided that he would rather spend his time in his home village. His older brothers, themselves secundaria dropouts, provided little incentive for him to continue. In the meantime, he was learning the trade of mask making from his uncle and knew that no secundaria certificate would be required for success in that endeavor. Just as Paco had begun his third year with a renewed sense of dedication to developing a schooled identity, Fidel had begun to question it altogether.

Paco's trajectory to his third year of secundaria had never been smooth. In his first year, he had almost failed a number of courses due to his penchant for playing hooky. Toward the beginning of his second year, Paco had temporarily transferred to the telesecundaria in his home village during the month-long teachers' strike at ESF. He might never have returned if the strike had gone on much longer, but his mother insisted. Then, Paco almost quit school after a run-in with the ESF principal, who suspended him one day for walking around school with an open shirt and no tie. Paco stuck it out, though, and by his final year of secundaria, he was clearly beginning to distinguish himself from other villagers as he became more integrated into the grupo. Most of his previous friends had since dropped out, and he was obliged to seek the guidance and camaraderie of his grupo mates. According to teacher accounts, his grades and attendance started to improve, although he could still be disruptive in class. His classmates noted that he had become more sociable. Paco also made use of his basketball skills, honed with the older boys on the central court of his home village, to become one of the grupo's premier players, thus garnering more prestige for himself. To the degree that he became comfortably incorporated into the grupo, he began to distance himself from some of the ideas and practices in his home village (except basketball!). In one telling conversation, Paco ridiculed typical village musical tastes, such as música ranchera. Paco instead extolled the virtues of contemporary rock and rap. These global-urban musical forms, dominant within the school, had more recently captured his imagination. Fidel, on the other hand, timidly yet steadfastly declared his preference for more traditional Mexican music.

Despite some of the contrary evidence that I have presented, negative talk about race and rurality was mostly muted within the school. Paco and

Fidel claimed they were never made to feel rejected as indios or rancheros. The way they told it, their earlier isolation had been a self-imposed choice to be with other students from the pueblitos who, according to them, had taken the mistaken path of truancy rather than hard work. Rather than belittling them, as I suggested during our chat, Paco and Fidel insisted that many in the grupo had tried to help them improve their grades and join the grupo's activities ("They helped us to stand out . . . to move forward in the grupo"; "*Nos ayudaban a que sobresaliéramos . . . a que nos fuéramos más adelante en el grupo*"). Some city students in 3B—girls mostly—even took it on themselves to give special assistance to village students. Fidel claimed that a girl named Gloria had single-handedly kept him afloat his first year:

> She's really nice to everyone. . . . In first grade, I finally started joining the grupo again—well, really all of us that had been skipping class—and she's the one who always helped me. Since we used to sit according to our roll number, she was number nine and I was number ten, so I sat behind her, and she would always pass me her homework . . . and I would say, "Gloria, look, how do you do this here?" or just, "I don't understand this," and she would tell me. I finished first year all right because she used to help me.

Paco and Fidel admitted that they had been rejected by some, but it was not for being indio or ranchero. Rather, it was for their lack of money or, more important still in their eyes, for playing hooky so often that they mocked grupo solidarity.

Why didn't Paco and Fidel sense the ambivalence behind these expressions of solidarity? Had they accepted the explanation, given by the 3B girls in the above section, that village-based students marginalized themselves in spite of other grupo members' gestures of acceptance? Had they internalized the discourse of adolescence and learned to blame their own personal weaknesses for the sense of marginalization that they had occasionally felt? Did most 3B members keep derogatory remarks out of earshot, or were Paco and Fidel merely reluctant to confess their struggles in the grupo to a snooping anthropologist, thereby rupturing the facade of grupo solidarity? Given the constraints of time and rapport, such questions must remain largely unanswered. Nevertheless, it was obvious to me that both boys had paid a price for being from the country.

The friendship groups that Paco and Fidel had formed their first two years, whether or not they recognized it fully, drew on ethnic and rural subjectivities not easily adapted to the reigning cultural center. While they attributed their initial discomfort in 3B to a vague sense of "not knowing anybody," the process of "getting to know" their grupo mates had been made considerably more difficult for them than the average city student. This was partly due to their relative isolation in distant villages, but it was also because the cultural center had been defined by urban mestizo tastes and subjectivities. By his final year, Paco had adopted such tastes and mastered such skills (basketball, rock music, and urban-slang Spanish). Along with his family's support, this adaptation allowed Paco to succeed socially and academically on the terms set by the grupo escolar. Fidel, meanwhile, was still more bound to village life and the prospect of mask making. In the absence of strong family support and personal desire, he remained more marginal to the symbolic center of grupo identity that 3B had constructed. He saw more clearly, perhaps, how grupo identification, even solidarity, implied a kind of homogenization, an accommodation to the center. Paco's evolving position in the cultural game of equality enabled elements of a new schooled identity to emerge, while Fidel's circumspection eventually defined his shortened school career.

THE PLAY OF GENDER IN THE CONFIGURATION OF DIFFERENCE

In chapter 3, I sketched out the gender practices constituting ESF's "gender regime," and in chapter 5, I did the same for households and families across San Pablo's varied intimate cultures. Here I examine the play of gender in student culture, where students' subjectivities constituted outside the school—in household relations, the church, the media, and so on—expressed themselves and occasionally took on new shapes inside the school's gender regime.

PLAYING WITH GENDER IDEOLOGIES

Something of the informal humor that pervades student life has already made its way into these pages. Nobody who works with teenagers in contemporary societies can miss the salience of humor as a mode of communication. Humor was the dominant communicative mode among secundaria students, and those students who learned to master the informal rules of humor stood a better chance of improving their social standing in the grupo escolar.[7] Likewise, teachers who engaged in classroom humor more easily gained both the attention and affection of their students (Levinson 1998b). Some teachers, in fact, used a brand of humor that brought out sexual and romantic tensions in the classroom. Mrs. Garfias often told gendered jokes or riddles that inspired hoots of nervous laughter from many students. She might even call out a boy and girl who were talking disruptively and suggest they were *novios* (a couple) to the delight of the grupo. Teachers also (hetero)sexualized interactions among themselves for the humorous benefit of the students. One day, Mrs. Garfias walked by a line of students waiting to be admitted into Mr. Cantú's room. She was nicely dressed this day, and as she passed, Mr. Cantú emerged from the classroom to salute her with a smile, an exaggeratedly loud, "*Buenos días, maestra,*" and a lingering gaze. Mrs. Garfias smiled coyly as many of the students let out a playful cry (a rising crescendo of "Oooooohh!") followed by laughter.

Yet humor held neither the same prominence nor the same meanings for all students. Boys' relationships hinged more on humor than girls', as they did for urban versus rural students. Few forms of humor were universally appreciated. Some might establish bonds of affection between teachers and students, or between all the students in a grupo escolar, but other forms could just as easily demarcate one friendship group from another. This was clearly the case for the Juanitos and the group of girls from 3B whom I presented earlier in the chapter. When the Juanitos made fun of Antonio's speech, they laughed heartily and unabashedly. Similarly, Gertrudis's comment about coming to school squeaky clean every day provoked a gale of laughter among her friends. In these instances, humor was enacted at the expense of another group of students. It seems obvious from these examples that humor often served to elaborate the identifications bonding a particular friendship group. Thus, jokes and wordplays were just as apt to reinforce social differences as to strengthen the ties of solidarity in the grupo.

It was also through humor that students most often negotiated the meanings of gender. Forms of humor that circulated in relatively closed friendship groups, such as the Juanitos, allowed students to perform, and thereby reinforce, certain components of their gender subjectivities. Among groups like the Juanitos, sexist banter formed the backbone of a hegemonic heterosexual masculinity (Levinson 1998a; see also Connell 1995). Yet in broadly public forms of humor, in social spaces such as the classroom or fiesta, the meanings of gender were more openly negotiated. It was in these contexts that students seemed to be trying on new gender subjectivities, often playfully challenging dominant gender ideologies. Humor could, as such, enact a playful gender politics through which students displayed and counterpoised the kinds of subjectivities formed in the family, school, and popular media. Such humor often experimented with the gender roles traditionally prescribed for heterosexual relationships and marriage.

In playful practice, students worked out their own orientations to such relationships. Here I will present just two brief examples. One rather simple kind of humor involved boys playfully asserting the male dominance encoded in long-standing gender roles and ideologies. I quote from my field notes taken during the latter half of a classroom session in the electricity shop:

> Many of the students in the shop have now gone outside or are wandering aimlessly around the room. I am sitting at the middle of a long table, mostly with a bunch of girls. At the end of the table, toward the door, there are about four boys. The girls are passing around a couple of magazines—one called *Notitas Musicales,* consisting mainly of short reports and photographs of popular musicians and teen idols; the other called *Quince a Veinte* (*Fifteen to Twenty*), a magazine for young women with fashion photos and tips, articles about sexuality, dating, and the like. I ask to view the latter magazine for a moment, kidding the girl who gives it to me, "Don't tell me you're already fifteen." "No." "Fine then, in that case I'm going to take it with me; you're not supposed to read it until you turn fifteen." The girl and her friends smile, not knowing if I'm serious (I'm not), and then she retorts, "It's really my mother's. She lent it to me." To which I respond, "And I suppose your mother is less than twenty-one [years old]? No way. I'm telling you I'm going to have to confiscate this." I leaf through the pages as the girls, now realizing my sarcasm, emit slightly mocking tones of protest. When the magazine's owner notices I've turned to an article about AIDS, she makes a statement on the topic to her teacher, who is standing nearby. Taking the cue, he launches into a short, authoritative account of how one can acquire AIDS, and two of the girls manage to tentatively interject a couple of things they know ("Hypodermic needles are really dangerous, aren't they?" "You can't get it from just hugging or shaking hands, right?"). The magazine owner also remarks that mothers can pass on the disease to their children. At this point, a small, impish boy further down the table who's been eavesdropping seizes the reference to "mothers" and interjects, "Women only know how to mop, sweep, and cook." The girls ignore him, so he repeats it a second

time. The three male friends around him are giggling, but the girls only shake their heads and direct them sharp glances of disapproval.

In this case, the boy, picking up on my own previous playful banter, made a rather lame attempt to interject relajo into a discussion that had turned quite serious. Yet his comment was really meant to knowingly perform a component of his masculinity, thereby consolidating his position among the surrounding boys. The boy obviously knew the regressive implications of his statement well before he made it. It was designed to energize his buddies and pique the girls. By asserting a traditional vision of male dominance and female domesticity, he playfully contested egalitarian aspects of the gender regime at ESF.

Periodically, ESF sponsored schoolwide fairs, called a kermés. At one kermés in late November, one grupo escolar diverged from the normal fare to sponsor a marriage booth (Registro Civil). Two girls from grupo 3E put themselves in charge of organizing this booth, and they enlisted the help of most of their female classmates. In the days leading up to the kermés, several girls were busily (and surreptitiously) typing up marriage certificates in their secretarial class. The marriage booth was undoubtedly the most popular at the kermés. It attracted a large and constant crowd, and cost only 500 pesos (about fifteen cents) to participate. Couples would arrive and fill out the Acta de Matrimonio (marriage certificate), exchange simple plastic rings, and then endure chants of "*Beso, beso, beso*" ("Kiss, kiss, kiss") from the gathering crowd. Sometimes they would even manage a feeble peck on the cheek to placate the onlookers. Meanwhile, well beyond the marriage booth, there was a quite active negotiation of possible marriages. Boys and girls alike ventured to "marry" the objects of their attraction, but often had to count on the good offices of a friend or cousin to broker the deal.

In her short story, "El Paraíso Perdido" ("Paradise Lost"), Mexican author Silvia Molina (1989) describes an occasion when she accompanies her young daughter to an elementary school kermés. Molina reconstructs the emerging consciousness of heterosexual affiliation and affection promoted by the children's Registro Civil. At ESF, however, the Registro Civil appeared to serve a more complex purpose. Aside from providing the excitement of allowing students to publicly display their affections (and heterosexual credentials), the booth also offered an ambivalent, subversive commentary on dominant gender relations in marriage. Especially the Acta de Matrimonio, composed by girls and recited by each prospective couple, both playfully challenged and contradictorily reinscribed dominant notions of proper gender roles in marriage—gender roles that largely crossed class and ethnic lines. On the following pages, I reproduce the original Acta exactly as it appeared, followed by a translation.

At first glance, it was obvious that girls had composed the Acta, for it represented a species of female fantasy. The "duties" of the husband and wife largely contradicted traditional conventions of gendered comportment and responsibility in the home. What made the Acta truly funny— and what made students laugh the most—was its ironic and outrageous reversal of dominant gender relations, especially the onerous requirements placed on men by both the husband and wife's duties. Husbands in this area of Mexico did not typically give their wives huge allowances or the opportunity to vacation while they themselves watched over the children. Nor did husbands normally complete household chores much less allow their wives an occasional lover. In the context of existing inequalities and double standards, the husband's duties stipulated by the Acta were rather revolutionary, indeed. Such stipulated duties, however, coexisted with more conventional ones. For instance, the wives' injunctions not to give the husband a divorce or allow him to deceive her were rather poignant yet sober observations of the (often legally sanctioned) imbalances favoring men in most Mexican marriages. On the other hand, duties number four and six required the woman to make her husband happy and give him some free time. These were fairly conventional demands that reflected, and perhaps even reinforced, Mexican marriage inequalities.

The Acta was thus a complex, contradictory document that in some respects playfully and humorously challenged dominant gender ideologies, and in other respects upheld them. Students staged the humor of the Acta as an opportunity for relajo, thereby announcing their awareness of dominant gender conceptions and attempting to articulate the alternatives. Yet the very occasion for the humor, a mock marriage ceremony, granted the status of heterosexual marriage as the proper paradigm for gender relations. Moreover, some elements of the marriage certificate contradicted the liberatory potential of its own humor and irony, validating more traditional arrangements of female subordination.

THE MASCULINE PREROGATIVE IN LEADERSHIP

While girls in fact took on many of the leadership roles in the grupo escolar and elsewhere, they often had to manage the implications of crossing gender lines and taking on the masculine attitude associated with leader-

ACTA DE MATRIMONIO

Hoy lunes _____ de noviembre de 1990. Contraen matrimonio _____

_____ y _____

DEBERES DEL ESPOSO

1. Querer, amar y respetar a su esposa.
2. Darle por lo menos $500,000 pesos a la semana.
3. Cuidar a los niños mientras ella pasea.
4. Hacer el aseo de la casa y la comida.
5. Dejarle tener por lo menos un amante.

DEBERES DE DE [*sic*] ESPOSA

1. Querer, amar y no serle muy fiel a su esposo.
2. No dejar solo a su esposo tanto tiempo.
3. Nunca darle el divorcio.
4. Hacerlo muy feliz.
5. No dejar que la engañe.
6. Darle por lo menos un día libre a su esposo a la semana.

TESTIGOS DE LA ESPOSA

_____

_____

TESTIGOS DEL ESPOSO

_____

ship. Girls on the whole showed themselves to be just as competent and assertive in school activities, but more than boys, they ran the risk of being accused of standing out from the group, or being tagged by boys as a *marimacha* (tomboy, "macho" woman). As we have seen, students who were singled out by their classmates as arrogant (fachosa), specifically for their manner of presenting themselves in class, were almost invariably girls. Often with their mothers' encouragement, girls saw schooling as a route to escape and independence from the oppressive gender relations of family and home. They sought to excel accordingly, and this might require some self-promotion.

The qualities of leadership that students generally admired did not

218   We Are All Equal

MARRIAGE CERTIFICATE

Today, Monday the _____ of November, 1990, _____

and _____ agree to enter into marriage.

DUTIES OF THE HUSBAND

1. To love, honor, and respect his wife.
2. To give his wife at least 500,000 pesos ($160) a week.
3. To take care of the children while she goes for a stroll
   [*pasear* can also mean a "drive" or "trip"].
4. To clean house and make lunch.
5. To let her have at least one lover.

DUTIES OF THE WIFE

1. To love, honor, and not be very faithful to her husband.
2. To not leave her husband alone for very much time.
3. To never give him a divorce.
4. To make him very happy.
5. To not let him deceive her.
6. To give her husband at least one free day a week.

WIFE'S WITNESSES

_____

_____

HUSBAND'S WITNESSES

_____

_____

include this kind of self-serving promotion. In occasional discussions, I asked students what qualities a leader should have, and whether they thought a girl or boy was more suitable for such leadership. According to them, leadership in the school context demanded, on the one hand, discipline and orderliness (seen largely as the special quality of women, at least at this age), and on the other, fairness and forcefulness (seen largely as the province of men). Interestingly, girls promoted their sex more than boys in these discussions. They argued that girls were morally superior, and given this, better suited for leadership roles in the secundaria. They tended to complain about leaders (mostly boys, but sometimes girls) who could not discharge their functions with sufficient discipline or fairness. Boys, for their part, often admitted that the best leaders in their grupo had been girls, yet they might complain about leaders (mostly girls, but sometimes boys) who could not fulfill the need for initiative and force.

In other ways, too, students revealed the subtly gendered criteria by which they judged qualities of leadership. In the 1990 election for student body president discussed earlier, Iván, head of the white planilla, beat out two other planillas headed by girls. Iván did not meet the criteria of good academic and social standing required to run; yet because of pressure from classmates, the principal eventually decided to let him be a candidate. Most students I spoke with agreed that Iván had won because of a uniquely gendered campaign strategy: an older and popular boy with a reputation as a good street fighter and fearless "protector of the people" (*bravucón del pueblo*), Iván had drawn on his aura of masculine vigor to convince students he would confront the authority of the principal and push through a number of student demands. His two female opponents, in the meantime, had been put forward on the basis of their general amiability, good records of discipline, and academic achievement. In comparison to Iván, they appeared to offer only the same kind of weak, deferring leadership the students had known in the past. Iván won the election, in large part, because he exuded the confidence and force judged necessary to advance student rights and demands.

Furthermore, the boys themselves, while they publicly endorsed girls' rights to serve in various leadership roles, would privately confide to me their reservations. In casual contexts with boys, I often heard them argue that girls were unfit to serve as student body president, carry the flag during parades, or otherwise fulfill leadership roles where masculine force was needed. The boys sometimes made reference to the all-male principalship of the school, and articulated a vision of masculine force as necessary to get the really tough jobs done. As Iván himself put it rather succinctly in assessing his chances for the presidency: "I'm *going* to win. . . . I'm up against two women, and everyone knows that the women won't be able to organize dances well, they won't be able to do much of anything."

ROMANCE, MARRIAGE, AND THE PRODUCTION OF SOCIAL DISTINCTIONS AMONG GIRLS

On any given day, I always knew I could find Andrea's friendship group (from 3A) over behind the drafting building at recess time. Rosita's group (3C) similarly occupied the grassy knoll between carpentry and classroom two, which they shared with the younger 3C boys (see figure 2). By contrast, Leticia's group of friends from 3B, some of whom were briefly introduced in the last chapter, often roamed the school grounds. They did not claim any single spot, choosing instead to flirt with different groups of boys, hit a volleyball around, buy various snack items, and occasionally ditch school altogether in search of a little adventure or some food not available at ESF. Meanwhile, Nidia's (3F) small group of three or four girls could usually be found far from the normal recess hubbub. After buying snacks, they typically migrated back to an area close to the classrooms, often entering the classrooms themselves to eat and chat.

I highlight these four friendship groups because they included some of the focal girls with whom I most frequently interacted. Moreover, my own unique relationship with each friendship group, and the particular girls in them, gave me an interpretive window onto the reasons for how and why gendered social distinctions were produced, maintained, or even accentuated. Not all these groups were equally stable and bounded. They seemed to have a core membership around which different constellations of girls would attach themselves for different periods of time, perhaps a few days, perhaps a few months. Nidia and Andrea's groups generally stayed intact throughout the year, though Andrea herself eventually dropped out. Leticia and Rosita's groups were more fluid. By the middle of the school year, both Leticia and Rosita were spending more time in smaller dyads or triads, and "visiting" across several different friendship groups. Nor were these girls' groups organized principally around the pursuit of romance. They were, in part, distinguished from one another by the degree and quality of their engagement in the burgeoning world of heterosexual romance. Most important, and in contrast to the jokes and roughhousing that prevailed among the boys, these girls spent a lot of time talking about their "problems," as they put it. To varying degrees in each of the friendship groups, these problems included relations with boys and struggles with parents over the right to pursue romance.

Most of the girls in Andrea's group got mediocre grades, at best, in school. During the time I spent most with them (November–December 1990), they were all fourteen years old, except for two who had just turned fifteen. Andrea's group was somewhat unusual in the relative uniformity of the girls' academic standing. As I've noted, friendship groups typically coalesced around varying tastes and subjectivities, and often included students with rather different kinds of school achievement and orientation. This was not true for Andrea's group. In fact, by the middle of the school year, the only two girls who had maintained higher grades and developed strong career aspirations eventually split off from the group and formed their own dyad.

What Andrea's group also seemed to share was a common orientation to romance and sexuality rooted in their lower-class experience and subjectivity. Several of the girls claimed to have steady boyfriends who were hard workers, as they liked to emphasize. Their view of relations with these boys, and men in general, had a distinctly guarded, practical quality—a result, I surmised, of these girls' greater exposure to alcoholism, underemployment, abuse, or abandonment. Andrea had already hinted at such experience herself when I was negotiating our first interview. At that time, she insisted we chat well in view of other adults because she had seen what men could do to unsuspecting girls. Other members of Andrea's friendship group eyed me suspiciously my first month in the school, and I learned later that few of their fathers still lived at home.

In a series of recess chats, a rather telling picture of this group's outlook on romance and gender relations emerged. I have already presented a part of these conversations in chapter 5, where these girls discussed their aversion to the boys in the plaza chica. That exchange was punctuated by numerous outbursts of nervous laughter and disagreements about certain details, but some kind of consensus was almost always orchestrated around my questions. When I asked the group how a man should be, they responded mostly with a series of negatives. First and foremost, they agreed, he should not drink too much or have other vices; he should be a hard worker; and above all, he should not be a womanizer (*mujeriego*), even though as Gisela resignedly put it, "All men are big womanizers, no?" ("*¿Todos son bien mujeriegos, verdad?*"). Did they think much about getting married, and if so, at what age? After Edna said they might not even get married, and I asked why not, Gisela commented sardonically, "Because they say that's how the world ends for you" ("*Porque dicen que así se va a acabar el mundo*"). After I tried to press them on this question and they waffled, saying that sometimes they felt like getting married and other times no, I tried a different angle:

> BL: What would appeal to you about getting married? What would be good about getting married? [lots of laughter].
> CLARISA: Well, the husband, right? [more laughter].
> GISELA: To form a family, right?
> BL: So that interests all of you? Having a family?
> EDNA: I'd say so.

CLARISA: I say it's nice to get married as long as the man fulfills his obligations [*siempre y cuando el hombre te cumpla*], you know?

GISELA: Honest and hardworking.

CLARISA: Honest and everything, and a hard worker, and that he provides all the necessities, the food and everything, in other words, that he gets everything for the family [*les arrime todo*].

CONCHA: Even if it's just so you can eat beans [*Siquiera para que comas frijoles*].

CLARISA: Every day.

FÁTIMA: Even if he were poor, if he's honest then it would be enough to eat beans [*aunque sea pobre pero honrado, bastaría de comer frijoles*].

CLARISA: As long as he's not arrogant [*arrogante*] or anything.

CONCHA: Yeah. Or a crook [*ratero*].

EDNA: Because sometimes there are some who go, for example some say, "Ajá, that guy has money so I'm going to throw myself at him," right? and I say what do they gain if he's rich, but then there are nothing but punches? I mean, they beat them and don't feed them well [*Qué se ganan que sea rico y todo si nomás hay trancazos? O sea, les pegan y las tienen mal comidas*]. . . . The thing is that some people get married because they're interested in the money, without loving, without there being any love or anything [*se casan sin querer, sin que haya pues amor ni nada*].

CLARISA: Well, as for me, I'm not like that.

FÁTIMA: Ay, well I'm not either.

CONCHA: Ay, me neither.

EDNA: I don't like to be like that.

ANDREA: Ah, me neither, me neither.

EDNA: If I have money, that's fine, if not, that's okay, too.

CLARISA: If I get married, as long as . . .

CONCHA: You can eat beans.

CLARISA: As long as I eat beans, that's enough [*Conque coma frijoles y ya*].

FÁTIMA: As long as one doesn't die of hunger [*Conque uno no muera de hambre*].

CLARISA: As long as [my husband] doesn't go around with different women . . . and he doesn't get drunk [*Conque él no ande así con mujeres ni nada, y que no sea borracho*].

I have reproduced this remarkable exchange at some length because it shows the kind of alternating tension and collaboration in constructing a common group position. Certainly, the girls dramatically brought forth irony and contradiction, perhaps even exaggeration, in their account, especially toward the end where they articulated a rather ascetic vision of marriage. Still, there were no clues in their tone or gesture to indicate they were deliberately putting me on, even if they had a little relajo at my expense. In contrast to the romantic dreams of other girls, this group advanced a rather practical view of marriage and courtship. Their expectations for romantic fulfillment were exceedingly modest. To be sure, they chided any girl who would pursue a marriage for money and not love. Yet just what this "love" might entail never became apparent, even after further questioning. In effect, the girls voiced a class-based critique of "rich" men who didn't work, got drunk, and abused their wives. Most strikingly, at different moments Andrea's group expressed a survivalist approach to marriage (what I came to consider the "beans-as-bottom-line approach"). The emphasis on beans, perhaps the most basic and modest of Mexican foods, signified the contrast between working-class simplicity and honesty, and the dangerous arrogance of wealth.

Other interactions with these girls provided further evidence for this view. On the second day of four consecutive recess chats, I asked the girls what they had been talking about before I arrived. They told me that they had been discussing what life might be like "*por allí*"—in the United States. None of them had ever crossed the border, but several had close relatives, even fathers, who had lived or were presently living there. Concha's family was making plans to take her there after she completed secundaria. When I asked if they had reached any conclusions about the United States, Gisela responded that it would be both better and worse in some respects. It would be worse, she said, because there are so many drug addicts "and all that." On the other hand, it would be better because "the women have advantages" ("*las mujeres tienen preferencia*"). I asked for clarification. "Well, for instance, I've heard that the government helps out the women who've been left by their men." In light of the conversation above, it seemed to me significant that of all the positive points about life in the United States that they could have mentioned, the girls chose the system of welfare support for abandoned women. On balance, the girls' aspirations for marriage, as well as their interpretation of gender relations, betrayed an uneasy assimilation of themes in the popular media (the importance of romantic love) to their more practical experience of gender subordination in a lower-class intimate culture.

Tellingly, the girls in Andrea's group also rejected boys from the morning shift of ESF as possible romantic partners. When I asked why these boys didn't attract them, they first proclaimed, in unison, that the ones in the afternoon shift were more handsome than those in the morning (they had obviously arrived at this assessment much earlier). "Only because they're more handsome?" I queried, incredulous. "There aren't even a few handsome ones in the morning?" Clarisa responded, "Some of them are really stuck-up, they think too much of themselves, as if they were the only ones around [*se creen bien harto como si nomás ellos fueran*]." Concha then chimed in, "Lazybones, lazybones! [*güevones*]," and Gisela concluded, "They don't work or anything." The generally poorer yet maturer profile of the afternoon students probably made them more attractive to the girls, who valued hard work over "lazy" and arrogant class pretensions. While these girls plainly valued schooling, and continued to demarcate themselves from the unschooled (recall their criticism of Andrea in chapter 5 for her dropout boyfriend), they were drawn toward boys who had completed secundaria or still worked during the day and studied afternoons. Choosing these boys as their objects of attraction appeared to reconcile their positive valuation of schooling with a class-based work ethic. It also provided them a valuable shield to parry the occasional snobbery of the girls in the cultural center.

Of the three other girls' groups I mentioned at the outset of this section, Nidia's from 3F came closest to Andrea's in its attitude toward gender relations and romance. Rosita's group from 3C, and Leticia's from 3B, on the other hand, expressed the sentiments more common to the girls of the cultural center. It was certainly no coincidence that Rosita and Leticia's groups attended the same parties and even chatted at school events, while interacting little with groups such as Andrea's. The contrast between such groups was instructive. Expressed orientations to gender relations in Rosita's group, for instance, emphasized different aspects of marriage and romance, including more egalitarian arrangements in the home. Echoing some of the concerns displayed in the Acta de Matrimonio, the girls from Rosita's group told me that they thought a husband should, above all, respect and love his wife, "understand her [*comprenderla*] and help her if she has any problems." In response to the same question that I posed to Andrea's group, the girls in Rosita's group agreed that a man should be "sincere and straightforward. . . . [H]is looks don't matter so much as his feelings, his inner beauty [*belleza interior*]." Rosita's group seemed less concerned about finding a man who would "put food on the table" or avoid alcohol; they were looking for a sensitive partner in romance and marriage. Such a sensitive partner included one who could communicate his feelings and share in the woman's "problems." Partners in a marriage, they said, should also "treat each other equally." If not, the woman should always "defend her interests" in the relationship ["*defender sus intereses ante el hombre*"].

The differences between the friendship groups mostly reflected class differences in gender experience and educational outlook. Their differential valuation of masculinities—loyal, honest, and hardworking, versus thoughtful, communicative, and affectionate—revealed significant social distinctions. While the girls in Rosita's group mostly had aspirations to study a professional career at a university, those in Andrea's group planned to pursue careers as clothing designers, hairstylists, secretaries, or preschool teachers—all highly feminized jobs requiring no more than two or three years of further study beyond the secundaria. There was actually relatively little difference in the socioeconomic status of these girls' groups. None of the parents in Rosita's group had ever studied at a university, and few had appreciably more resources than most of the parents in Andrea's group. The difference lay in two key factors: the upwardly mobile intimate cultures into which the families of Rosita's group had inserted themselves, and more important, the position each group of girls adopted vis-à-vis the game of equality and assumptions of the cultural center.

An expanded treatment of the relations between different girls' friendship groups would be necessary to document this point more fully, yet I wish to move on to a related set of issues. If different orientations to marriage and romance helped reinforce one set of distinctions among ESF girls, so too did the varied interpretation and discursive construction of female sexuality. I have already presented evidence of tensions between girls around involvement with boys and the expression of sexuality (even through "strong" jokes) in the school. In this aspect of student culture, social distinctions of class, ethnicity, and family background were accentuated, thus making common identification more difficult.

As the social studies teachers suggested in the conversation that opens this chapter, upper-class girls' ability to cross class and ethnic lines in forming friendships was more strongly circumscribed by parental sanction. While I observed few "bourgeois" friendship groups among the girls in my year of research, I did note that age seemed to be a much less salient consideration in girls' friendships than among the boys. In other words, girls formed close and lasting friendships more often across age (and grade) differences, while boys crossed ethnic and class lines more easily than age. This difference seemed largely due to the family-based socialization both teachers described in the conversation. Families of long-standing wealth, especially, tended to socialize girls' habitus to maintain status distinctions as well as to uphold the family name and honor. Yet other, equally wealthy parents had acquired their money more recently and through different means. These parents were less likely to guard their children from such contact; indeed, they were much more inclined to send their children to public schools precisely for the social mixing it afforded.

If lower-class and village girls kept themselves apart, on the other hand, it was due more to gender than class or ethnicity per se. Their parents and intimate cultures socialized a modest and retreating demeanor; they generally sought to control the girls' sexuality and limit their contacts with boys. Families from the outlying pueblos were especially conservative in this regard. Rural Indians and mestizos alike seemed determined to shield their daughters from what they perceived as the rather brazen conduct of city girls. If conservative or traditional families (as the girls themselves labeled them) guarded their daughters from the so-called liberal tendencies in the school, even those families considered most liberal would occasionally intervene to steer their daughters away from negative—especially sexual—influences. It was not uncommon for mothers (and even some fathers) to appear at the school and enlist teachers in efforts to keep their daughters separated from flirting boys or fickle girls.[8]

Discourses and practices around romance and sexuality fundamentally constructed girls' bodies as objects of boys' attraction, and this divided girls' loyalties and sympathies in ways that were not true for the boys. While the school's discursive emphasis on solidarity could powerfully mobilize girls to submerge their individual or factional interests for the benefit of the grupo escolar, instances of cooperation and solidarity between girls were in fact relatively rare.[9] More often than not, girls came together within their smaller friendship groups to press claims against teachers, organize student events, or negotiate assignments. However, these friendship groups often developed mutual antipathies toward one another, as we have already seen. Ironically, boys were fond of pointing out that girls "naturally" squabbled, especially over romantic rights to boys. In 3A, for instance, several boys enthusiastically appropriated Mr. Cantú's sexist wordplay and went around calling a group of girls the UVA, or Unión de Viejas Argüenderas (Group of Old Gossips; *uva* also means "grape" in Spanish). In the boys' view, girls' tendency to gossip created the conditions for regular infighting. Girls from outside San Pablo, moreover, carried a double stigma, for the prevailing urban image of insular rural life characterized the pueblitos as particularly fertile breeding grounds for gossip. By basing their interpretation on a naturalized gender ideology, and then compounding it with a stereotypical image of village life, ESF boys avoided facing their own complicity in a system of gender relations that compelled girls to compete for boys' affections.

As might be expected, girls were more subject to parents' censure than boys. Boys were allowed, indeed expected, to pursue their sexual impulses as they developed in adolescence. They were seen as more independent, volatile, and difficult to control. Girls, in contrast, were supposed to be modest. The dominant gender ideology stipulated that women should restrain their sexual impulses and concentrate on the appropriate domestic (or school) tasks at hand. While this gender ideology retained a strong hold on students, it was also contested in a number of ways. The subjective basis for such contestation often formed outside the school itself. The growth of a more significant professional class in San Pablo, and a rise in the number of adults who had migrated seasonally to the United States, had by the 1980s led to more permissive parenting practices and a relaxation of the control over daughters' sexuality. Furthermore, students' increased consumption of television, movie videos, rock music, and teen magazines—cultural commodities that tended to portray heterosexual romance in more democratic terms—had encouraged the reconfiguration of traditional gender roles and provided girls with resources for more active participation in the courtship process.[10] Within the school, then, one could see a wide range of orientations toward romance and sexuality, and a corresponding spectrum of masculinities and femininities. Some girls maintained their distance from boys and dedicated themselves entirely to schoolwork, mostly following parental dictates. Others actively sought interactions with boys, even flaunting their sexuality in flirtatious gestures and suggestive repartee. As one teacher who worked summers in the United States told me in the presence of the latter, "Some of our female students are very liberal, like American [U.S.] women" ("*Algunas de nuestras alumnas son muy liberales, así como las americanas*").[11]

Most important, students themselves undertook to police and manage the expression of sexuality in the school. Girls in the cultural center helped to define a kind of normative standard around questions of romance and sexuality. They were active in promoting romantic themes and interactions with boys, yet they patrolled the boundaries of acceptable expressions of sexuality and romantic interest. Poorer and rural girls shied away from the supposedly liberal practices of the cultural center, which included talking to boys, dressing in jeans, and dancing suggestively to rock music. Center girls tended to deride or ignore the girls who eschewed such practices. Yet the center students, in turn, stigmatized other urban girls for being fickle, promiscuous, or overly permissive in their relations with boys—for transgressing, in other words, the boundaries of acceptable expressions of sexuality and romantic interest.[12] In one case, two girls in 3B broke off their friendship with Mónica because, according to them, she was too boy crazy (*noviera*), and would go quickly from one boy to another, daring to kiss them ("*Se besaba con un chavo y se besaba con otro*"). In 3C, a number of girls distanced themselves from Alejandra, who at sixteen was much older than the norm and perhaps unjustly considered sexually precocious. In a private chat with me, Alejandra, in turn, defended herself against the charges and accused Inés of the same behavior:

> Reyna [the jefa de grupo] saw that all the boys in the grupo were grabbing Inés and everything, and Inés wasn't telling them anything [that is, complaining], so Reyna told us, "Look, don't hang out with Inés because you're gonna start getting burned" ["*No se junten con ella porque luego se van a quemar*"].

I asked Alejandra what she meant by getting burned, and she said that others would think of you in the same terms. To spend time with a provocative Inés was to risk guilt by association.

Two other girls in 3C, Rosita and her friend Guillermina, confirmed this impression. I noted that Rosita's friendship group had been reconfigured by the end of the school year. Rosita and Guillermina no longer joined the other 3C girls by the carpentry shop. Now they tended to roam the school grounds at recess. When I asked them why they didn't associate with the other girls anymore, Guillermina did most of the talking, with Rosita nodding her head:

> GUILLERMINA: The thing is they really are too much; sometimes they use a lot of vulgarities, with their bad words and everything [*Es que de veras son bien llevadas, a veces dicen muchas groserías, con sus palabrotas y todo*].
>
> BL: Are all of them like that?
>
> GUILLERMINA: Not all of them, but Inés, Silvia, Kati, and Patricia, those ones yes, they're the ones who get too carried away with the guys, and that doesn't sit well with us [*son las que se dejan llevar con los*

hombres, y eso no nos parece]. . . . Also, we don't like to be in the middle of so much gossip. We're neither little saints nor big goof-offs [*no somos ni santitas ni muy relajas*]; sure, we like to echar relajo and everything, but in another way. . . . And Vivian is a big gossip, a busybody, she sticks her nose in things that are none of her business, and Virginia, ooohhh! where does she *not* go to tell her gossip?

This exchange was fascinating for the way it defined the normative center ("*ni santitas ni muy relajas*"). Guillermina and Rosita were navigating a middle ground between the *santitas*—literally "little saints," and a code for the girls of more conservative families who kept mostly to themselves—and *relajas*—a code for the girls who overstepped the bounds of appropriate interest in boys and self-expression. Of note, too, was the way Rosita and Guillermina combined a condemnation of the girls' excessive interest in boys with their tendency to gossip. Rosita and Guillermina did not claim their friends' gossiping was natural or inevitable—like many of the ESF boys did. Rather, they saw it as somehow related to the girls' excessive interest in boys. Girls who allegedly gossiped were often the same girls who used vulgarities and got "carried away" with the boys.

The normative center of proper female behavior was also constructed in contrast to gender practices in other regions and schools. Indeed, given the enduring Catholic conservatism of the San Pablo region, some ESF girls' modest challenges to traditional gender roles could be seen as relatively tame compared to changes in other areas of Mexico. Certainly that's how a number of the girls themselves saw it. In March 1991, I accompanied a group of student athletes to the state track and field championships in a large city several hours from San Pablo. I would say that more than half of these students could be located in what I have been calling ESF's cultural center. We first arrived at a working-class secundaria federal, and for more than an hour, the ESF students mingled with their counterparts. Many of the teachers at this school were on strike, and few classes were actually in session, so the local students roamed the school grounds, playing or chatting. When they saw our contingent of some forty students arrive, many of them gravitated toward us. Several of the ESF girls were taken aback by the amount of makeup their counterparts were allowed to wear, and by their brazen manner of approaching the ESF boys. Nita, a precocious ESF first grader who sometimes endured accusations of flirting too much with boys, pointed at them and commented, "Do these seem like schoolgirls [*alumnas*] to you? They don't seem like it to me." Moments later, a large, rambunctious circle formed outside the school offices, and two of the more adventurous girls from ESF started rap dancing to the latest tune by Vanilla Ice. This rap dance included a good deal of hip swaying and other sexually suggestive movements. Very quickly, boys from the host school jumped in the circle and joined in the dance, with equally suggestive movements, while their classmates howled and egged them on. The ESF girls seemed completely unprepared for this. Their faces expressed concern as they moderated their movements. An ESF teacher, on seeing how agitated the crowd had become, intervened to stop the dance, much to the girls' apparent relief. When I caught up with the dancers later, they shook their heads in disbelief, and one of them ventured, "They really are a little wild here" ["*De veras que son bien loquillos aquí*"].

On another occasion, Matilde had just arrived from a family trip to Mexico City. I considered her among the more actively involved in the pursuit of romance since she spent a great deal of time attempting to win over a particular boy in her grupo and frequently wrote love poems in a spiral-bound notebook. Certainly, she could be placed in or near the cultural center. When Matilde and I met at a small party just after her trip, she commented on how wild the students were at a comparable party in Mexico City: "They have another way of thinking, they're more liberal. . . . Gosh, I saw them doing some things that just didn't seem right to me for kids of that age." What had bothered her most was the boundless use of alcohol, cigarettes, and drugs, as well as the unashamed (*descarada*) display of attraction and affection—open kissing and petting, and most of all, girls' rather revealing dresses.

In short, the cultural center girls tended to occupy a kind of gatekeeper position at ESF in large part because their moderation most closely corresponded to the school's gender regime. Most teachers tolerated, even playfully encouraged, heterosexual romance, as long as it did not interfere with their pedagogical mission. Moreover, at least one of the center girls' parents was usually still a sexual conservative, and exercised considerable force in their daughters' lives.[13] Through mutual avoidance and stigmatization, therefore, ESF girls enacted the differences posed by sexual maturity and conduct. Using the resources of discursive labeling (relajas, santitas, *llevadas, quemadas, loquillas*) and social distancing, schoolgirls constructed meanings about appropriate sexuality and romantic engagement. In this fashion, social distances between girls were culturally produced and reproduced around symbolic distinctions not completely reducible to class or ethnicity.[14]

At ESF, historical promises of gender equity were perhaps most seriously challenged in the student culture. The relatively progressive components of the local gender regime, given greater force by female teachers historically empowered by the State (Vaughan 1994, 118), were nonetheless subject to students' appropriations. Ironically, many student practices tended to produce or exacerbate social divisions between the girls themselves. This process reinforced the split between children of different intimate cultures. The peer-based system of gender relations provided an important arena for girls to work out conflicts and positions in their respective families concerning sexuality, marriage, work, future studies, and a possible career. Given this, the position they negotiated for themselves in the peer system of gender relations either challenged or reinforced their position vis-à-vis gendered tasks, responsibilities, and expectations at home.

Moreover, assumptions of hierarchy embedded in gender ideologies often disrupted school-based practices of equality. While teachers generally primed boys and girls alike for leadership roles, the quality of leadership was actually a contested matter in which deeply entrenched and naturalized notions of masculine power and force usually held sway. Young women often appeared to negotiate away their own leadership rights in exchange for endorsing a "good patriarch" who might best represent the interests of the grupo escolar (Mallon 1994, 19; see also Stern 1995). Humor and playful commentary also provided a discursive arena where students could challenge, modify, or reinstate dominant constructions of gender.

The strategic practice involved in the play of gender at ESF could thus have serious consequences for all involved. In fact, given the horizons apparently opened up by secundaria study, it surprised me that more girls didn't move toward the cultural center and "playfully" challenge the limitations their families placed on them. Even for so-called traditional girls, the secundaria offered a freedom greater than any they would likely encounter again. The relative insulation of peer group activity coupled with the discourse of adolescence allowed most to stay in the public sphere for longer periods of time than either younger girls or adult women. Given the few opportunities for women's independent public life in San Pablo, the spectacle of secundaria girls roving the streets in small groups was remarkable, indeed. As they grew older, women who no longer studied or developed a professional career were likely to find themselves increasingly cloistered in the house. Most ESF girls acknowledged their desire to have children, and even those with professional aspirations confessed it might always be the woman's role to take primary domestic responsibility.

I couldn't help but agree with Leticia when, in the notebook she kept, she sounded a note of frustration that some of her female classmates would not be able to continue their studies beyond secundaria:

> In the case of this one girl, she wants to keep studying and I think she's quite capable, but her parents won't allow it. What a drag [*Qué mala onda*]! Even though she's resigned to her parents' will, this [situation] just shouldn't be. She doesn't take it this way, but I think she won't be able to develop herself and show what she's capable of, and above all, she won't be able to become who she wants to be [*no podrá desenvolverse y demostrar de lo que es capaz, y sobre todo realizarse a su manera*].

It is interesting to observe amid Leticia's indignation that the girl in question apparently felt little conflict. From Leticia's point of view, her classmate had abandoned the liberal promise of individuation and self-development. Instead of showing the same disappointment ("she doesn't take it this way"), the girl "resigned" herself to the fate of family and service. Perhaps Leticia's friend was unwilling to express her deeper wishes; perhaps she was genuinely faithful to her parents' "will." Then again, the household economy might not have been able to sustain her studies. Whatever the case, Leticia's statement brings into focus the poignant consequences of a frustrated discourse and practice around gender equity.

The 1990–1991 school year concluded with little fanfare. In the end, the more severe work stoppages threatened by the so-called democratic teachers never materialized, and classes were only canceled a few times. The democráticos promised more political action against a national plan for educational modernization scheduled to take effect the following year. This plan would eventually succeed in decentralizing educational administration and making secundaria attendance compulsory, among other things. Yet the democráticos would also succeed in winning the local state's education offices, thereby maintaining some control over the implementation of national educational reforms. Meanwhile, the school closing and graduation ceremony went ahead on the grounds of ESF as planned, despite the grumbling opposition of many parents and students. Some of my focal students could not attend. Iván, Abel, Vicente, Paco,

Graduating students take their seats with their ritual sponsors (*padrinos*) for the graduation ceremony

Socorro, and Andrea had all failed to complete their requisites for a secundaria certificate. They would need to pass the special exams in August in order to receive this degree. After the ceremony, I raced from a party with 3C to a collegial gathering of ESF teachers. I had already begun to feel nostalgic for the friendships I would soon be leaving behind.

Gestures of departure often leave the deepest imprints on the mind, and I still remember the day I left San Pablo in July 1991. My girlfriend and I had already spent more than a week in San Pablo gathering up my things and saying our good-byes. The morning of our scheduled departure had arrived all too soon, and we found ourselves scrambling to pack the car and still make an early exit from town. I had already said my final farewell to my host and mentor, Mr. Solana, the night before, amid fellow teachers and plentiful toasts. It was now a Saturday morning, and as usual, Mr. Solana had arisen with the sun and set off to tend his family's fields in a village just a mile or two out of town. He was gone by the time we sat down to a hurried breakfast. Mrs. Ramírez was alternating between shepherding us through final arrangements and breaking into tearful fits of farewell.

We now only had to get on the road, but something made me want to visit Mr. Solana one last time. I made a short detour before heading out on the main eastern highway. We found Mr. Solana, as expected, toiling in his beloved scraggly patch. He seemed pleased to see us and took a few minutes to show us around, explaining his planting patterns, identifying crops (squash, corn, lentils), nodding proudly toward the fruit trees and rose bushes, and scowling irascibly at signs of rot or insect invasion. We made signs of haste, so he hustled us back toward the car, wished us the best of luck, bid us to send our greetings to our respective parents (always the consideration of extended family), and waved us on. But as we were finally bundling ourselves into the car, he suddenly urged us to wait and turned back toward the field. We saw him approach a hedge and clip a perfect pink rose. When he returned with the flower, he presented it to my friend, smiled, and told her to keep *it* in water and *me* out of trouble (*que se porte bien*). I laughed and tried to defend my honor, but Mr. Solana had already dismissed me with a slight wave of the hand and turned once again toward the field.

The evidence provided in this chapter raises fundamental questions about what I have called the cultural game of equality. If a cultural center exercised a hegemony of taste, if students were forming exclusionary friendship groups, and if derisive discourses of otherness continued to separate students, then what sense might equality and solidarity still have? How could students still identify with one another through tropes of equality? We have seen how the shifting formation of friendship groups, the emergence of a local youth culture, and a vibrant cultural center at ESF acted to produce and reproduce social distinctions that undermined egalitarian identifications and a common schooled identity. Senses of difference rooted in class, ethnicity, age, and gender, not to mention the divisions of romantic orientation, cut against the grain of the equality and solidarity prescribed by school discourse and practice. There was evidence that, in 1991, then, the convergence of subjectivities in the collective project of the grupo escolar had made modest inroads into the existing sense of social distinctions outside the school, but had not displaced them. Students' variable positioning in the game of equality and around the cultural center, in conjunction with their family's involvement in schooling, determined the kinds of aspirations they would be forming. How many of the students truly felt that "we are all equal" by the end of their time at ESF? Would the sense of shared nationality, of secondary schooled identity, persist well beyond the secundaria years? Where would students end up and how would they remember their time in the secundaria? To begin answering these questions, we turn to the next chapter and the stories of the focal students I followed for seven more years.

7. Political Economic Change, Life Trajectories,

and Identity Formation, 1988–1998

Most commentators identify the year 1982 as the end of the Mexican economic boom. The great dream of a permanent prosperity, buoyed by extensive oil reserves, seemed to wash away with José López Portillo's infamous tears as he handed the presidential sash over to Miguel de la Madrid. The oil fields, it turned out, were not as extensive as first thought; the peso went into a tailspin, investors lost confidence, and Mexico could barely meet its debt payments. Production crawled to a standstill, and unemployment rose while wages stagnated. The new president responded with fiscal austerity—State spending plummeted—and a plan to open Mexico to greater private investment. Nationalist protectionism would give way to an opening of the markets. These so-called neoliberal reforms seemed to turn things around at the macro level, as the peso eventually stabilized and economic growth began a slow upward swing.

The neoliberal agenda would gain further momentum with another presidential shift in 1988. Carlos Salinas de Gortari pursued an even more aggressive program of privatization, attempting to sell off long-standing para-Statal enterprises in transportation and communications. He also consummated the North American Free Trade Agreement in 1992, an important step in the move toward globalization. Yet even as foreign investment, trade, and production growth shored up the general economy, the average Mexican still struggled. Small-scale farmers could not afford credit, money was scarce, and most new jobs were woefully underpaid. As far back as 1982, Mexicans had been talking about *la crisis,* and for most families there was indeed a crisis of available funds. Then, in 1994, as President Salinas was basking in the praise of global investors, another severe peso devaluation brought Mexico to the brink of financial collapse. The dream of free trade prosperity again came crashing down, and average Mexican families, like most of those I knew in San Pablo, bore the worst of the renewed crisis.

Was there a corresponding crisis of confidence in government and educational provision? After all, neoliberal reforms had been undertaken by the same ruling party that had governed Mexico since 1929. The Partido Revolucionario Institucional (PRI) had helped build a proud national culture around the institutions and policies—many educational—of the State. Now, the State was decentralizing educational administration and globalizing economic flows, while backgrounding the discourse of the nation as a key reference for work and citizenship. On the one hand, it is demonstrably true that State legitimacy, especially in the guise of the PRI, suffered throughout the 1980s and 1990s. Opposition parties gained ground across the political spectrum, while nonaffiliated citizen and workers' movements grew apace. As discussed earlier, the official teachers' union—the largest union in all of Latin America—struggled for viable salaries and internal democracy, and by the late 1980s, secondary education experienced an enrollment downturn. Yet it is not clear if such skeptical popular response would remain deep and thoroughgoing in local life. After all, these political economic shifts were felt unevenly by different families and intimate cultures in the San Pablo region. Moreover, the culture of educational mobility was still deeply rooted. If economic conditions prohibited more and more families from pursuing further studies, the faith in public schooling, fostered by the educational policies of the boom years, seemed to persist.[1] There was ambivalence about the value of schooling, yes, perhaps even cynicism, but seldom was there outright rejection.

It is essential, then, to know how students' identities and aspirations developed in relation to these unique circumstances of the 1990s, as well as whether and how students' secundaria experiences had significant effects in their later lives.

For better or worse, by the spring of 1997, the symptoms of globalization had extended throughout San Pablo. In the midst of ongoing economic crisis after a severe peso devaluation, tourism seemed to be the only thing booming. A number of new restaurants and money exchange houses (*casas de cambio*) had opened, and I had never before seen so many gringos walking around. Some local businesses abandoned traditional Mexican cuisine for the cross-cultural palate. There was a bizarre kind of familiar pleasure now available to me: on one side of the central plaza, I could breakfast on bagels and scones; on the other, I could supper on soy burgers with whole wheat buns. Meanwhile, the depression of wages had brought a frantic search for hard cash. Nearly every residence, every doorway onto the street, sported a type of sale or service. In the notorious informal economy of the new world order, every family strove for some minor comparative advantage.

A number of San Pablo residents ventured that the casas de cambio had sprouted up not because of tourism but to service the growing drug trade with the United States. For some years now, regular confiscations of marijuana and poppy had occurred on the highways around San Pablo. Police and army roadblocks were common. The father of Antonio, the Juanitos's "benchwarmer," had been arrested for trafficking. People were now able to openly discuss what had only been gossip about the sources of Antonio's sudden wealth. Some residents even said the elected city treasurer was in the drug trade. He'd had no history of party affiliation before his candidacy, but he was worth a small fortune. There was still a high turnover of stores and restaurants in town, as would-be entrepreneurs crowded into a tight market. Franco's flour *tortillería* now had competition on the other side of town. Cable television made satellite dishes obsolete and allowed relatively easy access to previously forbidden cultural material. The newly finished and expanded highway to the capital made frequent travel easier, and brought in even more transient tourists. Finally, the signs of increased transnational migration were everywhere. Many of the youths I had first met in 1990 were either in the United States or recently returned from there. Assorted U.S. license plates (California, Oregon, Illinois) adorned a greater number of cars around town, and I was informed that regular nonstop flights now ran between the state capital and major U.S. cities like Chicago and Los Angeles.

What had happened at ESF since 1991? The principal had been promoted to a higher regional position while the vice principal Mr. Alvarez took over at ESF. In 1996, Mr. Alvarez said, about 640 prospective students had taken an admissions exam, of which only 480, or 70 percent, were accepted to the school. Most of those rejected would enroll in one of the two técnicas, where they rarely turned students away. So the late 1980s' reduction in applicants had soon reversed itself with a more or less steady increase. Meanwhile, the new plan of studies had been implemented along with the modernization initiative in 1993, and some teachers were happier with it than others. The new *carrera magisterial,* an optional salary and promotion incentive plan for "career" teachers, was embraced by some but maligned by most, who found it corrupt and divisive. Among the students, the new elective courses (*optativas*) in the third year seemed most popular. They included one or two hours a week of regional history, state history, ecology, so-called citizenship education, selected topics in physics or chemistry, indigenous language, or soccer.[2]

Materially, the school seemed to slowly improve. Mr. Alvarez had managed to get a new set of desks supplied by the state. The basketball courts and playing field had been improved in part through grants from Pepsi and Coca-Cola, whose logos were painted on the cement and backboards. A veritable cola war was now being staged on school grounds. At the same time, a modest computer workshop had replaced the printing press taller (shop), but in 1997, the talleres of carpentry and clothing design had been canceled—their teachers on political or medical leave. The tragic shortage of funds prohibited the hiring of substitutes, and the students from the closed talleres had to be crowded temporarily into others. One other operational change intrigued me: as of 1996, the Tuesday through Friday morning lineup had been eliminated. The student government had requested this change, arguing that they lost class time while standing in the sun. The petition was subsequently approved by the Consejo Técnico, the principal's advisory council. I thought Mr. Alvarez would be disappointed to lose this opportunity for moral instruction and discipline. He surprised me by saying that the administration was pleased. Teachers would now have to arrive promptly to their first classes instead of giving themselves the excuse of an extra ten minutes. The elimination of the morning lineup had improved teacher discipline!

In spite of some positive changes, then, an atmosphere of disillusion and defeat seemed to reign in 1997. Above all, the students were just not meeting the teachers' expectations. As I discussed in chapter 3, teachers were already noting the apathy of most students in 1990. They attributed this to the lack of firm guidance in the home and a pervasive ambivalence about the economic value of schooling. As Mr. Carrizo put it in a joint interview with the technical drawing teacher,

> We don't know how to motivate the kids. We think the kids all by themselves will be dedicated to the objective of increasing their level of culture. But we know that because of the present circumstances in society, the kids are completely apathetic to the kind of dedication that we used to see. . . . From 1980 to the present is when the kids have entered into a stage of confusion with regard to their dedication to study. Why? Well, economics has become the fundamental factor. The parents themselves have led the student to believe that studying is no longer productive, that it's more productive to get into some business than to finish a professional career.

In 1997, the "problems of society" had apparently increased, and according to the teachers who used this phrase, such problems impinged even more negatively on the attitudes of students at school. Mr. Alvarez worried about the erosion of students' cultural heritage. Among other things, he said, students no longer paid much attention to patriotic symbols ("*No quieren tanto a los símbolos patrios*"). More important still, "It's as if the kids don't want to prepare themselves anymore . . . there's more commotion, more belligerence [*más intranquilidad, más agresividad*]," though he was quick to add that not all students fit this description. Another teacher saw student speech and peer relations as symptomatic of their belligerence. Boys were more likely to use urban slang terms such as *güey* (dude) and *cabrón* (jerk) among one another, and less likely to monitor such use in teachers' presence. In the past, this teacher reflected, school had always been more like a church, where you would be expelled for using such language. Now school was more like a cantina, he chuckled, a tough male barroom where a religious gesture, or the *failure* to use vulgar language, might get you thrown out.

When I asked him to suggest some of the sources of negative student attitudes, Mr. Alvarez ventured several: the occasional strikes and lack of dedication among teachers, family "disintegration," cable television and videos, tourism, even the new highway linking San Pablo to the state capital. Mr. Alvarez was especially worried about the constant availability of violent and sexual images on cable television. He didn't think the San Pablo youth were ready for such things, and to illustrate his point he recounted another story from the 1960s, when ESF's physical education teacher had proposed that girls start wearing shorts to school on the days they had physical education activities. Even though many schools in the country were already doing this, the San Pablo parents strongly objected ("They almost ran all of us teachers out!"). As he often did, Mr. Alvarez advanced a perceptive sociological insight: the recent changes and influences in San Pablo might be even more disorienting because they had come rather suddenly and in the context of a more conservative culture.

HOW FOCAL STUDENTS FARED

In the next section, I provide a brief synopsis of most of the focal students' life trajectories (see table 4) between 1991 and 1997 or 1998. In the section following that, I offer a fuller account of the other eight students I first introduced in chapter 4. The extent of my knowledge about each student remains uneven. I was able to interview some thirteen of the students in great depth, and in several cases I chatted with their families as well. Most of these interviews took place in the spring of 1997, although a couple were conducted over the phone as late as the summer of 1998. I was only able to speak with some students for a few minutes, while still others—like Andrea and Ivonne—supplied me with only the barest outlines of the paths their lives had taken.[3]

In addition to asking the students about their lives since 1991 and plans for the next five years, I encouraged them to reflect on their time in the secundaria. What and who had they remembered of those years, and why? What lessons had they learned, and what knowledge had they found most useful? Were they still in touch with their former classmates? It turns out they were more out of touch than I had expected. The intervening years of work and study had led them away from each other, and new friendships had formed in other schools or workplaces. Some of the women had married and now found themselves bound to the home. A few students still remembered their classmates and greeted each other warmly, while others didn't. In the meantime, I had become a point of contact, an intermediary between former students who had fallen out of touch. As I went around interviewing students, I found myself prompted to speak almost as much as I listened. Especially after the first few weeks of my 1997 visit, I had accumulated much information about the location and activities of former students, and was asked to share this knowledge.

I also went around showing a large stack of photographs to any former ESF student who I happened to run into on the street. The photos evoked a variety of responses, most of them focused on their fellow grupo mates. With each photo, the former student would typically pause and say, "That one I don't know about" ("*Ese ya ni sé*"), or "That one got married and has a child" ("*Esa ya se casó, tiene niño*"), or "That one's studying law in the state capital" ("*Esa estudia Leyes en [la capital]*"]). In a couple of cases, students felt snubbed when their former classmates no longer seemed to recognize or greet them in passing ("*Ese ya ni me saluda, se puso bien sangrón*"). The comments elicited by the photos highlighted the former students' current marital or work status. Most strikingly, university studies and marriage seemed to preclude one another. Former students were said to have either married or be studying for an advanced degree. Typically, a male student who had married "doesn't study anymore; he left school to work" ("*ya no estudia, salió de la prepa para trabajar*"). A female student who had married was not even cited as working; she either had a child or would soon have one, and was expected to stay at home.

The educational trajectories of those who did continue studying varied a great deal. They attended one of several high school–level institutions like the CONALEP (vocational), the CBTIS (mixed), the semipublic preparatoria, a church-run "business" program, or one of two new private preparatorias. A number went on to university studies, most at the central public university in the state capital. There were a few surprises. For instance, in 1997, some six members of the former 3C, including Rosita, were enrolled in law classes at the same university. This is probably an unprecedented coincidence, though as an administrative center, San Pablo inspired many of its graduates to seek careers in law, and there was some evidence that these former grupo mates had challenged each other to pursue the same path. Yet not all former ESF students' educational trajectories had gone smoothly. Some students had to drop out and repeat a year of study. Others began a university career only to find it too difficult or unrewarding. After a year or two they would have to start all over. Even the 3C law students had followed different paths. At least two had lost a year or more of study and were not at the same stage as their former grupo mates.

I also noted a telling shift in the quality of my communication with the former students. In general, it became comparatively easier to talk with the young men and harder with the young women. In 1990, by contrast, few of the boys could be bothered with the curious anthropologist. They were too busy horsing around to engage in serious reflection about their lives, and many lacked the confidence and verbal skills to do so. The intervening years had seen the boys grow into men and shed their juvenile personae. By 1997, they had matured considerably, and with only one or two exceptions, seemed eager to discuss their lives and reflect on their years in the secundaria. When I finally tracked him down in Oregon, for instance, Isidro spoke at length about his experience in a U.S. high school and work history. Likewise, Fidencio was startlingly forthcoming about his drug addiction and attempts to rebuild his life. Neither of these boys had invited such trust while at ESF. Now, they showed quite an ability and desire to recall specific persons and events. I was also amazed to learn that most had valued my presence and friendship far more than they had ever led me to believe.

The girls were just as hard as the boys to track down, and perhaps even more difficult to pry open. To be sure, most of these young women remembered me fondly and renewed our rapport. The talk still flowed with Rosita, Leticia, and Matilde, though both Rosita and Leticia seemed more reserved than they had been at fourteen years old. They had grown even more serious and pensive, and our lapses in contact had clearly deteriorated some of the trust we had built up. On the other hand, some of the young women, like Matilde, Antonia, and Dalia, seemed even chattier than ever. Most disconcerting of all, after 1995, Andrea and Ivonne could not speak to me at all. Both had recently married and given birth, and their husbands prohibited them from talking to me. Despite my assurances and mild protestations, I could not reach them. I also began to notice that my more casual encounters with other ex-students differed by gender as well. Young men stopped to converse with me at ease, but few young women did. If I spotted a former female student in town, she often averted her gaze or gave only perfunctory greeting. This was in marked contrast to 1990, when the female students would more frequently smile and greet me, perhaps stopping to talk a while. Of course, part of the explanation for this change may have been in the relative busyness of the women. They typically had more chores and errands to do, while the men could luxuriate in free time. Nevertheless, in light of my experience with Andrea and Ivonne, I could not help but ascribe some of the women's distancing to the local politics of sexuality. The secundaria years had prescribed an ethos of relative innocence, where girls qua girls could still flirt and associate more freely. As young women, the ex-students were now expected to avoid most men in the street and go about their business discreetly. I suspect that some of them feared negative retaliation from jealous boyfriends or husbands.

Table 4. Focal Students in 1997

Name and Grupo	Age in June 1997	Occupation/Activities	Siblings' Schooling and Occupations	Level of Schooling Achieved
Franco (3B)	21	Helping in parents' tortillería; applying for university veterinary program; studying English	Younger sister studying law in university; other younger siblings still in secundaria or prepa	Completed prepa, then dropped out after one-year course at technological university
Iván (3c)	22	Married with two daughters; head mechanic in small engine repair shop	Older brothers and sisters mostly married, working as bank clerks, pharmacy delivery persons, and similar local jobs	Dropped out after one year at CBTIS
Abel (3B)	21	Helping out in family grocery stores; eventually becomes owner of San Pablo store	Four older sisters all completed university degrees (tourism, teaching, dentistry, law); two married with children; two working as professionals	Dropped out after three months of law program at state university
Isidro (3F)	21	Married with two children; Airborne Express driver in Oregon	Older brothers and sisters married with children; two residing in Oregon; four driving buses or taxis in San Pablo	Graduated high school in Oregon
Alberto (3F)	21	Soon to finish medical degree at state university	Two older brothers married and working as doctor and architect; another older brother, unmarried, working as lawyer and nursery owner	Still studying

Fidencio (3A)	21	Starting second year of program in industrial administration at distant polytechnic university	One younger brother, nineteen, at a restaurant in Massachusetts; youngest brother, seventeen, married and in family business	Still studying
Vicente (3c)	21	Working in automobile body shop	Older brother, mechanic, in United States; younger brother studying at CBTIS; sister working at health clinic	Barely completed secundaria
Enrique (3A)	20	Working in nut orchard and cannery in Oregon	Younger siblings all studying in primaria, secundaria, and prepa	Completed one year of prepa, then dropped out for economic reasons
Paco (3B)*	21	Working in southern California	Older brother married and working in California; younger sister completed secundaria	Barely completed secundaria
Socorro (3F)	23	Clerk at brother's pharmacy outside Mexico City	Two older brothers married and owners of two pharmacies; one sister married with children; younger brother completed prepa and working in pharmacy	Barely completed secundaria

Table 4. *Continued*

Name and Grupo	Age in June 1997	Occupation/Activities	Siblings' Schooling and Occupations	Level of Schooling Achieved
Fidel (3B)	21	Carving furniture in his home village	One older brother in army; another older brother married and woodworking in the village	Completed secundaria
José (3A)	20	Public health inspector for San Pablo region	Younger siblings in primaria, secundaria, and prepa	Completed accounting track at CBTIS and part of one year at university
Rosita (3C)	20	Soon to finish law degree at state university	Younger sister in private prepa, wants to study architecture	Still studying
Antonia (3B)	21	Clerk at telecommunications service	Younger brother in prepa; younger sister in primaria	Finished only one year of prepa, then completed two separate one-year cosmetology courses
Lidia (3F)	21	Analyst and clerk for highway construction company	Two younger siblings still in secundaria and prepa	Completed tourism track at CBTIS
Dalia (3C)	20	Studying to be an early childhood educator at state normal school	No siblings	Still studying

Name	Age		Siblings	Education
Leticia (3B)	20	Studying to be teacher at state normal school	One older brother married, working as biologist; one older brother partner in father's business; one older brother with medical degree; one younger brother in prepa, likes chemistry	Still studying
Nidia (3F)	23	Quality inspector at electronics factory in Mexicali	Older siblings all married with children; several younger siblings still in primaria and secundaria	Finished course in comercio at local colegio
Andrea (3A)	20	Married with one child; living in Oregon	Older sister possibly working as teacher	Completed secundaria through evening adult courses
Ivonne (3B)	21	Married with one child	N.A.	Completed nursing degree at CONALEP
Alejandra (3C)	23	Secretary working temporarily in a border town	N.A.	Completed comercio at private colegio
Matilde (3B)	20	Secretary at computer printing shop	Three younger sisters in secundaria or prepa	Completed secretarial track at CBTIS

A BRIEF RENDERING OF SOME LIVES

ABEL

When I went to his house in 1993, Abel took me over to the nearby cabaña, or ranch-style cottage that his family had been building for some years. This was his refuge, and he had brought me here before. At one point, he grabbed a pack of cigarettes from behind a post and smoked one quickly in the kitchen. He informed me that he smoked about five a day now, and also drank more than he ever had in the secundaria. His parents didn't know about any of this, he assured me. While showing me around the cabaña, Abel told me how he had fallen two years behind in his studies. In 1991, he entered the prepa but had to leave after a semester because he never "paid" the extraordinary exams he owed at ESF. He then enrolled at a private church colegio to repeat his third and last year of secondary studies. This year went poorly, too. Abel met up with his old ESF buddy Flaco, and together they were expelled for echando relajo in the back of the room ("You know, the sisters don't put up with that kind of stuff"; "*Ya ves que las madres no soportan eso*"). They let him enroll there again the next year, while Flaco transferred to the progressive institute outside of town. So Abel had managed to get his secundaria certificate just this year, and was planning to attend the prepa at the institute, yet he still had no clear career ambitions.

We returned to the cabaña in 1995, and Abel was still struggling to get through a new private prepa in town (the institute had shut down), though he had been able to pass each of his first two years (actually, he still owed a couple of subjects). He had a large patch on his forehead from an injury sustained in an alcohol-related auto accident just a few weeks earlier. His only serious girlfriend in recent times had turned out to be too "serious," indeed. She reproached Abel for his poor grades, friends, and relajo at the weekend discos, and they split up. Still, Abel was studying in the social sciences and humanities track in order to begin a law degree at the state university. He wanted to eventually join his former classmates there.

I played cat and mouse with Abel in 1997, trying to hunt him down for a talk. When we finally made a date to have coffee in the plaza, he rolled by in his car with a friend and said he had to pick up some items in the capital. Did I want to come along? Recalling Abel's automotive mishaps, I politely declined. It wasn't until July 1998 that we were able to chat at some length. With a raging San Pablo storm threatening to cut off our phone call, Abel told me of his definitive exit from formal education. After finally graduating from the private prepa, he had entered the law program at the state university but had lasted only a few months. Abel wouldn't say why he had dropped his studies, only that he'd had a few "little problems" that intervened. In the meantime, he had already started working fuller hours at one of the two small grocery stores that his family operated in the capital and San Pablo. He often ran deliveries back and forth between the stores. By the end of 1997, Abel's brother-in-law had signed over the deed to the San Pablo store, and just as his last sister was about to complete her university degree, Abel accepted his provisional fate as a small business owner. Amid thunderclaps, Abel told me he still thought he might study at the university some day, but for now he would live with his parents and open the store up front each morning at eight.

ISIDRO

By 1993, I knew that Isidro had left for Oregon to be with his father, but I didn't speak with him again until the summer of 1998. Isidro had not studied beyond secundaria in Mexico. After graduating in June, he worked as a construction laborer (*ayudante de albañil*) until November, then crossed the U.S. border illegally to join his family. When he first arrived in Oregon, he said, he felt strange (*extraño*) because he couldn't speak English and had no friends. He went to the local high school on a Monday and Tuesday, but by Wednesday refused to go anymore. It was his older sister who convinced him to persevere when he was already planning his return to San Pablo. The next Monday, he returned to school and never looked back. He hooked up with other Mexicans in school, graduated, and eventually, in 1997, married a sweetheart he'd met in his first year at the school. While he studied, Isidro said, his father refused to let him work during the school year. He only helped his father in the pine nurseries and fruit orchards during summers.

On graduating, Isidro kept working with his father and then got a job as a U-Haul rental dispatcher. He switched to working as a driver for Airborne Express in 1997. Isidro's son was born in early 1997, and a daughter was born in April 1998. Though he still didn't have his legal residency, Isidro hoped to arrange it soon and switch to a job with a phone connection service that offered benefits. His Mexican wife, already a permanent resident, got benefits through her job as a customer service representative at an employment office. Isidro's mother and mother-in-law took turns caring for the young children during the day. They would do so until the children were in school. I asked Isidro about his family and his own plans for the future. All of his brothers and sisters had come to Oregon at least once, though most had returned to San Pablo after just a few months of work. His parents would probably return for good in several years, after saving enough to build a new house. He figured he would return with his family eventually, but for the moment was content to stay.

FIDENCIO

I didn't see Fidencio again until I ran into him at the plaza grande in 1995. He told me how he had gone to the private institute after barely graduating from ESF, and when that school closed, he transferred to the prepa. Now he was more than a year behind, and ever since his prepa class had gone on an international exchange trip, he had dreams of going to Detroit to finish his high school degree. Another day, Fidencio called me over as I was walking by his family's furniture store. He focused our conversation on the United States again, this time telling me about another exchange trip where he visited "*el barrio de los gays*" (the Castro district) in San Francisco. On yet another day, I caught Fidencio at the store as he was preparing to drive a furniture order to the capital. He once again tried to impress me with the places he had been in California and Michigan. What really did impress me was his knowledge about the wood and production process of the furniture, though he confessed to disliking the work in the factory.

Fidencio still wavered about what he might do in the longer term. Almost in the same breath, he expressed interest in mastering English and studying in the United States or wanting to join the training program of the Federal de Caminos (Highway Patrol). These were both fairly common male aspirations in his ESF class and cohort. He also spoke animatedly about opening a new discotheque with a wealthy friend.

I couldn't tell just then, but Fidencio had already begun his slow descent into a personal hell of drug and alcohol addiction. When I tried to contact him in 1997, his family told me he was studying in a city some three hours away. I called him from my office later that summer, when he had returned to San Pablo for a visit. Fidencio was quite frank about what he had been through: "There's nobody to support you, or maybe you don't want to see who's there to support you, you just close yourself up. It was something I started falling into, I was falling, until I became an alcohol and drug addict." He said that the prepa had been his downfall (*perdición*), that he got into a bad crowd and barely graduated. It took

Fidencio a while to realize what was wrong. Eventually he accepted his family's help. He got treatment and then enrolled in an introductory course for a private technological school, where he would be studying industrial administration. Fidencio did not know if he would ultimately go into furniture sales with his family or branch off on his own. He still talked about spending more time in the United States. Above all, Fidencio reiterated, he would remember that to stop studying was "bad."

In July 1998, I was able to chat at greater length with Fidencio. He had managed to finish his first year of studies, but had also gotten back into drugs. Now, however, Fidencio showed little remorse, laughing instead about the pettiness of San Pablo and indifference of his friends. Citing Cervantes, Fidencio compared himself to Don Quixote, a maligned and misunderstood figure. He felt more comfortable in the large city where he now studied because of the anonymity it afforded. In San Pablo, on the other hand, he could sense the weight of judgment: "Here [in San Pablo] the people think I'm just a crazy kid. They don't accept me. But I am who I am and I'm not going to change." Somehow Fidencio had performed well enough to pass his courses. He admitted to staying up late and having poor study habits, yet he also confessed to feeling "obligated" by his family to do well (*"Pues tu sabes, se siente uno obligado a pasar"*). Meanwhile, Fidencio's two younger brothers had never studied beyond the secundaria. Now twenty, one of them had been working at a Massachusetts restaurant for over a year. The other, eighteen, had never even finished the private secundaria into which his family had placed him. He'd gotten married last year and now worked in the family business. Fidencio's laugh continued to haunt me. Once a sign of playful abandon, now it seemed equally tinged by tragedy.

VICENTE

Among the male focal students, Vicente had turned out the most diffi- cult to engage, even back in 1991. He remained taciturn through most of our interviews and never invited me to his home. I knew that he had barely made it through the school year and had continued working in the same auto body shop (*hojalatería*). His father continued to specialize in ironwork (*balconería*) out of his own home. Circumstances conspired to keep us from chatting at length after 1991, but an assistant finally tracked Vicente down in April 1998. Vicente's father now had a job with the Secretariat of Public Works, and his older brother, a mechanic, had been working in the United States for some time. A younger brother was still studying at the CBTIS, while a younger sister worked at the public health clinic in town. Vicente had continued working in the auto body shop, and now aspired to open his own business. To that end, his parents had bought him some of the tools to get started, but other costs were still prohibitive. All the while, Vicente's older brother had been inviting him to join up in the United States. Vicente thought about it, and his parents even half joked about moving the whole family to the United States, but Vicente would not want to leave other family and friends behind. Besides, he was already planning on marrying soon.

PACO

It always seemed to me that Paco, who had struggled to be a part of grupo 3B, had undertaken a difficult project of self-transformation. He understood yet could not fluently speak his village's indigenous language. He had learned to make straw hats and relished showing me the technique, but in school he would not admit to having the skill. Despite his efforts, some schoolmates persisted in highlighting his Indianness. (Some of these remarks had a jocular quality, and Paco took them in stride. In the back of class one day, Abel ribbed Paco about being from a pueblito where everyone smelled of fish. Paco smiled and shot back that Abel was a fat clown—*payaso panzoso*). In the midst of all this, Paco managed to construct his aspirations for a legal career with the money his older brother regularly sent from California. Thus, I was surprised in 1993 when Paco's mother informed me that he had joined his older brother in Santa Maria, California, shortly after I had left in 1991. He hadn't been back since. The two brothers had sent their mother a good deal of money, and this got her through the cholera scare of that year, when fish sales were low. Their mother also used the money to set up a modest home in one of San Pablo's new peripheral colonias, thereby eliminating the hour-long commute each way. Her daughter Riki, whom I felt so sure in 1991 would go on to further studies (see chapter 5), had sat the last year out but said she planned to finish her final year at ESF soon.

I made the trip out to his village in 1995 to see Paco for the first and only time I would after 1991. His former classmate Leticia had told me that I would find him more talkative and self-confident, and she was right. Paco answered the door with a warm welcome, and we immediately sat down to chat about ESF and his time in California. Crossing the border in the trunk of his uncle's car, Paco first found work as a dishwasher at a Denny's restaurant in a central coast city. Later he was promoted to busboy, a position that afforded him more visibility and a share of the wait-resses' tips. Paco had also enrolled in English classes to help his communi-cation at work. He observed, in passing, that some people in the United States—"blacks," especially, but also the English-speaking Mexican *pochos* who denied their Mexicanness—did not like to work very hard. He saw many of them come and go in his time at Denny's. In contrast, Paco worked harder and harder. He took on extra shifts at another chain res-taurant, and found time for odd jobs such as housepainting. He had bought a 1986 Mazda and modified it à la pocho (pocho, or Chicano-style), low-rider with bass-heavy speakers.

Paco left the Mazda behind, but now drove the car he had bought together with his older brother, a black Pontiac Firebird. The car virtually transformed Paco when he displayed and drove it. Like so many U.S. teenagers, Paco took obvious pride in the sports car's flash and style. It was the only one of its kind in his village, perhaps in the entire region. Never mind the incongruity, the mag wheels parked on a grassy field at the village outskirts. Paco had also acquired an even deeper love for hard rock music "in English"; he showed a fascination for video games like Nin-tendo and Mortal Kombat, which he played on a machine bought abroad as well. Finally, Paco took me out to the area beyond where the car was parked, where a modest brick structure and a pile of cinder blocks stood. This was the house he was building for himself and his future family. The new road around the village would pass in front, and he would have an "American"-style front yard with a driveway.

I was startled to learn that Paco's brother Toño had encouraged him to come work in California, since he had always been cited as an important influence on Paco's study plans. In 1991, Paco and his mother had quoted Toño as saying that he had made the sacrifice as older brother to permit his younger siblings a chance at university careers. Yet by 1993, even Toño had begun doubting the economic wisdom of a professional life. The pickings were just too good in California. Now twenty-five, he had only completed one semester at the university before heading to the United States some six years ago. Toño's dreams of becoming a teacher had been thwarted because the economic situation then wouldn't allow him to continue his studies. Just this year, he had married a young woman from the village whom he had met some time back on one of his visits home. When we walked around the village in 1995, Toño commented on the irony of the local language: few people spoke it in public because it was not encouraged in the allegedly bilingual primary school, even though the teachers were themselves supposed to be indigenous. He also noted the minor boom in the local hat industry, which had made a few people some money. Meanwhile, Paco still entertained notions of studying at a prepa and eventually finishing a law degree. When he drove me back to San Pablo, he said he wanted to enroll in August. This was when I also learned that he had only recently presented his extraordinary exam for Spanish at ESF and would not be getting his secundaria certificate for several weeks yet!

Yet when I returned in 1997, I found that Paco had already been in California again for more than a year. He was living in an apartment just two miles from the house where I had grown up and where my parents still lived. When I visited my parents in June 1997, just after I had been in San Pablo, I called the number that Paco's mother had given me. He answered the phone and sounded pleased to hear my voice. Indeed, he was living close by. Paco told me the nearest major intersection, and we agreed to meet in a few days. Then I made my fatal mistake; I failed to get his address, saying I would call again on his day off. Two days later, his phone line had been disconnected. I never got to see him again.

SOCORRO

I couldn't get any news about Socorro in 1993, but in 1995, I finally met much of his family at their modest house in a peripheral colonia. His father immediately dominated the conversation, pulling up a seat for me in the improvised outdoor kitchen. I learned that Socorro had passed the few extraordinary exams he still owed in August immediately after school graduation, then went to the outskirts of Mexico City to help his two older brothers in their pharmacy. He hadn't really been doing much since he returned to San Pablo. As his father and older sister repeatedly pointed out, "There just aren't any jobs." Socorro's father explained his own commitment to education, for he had moved the family to San Pablo from a small village in order to take advantage of the schools. Yet he didn't seem disappointed that none of his children had gone beyond preparatoria. His oldest daughter—a savvy, articulate twenty-four-year-old who listened in and occasionally intervened as she cooked nearby—had become pretty cynical about the value of schooling. She had only completed one year of the secretarial course at the CBTIS herself, but she said most places in town were hiring primary school graduates as secretaries in order to save money. No CBTIS graduate would accept the miserable salary they were offering.

In 1995, it was still not clear what income sustained Socorro's family.

When I returned in 1997, I found Socorro's father alone in a rather barren house. He gave me a confused story about how the family was forced to flee to Mexico City the previous year because of his daughter's vengeful husband. He also said they had acquired a lot of money and built a nice house to accompany their pharmacies in the city. I wondered if the story also indicated an illicit gambling profit through cockfighting, his confessed former occupation. When I asked why they didn't just sell the San Pablo house, Socorro's father said it continued to have special meaning as it had supported his children's studies for so many years. He showed me with pride a recent wedding picture of a younger son (seventeen years old) who had just finished training to be a teacher. Then I inquired if any of his children had ever studied at a university, and he responded defensively but in his resolute way: "Look, this is what I see, I'm going to tell you how things are: the government really doesn't want to give work to professionals. So you can do a lot better starting some businesses than studying so much" ("*Yo veo una cosa, mire Usted, le voy a decir como está el asunto: el gobierno realmente no quiere darles trabajo a los profesionistas . . . entonces, uno sale mucho mejor poniendo unos negocios que estudiando tanto*").[4] He said his son Socorro was smart (*listo*), and that's why he made a good pharmacy employee in Mexico City.

So I telephoned Socorro a few months later from my office in Indiana, and his voice brightened when he recalled our time together in the secundaria. For most of the time since he had graduated ESF, Socorro had worked in one of two pharmacies owned by his older brothers and cousins. This work was only broken up by occasional visits to San Pablo and one ill-fated journey to the state of Oaxaca at the age of nineteen. Setting out for Oaxaca's beaches, instead he ran out of money and had to seek work in small factories making straw hats and brooms. Unable to sustain himself, and with his clothes wearing thin, Socorro returned to Mexico City after a couple of months. Now his goal was to save enough money to purchase a plot of land and build a modest home with his younger brother (nineteen), who had studied in the prepa but then came to work in the pharmacies, too. He also hoped to start his own business, maybe a small grocery store, with this same brother. When I asked if he had any plans for marriage, Socorro just laughed and said he had no time. He reminded me that he worked in the pharmacy all day, every day, to save enough for his future plans. The work wasn't hard, he admitted, but the constant enclosure of the store made him feel like an exhausted prisoner ("*Es un encierro muy matado . . . has de cuenta que estás en una celda, en una cárcel*"). Socorro also expressed interest in pursuing a school career, perhaps even architecture, although he had not taken any steps toward this. In almost the next breath, though, Socorro described his "curiosity" to work in the United States. A brother-in-law had spent some four years there, and been able to save enough to build a house for the wife and children he had temporarily left behind. Now he was living well in Mexico and encouraged Socorro to take the same route.

Finally, I asked Socorro to reflect on his years in the secundaria, and he said he'd like to return. He still had nice memories and would often recall the pleasant times, in spite of the "sacrifices" it took for him to get his certificate. When in San Pablo, he occasionally sought out two old friends from 3F who had lived in his neighborhood. Socorro had not seen them in a long time, but he knew one of them, at least, was close to finishing a law degree. About this he commented: "You know, it does make me sad to know they've become something and I'm not anything. Well, in the end, everyone has their own fate, no?" ("*¿Sabes qué? Me da tristeza saber que ellos son algo y yo no soy nada. Total, pues es la suerte de cada quien, ¿no?*"). I challenged Socorro by asking just what it means to "be something," and his opinion wavered even as he tried to clarify:

> I'm referring to what they'll have one day, I mean a degree, in other words to be someone more. I don't feel less than them, but with the simple fact of their having a degree, I don't know, it's already something more, let's say it counts for something more. But that's just the way things are. I have to be [considered] something too, you know. [*Me refiero a lo que ellos van a tener un día, o sea un título, o sea ser alguien más. Yo no me siento menos pero ya con el simple hecho de ellos tener un título, no sé, pues ya es algo más, total ya cuenta más. Pero pues ni modo, yo tengo que ser algo también, fíjate.*]

Socorro sensed my challenge and backpedaled to confirm that he was "something," too, but not until after he had affirmed the higher value of a degree (*título*). Thus, in spite of his father's cynicism about professional degrees, Socorro's own secondary schooled identity, once a source of identification with schoolmates, now informed his sense of relatively low status vis-à-vis those with university studies.

ANTONIA

Her father had been killed in a tragic automobile accident in March 1991, when I was still at ESF—an event that changed Antonia's life forever.

Her family's fortunes reversed almost instantly, and in 1997, I noted her mother was selling candies from the front door of their home in a desperate effort for household cash. After graduating from ESF, Antonia entered the local prepa, but she quit after just one year, deciding not to pay the two subjects she owed. Then she moved on to the CBTIS, where she didn't even get past the first year of accounting. In 1995, Antonia explained that she did not have "the head" for this subject, yet in 1997, she claimed to have lost all desire to study. Her father had always been the one to encourage her studies ("*él me impulsaba a lograr mi meta*"), and without him she admitted she had fallen apart ("*me descontrolé . . . siento que me hace falta el calor de un padre*"). So Antonia then had to settle for a one-year cosmetology course. She received her certificate there and completed another half-year course in facial makeup with a specialized cosmetic company. She studied another year in an even more advanced cosmetology school, but when the school closed down unexpectedly she could not finish the three-year program. Her dream was to finish the advanced course at a school in the state capital, but she couldn't afford it. Thus she began working as a cashier at the local movie theater, followed by a stint in a building supplies store for almost a year. During this time, she was also hatching a plan to open a small boutique with an aunt in Guadalajara. When that fell through, a friend told her about a job with one of the small communications services that were opening all over San Pablo. She would put through long-distance phone calls, and send and receive faxes. In 1997, Antonia's brother had finished his first year in the prepa, but he talked of driving a truck or joining some branch of the military. Their mother insisted that he complete his studies through prepa, that he prepare himself to "be someone in life," even with a "short" carrera. Antonia's other sister was only in fifth grade and planned to attend ESF.

Antonia's dream now was to enter the prepa again and study communication sciences. She was also in love with a young boy her age who had finished a computer course at the local CONALEP. He had spent a couple of years in the United States and was now looking for work in San Pablo. Antonia commented that they had talked about marriage, and I wondered how that would affect her study plans. She was coy yet insisted that he had agreed to let her study if they married. At this point in our talk, I asked Antonia what she liked to do in her spare time. I already knew she was an avid dancer at the local discos, for many of her ex-schoolmates claimed to see her there often. Yet she also spoke at length about a book she had been reading, *Éxtasis de Juventud*, that used a male protagonist with syphilis to present what sounded like a cautionary tale about the problems facing youth around the world. Then, she surprised me by discussing her fascination with *música de banda*—a uniquely Mexican form of traditional rural music. When I expressed my surprise that she preferred banda over pop music, Antonia expounded at length on the benefits of banda and pitfalls of pop. Pop music was best for its rhythm, she said, but the lyrics were silly, incomprehensible, or downright dangerous. Her conservative side came out when she discussed the pop music played by groups like TRI or Gloria Trevi, two notorious examples of Mexican rock irreverence. Antonia thought such music agitated youth (*los alborota*) to rebellion in a way that could damage society. She liked a good lyric, Antonia said, and música de banda had healthy (*sana*) lyrics with "sentimental" meaning that went straight to the heart. I had always admired Antonia's comic irreverence in the secundaria, yet her spontaneous, lighthearted persona even now occluded a thoughtful, serious stance toward the world.

LIDIA

I only saw Lidia briefly in 1993. Along with a couple of former ESF compañeras now attending the local CBTIS together, Lidia was dressed in a traditional indigenous costume, with petticoats and braided hair. They had agreed to help form a welcoming ceremony for the state governor, due to arrive in San Pablo any moment now. We were gathered along one of the central streets when a caravan of white Chevrolet Blazers made its way toward us and a teacher cued the young women to sing an indigenous song. They seemed to articulate the lyrics well. People around them smiled and swayed to the melody, and the singers giggled in mock embarrassment when they finished. Meanwhile, the governor was emerging from a van and, amid rocket shots and handshakes, walking toward the far corner of the large plaza, where a stage and set of tarps had been improvised against the possible rain.

Lidia was in a rush to deliver a fluid sample for the public health service when I saw her on the street in 1995. Like José (below), she was doing her social service at the local public health center. A year behind, she was just finishing her tourism degree at the CBTIS and planned to begin university studies the next year. She had a serious boyfriend (as usual) and confirmed what others had already told me—she had triumphed as Reina Estudiantil (student queen) of San Pablo the year before.

When I finally tracked her down again in 1997, Lidia told me she had finished her tourism degree at the CBTIS and immediately found a job as a clerk with a construction company. She had switched between one or two other jobs, and then found her present work with another construction company, where she had been for eight months now. Lidia would move soon to the next city over, some three times the size of San Pablo, until the completion of the highway her company was building. While her father continued traveling a lot (selling encyclopedias, utensils, and the like), Lidia's mother stayed in their modest government-built home with her other daughter, eighteen, and Lidia's fourteen-year-old brother. When I asked about her future plans, Lidia said that she just hadn't felt like studying beyond the CBTIS, though she did say that it was necessary to move beyond San Pablo in order to grow as a person (*superarte*). Over and over, Lidia called herself restless (*inquieta*). She was always thinking about new things she wanted to do, "to go out and visit a lot of places, not just stay doing the same thing all the time." Her work now was a bit stifling, as she stayed from 8 A.M. to 8 P.M., with only a 2 to 4 P.M. lunch break. Yet the work was important for her to help her family while also establishing her independence. When I showed her the photos, Lidia commented about a few of her classmates' marriages and wondered if something was wrong with her. She admitted to being picky (*exigente*) about her boyfriends; since she was so inquieta herself, she wanted someone who was mature and focused (*centrado*), and yet dynamic. None of her boyfriends had lasted more than two years, and she'd had to turn down the proposal of a thirty-year-old engineer the previous year. Above all, Lidia insisted on her independence. She wouldn't consider marriage or children until she turned twenty-five.

DALIA

When I finally interviewed her in 1997, Dalia was honest in recounting the failure of her first year in the prepa. As she put it, she had started school at a young age, entering first grade with her schoolteacher parents when she was still only five years old. Thus, when she finished secundaria, "I had barely begun to be an adolescent" ("*apenas salí siendo una adolescente*"). She had been too shy, too "closed" ("*cerradita*"), and in the prepa she paid for it: "My very classmates took advantage of my shyness, and I didn't know how to defend myself." Dalia's grades went way down and she failed a class or two. She managed to finish a full year at the prepa, but she didn't want to go back. Then a friend she had met through her participation in a church choir recommended that she join her in studying nursing at the CONALEP. By now best friends, the two entered CONALEP the following year, but Dalia soon had to confront her fear of blood. She finished only one semester and decided not to return. At this point, Dalia was demoralized and frustrated. She had lost two years of study and still didn't know what to do. Her parents arranged for her to complete some questionnaires in vocational orientation, and she "discovered" that her desires and talents lay in teaching young children (her parents' profession). Not willing to confront her former prepa classmates, now two years ahead of her, Dalia applied to the only remaining public option in town, the CBTIS. She enrolled and completed three "wonderful" ("*de maravilla*") years there, majoring in tourism for the chance it offered her to learn to relate to (*relacionarse con*) other people.

In May 1997, Dalia was just finishing her first year of a teacher training program at a small private girl's college in the state capital. She had managed to overcome a profound case of homesickness to persevere in a modest student house. Returning on the weekends, she would visit her boyfriend of some two years, an electrician she had met in the junior choir. Dalia was coy when I asked her about marriage. Reflecting her mother's spirituality, she took a philosophical view, saying she did not believe much in "plans," and preferred to leave things to destiny and God's will. At the very least, she said, her studies would come first.

Dalia felt she had suffered a lot from the "abuse" of her secundaria mates. She challenged my view of grupo unity, insisting that it was a laudable ideal torn asunder by the pettiness of adolescence. What she remembered most was the salience of cliques and factions, the *grupitos* within grupo 3C:

> There were a lot of small groups composed of friendships [*los grupitos entre amistades*], and this made it difficult for the grupo to be solidly united. . . . In the secundaria everyone was cataloged, "If you're popular you get into this group of friends." There were little gangs [*pandillitas*], little gangs, and "this one is the most famous little gang in the whole school, this is the least famous one, this one is more and this one is a little less." So in order to be admitted into all of that, you had to do pirouettes [do tricks and ingratiate yourself].

Toward the end of our chat, when I asked Dalia what experiences stood out most for her in the secundaria, she recounted in detail the painful story of her marginalization in 3C. In the middle of her first year, one grupo mate had spread confidential gossip about another mutual friend in the grupo and then thrown the blame onto Dalia. At a grupo gathering to celebrate Valentine's Day (*Día de la Amistad*), the victim rose to denounce Dalia, accusing her of "treason." Dalia had wanted to defend herself, but she was still too timid, too foolish (*"bien mensota acá,"* as she put it). From that moment on, Dalia suffered the disdain of her grupo mates. Now I understood why Dalia had felt so little grupo unity in the secundaria. From her position, the grupo was riven by petty factionalism and the ritual gestures of acceptance. She remained on the outside of these dynamics. Still, after all this, Dalia finished her stories about grupo life by recalling her sadness on graduating. Even if there had been little unity, Dalia missed the camaraderie of secundaria life. She rarely saw her ex-classmates anymore, and that felt like a loss.

ANDREA

When I least expected it, in 1993, I ran into Andrea standing in front of her grandfather's house. Her older sister, just graduated from prepa and planning to enroll in an institute for early childhood education (Normal para Educadoras), stood with us and played with an infant niece. Andrea no longer harbored dreams of becoming an *educadora* herself. Her inability to complete the work for the secretarial class had come back to haunt her. She never got her certificate from ESF. Instead, she tried to repeat her third year at the técnica nearby, but because of her age they would only admit her to the afternoon shift. This just didn't suit her—Andrea wouldn't say why—so she had enrolled in a secundaria for adults, where she studied three to four hours every afternoon. The pared-down adult school offered only core academic subjects, thus Andrea would not be thwarted by the secretarial shop. On graduating, however, Andrea would not be able to enroll in a regular prepa either, and as her sister noted, this would prohibit her from later studying at the Normal, too. So Andrea thought she would join her older sister in the capital and study some still undecided *carrera corta* (short course).

As Andrea indicated, there were two other crucial developments in her life. Just as I was leaving in July 1991, her father had left for Oregon to work in a restaurant whose owners his brother had managed to impress. By April 1993, her mother and youngest brother had made the journey to join him. Yet Andrea's parents insisted that she and her older sister stay in Mexico. They would send money for their schooling while the two young women lived with their grandfather. Perhaps most surprising, Andrea had dumped her old boyfriend a few months back. He had never returned to his studies like he said he would, and anyway, she had caught him one day with another girl. This guy, it seems, had turned out just like Andrea's 3A detractors said he would! Andrea quickly acquired a new boyfriend, though. He lived nearby, and they'd only been novios for a few months now. She admitted with a silly grin that her new boyfriend was both lazy and belligerent (güevón and *buscapleitos*). He had only completed fourth grade because his teachers had not been able to control him. Andrea just shrugged her shoulders when I asked why she would like such a man. Clearly, her secondary schooled identity had never fully developed.

The next time I saw her, in 1995, Andrea was cradling her nine-month-old girl in her arms. I had bumped into her older sister, and she had given me Andrea's address in a poor colonia. Andrea emerged from the simple cinder block house with a welcoming smile and spoke freely. She had married her husband one and a half years ago, but he had quickly gone off to Oregon and left her at home with several in-laws. Andrea insisted that marriage and children were never really in her plans. She'd only had one semester left to complete her adult secundaria, and then she was planning to move to the capital to study for a secretarial or early childhood (educadora) degree. But her husband had come with his brothers to "rob" her for marriage, and her parents in Oregon were powerless to intervene.[5] Andrea accepted her fate and made the best of it. She claimed not to really regret anything, but likewise, not to miss her husband much. He was off in Oregon for three years, saving enough money to build a home of their own.

In the meantime, Andrea spent most of her time caring for her child. Her in-laws ran a small sawmill next to the house, loading crateboard onto flatbed trucks. As we chatted, her father-in-law emerged from the house and grunted his greeting when Andrea tried to introduce us. Some young women I presumed to be her sisters-in-law periodically opened the front door and urged her inside. Pointedly, neither Andrea nor any other family member invited me in. I surmised that Andrea was violating some marital rule of prudence by standing and talking with me, and I was probably right. For when I phoned her again in 1997, a young man aggressively steered me away. "What do you want her for, huh?" ("*¿Para qué la quiere o qué?*"), he shouted, and when I began to explain our research relationship, he cut me off with, "Well, she doesn't live here," and hung up. I didn't pursue the interview, because I feared for Andrea's (and my) safety. A year later, my female research assistant reported a similar reception. She was told that Andrea was now with her parents in Oregon. That was the last I heard of Andrea.

IVONNE

In 1993, I ran into Ivonne and her former classmate Nancy on a city bus. Both were studying at the local CONALEP: Ivonne took nursing, while Nancy, after a year off from the "exhaustion" of school, took data processing (*informática*). I didn't speak with Ivonne again until 1995, when I stopped by her house. She had gone straight through the three years of CONALEP and was just finishing her last year of social service before she could gain full title as a nurse. Ivonne claimed to be happy with her work and had a serious boyfriend working in the United States, "supposedly saving money so we can get married." Excusing herself to continue her housework, she reluctantly agreed to a joint interview with her mother the following week. As it turned out, Ivonne stood me up then.

In 1997, I sought her out again at her home, and her mother informed me that she lived nearby with her husband and a newborn child. Ivonne's husband, whom she had known in the neighborhood since childhood, had returned from the United States and now worked hauling wood like Ivonne's father. Advising me that her husband was a jealous sort, Ivonne's mother promised to vouch for my character and request an interview on my behalf—in the husband's presence, if necessary. When I returned two weeks later (they had no telephone and lived a good distance from the city center), Ivonne's grandmother was lying in wake, her mother grieving. I couldn't press my agenda, and I never saw Ivonne again.

FIDEL

I found Fidel in 1995 carving furniture in his home village. His oldest brother was doing the same kind of work and had built a modest house next door, while his next oldest brother had joined the army a year ago. Fidel said he got paid to carve predrawn designs on furniture pieces supplied by a U.S. citizen in the capital. It would take him about an hour to carve each piece, for which he was paid 10 pesos, or about $1.50. Fidel admitted he was sorry about abandoning his studies for the first year or two after graduating from ESF, but now he didn't really care much. He would have to keep working to support himself anyway, and with school he'd have had no time at all to enjoy himself (*divertirse*). This way, he would be working enough to begin building his own little house on an adjacent piece of land. Fidel also mentioned that his mother had urged him to keep studying, yet this was not enough to convince him after his father had died. Confirming what ESF teachers often said, Fidel commented, "A mother's not the same as a father who's demanding and telling you to go to school, so that was that" ("*No es igual una mamá que un papá que te esté exigiendo y te esté diciendo que vayas a la escuela, y pos ya*").

JOSÉ

José had talked a lot about becoming a national highway patrolman (federal de caminos), and when I stopped by his house in 1993, his mother said he was still taken with the idea. She and her husband, who still drove a van in the urban transport system, preferred that he finish his final year of prepa with an eye toward university studies. A week later I found José at home, and he confirmed his continuing interest in becoming a federal de caminos. In the meantime, José had begun to enjoy the challenges of his work at the Centro de Salud (Public Health Center), where he was doing his social service.[6] He had been put in charge of health and sanitation inspections for parts of San Pablo and several other zones in the central part of the state.

It was not until 1995 that I met José's father for the first time. He disassembled and repaired a clothes iron while his wife complained about the rise in prices and absence of work. At one point he mentioned his new regular work, hauling finished wood products on a flatbed truck to cities as far as Ciudad Juárez on the Texas border. Work had been sporadic since the peso devaluation because orders for wood had plummeted. He chided me playfully for my country's role in Mexico's woes. Then José's mother told me that her son had finished his first year in accounting at the state university, but had lost the first semester due to illness. Given this, José had used his old contact at the Centro de Salud to secure a part-time job as an assistant accountant. His work would include assisting in a new regional education effort about cholera. When I finally met José in the plaza grande a week later, he confirmed his hope to keep the job even when he returned to the university in the fall. I also noted José's reserve, his social conservatism among his slang-speaking, knuckle-rapping, cigarette-smoking friends in the plaza. He even commented that he would rather commute each day to his studies in the capital because he had seen too many male classmates take to drinking and carousing, losing their focus. Meanwhile, José's friendships with his fellow public health workers continued to deepen. Together, they even talked about opening a video café "with a great sound system" or perhaps a special pharmacy in San Pablo.

I visited José's family for lunch in 1997, and his father was happy to report that he now only had to work a few days a week hauling wood to a city some three hours away. The family was also selling rolls of toilet paper and containers of bleach out of their house. José, meantime, had grown tired of going back and forth each day to the state capital for university classes, and his family just couldn't afford to keep him there on a daily basis. After missing much of his first year in accounting, José tried to study law his second year. Yet his accounting specialty from the CBTIS made this transition difficult, so now José seemed content to work full-time for the Centro de Salud, carrying out vaccinations and other related jobs. Pointing to one corner of the room, his parents joked that he spent most of his money on CDs and a new stereo to play them on. José arrived late for lunch with his girlfriend, a small, quiet girl who was studying the secretarial track at the CBTIS. I made plans to chat with José the following week, but an illness on my part canceled our date, and I only learned more about him when my assistant contacted him in June 1998.

Among other things, I was amazed to discover that José had changed jobs, gotten married, and fathered a baby boy by the end of the previous summer (apparently, his future wife was already well into her pregnancy during our short lunch visit). Because the Centro de Salud had wanted him to concentrate his work in remote and dangerous zones, José switched to a job as a price and inventory controller for a local grocery distributor. When my assistant interviewed him, José had just opened his own small grocery store with money saved from previous jobs. He hoped to improve the business and then turn it over to his wife in order to pursue yet another job or career. He also wanted to see his younger siblings go further in their studies, even as he recognized that a family business such as the grocery store was necessary to "survive, since a degree doesn't guarantee you anything." Always one to acknowledge his connections and debts, José attributed much of his recent success to his wife and former employers at the grocery center. Without their "support" and "motivation," José thought he'd have much less now in life.

EIGHT LIVES: THE ARC OF IDENTITY AND PRACTICE

FRANCO

On graduating, Franco enrolled in the local prepa, and by 1993, he had decided on a specialty of physics/mathematics. I ran into him one night in 1993 keeping company with his friend Miguel, who attended a newspaper kiosk in one corner of the plaza chica. He said he was just "watching the women pass by," and while I showed him some photos and asked about his studies, he continued to ogle the young women, inciting me to join him. The next day, I stopped by the tortillería, and Franco's father said that he wished Franco would take his studies more seriously. His oldest daughter had just graduated from a well-known public secundaria for girls in the capital, and Franco's next younger sister was set to enter that same school. Both were expected to continue their prepa studies as well.

The tortillería was still booming in 1995, but now there was competition on the other side of town. In order to finance all their children's studies, Franco's family had begun selling avocados, prepared chilies, and other items at the counter as well. Franco and his mother continued the repetitive motion of throwing small balls of dough onto the tortilla press and removing the circular patties that resulted. Through the noise of the press, Franco informed me that he was about to finish at the prepa and hoped to begin a computer course at a technological college in the state capital. If I wanted to talk more, he said, I could find him most afternoons playing video games at a downtown store or most evenings playing pool near the bus station.

In 1997, I saw Franco riding his motor scooter around town several times before I had a chance to stop by the tortillería. Franco had already told me that the scooter was meant for tortilla deliveries, but it was clear he had commandeered it as his personal vehicle. He had also told me that he had failed out of the technical college and was looking into studying veterinary medicine—his father's career. At the tortillería a few days later, Franco's parents made snide-sounding comments when I asked if it was true that he would study veterinary medicine ("This one doesn't have any idea what he wants to do"; "*Este ni sabe qué quiere hacer*"). They seemed exasperated with Franco's waffling performance, and Franco intervened to say without conviction that he was now "looking into" the chemical engineering degree at the state university.

Franco seemed eager for me to visit his afternoon English class. His parents had encouraged him to take up this activity to prepare himself for a scientific career. When I finally agreed to meet him in class, Franco showed up half an hour late. We went in, and I said a few words to the class. Afterward we went to a small café to chat. Franco started by telling me how he had failed a number of classes his final semester of prepa and had to repeat the year. He attributed this downswing to his family's economic problems and the increased demands for his labor in the tortillería.

Eventually, Franco finished prepa and began a career in "materials engineering" at the technological college in the capital, although it didn't go much better there. He went for a year and a half, but he never could pass one of the most difficult classes of his first semester. Part of the blame, he said, lay with the professor's enigmatic style of teaching. To make matters worse, his younger sister had just finished a shining career in the prepa and was about to finish her first year in the law program at the state university. She was clearly going to upstage her older brother. So Franco had gotten the idea to study veterinary medicine. His father had lots of old books and catalogs, and might help him with his studies. Besides, Franco knew there was little student interest in this profession now. The university would probably admit him even with his tangential physics/mathematics specialty from the prepa.

As his parents observed, Franco still seemed confused about what he wanted to do himself. He had learned to manage all aspects of the tortilla business, yet still internalized his father's messages about finishing a university career. In fact, in the following remarks it was not clear if Franco was reporting his father's words or assuming them himself:

Sometimes I think I should stop studying and devote myself to making flour tortillas, but then I see how my father doesn't like to exert himself much and it's like you get stuck there. The other day I told my father [or he told Franco?], I said why wasn't he exerting himself more ["*la otra vez le dije a mi papá, que por qué no le echaba más ganas*"], because I've seen a lot of people who study and don't have much money, and still they manage to keep studying a career. I don't respect someone who starts a career and then at the age of twenty or fifteen forgets the career for good. When I was in the technological college, I did see that the teachers were good and I liked to follow their example, that's why I have more desire now, because they kept at it.

On a second listening of the tape, it was difficult to make out the middle part of this little speech. It seemed, at first, that Franco was reproaching his own father for not working hard enough, for not having followed through on his veterinary career. Yet he was advancing the very same words that his father often used to motivate him. After all, Franco was the one who, at the age of twenty, was close to "forgetting his career for good." Franco's father had at least managed to finish his university coursework against great odds, and when he was much older than Franco. He did work as a livestock inspector for several years. Curiously, even though

Franco was not presently in school, he claimed to take heart in the example of his former college professors. This was a fairly typical confusion of voices for Franco. In our conversations, he would try to work out a response that made sense to him, often incorporating the prompts of parents and teachers. Even his newfound interest in veterinary medicine had emerged suddenly, and only then through suggestion from his parents and siblings. Franco admitted that he had never spent much time with animals, but now he wanted to work on a ranch to learn all about their reproductive cycles and eating habits. I couldn't help but wonder if Franco would ever find something he felt compelled or called to do.

IVÁN

By 1993, Iván had finally married his fiancé and resigned himself to a full-time job at the small engine repair shop where he had always worked. I happened across him fixing a lawnmower in front of the shop one day, and he informed me that his first child, a girl, had just been born a few months prior. Iván looked even older than his years now. He had gained a lot of weight and probably lost his fighting edge.

In 1995, his daughter would soon be turning three, but Iván still managed to visit occasionally with his former 3C mates, the Potrillos, at Benito's family's chili stall in the market. Incredibly, three of the former Potrillos were now studying law at the university. Iván had completed a full year at the CBTIS in electricity before dropping out to get married. As he put it, there just wasn't enough money to do both things. I continued to admire Iván's knowledge and skill around the shop where I would visit him. He was now in charge of two assistants, and managed to keep them motivated with jokes and spicy banter. At one point, a man who came to retrieve an electric trimmer was told they would have to send it off to Mexico City because the shop didn't repair electric items. When the customer grew irritated at not having been informed of this in the first place, Iván employed a picaresque insult about the employee who had originally waited on him as a way of smoothing things over. Iván seemed as skilled in customer relations as in small engine repair!

I made a date to have dinner with Iván in 1997, and he arrived with his hair slicked back and smelling of strong cologne. He seemed more eager to talk, more straightforward, than I had ever seen him before. Iván had entered the CBTIS but never got beyond the start of his second year. He had continued to work at the engine repair shop throughout this time, trying to save enough money to quit the job, "rob" his girlfriend, and marry her. He achieved this in December 1992. Summarizing his account of a once-thwarted, harrowing elopement, Iván said he had dropped his studies only because he was so powerfully in love. Otherwise, he would have stopped working and pursued a career.[7]

For six months Iván tried to make it on his own. At first, he opened his own shop with tools that he had accumulated over the years, but he barely made enough to cover his rent. He closed the shop after a few months and went to harvest avocados about one hour from San Pablo, yet the difficulty of the work made him leave after just one week. Then he lasted only a week assisting a bricklayer, and went on to work in his father's print shop, a job he had never really liked. Eventually, Iván sucked up his pride and went to ask for his old job back. The owner of the engine shop recognized his talents and brought him on board. He has worked there ever since.

Iván and his wife had spent the first few weeks of their marriage living with Iván's parents, just enough time, he said, for them to get some things together and rent a modest house. With the failure of his own small shop, however, they had to abandon the rental and return to his parents again. Throughout this period, Iván's wife was doing her social service in order to get her nursing degree. By the end of the year, though, she was well into her first pregnancy, and they moved in with her parents shortly before the birth. A few months after the healthy delivery of their first daughter, Iván started bickering with his mother-in-law and once again sought to rent a small house. At the same time, Iván began donating a larger share of his salary to a social security fund in order to qualify sooner for government-subsidized housing. His boss advanced a significant part of his salary so he could channel it into his point total, but this process put a real squeeze on the family's economy. Iván endured nearly a year of extremely low real wages. "It was looking black, really black" ("*Me las ví negras, negras*"), he said. "The money wouldn't even cover a week's worth of meals. All last year the situation was very hard." They were always reluctant to call on their parents for assistance: "Sure, they helped us out with a meal here and there, but to completely depend on their help? No" ("*Sí nos ayudaban con un taco, pero ¿así totalmente enclavarnos a ellos a que nos ayuden?, no*").

After occupying the government-subsidized house, Iván's second daughter was born under dangerous circumstances. Only a cesarean section and partial hysterectomy saved her. Iván's wife had wanted to deliver him a boy, and they had originally planned a family of three or four. She even told him that he could go have another child with someone else ("*por otro lado*"), but Iván claimed to be perfectly happy with his two daughters.

I asked if he would want his wife to work, and he said she would after their youngest child entered school. He noted tenderly his wife's influence in cultivating his sense of responsibility: "It was my wife who made me who I am today. She made me mature, because I was still very young when we got married" (she was one year older at seventeen, although two school grades ahead).[8]

Would Iván stay to repair chainsaws and mowers the rest of his life? Already he had been tempted to take a job as a supply van driver for a national snack food company. His wife's uncle had also enticed him with jobs washing cars during the day and dishes at night in Denver, Colorado. But Iván could not bear to "abandon" his daughters so young. He still left the option open for several years down the road. Meanwhile, the owner of the engine shop had worried that she might lose Iván, and offered to let him train in fixing and preparing a new kind of bandsaw. When he had mastered this piece of equipment, she would let him try to sell it on the road; Iván would keep his base salary and work on commission. This arrangement was enough to keep Iván satisfied for the time being. Still, Iván said, he would stay on the lookout for something with a higher salary and ultimately wanted to establish his own shop: "Even if I already failed once, even two or three times don't matter, until that darn shop gets well established. That [project] still remains in my plans" ("*hasta que quede bien ese mentado taller. Eso sigue en pie todavía*").

From his time in the secundaria, Iván remembered his friendships the most, above all the mischievous pranks (*travesuras*) he would carry out with them. He still considered the secundaria years a special time:

> I think it must be the most valuable moment that an adolescent can go through, no? [¿*Es la etapa mas apreciada que pueda tener un adoles-cente, no?*] Not so much for what [the teachers] used to teach me, but for the nice time I got to spend there. It was the friendship as much as the enmity, yes, that's what attracted me the most, the friendships. I'm telling you, my little gang [*mi palomilla*]. I say my gang because they really were my gang.

Iván insisted on his own leadership and recalled a number of pranks that he initiated himself. He also recollected that the palomilla rarely extended beyond the school. Benito would go off to watch over his family's chili stand, Valentino would hang out with his friends and girlfriends in the distant colonia where he lived, Matías would study in the library, and Andrés would work in his family's bicycle shop. The palomilla was only a school-based phenomenon, and Iván was sad to see it disintegrate on graduation. He rarely saw his former friends, spending all his free time now with his family, especially watching television and rented videos. Yet he still wanted to make Benito his *compadre* some day: "That Benito, I like him, I like him a *lot.*"

I suppose I should not have been surprised when Iván then described his deep religious faith. To be sure, his parents had always conditioned his weekday liberties on faithful weekly church attendance, yet by the time he got married, this perfunctory ritual came to have new meaning. The church had sanctified his love, and during difficult times, he and his wife would take out their altar stones and ties from the marriage to pray for relief. It seemed to have always worked. Iván had already made a couple of pilgrimages to pay off his "debts" to a powerful santo. Then he prayed to the Virgin of Guadalupe for his youngest daughter's well-being when she was born prematurely. When she recovered, he made the trip alone to "see" the Virgin at her sanctuary outside Mexico City. Now, he was a confirmed devotee of the Virgin and attended services at the local Guadalupan church whenever he could.

ALBERTO

When I knocked on Alberto's door in 1993, he answered with a quizzical look and swore he'd just been thinking about me while listening to a Paul Simon song. Along with a few other workers, he was in the midst of painting his family's house. Alberto told me he could not really start his summer vacation until the job was finished. Throughout our twenty-minute chat, the large-screen television in the opposite room blared MTV music brought in by a satellite dish. Alberto informed me that he had transferred from the public prepa to the institute outside of town. His best friend and former Juanito Constantín joined him there. Alberto's middle oldest brother, the architect, had gotten married and moved into an apartment on the second floor of his father's medical office. The brother immediately above him in age had transferred from an elite law school in Mexico City to a new private college in the state capital, where he had also started a carwash business that appeared to be thriving.

Alberto caught me having my afternoon coffee on the plaza grande in 1995 and was eager to talk. Among other things, he told me about his frightening bout with cancer. Since he'd had a malignant tumor removed last year, he had become even more "Catholic," though he didn't elaborate. He was also more committed than ever to his medical career. Now one year into the medicine program at the state university, his dream was to assemble a team of specialists and work somewhere in a large, well-equipped hospital. Alberto also updated me on some of his relationships. He talked about fighting his old classmate Antonio in what he characterized as a stupid, drunken showdown on the grounds of the preparatoria. Alberto described his mother as a lifesaver for having recognized the poisoned environment of the prepa and insisting he transfer to the new institute outside of town. In the prepa, Alberto was drinking a case of beer nearly every day with his buddies. He was really going downhill. At the institute, he said, they kept much stricter control, and his grades improved immediately.

A couple of weeks later, I spent the better part of a day in the state capital with Alberto. He took me to see the well-appointed apartment he shared with his older brother, who was still studying law. Then we went to see the latest version of *Batman* at the local cineplex. We discussed the special effects and most recent technological advancements as he drove us around town in his red Volkswagen. The next day Alberto took me to the bus station. The deluxe highway coach that transported me to Mexico City played the video *Buffy the Vampire Slayer* on a closed circuit television as midsummer cornfields and swollen burros passed by my window. I wondered if Alberto would appreciate this juxtaposition of campy U.S. popular culture with rural Mexico.

I did not think I would see Alberto at all in 1997. When I stopped by the house in San Pablo, his father answered the door and updated me on Alberto's three brothers: the oldest would soon finish his specialty in internal medicine in Guadalajara, the next was still an architect doing well out of his own local office and also selling building materials, and the one just above Alberto was about to receive his license in law. Alberto himself was hardly returning to San Pablo for visits these days, his father revealed sadly. Exams and papers were keeping him busy full-time. When I fell ill and left San Pablo shortly thereafter, I knew I wouldn't visit Alberto. Still, I called him up in early June, and we had a nice chat. Among other things, Alberto told me that he had already begun specializing in surgery. When I suggested at one point that having three older brothers as *profesionistas* had helped pave the way for Alberto, he did not protest, although he mentioned that both his father and oldest brother had actually tried to dissuade him from medicine at first. They wanted to extirpate his romantic vision, to show him the pain and sacrifice involved. To that end, Alberto's father sent him to live with his brother for a month while the latter was doing his social service in a remote rural area. But the experience only strengthened Alberto's resolve.

In the past two years, Alberto had overcome several obstacles. He sustained his own injuries in an automobile accident followed just a week later by the death of one of his best friends in a similar accident. This caused his grades to go down, and he had set himself the goal of raising his average in the present school year. More recently, he had begun dating a classmate he'd known from his first year in medical school. Her father was a cardiologist, and together she and Alberto dreamed of starting their own medical practice. Alberto insisted on finishing his career first, and that meant another year of classes followed by a year of internship and then a year of social service. Only then would he consider marriage in his immediate plans.

Before I knew it, Alberto and I were seriously discussing a visit to Indiana, where I was living, and we made the necessary arrangements. Over the course of his nearly two-week stay in July, I was able to appreciate other sides of Alberto. For one thing, he was hardly surprised or impressed with most of what I showed him. He had already seen so much on a month-long trip to California and in his middle-class milieu back in Mexico. He was not intrigued by my computer or Web skills, since he had spent a lot of time on the Web with his equally powerful computer. In fact, he'd been asked to contribute a regular column on related Web resources for his university's medical school newsletter. Nor was he terribly excited to accompany me on a motorcycle ride, since he had ridden much bigger and better bikes in Mexico.

Alberto also displayed a keen entrepreneurial spirit. He closely tasted and observed our vegetarian food, then considered seriously the prospect of starting a chain of vegetarian restaurants in Mexico. In politics, Alberto clearly favored the conservative, free-market Partido de Acción Nacional, a leading opposition party. He confessed his disillusionment with the "political farce" of the dominant party, the PRI. His family had always been *priista* as far back as he could remember, but the corruption had become too much for him. Besides, he said, his experiences as a medical student had opened his eyes in other ways, too: "There are a lot of shortages, you know. And I see it from the point of view of health. We can and should have politicians who in reality cover the people's needs, right? Above all the basic needs, and one of those basic needs is health." Alberto similarly expressed strong sentiment in favor of policies designed to assist the poor and create equal opportunities.

Showing a good deal of intellectual curiosity, Alberto also wanted to know more about my research and assess my interpretations (like a few of the former students, he has reviewed this summary). When we walked along the shores of Lake Michigan in Chicago, he asked me about my understanding of God. He was intrigued by my agnosticism yet challenged it as well. Alberto remained firmly in the Catholic faith, quoting his father as saying that you had to believe in something larger than yourself. Otherwise, in times of trouble, whom could you always turn to? Though he confessed to having been "indoctrinated" into Catholicism as a child, later he accepted it through reason and conviction. In our phone call a month earlier, Alberto had confirmed that his survival of cancer and the events of the last year had deepened his conviction. Since 1994, he had devoted himself to a powerful San Pablo "virgin" (saint image) who lent him her healing powers. Even if he rarely attended church, when in San Pablo, Alberto would always try to visit the virgin's sanctuary. She had helped him "turn his life around" and "put things in order" this past year. Nevertheless, Alberto's growing experience with medicine had sometimes shaken his faith. He had been to a hospital and seen a few young children die, wondering why they had ever lived, and his study of medical biology urged him toward a more mechanistic view of the universe. Alberto continued seeking answers to his many questions.

ENRIQUE

When I went to Enrique's house in July 1993, his parents told me he was working as a mechanic's apprentice. His father had been driving a public transport van the last couple of years, but he was thinking about heading up north again, to join a brother in Nebraska or catch shrimp off the Alaska coast. His mother appeared to be pregnant with her seventh child. According to his parents, Enrique had not wanted to continue his studies. He began working in a mechanic's shop soon after graduating from ESF. He was thinking now about joining his father for the illegal trip to the United States, or perhaps joining the army. He had a serious girlfriend of some five months. She was a year or two older, and they'd met right there in the poor colonia where they lived. Since she was moving to the state capital soon to study, Enrique thought an army placement in the capital possible and desirable.

I stopped by to see Enrique at his workplace just a couple of days later. He came out to greet me with his blackened clothes and an oilcloth in hand. The most immediate decision he faced was whether or not to accompany his father to the United States. Perhaps in a gesture of masculine cavalier, he confessed he wouldn't let his girlfriend influence his decision. Enrique told me that he had almost completed a whole year of preparatoria. He was doing fine until the second semester, when he started forgetting everything he had learned in secundaria. Besides, he said, the principal tried to trick the students with a sudden monthly tuition raise, and Enrique wanted to stand his ground on that. As we departed, Enrique commented that he didn't know if he could stay with his father on a long sojourn in the United States. "I don't like the way he acts. . . . [I]t's that he's really a womanizer [mujeriego]." His remark proved ironically prophetic. Within three years, Enrique would be on his own in the United States, and his father would abandon his mother to establish another San Pablo household with a younger woman and their two small children. As the oldest child, Enrique had become the most secure breadwinner in the family.

I spoke with Enrique a few times when he was still in Oregon. He seemed restless away from his family. His father had returned to San Pablo the year after they had arrived together in Oregon, but Enrique stayed on with an uncle. He eventually found an apartment to share with a few young Mexicans, and this enabled him to send more money home. His mother, whom I visited in May 1997, emphasized what a good son Enrique had always been. He had always shown great concern for his younger brothers and sisters (seven in all, from a seventeen-year-old brother to a two-year-old sister), sending even more money when he learned his father would cut back his contribution. Indeed, he managed to send enough money for his mother to buy the vacant lot next door so Enrique could later build his own house there. He was thinking about coming back soon, but now that he had spent most of his extra money on the lot, he would probably work at least another year to save some more money.

Then, too, I admired Enrique's mother's command of the household. While I visited, she was cleaning beans for the afternoon meal, taking frequent breaks to scold the children, hurry them off to school, and arrange the hair of the two girls who would soon be off to the afternoon shift of the primaria. Yet Enrique's mother also took moments to say sweet things to the children, joyfully noting some of their innocent and funny phrases. I observed how the siblings watched after each other. At the same time, Enrique's mother filled me in on the family. Her next to oldest son had studied a year at the CBTIS before dropping out to work for a couple of years to help support the family. Now that Enrique was sending more money, this son had joined his younger brother at the CONALEP. Neither boy had ambitions to study beyond that. They would become computer and automotive mechanical technicians, respectively, in order to work right away. Another brother was in the nearby secundaria técnica, and two sisters traveled an extra distance to attend one of the best primarias in town.

I finally spoke with Enrique at some length in August 1997. He had moved from working at a nursery to a nut orchard. He still harbored hopes of continuing his schooling one day—in computer programming perhaps—but for now, he would stay in Oregon and look for better work at a new cannery that was due to open soon. Enrique claimed he had always wanted to keep studying, but that mixing studies with work was too difficult for him, especially when his father had stopped supporting the family. Now twenty-two, he remembered his years in the secundaria fondly. One day, on a whim, he had called his old grupo mate Edna, a modest girl from Andrea's friendship group who had been Enrique's closest contact among the girls. She was surprised to hear him calling from the United States, and together they reminisced about ESF while Edna brought him up to date on the doings of their former classmates. Enrique recounted one exchange between them that had stood out:

BL: And what about [Edna], she didn't get married?
ENRIQUE: No, not yet. I asked her, "Are you pregnant?" and she said, "No." And then [I asked], "Your boyfriend?" "No, I don't have a boyfriend." "Why not?" So she says, "No, there aren't any men around here." I told her, "Ay, I can't believe that. . . . Well, what can you do? All of them are up here [in the United States] now!" ["*Bueno pues, ni modo. ¡Ya se vinieron todos para acá!*"].

After recalling more of his former classmates, Enrique discussed with obvious delight the mischievous reputation that had always followed 3A: "In our second year, they supposedly gave us the most demanding teachers, the strictest ones and all that, but the students came out on top once again. No, but truthfully, it was a really nice time in the secundaria. Sometimes I'd like to go back in time and be there again." Perhaps because he'd been unable to develop more lasting friendships in the preparatoria, Enrique still made primary reference to the connections rooted in his grupo escolar.

Enrique had been among the poorest students at ESF, yet he didn't cower among his richer classmates. Even back then I had noticed that he was virtually the only ESF student who chose to frequent the plaza chica on weekends. When I reminded him of this in 1997, Enrique defended his choice of the plaza chica over the plaza grande, claiming its atmosphere was more "joyful" ("*alegre*"), more pleasant. Only the "bourgeois" ("*burgueses*") really favored the plaza grande. Citing the popular singer Thalía, Enrique said the plaza chica was the place for the "folk" ("*la raza*"), the "poor ones on this side [of the border]" ("*los pobres de este lado*"). I suggested to Enrique that most of his classmates had preferred the plaza grande because it made them feel of higher social standing, and he agreed by recounting his own response to the pressure these classmates had exerted:

> Sometimes that used to happen [imitating a classmate's voice]: "Listen, why are you going over there. The [real] plaza is here." So I told them, "Look, I can't be over there where you are. I can be over here, because I see all people as equal." I told them, "Look, you take out your wallet, you carry a lot of money. I hardly carry any money, but why? What do you really gain [have over me]? We're all equal" [*Le digo, "Mira, tú sacas tu cartera, traes mucho dinero, yo traigo muy poco dinero, ¿por qué? ¿Qué te ganas? Somos iguales.*"]

Like his grupo mate Andrea, then, Enrique appeared to use the rhetoric of equality drawn from school culture to challenge the inequalities presumed by a schooled identity (see chapter 5). He asserted a democratic conception of social membership that ignored differences in wealth and education.

Then, because I had seen it happen with so many others, I asked Enrique if after four years he had become attached to the "luxuries" of U.S. life. He admitted his passion for soccer, and enjoyed the well-kept playing fields in Oregon. Yet Enrique said he was looking forward to seeing Mexico soon. He hoped to return in December, and didn't know if he would see the United States again. Just as his mother had said, Enrique showed a remarkable commitment to his family and their sentimental bonds. As Enrique put it, "In general, sometimes material things don't interest me much. I've decided to be happy with myself and happy with my family." Late one night in December 1997, I was awoken by Enrique's phone call from Oregon. He just wanted to say good-bye because he was leaving for San Pablo the next day.

ROSITA

Still early in the school year of 1990, Rosita called me over during recess and said she wanted to consult with me. She proceeded to tell me about the quarrel her parents had had the night before. She claimed to have successfully blocked out the details of it, even though they had been arguing close to where she was doing her homework. After a few minutes, she said, her father asked her to bring him his coffee with some cookies because he was going upstairs to rest, but her mother blurted out a defense, scolding, "Why don't you do it yourself? Your daughter is not your slave. If you're already down here, why can't you just serve yourself?" Rosita said this whole episode caused her to stay up all night with worry.

The conflict between her parents would become a dominant theme in Rosita's final year of secundaria, and it became clear that Rosita felt somewhat responsible for it. One day shortly after the discussion described above, I noted that Rosita looked distracted and upset. She hardly looked at me, and when I asked her if she was angry, she only managed, "I had a big mess [relajo] at home." When I finally caught up with her after school, and we walked alone for a stretch, she told me her parents had upbraided her for her grades, which were much lower than usual during the first grading period. Then they had argued with one another. As I observed in several other households, the father had blamed the mother for insufficient vigilance over their daughter's studies, and the mother had defended herself in turn. In the manner of an unspoken agreement, the father felt that his material provision of the family obligated the wife to take care of the home, and by extension, monitor the conditions allowing for school success. Rosita thus felt she had occasioned an uncomfortable fight between her parents.

Both of Rosita's parents were strongly committed to her education. I learned this when I became quite close with Rosita and her family, visiting often. If her father was home, I was invariably obliged to sit and chat with him, while Rosita and her mother sat on the margins of our conversation and listened or went about their household chores. Rosita's mother often chipped in her comments, but did not otherwise take a leading role. Because of this, I relished the opportunities to speak with Rosita's mother at length, when her husband was outside the home. It was during these talks that I learned why she so adamantly upheld her daughter's right to choose her own friends, leisure activities, and eventual career. She spoke with a sense of sadness and loss about her own missed opportunities (her parents would not support her continued studies), and her too-early marriage to a man who turned out much like her own domineering father. Rosita's mother was struggling in a marriage, and a web of affinal kin, that she regretted in many ways. Her solution, it seemed to me, was to invest in her own daughters' happiness and freedom. That is why she enjoined her husband to give Rosita more independence, and why more overt household conflicts had begun to develop as Rosita matured.

Early in the 1990–1991 school year, Rosita's mother hoped that her husband, through his union position with the truck drivers, could get them a subsidized house in the state capital. That way, they could start saving and send Rosita to the capital as early as preparatoria studies. Yet just a month later, the mother revealed to me that once again Rosita had returned from an activity much later than they had agreed. Now her mother was convinced that Rosita still lacked the "responsibility" she had so diligently tried to impart. This meant they would not be able to let her study her prepa in the capital. I noted that responsibility here implied obeying parental orders, and especially, guarding her female sexuality and propriety.

Nonetheless, in 1993, Rosita had grown more certain about her career while in the San Pablo prepa. She had decided to study law, but with an eye toward public relations or journalism (*ciencias de la comunicación*). Her father had his own ideas about her career, and endorsed the choice of law and politics. Her mother remained supportively neutral: "We'll support you in whatever you decide to study." Rosita also explained that her father had grown more "accessible" with a diagnosis of diabetes and the recent death of his own father. She had seen him cry for the first time, and shortly thereafter, he finally agreed to a big fifteenth birthday party, which they eventually did up in style.

In 1995, Rosita was finishing her first year in the law program at the state university. She lived in a student boarding house with some five other young women, and claimed to spend little time outside the house. When I visited her family in San Pablo, the father dominated the conversation as usual. He challenged my liberal views on Chiapas and the Zapatistas, alleging that they had brought on the devaluation by scaring away foreign capital—he was more progovernment than ever. Rosita and her mother managed to break in to show me some photographs from both her fifteenth birthday party and class exchange trip to Detroit. The mother related her surprise that Rosita's father had given permission for the trip to the United States altogether.

By 1997, Rosita had grown even more serious and expressed great satisfaction in the law career she had chosen. Soon to finish her third year of classes, she would go observe proceedings in the state legislature and do her social service in a law office every weekday. She was amazed to learn that the law included so many complexities and did not know yet what specialty she might choose, though criminal law and the question of human rights interested her a great deal. Rosita asserted that she rarely went out with friends; her studies occupied virtually all her time. For over a month now, she had spent time with a young man she called her novio, but insisted it was mainly a supportive friendship. Rosita had put all thought of marriage out of her mind until she felt fully "developed" as a person. Her career came first. When I asked her how she had come to this decision, her response was immediate:

> Well, my parents. Ever since we were little children they would always, always tell us that school comes first, that school is the most important thing. And, well, it's like you gradually acquire this idea of what's the most important thing, the purpose [*sentido*] of your life. And that's what we've done. I don't start counting my career from three years ago [the beginning of her university studies] to the present. Rather, I think of my career as having started in kindergarten and gone on to primaria, secundaria, preparatoria, up until now. And if they were to tell me, "Know what? Everything you've done up until now is worthless, you've got to start all over again," I would start all over again.

The constancy of her parents' prodding was evident. Rosita had every-thing worked out. She would take a government post for at least a couple of years after her degree, getting a pension and "fixed salary." Then she might try to open her own law practice. She figured she would get married in seven years, and when I ribbed her about the exactness of her calcula-tions, she hedged just a little, admitting that if she were to fall madly in love she might move it up a couple of years. Still, nothing would divert her from gaining her professional title. She would even have two children eventually, but only "in due time."

Rosita's reflection on what she had gained from her secundaria years was notable for its adoption of the adult viewpoint. It also showed just how different her experience could be from her former grupo mate, Dalia:

> [Secundaria] is when you change, when you stop being a child in order to be an adolescent. It's when your ideas are being molded, when you establish your sense of right and wrong, you establish yourself as a person, it's when you lay down the path you'll follow. It's the most innocent age because nothing you do is done out of malice or [the] desire to hurt someone. You do it in order to feel good, to have fun, to

be yourself. . . . It was the age when I felt I could do anything, that I could go over here and over there; it's when I met my friends and knew they were my friends and would never leave me. You're not so neurotic, so full of social vices, like envy, anger—there wasn't any space [in the secundaria] for all that. It's a very nice time, very different from all the others. It's where you feel change the most, it's where you feel the whole world is against you, but you're also against the whole world in that phase, because it's when they scold you the most, you rebel, it's when you learn a whole lot of things.

Rosita went on to discuss how the secundaria had been distinctively different both for the quality of her teachers and that of her relations with her classmates. She distinguished the former from her primaria teachers, saying:

In the secundaria, you start to make your own plans and it's not so much whether you love the teacher or not but what the teacher's position represents [*lo que representa esa figura*]. Because it's a person with advanced studies, who knows what he/she is talking about. So that encourages your own responsibility, your desire to keep studying. [The teacher] helps you forge your own goals, orients you; in fact, many of the teachers would orient you for that same reason, because they had studied and knew all about these things. They helped to make you responsible.

Because of the unquestionable dedication to schooling her own parents had imparted, Rosita was ready to receive the lessons of schooled identity offered by her teachers. She was able to identify with the knowledge and social position "represented" by the secundaria teachers. Yet Rosita still valued the quality of peer relations that would sometimes challenge teachers' attempts to form "responsible" behavior.

When I asked her what event she most remembered from her secundaria years, she didn't miss a beat in recounting the episode with Mr. Carrizo I presented in chapter 4, citing it as a fine example of compañerismo and *unión de grupo*. These dynamics distinguished the secundaria from what came after:

In the secundaria, camaraderie is a general rule. It's like saying if we're not together or if you're not with us you don't survive, if we're not together you go down. . . . By contrast, in the preparatoria . . . it's all very individualistic, there it's "think only of yourself." [*En la secundaria es una regla el compañerismo. Es como decir si no estamos juntos, o si no estás con nosotros no sobrevives, si no estamos juntos te hundes . . . En cambio en la preparatoria . . . es algo muy individualista, y allí es "piensa en tí mismo."*]

Unlike Dalia and some of her other classmates, Rosita still highly valued the camaraderie of her time in the secundaria. This was a value that would persist throughout her life.

Rosita had always struck me as one of the most religious students I had known. She had gone through all the major Catholic rites, frequently made reference to God, and said she prayed for her family's health and well-being. So when I asked her what role religion had played and still did play in her life, she emphasized the change in her conception of it:

> I don't know quite how to tell what has changed because before I was very, well, let's say I had too much faith. . . . I didn't used to open my mind to other things, other types of religion. I haven't looked into other religions, what saints they believe in and that kind of thing, no. But now in saying, "I believe in this and have faith," it's like saying, "I believe in what I can do with the help of the security that this God or this saint provides me." It's no longer so much a matter of one being Catholic and the little blows [*golpecitos,* or self-flagellation] and so much prayer.

Rosita now claimed religion represented a form of "protection," security. Most strikingly, she considered her own religion against a broader field of beliefs. Her schooling experience had produced in her an appreciation of "plural convictions," for Anthony Giddens (1991) a defining feature of modernity. No longer could she remain "stuck" ("*aferrada*") on her own God. Significantly, Rosita cited the transition from a private religious colegio to the public secundaria as the determining moment in this dawning awareness. In the colegio, the sisters had taught a closed kind of faith, but in the secundaria, Rosita encountered a greater variety of customs and beliefs.

Finally, like so many of her former classmates, Rosita had become a jaded pragmatist regarding politics. The political arena was defined by corruption, she said, and one could not get very far by honest means. Opposition parties had to play the same game. At least the PRI had "experienced people" ("*gente preparada*") and got things done, she rationalized. More specifically, she admitted, it was to her own advantage (*me conviene*) to support the PRI. Since they would hold the reins of power for the foreseeable future, her own desire for a government job depended on her demonstrated loyalty to them.

NIDIA

I got some help from two of Nidia's old ESF schoolmates when I tried to find her in 1993. They saw me walking around the plaza grande one morning and hurried me over to an accounting office around the corner. There I found Nidia huddled over some books, and she seemed happy yet flustered to see me. She took a break from work to tell me about her plans. She had one year left in a comercio (accounting and secretarial) course at one of the private colegios. Her work in the office was part of her social service for that degree. When she graduated, she said, she would probably have to leave the area to find work. She thought to go live with an aunt in Mexicali, but that aunt was even stricter than her own father. Or she could live with her grandfather in Monterrey, and he would be less strict. I noted the emphasis on finding a place that would permit her a measure of freedom. Yet later, Nidia would tell me that it was during this time, as she was finishing her degree and her older sisters were leaving the house, that her mother became her "intimate friend." Together the two gathered frequently in church, where Nidia formed part of the *coros* (choir) and enjoyed hearing the talks given by the padres. She claimed to feel best during the time she was in church. Nidia's desire to free herself from her father's control must have been great indeed to leave all this behind.

I did not speak with Nidia again until August 1997, when I called her in Mexicali where she was living with her aunt. After graduating in June 1994 with a degree in comercio, Nidia began working as an accountant in a store on San Pablo's main plaza. Just six months later, she had to be let go. Her aunt was visiting from Mexicali around that time, and Nidia returned with her to see if she would like it there. It was not long before she got a job as a cashier in a Mexicali bakery. After having worked there for more than a year, she got a job inspecting computer chips for a border factory (*maquiladora*) that manufactured consumer electronic goods. Her high school degree in comercio had helped Nidia keep books for the bakery owner, but her present job drew little on her formal school knowledge.

When I asked her what life was like in such a large border city, she commented that she still didn't have any real friends, just friendly mates at work. She continued to be shy and spend time alone, calling her parents at least once a week. We both laughed at the irony of her "escape" to Mexicali. Nidia's two older sisters had gotten married quite young, so she was now considered the oldest (mayor) of the remaining children. By letting her continue living in Mexicali, her parents had accorded her a trust and freedom never given to her older sisters. Nidia wanted to control her own destiny, but she admitted that she monitored herself as much as her own father might. She was as determined not to disappoint (*defraudar*) her parents as she was to find her own way: "I was always shut up in the house back in my village and even though my father denied me many things [dances, parties], now that I'm here on my own I deny myself in the same way, but at least I make my own decisions [*me mando sola*]." When I asked her what she might be doing in the next three to five years, Nidia hesitated, saying only that she would like to keep moving ahead (salir adelante) and eventually "triumph." Concretely, that meant she would ultimately get a position corresponding fully to her training and aptitude. Still, she was happy enough with her present job; she was not looking hard for another but might consider an opportunity that appeared:

> You can obtain the right job with practice and above all if [the employers] know you; in other words, sure they give you work, but sometimes nothing more. They don't trust you enough, you know? Sometimes I think it's not like that [in San Pablo], that here people are more distrustful . . . and [in San Pablo] on the other hand, they aren't.

Because of her low and recent social profile in a big city like Mexicali, Nidia was having difficulties navigating the notoriously personalized Mexican labor market. She interpreted this as a difference in the essential qualities of the residents (distrustful versus trustful) rather than a difference in her circumstances and position in that city.

Nidia did say that she would like to get married, but not nearly as young as her two older sisters. She even reflected wistfully that if she had stayed in her village, she would probably be married by now. So I was surprised to learn that she did have a serious novio with whom she had fallen in love through a neighbor's photographs! This neighbor's son, some twenty-seven years old and originally from Mexicali, now worked in a Nebraska meatpacking plant. Occasionally, he got to use his studies as a mechanic by driving and repairing the plant's big rigs. He came to visit at least once a year, but stayed for just a few days. I must have sounded incredulous when I asked Nidia to confirm that she had only spent a few hours of a few days with her boyfriend, yet she was eager to admit it. Nidia said she would like to visit the United States, perhaps even live there, but she was not willing to cross the border illegally, and her novio hadn't asked her to—she was instead trying to apply for a legal visa. Nidia also expressed a desire to have children with her eventual husband, although not anytime soon. Then I asked her where she thought they might live, and she surprised me again by suggesting it was proper for her to follow her husband wherever he might want to go: "Well, I say whatever he says goes, and that if I love him, I'm going to follow him wherever he may be, right?" This sentiment seemed to contradict much of what she asserted before and after. For instance, when I commented on the difficulty I had getting around jealous husbands to speak with some of her former schoolmates, she agreed that people were sometimes "closed" ("cerradita") like that, especially in her home state. In Mexicali, Nidia said, women had a much greater say in these kinds of matters, and that's the way it should be. So Nidia showed a shifting combination of desire for personal freedom and satisfaction, and a desire for the security and satisfaction of a family.

LETICIA

While still in the secundaria, Leticia already had an acutely developed sense of social justice. She worried about the problems of the world, and sounding the themes of peace and compassion, often berated her classmates for considering themselves before others. I identified closely with her youthful idealism and told her so. Leticia also reported that she was generally a happy person with a secure sense of herself. Nevertheless, about midway through the 1990–1991 year, in the notebook she shared with me, Leticia recorded an inexplicable change:

> Lately I've been feeling insecure, nervous, like I'm not content anywhere, and this is unusual for me . . . because I've always been a resolute girl who makes decisions for herself. . . . Now I don't know what's happening to me. It's difficult for me to make a decision; I contradict myself and don't know what I want. . . . It's quite logical to think this is because of adolescence, since that's the stage I'm in, but many teachers have explained this to us and it's not exactly what I feel.

Eventually Leticia would emerge from this funk, but it would reoccur throughout her young life. Most telling was her entertainment and then rejection of the discourse on adolescence as a means of explanation. Although this seemed "logical" given the circumstances, Leticia thought her experience did not quite fit the model.

In 1993, Leticia's father was now managing two auto parts stores and a small mechanics shop. Her oldest brother was living in the state capital and writing his college thesis; her middle brother had dropped out of his college-level agronomy program and worked at one of her father's stores, saving for marriage; the next youngest brother (still a few years older than her) was studying medicine in the capital; finally, her younger brother, just entering secundaria himself, was having difficulties in school because of what Leticia's mother called his "hypersensitivity." Leticia herself had been spending most of her summer days at the new auto parts shop opened in a peripheral colonia. She was still wondering about her studies and career. Along with several of her ESF friends, she had chosen the social sciences course (bachillerato) at the prepa, but still had time to switch to the economic/administrative or pedagogical specialty. As she explained it, the social science degree mainly prepared her for a teaching career, although most teachers she'd asked had tried to dissuade her from work that had such low pay, low prestige, and difficult conditions. She was even considering medicine. At the same time, Leticia continued to lament the fates of some of her former female classmates. Her cousin Sara, an ESF second grader in 1990 and now only fifteen years old, had stopped studying and was poised to marry.

In 1995, I found Leticia cleaning house with her mother, bored and anxious about her future. On her father's prompting, and because of the economic security it seemed to offer, Leticia had entered the accounting program at the public university. By the end of the year, though, she was painfully bored with her classes and receiving what for her seemed like poor grades. She dropped out in desperation. Now, she was biding her time in the house or at one of her father's auto parts stores. Leticia worked as secretary for her older brother who managed the stores, helped her younger brother with school projects, cleaned house, and listened to music. She was thinking again about teaching social studies at the secondary level, but she had been told that to do this she'd first need to graduate from the regular Normal school, teach primary school for five years, and return to the Normal Superior for advanced training. Meanwhile, her oldest brother, the biologist, was working for the Federal Water Commission in the capital, while the brother above her, a doctor, had just begun his medical residency in a nearby city.

Leticia and I finally got a good chance to sit down and chat in May 1997. We reviewed her life over the last few years, and the first thing Leticia did was to clarify why she had begun studying accounting and how she had come to drop it. Leticia had thought the accounting major at the university would be relatively easy in the academic sense, that she would not have to "kill herself" studying because the course was rather "mechanical." She was philosophical about why she had continued with a career she knew would not fulfill her: "I feel that you can't always do what you'd like, above all when you're in the conditions like I am now, and like so many people here in Mexico. I came to think that I would be able to substitute some things that I like [for the career I didn't like]." In other words, Leticia had made a strategic choice to pursue a practical career that cost little yet provided greater economic return. This would enable her to do other things she enjoyed. She said she liked to go out and dance, for example, but as a teacher, she would never have the money or time to go dancing, even while she was still studying. Nevertheless, accounting quickly became a big disappointment. Leticia felt like she was wasting her time there, burdened with tedious assignments and exams that bored her. Besides, she was only getting mediocre grades and knew herself to be capable of much greater things.

Although Leticia had eventually chosen the economic administrative track at her prepa, she was now able to switch over to the urban Normal school for a teaching career because it was the final year before the school began requiring a social studies or pedagogical specialty (bachillerato) to be admitted. For the last two years, she had been living with an older brother in the state capital and enjoying her education courses. Leticia felt pleased with her current studies and confident she would like her future work. As a teacher, she could continue learning about matters of great interest. Her only apprehension was the political turmoil that still wracked the teaching profession. She had no desire to get involved in politics and protest.

Leticia's family had continued on a similar track. Her oldest brother still worked for the Federal Water Commission and his wife, an assistant to a bank manager, also kept the house and cared for their baby daughter. The next oldest brother had given up on his agronomy studies and bought half an interest in their father's auto parts business. The second store they had opened had failed, and now they were trying to build up the first one. As well, he was due to marry a CONALEP graduate of secretarial studies in just a few months. Another older brother had just finished his degree in medicine and continued to do his social service while he looked to apply for a specialization in internal medicine. Leticia's younger brother was just as "disordered" as ever. Close to finishing his first year in the new private

San Pablo preparatoria, he would probably choose a science specialty and go into pharmacology. As for her parents, Leticia said her mother "has always been a homebody. Her illusion, her triumph, her happiness or sadness always depends on her children." Her father had always been much more distant, and the biggest change most recently had been Leticia's growing economic dependence on the brother that ran the auto parts store rather than her father. Leticia had even taken a part-time job recently as a receptionist at a small etiquette school for models and ushers (*edecanes*). She chuckled as she recalled her three-month stint there because it required her to be in so much contact with young, pretty women. The job had also enabled Leticia to support herself completely for a while without having to "ask" for money back home.

Leticia's overwhelming goal now was to finish her studies and join the teacher corps. Then, too, she hoped to travel and visit new places before settling down. Though she had been with her soon-to-be doctor boyfriend for six months now, Leticia had no thoughts of marriage or children. She would not even consider it until she had turned twenty-five, and even then she wondered whether she would feel "prepared" for such a new phase in life. As she put it, "There are a lot of things I still want to do before getting married and right now it's not part of my interests. . . . I feel I'm not ready to get married, much *less* have children."

Reflecting on her values, Leticia insisted she was a little different than most. In the secundaria, she had yearned for someone with whom she could discuss her intellectual doubts and questions. It was not until preparatoria, however, that she, like her classmates, had really begun to establish her "*own* set of values" ["*mi propia tabla de valores*"]. In college, Leticia was attracted to critical theories, and she confessed to being more than a "little marxist" ("*medio marxista*"). Applying those concepts, she even described her parents as always having been Catholics "in theory but not in practice." It was no surprise, then, that Leticia considered the social aspects of religion "manipulative" and deceiving. Still, like Rosita, she was accepting of other people's faith. She even claimed to have "wanted to believe" at many times in her life, especially toward the end of secundaria. Leticia whimsically recounted this time with a huge smile on her face:

> You should know that I really had a strong drive to believe in a religion [*fue mucho mi afán por creer en una religión*]. . . . It was at the end of secundaria and it only lasted a short time. I even went to church like three or four times. I read the Bible, I was trying to believe, but I think

in spite of all this it's really good to have faith in something, and it's really great if you identify with a religion. I imagine it makes you feel accompanied in your faith and really that's great. But I just couldn't have [that faith] even though I wanted it, and the truth is I really did try.

She was describing a moment of profound awakening but also profound pain, and as a narrator, she could only look on bemusedly as if she'd had no control over the values she might adopt. Without judging others for their beliefs, Leticia recognized that her growing social awareness precluded the kind of faith most others seemed to have. This was a dilemma she would probably face the rest of her life. As Leticia said with a self-deprecating laugh when I first asked her about it, "It's a little difficult [*conflictivo*] for me to think about religion."

MATILDE

Matilde seemed absolutely delighted to see me when I came to her house in 1993 for lunch. We had an hour to talk before her parents arrived, and she immediately launched into stories about the two relationships that she'd had since we'd last spoken in 1991. The first one lasted seven months (she always mentioned these time spans); the second one had been ongoing for some six months now. Matilde spoke with little compunction about having failed two subjects in her first year of high school (math and typing). She tried to keep it from her parents and pass the extraordinary exams on her own, but they discovered her plan. Her parents prohibited Matilde from leaving the house, and thus seeing her boyfriend, until she passed the exams, but her alternating tantrums and depression convinced them to soften the punishment. Matilde described this moral victory without a trace of guile.

Only recently had Matilde decided to study the specialty of executive secretary, one of the nonpreparatory tracks at the local CBTIS. She told me a few relatives had promised her a job at one of their businesses in Mexico City or the booming port town of Lázaro Cárdenas. When her parents arrived for lunch, they tried to enlist me in pressing Matilde to give more sérious attention to her studies. Wasn't it improper, they asked me to confirm, for a girl Matilde's age to fail school subjects because of a boyfriend? For general effect, they reminded us that young women needed a solid career to "defend" themselves in today's world. Yet Matilde had broken her parents' expectations of docile female behavior by expressing a strong mind of her own. Just as they planned to do for their three younger daughters, they had given Matilde all the *facilidades* (resources, support) to study, but she was not taking full advantage of her opportunity. Such support persisted despite the fact that Matilde's father had been almost two months without work.

By 1995, Matilde had completed her secretarial degree at the CBTIS, but her first work experience was trying, to say the least: she never even got paid after spending two months in a business that eventually failed. Soon after, though, she landed a regular job in the offices of a local union. Matilde's father was still struggling himself. Work had been inconsistent, and most of his orders required him to drive the truck to a region notorious for its growing rate of highway bandit assaults. Over lunch with the family, Matilde recalled some of her classmates' mischief at ESF. She also discussed those she considered the best and worst teachers. When I asked about her boyfriend, there was an awkward silence. As Matilde and I later walked back toward her work, she confessed that she had gotten engaged against her parents' wishes. Her fiancé had finished preparatoria yet was unable to continue his studies. His family owned a small furniture business and liquor store. Matilde said that when they got married, she would leave her present job and run the liquor store. Profits would be shared between both families. Though she might strain against her parents' preferences, Matilde always reinforced the importance of assisting them economically.

As early as 1990, Matilde had admitted her own propensity for "sentimental" entanglements, and by 1996, this weakness finally caught up with her. Matilde had since broken off with her former fiancé and entered into an ill-advised relationship with her boss at the union office where she worked as a secretary. Her parents never accepted the relationship because they knew this man had a child by another woman. Thinking she could win him away from his prior commitments, and attempting to avoid the reproachful glare of San Pablo society, Matilde accepted her lover's invitation to establish a household together in the capital and make efforts to have a child. She fled her parents' home early one morning and did not call for nearly two weeks, even then withholding her exact address. Her mother entered into a depression, and her father, who had gone nearly a year without work, threatened to take revenge on the man. Meanwhile, Matilde enrolled in a computer course and relished the few times each week she could see her lover. When her lover reduced the frequency of his visits, she slipped into her own depression. Her father then delivered an ultimatum about rejoining the family or risking permanent ostracism. Defeated and demoralized, she returned to face the judgment of her family.

Matilde summed up the story in May 1997:

> One day, my father called me up in the capital and told me it was my last chance to return to the house, that if I didn't return I might as well forget I had a family. You know that I'm very sentimental, so I said, "Well, I love [my boyfriend] a lot, I love him tremendously, but it's something that'll never be for me. It's like the rent for a house—you know the house will never be yours, and in the end you come out losing, no?" So then, with all the pain in my heart, I returned to San Pablo. I confronted problems with a lot of people, with my family, with everyone, trying to recover my self-confidence, to return to the way I had been. I changed a lot, let me be honest, I don't know, before I used to smile a lot, I was more cheerful, more everything. That girl with all the jokes, remember? I think they've all run out now [*Aquella chica de los chistes, ¿recuerdas? Creo que se han acabado*].

When I recorded these words, Matilde's wounds were still fresh. She had only moved back some three months prior and accepted a job as a secretary at a computer print shop in town, but her former lover still came looking for her, insisting that his other relationship had ended. Matilde knew that his child from another woman would always come between them, and despite the intense pain and fear of being alone, she resisted his supplications. Her reflection on how she could have fallen into such a relationship presents her own language describing the powerful pull of the "heart" over critical discernment:

> When I returned [to San Pablo], I returned with a lot of fear, a lot of uncertainty, because I didn't know what would happen to me. I was afraid to bump into people who knew me, who had found out about the problem. It was *so* difficult for me, I swear to you, because something like this is not well regarded in local society [*no está bien visto ante una sociedad*]. . . . I consider [the relationship] a mistake in the sense that it surprised me, in the sense that I was one of those people who used to most strongly condemn a relationship of that sort, I criticized it a lot, you know? So when I got into this situation, I said, "My God, why *me?* This was not in my plans." But you know that you can't control your heart [*en el corazón no se manda*], and even less with such a powerful feeling.

Her next oldest sister, Nadina, was among those who reproached Matilde the most. Now studying comercio at the private colegio, Nadina was still involved with the same boyfriend she'd had for over four years. She accused Matilde of reckless and selfish behavior, charging her with their mother's ongoing depression. Her mother, for her part, had warned Matilde she would be like "a cake already bitten into" ("*pastel ya mordido*"). Clearly, Matilde's actions had been an affront to her parents' deeply religious sensibilities.

I wondered if Matilde had really learned her lesson, because she told me that she had already begun to date an engineer ten years her senior who had known her before she left for the capital. When she asked for my advice, I could not help but suggest she spend more time alone recovering from her previous relationship and then find someone closer to her age. Yet Matilde claimed that her new relationship was different and helped her forget the pain she'd recently been through. Besides, her parents liked the engineer. He was respectful and did not judge Matilde for the experience she'd had. Matilde also laid down some conditions: she wanted someone to love and "comprehend" her fully, and she would save herself sexually for marriage. Her new boyfriend did not shy away from these demands. And Matilde also had further career plans. She admitted that she had always been lucky finding work. When she returned from the capital, it only took her a week to land her present job, although she also recognized that her father's friendship with the print shop owner had been decisive. She still wanted to finish the computer course that she had started in the capital and perhaps find a job working for the Secretariat of Public Education there. Her contacts in education through her mother might facilitate an interview, she said, but her computer skills still had to be up to par. Most important for Matilde was to have a permanent and secure job, preferably with the government, that offered benefits and a pension.

Yet immediately after relating these career goals, Matilde returned to her relationship with the engineer and the plot thickened. She spoke about her "other plans," if things worked out with the engineer. Apparently, he had suggested that they get married with the New Year. They would go to live in his hometown some two hours away, where the company had its headquarters. He would hire Matilde as his own secretary and the company would pay for her to complete her computer course. I stuck my nose out again and suggested that things might be going too fast. But Matilde insisted they were both looking for a more stable existence and the relationship would provide that for them. She would come to love him. I was struck by Matilde's practical turn, but it was clear she no longer trusted her "heart."

Reflecting back on her years in the secundaria, Matilde valued her friendships the most. Like Antonia, she recalled the solidarity of her grupo mates in 3B:

> If we were having some problem, we got together and solved it among ourselves . . . and the friendship we had was very solid, it lasted a long time. From the time we entered first grade of secundaria we were together constantly.

Yet unlike many of her former classmates, Matilde brought out a darker side to grupo life as well. She admitted to having been sensitive and "innocent." As a dedicated student, she often endured the taunts of her grupo mates who thought she was too studious and not generous enough in pasando la tarea. She also felt marginalized and "abused" for other reasons. For one thing, some of her best friends challenged her to enter into more serious romantic relationships (*vivir más rápido*) and ridiculed her for her innocence. "They made me feel less, because they would tell each other things that I still didn't understand because I hadn't experienced them yet." In addition, some of the boys she liked took advantage of her feelings and flirted in order to exploit her academic strengths. She felt more comfortable when she moved on to the CBTIS, where the students left each other in peace ("*no se metían contigo*") and went their own ways ("*cada quién por su lado*"). For at least a couple of years, she maintained close friendships with a number of former ESF schoolmates who now studied in other high schools. Such friendships sufficed to remind her of her schooled identity and the gratifying solidarity of secundaria life, even as she enjoyed the relative anonymity and respect that came with CBTIS studies.

WHAT YOUNG LIVES CAN TELL

The personal stories that I have updated here are partial and incomplete both in their living and telling. They are partial in their living because these former ESF students still retained hopes and dreams for a future better than the life they had presently achieved. Their lives could end tomorrow, several admitted, even hedging their comments with spiritual qualifiers ("*Si Diós quiera,*" "God willing"). Yet their lives should and probably would extend well into the future, and for that they had projects, intentions, plans. Making plans in the provincial Mexico of the mid-1990s was a risky business, and several former students had encompassed much wider spaces—Mexico City, Mexicali, Oregon—within their evolving trajectories. Some, like Rosita or Alberto, still thought their professional degrees would enable them to achieve the lifestyle they had always desired. Their aspirations might become mostly fulfilled. Others, like Leticia or Nidia, had downscaled their ambitions to meet pressing economic and social realities, while still others, like Iván and Enrique, had largely accepted the fates that earlier decisions or family circumstances had thrust on them.

These lives are of course partial in their telling, too. On the one hand, this means that the students selectively reported certain elements of their lives in the context of an evolving research relationship, and as a product of the situated remembering that occurs in conversations and interviews. Field notes and interview transcripts captured most all the students' verbal and even bodily expressions, but these moments were only snapshots after all—an arbitrary abstraction from life's practical flow. A great deal can be understood from such snapshots—especially those where students are seen pondering, remembering, and projecting—yet one must also remain humble about what of these evolving, complex selves has really been captured in the end.

And there is the artifice of the professional storyteller to consider as well. The students' selective stories have, in turn, been filtered through my own theoretical and literary screens. I have tended to highlight elements of their stories that I found most poignant or provocative, or that help illustrate theoretical points I wish to make. To be fair, the highlights recounted here generally correspond to those emphasized by the students themselves. They are not chosen gratuitously to demonstrate a preconceived theoretical notion. The stories I choose serve to illustrate themes and patterns I noted emerging through analysis of a large body of field notes and transcripts. Still, analysis itself is never complete, never seamless. No doubt other interpretations would be possible, too. You, dear reader, may want to supply some of these.

As early as 1993, I had begun to reflect more on the felt particularities of San Pablo as a place. I wondered what forms of subjectivity were encouraged among youth in that curious admixture of Indianness, colonial religious conservatism, backwater province, urban spunk, tourism, so-called modern cultural media, frantic entrepreneurialism, and international migration that together constituted the jumble of public life in San Pablo. Before 1993, my view had been focused on the school, from which I looked outward. Now, as I followed the students down their spatial and temporal tracks, I saw ESF as just one place and experience nested among many others, including the town itself. The students' lives told of a broadening swath of experience, but something unique to San Pablo, a certain regional configuration of sentiment and ideology, continued to make its imprint. No matter how close or far in person, the students remained without exception closely bound to San Pablo in mind and spirit.

Back when they were about to leave ESF, most students phrased their broader aspirations in terms of "becoming someone" through further schooling. They constructed a difference between themselves and those who had never completed secundaria—what I have called their distinguishing schooled identity. Yet even as they articulated such aspirations, many students betrayed their ambivalence. Some wondered if further schooling might be a waste of time: Fidel, for instance, thought making masks could afford him a comfortable life, while Andrea wavered in her plan to become a teacher at a nursery school. Others had more modest ambitions to finish vocational studies (*carrera corta*) and find a local job. Nidia, Matilde, and Enrique never really intended to go much beyond this. Still others, like Alberto and Rosita, held fast to a goal of university study, buoyed by ample household economies, strong family support, and a firm schooled identity. In any case, toward the close of the millennium the economic fragility of 1990s' Mexico, coupled with the unforeseen twists of personal biography, had most former students still scrambling for livelihoods and more certain identities.

What forces structured students' aspirations then, and how did their schooled identities hold up to the test of time? The press of economic necessity and family obligation combined with the media-purveyed dream of consumer abundance to produce a variety of strategies. Most obviously, migration to the United States or other regions continued to be an attractive option for many of these students. Almost immediately on finishing secundaria, Enrique, Isidro, and Paco had each gone to spend a few years in the United States, and by 1998, Andrea had apparently emigrated there for good. Meanwhile, Nidia and Alejandra moved to the border city of Mexicali, while Socorro joined his brothers in Mexico City. Other former students, like Fidencio, Iván, Socorro, and José, still talked about going to the United States for extended stays. Friends and relatives continued to suggest this alternative, and it was clear that migration to the United States had for some time exercised a strong influence on the young men's imaginations. Especially for those whose family culture or economy might not encourage further schooling, migration held out the possibility of adventure, earnings, and future prosperity. One could even say that in certain intimate cultures, such as that of the village where Paco's family lived, migration had become a rite of passage for young men. For young women, in contrast, migration to the United States held fewer independent attractions. They might go to follow a husband or join a family, but few would migrate to work and save. In either case, students' schooled identities appeared to recede in importance. They were now more than ever likely to live and work with those who'd had less schooling than them, and the perceived differences were not great. Yet some former students continued to express echoes of schooled identity. For instance, Enrique and Socorro lamented their failure to continue schooling, and still maintained dreams of making it some day to college. They sensed that they would not "be someone" until they achieved this goal.

Even as migration held such attractions to these students, many of them spoke longingly of settling down. Most strikingly, a good number of the young men had already begun planning or even building their own homes, regardless of whether or not they had serious prospects for marriage. Socorro, Enrique, Paco, Fidel, Iván, Vicente—all had imagined a modest house on a plot of land adjacent or nearby to that of their parents and siblings, if possible. Only Isidro and Andrea seemed candidates for permanent residence in the United States, and this because their parents or older siblings had already established themselves there. Such trends were not surprising given the ongoing strength of kin relations in this region. A house in San Pablo represented security, a kind of anchor in difficult times, as well as a modicum of independence from occasional feelings of family suffocation. Most former students wished to be close to their family, but perhaps not too close.

Among the young men and women alike, what stood out as well was the expression of a pervasive entrepreneurial ethic. Many spoke of opening or running their own businesses: Socorro a grocery store with his younger brother, Fidencio and José a disco in San Pablo, Antonia a boutique, Vicente a body repair shop, Matilde a liquor store with her first husband-to-be, and Iván his own repair shop. Remember that when he couldn't stay in school, Abel took over the operation of his family's store. Perhaps related to this, it was also clear that few students were working in jobs for which their schooling had really prepared them. Of those with terminal vocational degrees, only Matilde worked in the field of her degree—as a secretary. Lidia and Dalia had studied tourism at the CBTIS,

This young ESF graduate, now nineteen years old, helps out in the family business

but Lidia was now a clerk for a construction company, while Dalia was studying to be a teacher. Ivonne had studied nursing at the CONALEP, but got married before she could really start a nursing career. Vicente continued working at the same auto body shop where he had apprenticed as a boy. His secundaria certificate was superfluous for such work. Even Antonia did not work in the field of cosmetology for which she had taken several yearlong courses beyond the secundaria. The former students' work histories and entrepreneurial ambitions thus reflected the pressures of economic crisis and absence of large-scale employment in San Pablo. As a commercial center, San Pablo had few opportunities for waged work. Meanwhile, with its nationalist emphasis on equality and solidarity, secundaria studies prepared students better for industry than small-scale business. Most former students overcame this disjuncture between their schooling and work opportunities by drawing on family connections and a long-standing merchant culture to craft themselves an economic niche.

What about the effects of gender ideology in structuring life experiences and opportunities? Despite the relative empowerment accorded them by a secondary schooled identity, female students especially continued to struggle with the tension between work and study, on the one hand, and having a family, on the other. Those young women who continued studying at the university made self-conscious choices to postpone marriage until their mid-twenties. Establishing economic independence and a professional identity concerned them most, and family support in cases like Rosita and Leticia was critical in this regard. Yet what about the majority who had never made it to college? Unlike the men, international migration was scarcely a viable option.

In my initial judgment, many of the young women had fallen prey to their sentimental side, as Matilde might put it. Marriage and childbearing had prematurely terminated their studies or careers. When I mentioned my disappointment in this regard to a San Pablo friend, herself a poor woman who had married and bore children rather young, she attributed the trend to poverty. Young women whose economic circumstances prohibited them from further schooling looked to spouses and children for meaning and fulfillment. Yet something in this response could not quite account for students like Matilde or Ivonne. Several of these young women apparently had entered marriage in spite of future work and study opportunities. After all, Matilde's parents had been prepared to support her studies all the way to a university. Young women who desired such careers wrestled with the fact that the social position for single professionals was less viable in a city like San Pablo than it might be in a larger urban area. Some of these women seemed torn between marriage and further study, since the latter would inexorably draw them away from San Pablo and the people they loved. No doubt their scripted gender habitus (McCall 1992) made such professional ambition even more unlikely. It seemed to me, however, that the desire for marriage and children sprung from an even deeper place. It wasn't the default path when schooling no longer made sense. It was the alternative that would always present itself to work and further schooling. It was a key figured world for feminine identity continually nourished in local intimate cultures. Getting married and having children had always been a source of status and identity for women locally, and in the context of great economic uncertainty, this desire came to have greater weight for some women than the further uncertainties of career and schooled identity.

It bears mentioning that men were also subject to some of these same dynamics, though perhaps not to the same degree. For men as for women, cultural codes stipulated marriage and children as the fullest expression of adult status. Iván, after all, could be said to have ultimately conformed to such cultural codes, succumbing to the temptations of love. By his own account, the overwhelming desire to marry his sweetheart forced him out of school early and into a full-time job. Such feelings of love and attach-

A young female ESF graduate (with purse), now nineteen years old, poses with her family

ment, for both men and women, cannot be captured easily by the language of strategy. In Robert Connell's (1987, 112) terms, a "structure of cathexis"—the social construction of emotional attachment and desire—also moved students to important life decisions around romance and the creation of a new family.

A structure of cathexis continued to renew the former ESF students' bonds with existing family as well. I have suggested in previous chapters that an emerging San Pablo youth culture had opened up new ground for the influence of peer relations on aspirations and identity. Certainly, the peer culture acted to recontextualize discourses from teachers, family, and the media, forming a heady milieu for the cultural production of new desires and imagined worlds. The significance of the peer culture loomed largest for those youth who spent the most time in the school, workplace, or street, and whose family unity had been loosened by migration, infidelity, and/or separation. Yet in contrast to most youth studies in other countries, the family still maintained a powerful hold on student lives.[9] Someone like Enrique never stopped seeing himself as part of a family unit, his mother and younger siblings at the center of a moral universe defined by work and sacrifice. Matilde juggled the desire to find love, have children, and pursue a career with a compelling concern for her family's needs and judgments. Most former students articulated their life trajectories in terms of family commitments and expectations. There was ambiva-

Third-year boys pose during a break in physical education class

lence about such commitment, to be sure; it was an ambivalence wrought especially by the contradictory messages of individual pleasure and freedom supplied by the cultural media.[10] Yet through it all there persisted a powerful moral bond between these youths and their primary caregivers. They loved their families and wanted above all to do right by them.

In this chapter, I have explored how students' sense of themselves and their priorities in life continued to evolve in a kind of dialogue between the subjectivities garnered in their secundaria years—through the game of equality and play of schooled identity—and the conditions they later faced in unfolding time and space. Through their practice, students engaged the subjectivities formed in previous contexts in adjusting themselves to new circumstances. Such previous contexts included the diverse socialization sites of intimate cultures, the regional culture of San Pablo, the institutional and student cultures of ESF, and the hegemonic culture of the State; the circumstances ranged from personal contingencies of illness, opportunity, and loss to the global restructuring of economic relations (see figure 5). The students' trajectories reveal that the enduring features of habitus formed through intimate cultures did indeed have a bearing on how and where students' life paths unfolded. Were Andrea and Ivonne always destined for early marriages to relatively unschooled working-class men, despite their own schooled aspirations? Were Alberto and Leticia equally destined for university studies and fulfilling professional careers because of the example set by their older siblings and the cultural capital provided by their families? Bourdieu's vision of class reproduction would seem to hold true in these cases. Yet what about Abel, who according to most critical theories would have stayed on the fast track to educational privilege? And what about Dalia or Rosita, who remained in college as trailblazers of their rather modest intimate cultures. Habitus only established predispositions and tendencies that played themselves out in school (Davidson 1996; Eisenhart and Graue 1993) as well as through a variety of ensuing circumstances. In the next and final chapter, I develop a more explicit theoretical account of this interplay between social disposition and evolving circumstance, between aspiration, identity, and the emergent structures of social life.

8. Games Are Serious: Reflections on Equality
and Mexican Secondary Student Culture

Notions of equality were central to the meaningful games students produced and played at ESF in 1990 and 1991. Yet the roles and positions students took up in this game differed considerably. The play of student culture at this Mexican secundaria then had varying consequences for students' lives in subsequent years. In this final chapter, I propose some theoretical implications of the student culture I studied in 1990–1991, as well as the lessons learned from following some students' lives for another six or seven years. I revisit some of the questions posed in the introduction: How and why does a game of equality emerge at a provincial Mexican secondary school, and how and why does it help create common identifications among students across significant social differences? What are the organizational and discursive resources students appropriate to construct this culture? What is its power and influence relative to the moral forces of family, church, workplace, and other sites of adult authority? To what extent and in what manner does the school-based game then become part of students' broader identities and aspirations, influencing to some degree the trajectories their lives take? As I attempt to summarize answers to these questions, I remind the reader that appendix A provides a fuller elaboration of key theoretical issues and terms.

In the first part of this chapter, I interpret the school year of 1990–1991 as a structural moment that provided certain conditions for the development of student culture, identity, and aspiration. I look at organizational patterns and meanings—institutional structure—as these intersected with students' subjectivities and personal biographies. My main point here is to show how unique historical and institutional contexts (chapters 1 and 3) provided crucial structural and cultural resources for student practice. The next section considers the extension and transformation of student subjectivity in time and space as their lives unfolded in varying contexts. Here, I am more concerned to show the embedded and highly conditioned nature of the school's influence on subsequent life trajectories. With some variation, of course, the subjectivities and identities students exhibited in later years owed at least as much to family dynamics, personal contingency, and economic necessity as to the game of equality at ESF. Yet the game still showed its traces.

THE INSTITUTION AND THE PLAYFUL PRACTICE IN STUDENT CULTURE

I wrote my dissertation (Levinson 1993) immediately after a year of field research in 1990–1991. In that work, I accounted for the social and cultural dynamics I had observed during that time. Why were equality and solidarity so obviously important for both teachers and students? What kinds of strategies and understandings had students developed as a result of staying in school? Why were there no clear and enduring social categories or subcultural antagonisms within the school? The data I marshaled and interpreted to address these questions here form the better part of chapters 3–6. The answers hinged on applying theories of cultural production and practice to interpret these data.

Throughout this book, I have used the metaphor of the game and characterized student practice as a kind of play. My intention has not been to trivialize student agency but to theorize its fluidity in a world of multiple options and influences. When they entered ESF to begin their studies, San Pablo students already brought with them a rich stock of experiences and aspirations formed through the varying sites of intimate culture, media, church, work, and prior schooling itself (see chapter 5). Such sites had involved their own cultural games, their own structuring of subjectivity in varying extensions of space and time. Such structured subjectivity can be thought of in terms of Bourdieu's concept of the habitus and its field (1984; Bourdieu and Wacquant 1992)—with the latter defined as a social "space" for the action of the structured and structuring habitus.[1] For most students, the new site of practice—the institutional structure of

The author enjoys a lighter moment with the boys of grupo 3B, as they monitor the school's back gate during recess

ESF—represented a continuation of prior games and fields rather than a sudden break. The secundaria had already been incorporated into their families' socioeconomic strategies and cultural outlooks, and their habitus adjusted accordingly. Yet the secundaria also presented students with a novel combination of institutional demands, discourses, and options for the cultural production of identity, including the setting of the grupo escolar, discourses on adolescence and national identity, and the ethic of solidarity and equality.

Thus, even if students' existing subjectivities had already been formed through complex structural sites and discourses, ESF provided a new and significant site. In her study of a French rural village and school, Deborah Reed-Danahay (1987, 1996) draws on Bourdieu's concept of strategy to suggest how local actors within schools might negotiate these varying influences: "Individuals are not captives of either national institutions or local cultural traditions; rather, they attempt to manipulate, or negotiate, meanings in their dealings with national institutions through strategies informed by both national- and local-level sociocultural constraints" (1987, 89). Far from homogeneous itself, ESF encompassed a complex institutional history (chapter 1), varied teacher biographies and cultures (chapter 3), and a socially diverse student body (chapter 5). The reciprocal influence of student subjectivity and institutional structure (see Corsaro 1992, 1997) involved many different levels—conceptually, historically, and spatially. The game of equality at ESF was played according to the rules given by a historically complex institutional culture (liberal individualism, nationalist collectivism, regional conservatism, and so forth), students' varied intimate cultures of origin, and broader political-economic and media fields. Students played by such rules and simultaneously adapted them to their own site- and age-specific interests. They used the symbolic artifacts around them to create a culture, a "figured world" (Holland et al. 1998, 49 ff.) of equality through communicative strategies of solidarity: normative discourses about "selfish" or "stuck-up" students, but also practices like echando relajo and pasando la tarea. The students' cultural game, in turn, came to form a part of the school's institutional culture.

A key point here is to acknowledge the distinctiveness of the institution in structuring patterns of cultural production and practice. Critical ethnographies of student culture in Europe and the United States have tended to take the institutional cultures of the secondary school for granted. The unacknowledged backdrop to arguments about social and cultural reproduction appears to be the ideology of liberal individualism and the pervasive enactment of competition in schools (see Varenne and McDermott 1998). While critical ethnographic research in the 1970s and 1980s questioned the comfortable assumptions of reproduction theory (Apple and Weis 1983; Levinson and Holland 1996), it may have settled into its own zone of comfort regarding the liberal postulates of schooling. That is why the comparative perspective offered by Mexico and other regions (Demerath 1999; Luykx 1999; Schoenhals 1993; Stambach 2000) is so valuable.

The ESF example shows how an institutional culture takes shape historically and discursively. An analysis of historical contexts of State formation and national development locates the evolution of the Mexican secundaria as part of a global trend in educational differentiation and the schooling of adolescents (chapter 1). To be sure, liberal democratic ideologies and concepts of meritocracy have contributed to this evolution, yet so have uniquely Mexican constructs of solidarity, collectivity, and the hierarchical whole. Then, too, a look at a particular school such as ESF reveals the stamp of regional and institutional idiosyncrasies. As a secondary school, ESF shares key organizational principles with other secondary schools around the world, and as a secundaria, it shares a curriculum and ideology with other secundarias in Mexico. Yet perhaps because it is in San

Pablo, because it has had this or that principal, this or that teacher corps, ESF evolves its own discourses and practices (chapter 3). Broader historical and ideological patterns are uniquely configured at this local institution. This, in short, highlights the importance of historical and cultural contexts in the structuring of institutional practice. The school that ESF students encountered in 1990 was a complex historical product, part liberalism and part socialism, part global and part local. A central component of its ideological makeup was the trope of equality, and a primary component of its organizational structure was the socially diverse grupo escolar.

THE FLUIDITY OF STUDENT IDENTIFICATIONS AND THE PROBLEM OF RESISTANCE

Critical ethnographies of secondary schooling in Europe and the United States have also portrayed the existence of polarized subcultures as obstructing institutional goals of learning (see, for example, Eckert 1989; Solomon 1992; Foley 1990). Student subcultures or "symbolic categories" typically develop in response to differentiating practices at the school (Page and Valli 1990). Oppositional subcultures, at odds with the mainstream premises of school participation, try to assert a kind of dignity, a spark of meaning, in the stultifying school environment (Willis 1981b; Eckert 1989).[2] Yet at ESF, such polarized subcultures or symbolic labels failed to form. There were, of course, some mutually indifferent or occasionally antagonistic peer groups, and peer associations outside the grupo escolar tended to follow lines of gender, class, ethnicity, and/or age (chapter 6). However, these associations were more fluid and, above all, subordinate to the ethos of schooled identity and grupo escolar equality than the existing literature would lead one to expect.

ESF students were also learning the stance appropriate to being secondary schooled. They developed a schooled identity that they drew on to distinguish themselves from school dropouts or the relatively unschooled (chapter 5). This identity, activated most strongly in spaces outside the school, reinforced the sense of equality and solidarity constructed within the grupo escolar. In the United States, on the other hand, compulsory secondary schooling typically presents students with curricular and track options, tied in to future studies and careers. "Corporate structures" in secondary schools (Eckert 1989) promote competition and exclusion. The choices students must make about these options tend to differentiate them culturally and socially, since peer groups "incorporate concrete aspirations into their identities" (Eckert 1989, 11; see also Canaan 1990; Page 1987;

Varenne and McDermott 1998). This differentiation usually leads to the kinds of subcultural polarization demonstrably lacking at ESF. In U.S. and European schools, students seem to be learning, above all, a sense of ranking and distinction. Some, no doubt, resist this process and develop alternative cultural vocabularies for ranking, while others accommodate themselves to it in various ways. At ESF, by contrast, students appeared to learn a sense of belonging, of collective identification with the grupo, school, and nation. Some ESF students resisted this process as well, but the logic seemed reversed. It was not a competitive corporate structure, but rather a normative ethos of equality and solidarity within and against which some ESF students had to struggle.

The game of equality at ESF thus both enabled and oppressed. It continually produced a symbolic grid capable of incorporating difference into a common project, such as that of surviving or advancing academically according to the logic of evaluation. It encouraged students to recognize and construct points of common experience and identity that might otherwise never surface through local constructions of difference. But it also ran the danger of collapsing difference altogether. As we have seen, instead of fully accepting difference, students tended to police it more closely among themselves. Similarly, teachers' exhortation to solidarity was transformed by students into a practice of exclusion as much as inclusion, insofar as it was used to condemn those students defined as different or uncooperative. By suppressing the expression of alternative sensibilities, the common culture enforced a singular public identity. Like the tragic decision Mexican immigrant Richard Rodríguez made to eschew the "private identity" of his Mexican family for the "public identity" of the U.S. school (Rodríguez 1982), some ESF students had to mask or deny aspects of their identities to accommodate themselves to the culture in the school.

For these reasons and more, this study calls into question the typological notions of resistance and accommodation that pepper the critical education literature. What and who are students resisting or accommodating, after all? If the school does not clearly and unambiguously track students into existing social and occupational structures, what do students resist beyond the situational limitations on their freedom and self-respect? As a more nuanced conception of school structures and practices is developed, a correspondingly fluid conception of student action must be employed. The notion of resistance, almost always linked to a utopian political project (Liston 1988), is somehow too forward looking to capture the situated meanings of student action. It reads student behavior hopefully and tendentiously from a future orientation constructed by critical theory. It must instead be acknowledged that students position themselves strategically in the cultural game of equality as they work out immediate problems and existential projects in school. The reproduction paradigm, then, needs to be pried open and made far more fluid (see Mehan, Hubbard, and Villanueva, 1996). As I have shown, ESF's institutional structure sponsors more mobility than reproduction, partly because teachers are complex actors with multiple allegiances and formations (chapter 3), and partly because the State has tried to empower popular classes even as it has deepened its own rule. On the other hand, students' cultural productions are also complex, and as such, difficult to place in a simple rubric of accommodation or resistance. Rather, student culture ranges through multiple, shifting positions and ongoing trajectories.

This is reflected in the contradictory positions students took up in and around prevailing discourses of identity and difference. The cultural game of equality pervaded patterns of discourse and practice in friendship groups, sometimes encouraging students to mollify their disparagement of difference, as seen earlier. Perhaps the game of equality inspired some students to see themselves as more alike than they might have otherwise. The question is, Did such identification lead to more lasting social orientations? Typically, urban mestizo students, like Abel, Alberto, or Lidia (that is, most of what I've called the cultural center), would mark their differences from other students, even as they participated in the cultural game of equality. Perhaps they played the game partly to "euphemize" (Bourdieu 1977, 196) their privileged position in the school and regional society. By contrast, students from less privileged backgrounds, like José, Isidro, or Andrea, often formed their own relatively low-status friendship groups, even as they played the game to acquire a means of relative empowerment, of claiming the same cultural capital in the educational field (Bourdieu 1984). Still, members of the cultural center were perhaps most deeply invested in the game of equality and its associated ethic of solidarity. This would seem ironic, for center students brought into the school precisely those subjectivities normally considered dominant and privileged in the wider community. Yet in the school, the effect of teachers' discourses on solidarity and equality, coupled with the appropriation and rearticulation of these discourses through students' practice in the grupo escolar, was to create an environment where dominant subjectivities were not easily expressed.

While noncenter students also participated in the game of equality, their strategies were rooted in a different set of social circumstances: for instance, they sought to ensure a support network and minimum passing grade through the production of equalizing strategies within the grupo escolar (chapter 4), and to secure rights and recognition not ordinarily granted to those of their status in local society. On the whole, they were more astute about the balance of power behind the tropes of equality; they were more sensitive to how the game of equality was played from below. Members of the cultural center shared some of the same pragmatic interests, to be sure. Yet some, like Alberto, played especially strong roles in the game of equality in order not to let their privilege become too visible. Teachers and students alike constantly monitored student conduct for expressions of privilege or exceptionality. A discursive endorsement of equality deflected attention from practices and gestures that otherwise denigrated difference.

Such contradictions should not necessarily lead to a cynical interpretation. It is too easy to assume that the rhetoric of todos somos iguales was wielded cynically by all those students who sought some advantage from it. Certainly I have provided some evidence for such an interpretation. Alberto seemed to tout equality as part of a personal strategy to mask his economic and social privilege. Rosita endorsed principles of solidarity that would consolidate her position in grupo 3C. José worried that girls like Teresa would threaten the advantages of the equality that grupo 3A had managed to construct vis-à-vis its teachers. All of these seem like rather individualized tactics. Particular selves appropriated the discourse of equality to advance their own interests. Yet something else happens as part of this process. What seems like a personal strategy, at first easily pursued in one context to be dropped in another, becomes a social strategy with broader repercussions. Almost in spite of himself, Alberto discovered that maybe he was not all that different from other ESF students and, by extension, the secondary schooled. His personal investment in the game carried over into other areas of his life. This is true of many other students as well. No matter how students may have entered into and participated in the game of equality, the situated identification brought forth by it often entered more deeply into their senses of self.

At another level, too, numerous studies in Mexico have examined the contradictions of rhetoric on equality.[3] In her study of a primaria in a large rural community, Margarita Campos de García (1973, 193) concluded that the school functioned to denigrate local culture at the expense of national culture. The school attempted to incorporate marginal groups into a national culture by encouraging an identification with nationalist imperatives while discouraging the production and reproduction of local culture. Such symbolic incorporation is most notorious in the case of Mexico's indigenous groups. As Marjorie Becker (1989, 1995), Mary Kay Vaughan (1997), and Jane Hill (1991, 77–78) have documented for different regions, Mexican schools draw on aspects of regional indigenous identity and folklore to celebrate their part in national culture. Yet in so doing, the schools deny indigenous groups any measure of distinct and worthy identity (see also King 1994). Indigenous cultures are valued only insofar as they associate themselves with the overarching project of national culture. Discourses on gender equality seem just as contradictory. If women are symbolically incorporated into the nation, it is usually as the handmaidens, rather than the publicly recognized executors, of civic progress and defense.

Official discourse and curriculum at ESF confirmed these broader observations by valorizing the indigenous component of Mexicanness, ignoring or domesticating the virtues of women, and honoring popular class struggle in the making of the modern nation. For instance, social studies textbooks referred to the contributions of indigenous culture and patterns of class struggle in forging modern Mexico (these same textbooks rarely mentioned the role of women in Mexican history). Indigenous culture, however, was construed as the positive underpinning of a mestizo nationality rather than a distinct and present reality. Likewise, local indigenous culture was appropriated by ESF teachers for the purpose of symbolic display (chapter 3), but it was rarely discussed or analyzed outside the context of ritual performance.

For their part, teachers typically reinforced textbook messages, rarely supplementing them with alternative interpretations. Little attention was paid, in fact, to accommodating the varied backgrounds of the students themselves. Though some ESF students came from indigenous communities, it was not until 1994 that an elective class in the indigenous language was offered. When teachers had occasion to discuss indigenous culture, they almost never referred to those students at ESF who might still identify with one. Similarly, working-class and peasant struggles formed a major part of the social studies and Spanish curriculum, yet classroom discussion rarely touched on the concrete experiences of struggle some students brought to school.

For these reasons, as well as others I have discussed at greater length (chapters 5 and 6), an urban, male mestizo form of speech and conduct generally governed life at ESF. Students and teachers alike often discouraged signs of rural status. Girls who wished to obtain leadership positions in the school's public sphere often adopted masculine modes of expression, while female forms of public citizenship were rarely valued or represented in the school. The effect of all this was to call into question the State's vaunted commitment to a new cultural pluralism. While revolutionary nationalism had been clearly and emphatically premised on masculine and mestizo cultural codes (Bartra 1987; O'Malley 1986), by the late 1970s, Mexico had adopted a rather more pluralist strategy of national integration (Lomnitz-Adler 1992, 11). Supposedly, there were now many different ways of being and becoming Mexican. Yet despite this rhetoric, a male mestizo norm was still in evidence at ESF. Discourses on equality and solidarity often served to deny ethnic and class differences, encompassing them within a singular, homogeneous image of national membership. If the State had officially adopted a pluralist vision of the nation after the 1970s, it had yet to become a reality at ESF.

ORGANIZATIONAL STRUCTURES AND CULTURAL FORMS: SOME COMPARATIVE LESSONS

What do my findings reveal about the kinds of institutional structures and discourses that promote or inhibit democratic solidarity in secondary schools? How do certain school practices encourage student subjectivities that prize collaboration across difference and therefore empower all students to achieve success in school? On the other hand, which school practices encourage an individualistic, meritocratic ethos and thereby introduce rivalry into the learning process? Can such competition, ultimately rooted in liberal and neoliberal ideologies of development and progress, be reconciled in the school with the tenets of democratic solidarity. Or has the "school America builds" (Varenne and McDermott 1998), with its inlaid assumptions about success and failure, been exported successfully to Mexico?

Researchers in Europe and the United States have identified a number of school practices that differentiate students and inhibit democratic solidarity. Tracking and discourses of competition as a zero-sum game are foremost among these practices. In their synthesis of the U.S. research, for instance, Adam Gamoran and Martha Berends (1987, 430) find that "tracking appears to polarize students into pro- and anti-school factions. Polarization is said to occur as a result of interaction between teachers and students and among students themselves."[4] In a similar review, Gary

Natriello (1994, 137–38) draws attention to opposite trends—that is, those "unifying elements" of school practice that arrest tendencies toward student differentiation. Echoing my observations about school identification and schooled identity at ESF, Natriello observes that "the basic differentiation of members of the school from nonmembers may displace the processes by which students within a school differentiate themselves" (137).

What is unique, then, about the Mexican secundaria that I studied? Is the cultural game of equality really all that different from what might be found in any school with unifying discourses and a concern to create substantive equality across social differences on the basis of national or local identifications? For one thing, the structural history of such unifying discourses at ESF includes distinct moments of postrevolutionary State formation and the effort to achieve social justice while homogenizing diverse regional and ethnic cultures. Equality and solidarity serve the State's ideological purposes as much as the school's more pressing agenda for adolescent socialization. At ESF, unifying elements were structured around varying collectivities such as the grupo escolar and school as a whole (chapter 5). Group identification and affiliation were situationally activated around the goals of such collectivities, especially the grupo escolar. In other Western contexts, such identification has often been developed within smaller friendship groups and *in opposition to* the general student body, or to other emerging, informal student groups. In other words, the locus of group identification does not coincide with a collective structure provided by the school itself. Paul Willis's lads (1981b), for instance, may have developed an ethic of solidarity within their immediate subculture, but this did not extend to other groups or the school at large. The important point about this Mexican secundaria, however, is the way the value of equality gets taken up and fashioned in the grupo escolar—a social space officially designated for the production of good students and Mexican citizens.

In his critique of current works on identity, Roger Rouse (1995, 369) discusses the "relational sense of self" that existed among Mexicans before the State's introduction of schooling and other "scriptural and taxonomic activities . . . [and] habituating micro-rituals." Outside schooling, Rouse implies, rural Mexicans' relational sense of self asks fundamentally, "Where do I stand—and how should I conduct myself—in relation to others?" It is the modern State education system, as well as the rise of corporate consumerism, says Rouse, that historically came to promote "an individuating view of personhood that valued people more for the qualifications they possessed than for the nature of their ties to others" (369). This more recent view of personhood, one that basically asks, "Who am I?" is what Rouse calls "identity." Clearly, it is rooted in the rise of liberalism as a political and institutional form. Clearly, too, this kind of identity promoted in school relies on a "reflexive project of the self," a kind of individual life planning based on distinctly modern knowledge of distant and "abstract" systems (Giddens 1991, 5, 32).[5] One need only think of "vocational orientation" at ESF to understand how individual biographies intersect with highly complex economic systems.

Yet Rouse errs in viewing Mexican schools as vehicles only for this kind of liberal individualism. As I have insisted throughout this study, ESF's promotion of collective solidarity and identification drew on an existing relational sense of self in popular culture even as it undercut such solidarity with individuating discourses of competition and self-advancement. Only by recognizing such contradictions within the Mexican secundaria can comparative sense be made of school structures and their relation to student subjectivity. For just as the so-called liberal Mexican school still encourages solidarity through a relational sense of self, so too do some U.S. schools (Fordham 1991; McQuillan 1998)—schools that are presumably even more liberal than the Mexican secundaria. Across disparate national contexts, schools may both reflect and challenge the dominant tenets of liberalism. Local institutional cultures may uniquely configure dominant discourses.

The Mexican case described here can help to explain much about the comparative contexts of school subjectivity. The absence of tracking or ability grouping, the strong presence of normative discourses on equality and solidarity, and the growing popularity of a mediated youth culture not yet market-differentiated along subcultural lines occasioned students' production of cultural identifications across existing lines of social difference. Such identifications, it is true, were situated in concrete social contexts, and they were still challenged by cross-cutting discourses of competition and distinction in the family and school as well. Yet there is much that those of us in the more highly competitive and individualized North could learn. Thinkers concerned with the damaging effects of student factionalism in U.S. secondary schools have proposed cooperative school structures and activities remarkably similar to what I found in Mexico (see Aronson 2000).

Meanwhile, in Mexico as elsewhere, the challenge that remains, it seems to me, is to retain the best features of collective solidarity and national/school identity, while acknowledging the value of difference in the public sphere. What the secundaria needs is some sense of unity in diversity—an equality of respect and opportunity, not sameness. In this way, the relatively fleeting identifications of student culture might be transformed into the more enduring identities of a solid democratic citizenry.

THE FIELDS BEYOND SCHOOL: IDENTITY AND ASPIRATION UNFOLDING

Looking beyond 1991 and ESF, what were the forces that pushed and pulled at former students? What issues became of greatest concern to them, and how did their subjectivities and identities unfold in new circumstances? On balance, what is the evidence that playing the game of equality in the school and grupo escolar altered habitus and carried over into other spheres of life? Finally, what consequence might this have for the cultural reproduction of the Mexican nation itself?

The trajectories of my twenty-two focal students certainly show the impact of deeply conditioned habitus. Clearly, Alberto's chances for university study were greatly enhanced by his intimate culture and the cultural capital that his family supplied. Everyone expected Alberto to achieve professional status. Conversely, Andrea's chances for advanced study were hampered by the absence of such cultural capital. Her older sister managed to make it beyond prepa only with great effort and expense.

Yet many of these students' paths varied significantly not only by gender and class or ethnic origin, but also by singular contingencies of personality, birth order, family tragedy, and the like. While Mexicans themselves like to highlight the temperamental differences (*carácter*) among their offspring, most critical educational studies have ignored these differences. This study shows, however, that it is necessary to point to family idiosyncrasies and their corresponding psychological entailments as key components in the structuring of life trajectories. How else can Abel be understood other than through what his own mother called the "trauma" of being an underachieving younger brother of four outstanding sisters? Might Iván have continued his studies had he not maintained a tough masculine disposition and then fallen in love to marry at such a young age? How much did Franco's physical disabilities explain his vacillations in school? Andrea's bitter conflicts with her mother may have had much to do with her feeling of belittlement vis-à-vis her older sister, and thus a decision not to pursue an identity in the same educational field. And in

Antonia's case, the sudden death of her father obviously eliminated a crucial source of economic and emotional support.

I would suggest that differences of temperament and family history even accounted for rather distinct visions of grupo escolar life among students who otherwise occupied similar intimate cultures. For example, Dalia and Matilde each came from modest working-class homes located in outlying colonias. Both had strong mothers with some training as teachers. Dalia, to reiterate, often found ESF's grupo life divisive and difficult. Her younger age and socialization as an only child probably ill-prepared her for the rough-and-tumble compañerismo of the grupo escolar. When she eventually enrolled at the technical school, CBTIS, she saw her friends there as rather unified in comparison to the factionalism she had perceived at ESF. Matilde, the oldest of four daughters, said she suffered from some of the same exclusions in the grupo escolar. Yet unlike Dalia, Matilde still stressed the value of grupo unity. She did express relief on attending the CBTIS, but not because she found the unity there that had been lacking at ESF. Rather, at the CBTIS, nobody bothered her and "everyone was on their own." In all these cases, individual temperament and biography mediates a profoundly social dynamic.

As I have shown, the construction of a secondary schooled identity provided an important sense of self that ESF students variably appropriated to construct sameness and difference, to justify patterns of affiliation and distance. Yet the friendship groups students chose and developed had differing effects on their identities and aspirations. Some appeared to have a significant impact on students' aspirations and subsequent trajectories. Rosita, Leticia, and Nidia benefited from strong, supportive peer groups in their efforts as young women to continue their studies. Still, in most instances, friendship groups merely accommodated the sensibilities that students had already developed in their intimate cultures, thereby re-affirming aspirations already well in formation. In counterpoint to the peer group, the Mexican family continued to provide an overwhelmingly powerful site for identity and aspiration formation. With regard to the focal students, few of them established friendship groups that had serious long-term consequences for their development. Whatever tendencies the friendship groups at ESF fostered were quickly superseded by new contexts and relationships (including immigration, work, another school, marriage, or new forms of pop culture consumption). Perhaps because the friendship groups and other observable social distinctions at ESF were not stimulated or reinforced by school structures, they failed to have a more lasting impact on student identities and aspirations. For instance, distinctions did not necessarily persist according to who would eventually continue their studies. Most of the Potrillos were still studying at a university in 1997, but their leader, Iván, had not even finished high school. Similarly, among the Juanitos, Alberto and Constantín were becoming professionals, while Abel had dropped out and nobody could say what had become of Roberto. Such patterns highlight a crucial difference between this study and those conducted by U.S. and European researchers. Cliques and subcultures in schools like those examined by Penelope Eckert (1989) and Paul Willis (1981b) tended to form around common orientations—or common resistances—to school structures and discourses. Such friendship groups then reinforced emerging identities and aspirations. At ESF, though, friendship groups formed for different reasons and, apparently, to rather different ends.

Of course, some students never seemed to find a comfortable place in school. Andrea and Fidel, to cite two cases, never fully adopted the schooled identity under construction in and around ESF. But for those who did, subsequent experiences then intervened to influence the ongoing formation of subjectivity and identity. The habitus first formed through their intimate cultures and then subject to the positioning of ESF's cultural game now confronted new and different circumstances. For instance, the young women who got married or began remunerative work during their teenage years (Antonia, Nidia, Andrea, and Ivonne) obviously formed new kinds of allegiances and identities. Likewise for those who continued their university studies. This was not always an even trajectory, either, for some students repeated a year or waited as long as two years between courses of study. Economic circumstance and poor academic performance (Franco, Abel, Dalia, Leticia, and Fidencio) often conspired to postpone these students' professional careers.

The cultural game of equality at ESF positioned students in fields of national culture and socioeconomic mobility, yet such fields did not exhaust the symbolic resources available to students. As I have noted already, the images of glamour and wealth in media culture, as well as the promise of a better life through migration, pulled at students' sensibilities. Indeed, the ongoing expansion of migration to the United States opened up possibilities that made scholastic routes to status and economic security even more questionable. In a well-known essay, the anthropologist Arjun Appadurai (1991) comments on the importance of documenting these new "imaginaries" in the construction of identity and aspiration:

Ethnography must re-define itself as that practice of representation which illuminates the power of large-scale, imagined life possibilities over specific life trajectories . . . a new alertness to the fact that ordinary lives today are increasingly powered not by the givenness of things but by the possibilities that the media (either directly or indirectly) suggest are available. (200; quoted in Nespor 1997, 162)

Though Appadurai highlights the symbolic resources of the media, in San Pablo the lore surrounding international migration arguably exerted an equally powerful influence. The promise of international migration had, in effect, become lodged in youth's imaginaries. And clearly, those who migrated to the United States had their schooled identities challenged and altered forever. In this fashion, global flows of culture and political-economic trends provided powerful structuring resources for student identity and aspiration.

To sum up my points about students' unfolding identity and aspirations in the 1990s: The ESF students' varying involvement and positions in the school-based game of equality had some immediate and circumstantial effects on their aspirations in 1991. Through peer affiliation, grupo escolar life, and the occasional identification with national progress, many students substantially altered their habitus and embarked on life trajectories rather different from what their parents' generation had known. Yet new contexts and circumstances quickly intervened. The new contexts included the next level of schooling (preparatory or vocational high school), a workplace, a set of neighborhood relationships, or a different country altogether (the United States); the circumstances ranged from personal contingencies of marriage, illness, or loss, to the global restructuring of economic relations. The school-learned discourses of equality persisted most strongly in those students who had most avidly appropriated it to position themselves socially in 1991, or had since clung stubbornly to a schooled identity in order to justify or envision their further schooling. Those former students who continued to pursue a service profession, especially within public institutions, also showed stronger traces of having played the game of equality. On the other hand, students who got married, dropped out early, or emigrated to the United States, and therefore no longer participated in projects of national scope or ideology, tended to have withdrawn the most from the game.

Figure 5 represents the dynamics of student culture and identity formation discussed throughout this book. The three vertically defined areas

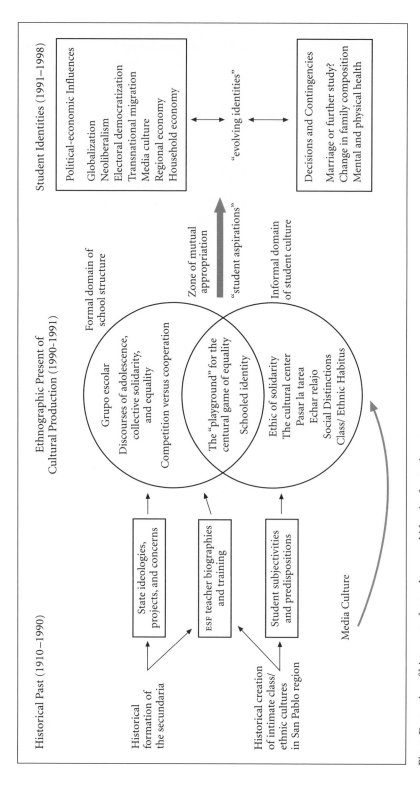

Fig. 5. Dynamics of history, student culture, and identity formation at ESF

(columns) moving from left to right—the "historical past," "the ethno-graphic present," and "student identities"—correspond to different time periods, or "moments," of cultural production. The middle area, on the ethnographic present, represents the dynamics between students and teachers described in the heart of the book, chapters 3 through 6. An overlapping zone of "mutual appropriation" is created by the interaction between the "formal domain of school structure" and the "informal do-main of student culture." The dynamics represented in the middle area have historical inputs coming from the left-most area, and the output of student identities and aspirations moving into the future, to the right.

The "historical past" represents the historical creation of beliefs, ide-ologies, practices, and so on that converge in the school. The two main elements are the secundaria as an institution, and the parents and children who attend the secundaria. The three boxes I've drawn in the space be-tween the left and middle areas correspond to the main "actors" that are historically produced and come together to interact in the school. They are placed between the past and the present to indicate the flow of time. On the one hand, there are "State ideologies, projects, and concerns" that give the formal domain of the school a certain shape in the form of textbooks, organizational structure, policies and discourses, and so forth. On the other hand, there are "student subjectivities and predispositions" that give the informal domain of student culture a certain shape. "ESF teacher biographies and training" are constituted in the meeting ground between the State and local intimate cultures, since many teachers come from local cultures but are trained by the State. Their training forms part of the school's formal domain.

The impact of "media culture" is a bit off by itself, with input into the informal domain of student culture, because it is neither wholly of the State nor of local intimate cultures, and because its impact is of more recent creation.

Finally, the arrow pointing from the middle area to the right-most area represents the unfolding of student identities and aspirations between 1991 and 1998. These identities and aspirations emerge out of the encoun-ter between the formal and informal domains of the school, and continue to evolve in response to two other sets of factors that I've represented here in the boxes, "Political-economic influences" and "Decisions and con-tingencies." The arrows drawn between these two boxes and the area of students' evolving identities are two-sided, to indicate influences moving in both directions.

To refine theories of cultural production and student identity, it is necessary to explore how students' sense of themselves and their priorities in life continue to evolve in a kind of dialogue between the subjectivities garnered in their school years—in this case, largely through the game of equality and play of schooled identity—and the conditions they later face in unfolding time and space. This study shows how these conditions may encompass the broadest forces of global political-economic restructuring, in which individual identification with national progress makes little sense, and in which the solidarities of transnational labor and youth culture may now resonate more with the old game of equality than the increasingly elusive goal of national unity.

CODA: THE STUDENT AND THE NATION

If transnational media and migration structured aspirations in new and different ways, what had become of students' faith in national political and spiritual institutions? As discussed earlier, the secundaria had been charged with forming national identity and socializing adolescent subjectivity for citizenship and political participation. Even though school officials maintained a strict separation of church and State, students generally declared themselves devout Catholics. In 1997, I asked students to state their political preferences and reflect on their religious development. The failure of the government to resolve the ongoing economic crisis, along with the impact of global media and migration, served to intensify the former students' doubts about their own place in the national project. They were mostly put off by official corruption and cynical about Mexico's political future. Few of them expressed strong attachments to the nation; they focused instead on the local and global. I was not surprised, then, to find these former students with generally strengthened orientations to the church, God, and the saints. To be sure, some students did not find church attendance necessary to express devotion to God. Yet nearly all of them confessed to praying and rendering homage to one of the many saints in the Mexican Catholic cosmology.

Does this augur a problem for Mexican solidarity and continuity at a national level? The question of Mexican national culture and identity, as I note in the introduction and appendix A, has occasioned a great deal of commentary over the years. Especially in light of the North American Free Trade Agreement and other signs of global integration, authors have speculated on its renewal and demise (Bartra 1993; Guevara Niebla and García

Canclini 1992; Valenzuela Arce 1992). In a provocative article, renowned journalist and historian Héctor Aguilar Camín (1993, 325) remarked on the growing contradictory tendency in postwar Mexico between nationalism and what one might call cosmopolitanism. While markets, media, and migration have brought Mexico closer to the world, and especially the United States, nationalist discourse continues to affirm the triumph of the collective sensibility and need for national sovereignty. Historians and anthropologists have frequently associated such nationalist discourse with a hegemonic project of the postrevolutionary State. In this view, the construction of a strong national identity has served to build allegiance to the State and diminish attachments to potentially hostile local projects and identities. National culture thus displaces, incorporates, or "articulates" local cultures.

Yet much of this has changed since the early 1980s. As critical intellectuals and opposition parties continued to demonstrate the insidious convergence of strong national culture with authoritarian single-party rule, the State itself took a strong rightward turn. On the heels of a fiscal crisis, State enterprises were sold off, markets were opened, and schools were defunded. National solidarity, while given mention in political programs and discourse, took a backseat to global economic integration and entrepreneurial ambition. Now critics of the State sought to revalue national identity, decouple it from the ruling party (PRI), and use it to offset the free market drift. Still, the State's revolutionary project of social justice through education seemed to be reaching a definitive end.

If my study is any indication, Mexican youth have become more pragmatic in outlook. They distrust the State, and perhaps for that reason rarely invoke national identity. They also derive meaning from an increasingly complex and varied set of possible values and life courses (Loaeza 1997, 82). Of course, there was never much evidence in 1991 that students felt strongly compelled by nationalist discourse. By 1998, despite the secundaria's insistent emphasis on national identity and solidarity, former ESF students continued to look elsewhere for frameworks of practical meaning.

Structure, Culture, and Subjectivity:

The Elements of Practice

One can only gain a clear understanding of the relation of individual and society if one includes in it the perpetual growing up of individuals within a society, if one includes the process of individualization in the theory of society. The historicity of each individual, the phenomenon of growing-up to adulthood, is a key to an understanding of what "society" is.—Norbert Elias, *The Society of Individuals*

Throughout this narrative text, I have attempted to weave the theoretical perspectives informing my study. Here I provide a more explicit statement about theory. I begin with a review of the literature that inspired my initial research design and move on to clarify my own approach. I finish with an extended discussion of key terms in critical cultural analysis. My goal here is to outline sufficiently reformulated concepts of structure, culture, and subjectivity that can provide useful tools for thinking about the strategic practice students enacted in their cultural game at ESF.

THEORETICAL AND ETHNOGRAPHIC PRECURSORS

When, in 1987, I first conceived of doing research in and around a socially diverse Mexican secondary school, I had a set of comparative questions in mind. Critical scholars of education in the United States and

Europe had already drawn a fairly elaborate picture of how secondary schools sorted and socialized their students for unequal positions in society. Many of these same scholars had also explored the ways students responded to such treatment by creating practices, identities, and cultures within and sometimes against the schools.[1] The dynamic interplay between school structures and student cultures was shown to influence the fates of most students. Clearly, the nature of the broader social order—most often conceived of as capitalist, sexist, and/or racist—structured this dynamic, though perhaps not as deterministically as earlier authors had initially postulated (Althusser 1971; Arnot 1982; Bowles and Gintis 1976).

I thought the story in Mexico might be different, but wasn't quite sure how. Mexico was an ostensibly capitalist society with a strong liberal tradition and growing need to differentiate students for a technical labor market, yet it was also a former colonial society that had articulated a strong commitment to quasi-socialist ideals of justice, solidarity, and equality emerging from one of the great revolutions of the twentieth century. Setting it further apart from the United States and Europe was its only recently expanded, noncompulsory secondary school system, a still-emerging youth culture, and a rather unique "authoritarian" (Smith 1991) and corporatist political system. Moreover, since the early 1980s, a forty-year economic and educational boom had fallen victim to severe monetary devaluation. In this shifting context, did most Mexican students wish to continue their education beyond secondary schooling? Did secondary schools attempt to differentiate students by class, ethnicity, or gender? If so, how did they do this, and how would students respond? If not, what kinds of practices and values did the schools most forcefully enact? Did students then do the work of differentiation themselves, and if so, how?

To begin answering these questions, I conceptualized a case study of a single secondary school. I wanted to know how a particular group of Mexican secondary students developed their sense of self as well as learned their future places in society through their encounters with relatives, teachers, and other students. I was especially concerned with examining how students from different kinds of backgrounds formed aspirations and practical strategies that confirmed, modified, or more substantively challenged the life circumstances they had inherited.

CULTURAL PRODUCTION AND REPRODUCTION IN SCHOOLING

The most significant body of work informing my research had come to be known as social and cultural reproduction theory. Back in the 1970s, a number of educational researchers had begun to mount a critique of schooling in advanced capitalist societies like the United States, Britain, and France.[2] These authors observed that while the prevailing liberal democratic rhetoric portrayed public schools in Europe, the United States, and Australia as fair and equal, the reality betrayed a system based on discriminatory social sorting. Rather than transforming entrenched structures of inequality, schools tended to *reproduce* these structures as well as the cultural assumptions underpinning them. For example, despite the schools' promises of upward mobility, most members of the subordinate working class eventually found that their children ended up in the same class, and that they had adopted the same values and meanings as the parental generation. Drawing on Marxist and Weberian theories of power, authors like Samuel Bowles and Herbert Gintis (1976), Michael Apple (1979), Pierre Bourdieu and Jean-Claude Passeron (1977), Christian Baudelot and Roger Establet (1975), and Michael Young (1971) developed compelling accounts of how schools performed the work of reproducing inequality.[3] These accounts differed in terms of the relative weight they put on factors such as tracking, examinations, teacher comportment, curricular knowledge, and so forth. Nonetheless, they all agreed that public schools in the capitalist nation-state by and large served to reproduce the status quo and socialize students to accept their appointed places in the existing political-economic hierarchy.

Yet even as this body of work was beginning to exercise considerable influence among scholars, there was growing unease about how schools were portrayed in such functionalist terms. The picture was too deterministic, the school too much an instrument of powerful political and economic interests (Liston 1988). Teachers and textbook writers appeared as guileless agents of the State or handmaidens of the ruling class. Students appeared as passive dummies, marching off to their respective fates. The school was still a black box, a space overfilled with theoretical assumptions (Connell 1983). Critical ethnographic research in schools sought largely to correct this imbalance (Anderson 1989; Levinson and Holland 1996; Mehan 1992). Paul Willis's (1981a) striking study of working-class students at a British comprehensive high school is often cited as a watershed in this ethnographic wave, but in reality, the 1970s and 1980s saw a flood of nearly concurrent activity (Anyon 1981; Apple and Weis 1983; Everhart 1983; Rosenbaum 1976). In these studies, both teachers and students demonstrated greater agency, the ability to intervene creatively in their circumstances and even "resist" the dominant script. Parents and teachers were brought more squarely into view in some cases—their interests and strategies made part of the more complex equation (Carlson 1987; McNeil 1986; Connell et al. 1982; Lareau 1989). Feminists and critical race theorists also broadened the question of reproduction to include structures of gender and racial inequality, focusing ethnographic research on the agency of women and racial minorities (Delamont 1984; Fine 1991; Fordham 1988, 1993; Lesko 1988; Valli 1986; McRobbie 1992; Gillborn 1990).[4]

Radical educational theorists meanwhile reflected on the findings of this ethnographic research and developed a more nuanced picture of how power operated within schools to shape particular student outcomes (Apple 1982; Giroux 1983; Morrow and Torres 1995; Shapiro 1990).[5] They attempted to understand the range and modalities of human agency in schools without losing sight of the structures and circumstances conditioning that agency.[6] Increasingly, ethnographers enriched theory by exploring the process of *cultural production* as the making of meanings by reflexive social actors in specific and diverse contexts of structured power (Levinson, Foley, and Holland 1996; see also Apple and Weis 1983). Theorists now agreed that social and cultural reproduction, if and where it occurred, could not be foreordained; it had to pass through the dynamics of cultural production, the consequential making of meanings.[7] Student culture has since been placed at the heart of the social reproduction inquiry, for it is now widely recognized that the meanings students make of their schooling experience have a powerful impact on their relations with teachers and parents, hence their subsequent life trajectories. Radical portrayals of the school as villain or instrument of domination must now pass muster with the implacable agency of students.[8]

Concepts of aspiration and identity formation help capture the important and dynamic relation between student agency and the structural conditions of schools. Aspirations and identities are both cause and result of the meanings that students make in schools.[9] I define aspiration as:

> an evolving commitment to a life course that is subject to both the structural-cultural position that individuals inherit (habitus) and the idiosyncratic conditionings of personal life history as these *both* manifest in the shifting developmental and institutional contexts of learning.

The school, perhaps especially the secondary school for so-called modern adolescents, is one of the most crucial of such developmental contexts. Identities form hand in hand with aspirations as a significant part of the educational process, in the broadest sense of that term, though identities are much more than aspirations (see below).[10]

What happens to students' aspirations when they encounter the modern secondary school?[11] To be sure, most ethnographic studies of student culture and secondary schooling have been carried out in the Euro-American context of liberal, pluralist democracy (including Australia), where secondary schooling has typically been compulsory and available for most adolescents at least since World War II. Nearly all these studies, moreover, emphasize the splintering of school populations into divisive and mutually antagonistic "status groups" or "student cultures." Such splintering takes place through the production of differential meanings around schooling, meanings that may be intimately related to class, race, and gender subjectivities imported into the school.[12] Douglas Foley (1990), Robert Connell (et al. 1982), and Penelope Eckert (1989) have been among those most attentive to how these student groups reflect structural divisions outside the school without always corresponding neatly to them. The meanings and dispositions that students bring with them into the school are reinforced, altered, or reconfigured through a complex interaction with school structures and teachers' practices (compare Davidson 1996). As Colin Lacey (1970, 56) put it, "external factors" such as social class must be "fed through the internal system of relations within the classroom." Student groups or subcultures are not "expressing" their subjectivities as a "product," an "accomplished fact" (Lave et al. 1992, 269; see also Hall 1990); rather, subcultures are intimately involved in the ongoing production of identities, vis-à-vis other groups engaged in the same kind of identity work. This is one of the primary ways that social difference gets continually reconfigured in the school.

Paul Willis (1981a, 1981b, 1983) provided an important statement about the way student groups were involved in the cultural production of meanings that then mediate the reproduction of structural inequalities. In Willis's study, the rebellious working-class lads drew on broader class-based discourses of resistance to challenge the school's false promise of middle-class mobility. In being creative agents of their own counterschool identities, they reproduced their subordinate class position through a willful practice, not a passive acquiescence. Willis, who wrote *Learning to Labor* while at the University of Birmingham Centre for Contemporary Cultural Studies (cccs), was one of the first to apply the Centre's emerging critical subcultural theory to the dynamics of secondary schooling.[13]

Yet while he described the antagonisms between the rebellious lads and their foils, the conformist "ear'oles," he never adequately explored how such difference emerged in the school context when all the students apparently shared the same class background.[14]

A number of authors in the critical educational literature have drawn on, modified, and expanded Willis's initial formulations in ways that are suggestive for the present study. Dorothy Holland and Margaret Eisenhart's (1990) study of women at two universities (one historically black, the other white) in the U.S. South demonstrates the power of a dominant cultural "world of romance" that obliges most women to adjust their career goals and identities, often subordinating them to the search for heterosexual romance and marriage. This dominant cultural formation—produced collectively by both men and women across a variety of social contexts at these universities—appeared to throw women back onto individualized strategies for social and academic survival. Holland and Eisenhart view the mixed peer group as the key site for the cultural reproduction of male privilege in gender relations. Structures of gender inequality, or patriarchy, therefore, are "mediated most virulently by the peer group—not by school officials who are socially distant in age and authority" (Holland and Eisenhart 1990, 221). In other words, patriarchy at universities is most powerfully purveyed in face-to-face peer relations in informal settings largely outside the scope of "official" institutional gender practices.

In Douglas Foley's (1990) study of a South Texas high school and its surrounding community, "youths practice, learn, and anticipate their different class identities and roles through the way they play football, display peer status, and horse around in classrooms" (192). Yet class identities articulate with ethnic identities in powerful, and often unpredictable, ways. Foley draws on the interactionist sociologist Erving Goffman to depict the school as a middle-class bureaucratic organization, "dedicated to stripping kids of their ethnic identity and replacing it with an institutional, mainstream identity" (161). In the face of this institutional action, Foley found that students "endlessly rebelled and created their own identities and spaces" (ibid.). He shows how class and ethnic identities—the stuff of social difference—get "staged" by students in the school as they attempt to creatively negotiate the dominant meanings of schooling. Students' "expressive practices" therefore represent institutionally situated forms of class-ethnic "communicative labor" through which they learn their "proper" place in local "capitalist culture."

In her study of diverse high school students "making and molding identity," Anne Locke Davidson (1996) shows how students, based on their minority status and perceptions of labor market opportunities, may have predispositions to resist or comply with school directives. Such predispositions, however, interact with a number of complex factors at the institutional level to mold behavior. Davidson is especially concerned with identifying those school practices that contribute to student "alienation" and the formation of resistant identities. Her book presents the extended narratives of six youths that represent a range of academic achievement. Through an analysis of these narratives, Davidson synthesizes the four factors that she thinks contribute most to student alienation (35–49). First, the practice of academic tracking, which separates groups of students and defines them as "academically or socially different," contributes to the social isolation of some students. Second, "significant speech acts" by teachers, including the labeling of students, discriminatory remarks, and proscription of behavior or symbols marking group identity, can elicit negative student response. Third, some schools are dominated by "bureaucratized relationships and practices," where the enforcement of hierarchy and status divisions between teachers and students, and the maintenance of silent communicative distance, can provoke student noncompliance. Finally, schools often tragically and unwittingly create "barriers to valued information." Davidson says that these school practices are "particularly relevant to the construction of identities" (1996, 214), and it is not difficult to see why. By framing the relation between student identity and academic achievement in terms of *engagement*, Davidson allows for an assessment of the complex relations between students and schools.

Aurolyn Luykx's (1999) recent work on a Bolivian high school for indigenous teachers-in-training demonstrates how students creatively respond to contradictory educational discourses around gender and ethnicity. Students seek to retain an indigenous identity while empowering themselves professionally, yet State discourses—exemplified in their own instructors' lessons and sermons—deny constructive dialogue around ethnicity and portray indigenous culture as irremediably backward. The Bolivian State thus equips its rural teacher-training schools to reproduce the class-ethnic subordination of its indigenous peoples, even as the very existence of such bilingual schools represents for such peoples an opportunity for socioeconomic mobility. Luykx reveals in vivid detail how students appropriate the language and social space of the school to produce cultural forms that serve as "weapons of the weak" (218), and as crucibles for the development of complex and resistant identities.

All these authors exemplify a growing concern with student agency in the production and reproduction of social inequalities, as well as the elaboration of sociocultural difference. Yet while the critical literature has assiduously documented the process of differentiation, few authors have examined the factors that might actually inhibit the development of clearly defined, mutually antagonistic, student cultures, even in schools that try to accommodate a rather full range of social and cultural differences. Rarely have ethnographers of secondary schooling described school-based processes that lead to greater common identification and solidarity, not differentiation. Nor have they fully addressed the way identity and aspiration can become reconstituted in quite unexpected ways. Only through closer attention to the interplay of structure and subjectivity at multiple levels can the contextual contingencies of such identity formation be appreciated. This is one of my principal aims in this book.

SCHOOLING AS STATE AND POPULAR CULTURE IN THE FORMATION OF NATIONAL IDENTITY

One of the great puzzles of the modern period is how the political form of the nation-state has been able to forge collective identifications—a common national identity—out of the multiple allegiances of locally rooted popular cultures (Eley and Suny 1996). Spurred on by Benedict Anderson's (1983) provocative work on nationalism as a form of "imagined community," scholars have investigated the means by which modern States have done the work of nation building with the raw material of these diverse popular cultures. Mexico provides a remarkable case. Recent explorations of the State and popular culture in Mexico have sought to describe and conceptualize the dynamic and mutually constitutive relations between them (Alonso 1995; Joseph and Nugent 1994; Beezley et al. 1994; Lomnitz-Adler 1992; Becker 1995; Rubin 1996). The debate between "revisionists" and "neopopulists" in Mexican historiography has largely been about the extent of "popular" participation in the formation of the postrevolutionary State and national culture (Joseph and Nugent 1994). The revisionists argue that the revolution of 1910–1920, although fueled in large part by regional popular uprisings, eventually culminated in the ascendancy of bourgeois factions that reinstated the model of centralized government and dependent capitalist development characterizing the prerevolutionary dictatorship of Porfirio Díaz (Gilly 1971; Córdova 1974).

The neopopulists, on the other hand, insist that the vitality of a popular presence during the revolution had a significant impact on the manner in which the postrevolutionary State developed a unique mode of governance (Knight 1986). I situate my study in the context of Gilbert Joseph and Daniel Nugent's (1994) attempt to bridge these two interpretations by examining more closely the everyday role of consciousness and popular culture in the ongoing formation of the Mexican State.[15]

Public schooling has played a crucial role in the formation of a Mexican national identity and the popular legitimization of the Mexican State. Until recently, it has been able to do this by providing both real, albeit unevenly distributed, opportunities for educational and economic mobility, and symbolic participation in a rich national heritage. Scholars like Mary Kay Vaughan (1997) have highlighted the State's fulfillment of popular demand and involvement in the construction of a positive nationalist sentiment (see also Rockwell 1994, 1996; Mercado 1985; Quintanilla 1996). Even as State bureaucrats used schools to extend control over local communities (Fuentes 1983; Becker 1995), they had to contend with the power of the popular cultures they encountered there. As Justa Ezpeleta and Elsie Rockwell (1985) put it in borrowing a phrase from Antonio Gramsci, the "traces" of popular claims can be found in many current school practices and structures. State action in the educational field has thus come to seem less a form of imposition and more a continually modified product of negotiation. In an important sense, then, public schools in Mexico have always served as key sites for the reciprocal production of forms of State and popular culture.

I have taken some inspiration from Philip Corrigan and Derek Sayer's (1985) highly original treatment of the way in which the English State, as a "form of [bourgeois] claim" to legitimacy, took shape over several centuries in the context of a "mutually formative struggle" with oppositional cultures (7). Through a "double disruption" of popular culture, Corrigan and Sayer argue that the State "erase[s] the recognition and expression of differences" (of class, gender, ethnicity, age, religion, occupation, locality) (4). Drawing on Michel Foucault's work, Corrigan and Sayer then maintain that this double disruption consists of both a "totalizing" project, in which the State represents people as members of the national community, and a project in which the State also tries to "individualize" subjects in specific ways—for instance, as taxpayers, jurors, consumers, and homeowners. In both of these disruptions, "alternative modes of collective and individual identification . . . are denied legitimacy" (5).

Recently, Derek Sayer (1994, 368–71) has warned against both generalizing from the English "case" and treating the State as a unified agency. Following Philip Abrams (1988), he suggests that the State is nothing more, really, than an "ideological project," a "claim" to rule that must be continually renewed. Yet the collection by Gilbert Joseph and Daniel Nugent (1994) demonstrates the power of a notion of "mutually formative struggle" between States and popular cultures. States may indeed make claims to rule, but they also must create and sustain the institutional forms necessary to making such claims. These forms do not represent any unitary will; they emerge out of a considered negotiation between elite members of the governing apparatus and popular political subjects. Indeed, as a more nuanced, relational, and historically informed conception of popular culture emerges in the field of cultural studies (Grossberg, Nelson, and Treichler 1992; Johnson 1986–1987; Morley and Chen 1996), no object, phenomenon, or process can be considered "popular" by virtue of its intrinsic properties. Rather, popular culture should be thought of as that set of cultural resources deployed by subordinate groups in a "dialectic of cultural struggle" (Hall 1981, 233) with a project of domination.[16] Employing this more relational and historical understanding of popular culture allows for a subtler appreciation of how the State "works" through schools.

As I hope to have shown here, the school is an important site where dominant and popular meanings are caught up in that "dialectic of cultural struggle" to which Stuart Hall refers. Such meanings provide a key resource for students to play their part in the game at ESF. Rooted in an everyday "form of life" (Hannerz 1996), popular meanings into a complex dynamic with the meanings imparted through domains such as schooling and the electronic media.[17] This book is, in large part, about the traffic in popular and dominant meanings at a secondary school, and how the identity work that students perform with those meanings has possible consequences for their eventual place in local and national life.[18] Indeed, secondary schooling may be an especially significant site precisely because it is one of the few social institutions (along with the church) where people from very different communities, and with rather different subjectivities, interact intensively in the same activities on a daily basis. Yet unlike the church, the school is formally a State institution—the ideological child of the revolution originally designed to displace church power. How, then, does the culture of the State intersect with other allegedly popular identities in everyday school practice and discourse? What kinds of identities and meanings does the school promote or censure? How does the cultural action of the State in schooling, mediated by students' own cultural productions, participate in configuring and reconfiguring power relations in local communities? In this book, I have shown how organizational and discursive practices emphasizing equality and solidarity at one school aim to create common, national identifications across social difference. Yet in so doing, the State participates in creating the category of a secondary-schooled educated person, which then helps restructure a broader field of class-ethnic and gender relations.

ANTHROPOLOGY, HISTORY, AND THE
LOCAL MEANINGS OF STUDENT CULTURE

European and U.S. Scholarly Perspectives. The critical ethnographic literature on secondary student culture lacks a body of comparative work from those societies historically on the colonial periphery of capitalist development and liberal democratic rule. This is partly because the questions of reproduction theory themselves have emerged out of the contradictions specific to liberal democratic discourses of individualism and equality, as well as capitalist imperatives of a differentiated race-class order. It is also because the criteria for social differentiation across a broader range of societies cannot be described easily by Western categories of race or class (Farrell 1992, 110; Stambach 1996).[19] As I soon learned when I first attempted to analyze my Mexican data, there is something deeply troubling about the application of radical European sociological categories to societies like Mexico. While I cannot claim to have escaped entirely the blinders such categories can impose, I have tempered my critical perspective with a broadened purview from anthropology and history.

Beginning in the 1960s, anthropologists of education had already begun to explore the dynamics of aspiration and identity-formation within the prevailing paradigm of modernization theory (King 1967; Spindler and Spindler 1973; for an overview, see Foley 1977). Prior to that, classic studies of education as basic cultural transmission, initiation, and observational learning were carried out largely during a period of relative anthropological innocence, when cultures were seen as uniquely bounded.[20] While often blind to the broader political and economic forces impinging on local cultural practices, early anthropologists nonetheless observed a world where modern schooling had yet to make itself strongly felt. Since then, as marginalized groups have become increasingly drawn into the modern nation-state and global economy, they have also been subject to the ideological action of mass public schooling. Almost universally, schooling has now come to be seen as the primary method of receiving an "education." This meaning of education is, of course, bound up with the State-sponsored goal of creating good national citizens and, in many instances, providing cheap skilled labor for economic development. The rise and expansion of State schooling has usually involved the rather sudden displacement of tribal or agrarian practices and identities (Levine and White 1986), transforming them through the cultural production of a new kind of "educated person" (Levinson, Foley, and Holland 1996).

In the last twenty years, anthropologists have begun to situate their ethnographic case studies of schooling in a critical comparative framework that examines local and extralocal relations of power. Most work continues to focus on elementary education.[21] Some anthropologists, however, have done pioneering work in secondary schools.[22] Even more recently, Janise Hurtig (1997), Aurolyn Luykx (1999), Thomas Shaw (1991, 1996), and Amy Stambach (2000), working respectively in Venezuela, Bolivia, Taiwan, and Tanzania, have examined the locally unique circumstances and cultural conceptions giving rise to new configurations of difference in secondary schools. Rather than validating the homogenizing myth of modern schooling, these authors recover history in order to demonstrate how schooling introduces new practices and contexts within and against which students may reconfigure their differences from one another. By showing how identity formation is subject to such historical-cultural shifts, these authors help broaden and refine the comparative insights available from such work.

Mexican Scholarly Perspectives. From my colleagues and teachers in graduate school, I learned to think historically and comparatively. I had similar lessons to learn when I went to Mexico. There I discovered a group of researchers who had already reckoned with the implications of social and cultural reproduction theory. Elsie Rockwell and her colleagues and students at the Departamento de Investigaciones Educativas (DIE, or Department of Educational Research) had taken on the task of understanding the enormous inequalities and frustrating contradictions in Mexican educational development. The seemingly monolithic character of the Mexican State, with its centrally controlled school system, prompted a critical analysis of educational domination and capitalist development.[23] Strains of social reproduction and dependency theories provided the context for some of the earliest writing and ethnographic work at the DIE (Rockwell 1991). Yet soon realizing the rather foreign and functionalist

(Liston 1988) character of reproduction theory, DIE researchers joined hands with other Latin Americans in elaborating an even more dynamic, historical, and locally informed conception of the State and school (de Ibarrola and Rockwell 1985; Madeira and Namo 1985; Tedesco 1983). Rockwell and her colleagues came to their critique of reproduction theory primarily through close attention to teachers' practice and agency. They rejected the tendency in reproduction theory to identify teachers' action and discourse with the ideology or agenda of the State. Opting to look phenomenologically (Heller 1984) at the various modalities of teachers' work in the everyday construction of school, they saw heterogeneity and contradiction, not uniformity and compliance (Rockwell and Mercado 1986; Rockwell 1995).

Following their lead, I tempered my comparative framework with an emerging understanding of the unique circumstances and dynamics of the Mexican context. I tried even harder to bracket some of my expectations about student culture informed by ethnographic work on cultural reproduction elsewhere. Soon it became clear that, as Rockwell herself had discovered, the assumptions of reproduction theory could not be easily transposed to Mexico without doing its complex educational reality some violence. After all, public schools in Mexico had been created as part of a revolutionary program of social justice, encouraging popular participation in a variety of formats (Vaughan 1997). Reproduction theory's rather more sinister view of education as ruling imposition did not easily square with this popular history. The emerging cultural history of the Mexican Revolution had begun to show how the State was formed through everyday practices and negotiations with popular groups. Clearly, the State was no simple instrument of domination. It had also become obvious, moreover, that the structuring of inequalities in Mexico took rather different forms from what had been found for advanced capitalist countries. My understanding of student culture would have to be informed by these locally defined configurations of difference.

Furthermore, I began to see that in Mexico, the study of student culture could play an important role in offsetting conventional explanations of school failure or attrition (Muñoz Izquierdo and Ulloa 1992). Most scholarship on Latin American education attributes the phenomenon of school attrition to family or household dynamics. Like the teachers themselves (see chapter 3), most scholars find that students abandon their studies because parents lack the time to guide their children properly, or because the household economy may not be able to sustain a child's studies beyond a few years. Opportunity costs can be too high: children may be needed to work the fields, care for younger siblings, sell merchandise, or help in the family business, and parents simply cannot afford to lose this source of labor, much less pay out more for books, uniforms, and transportation. There is, of course, much truth to these explanations. A great deal of evidence shows that poverty does indeed limit school attendance (Martin 1994b). Still, there is more to the story than this. Especially at the secondary level, I found that student culture comes to have a powerful influence. The research on household economies and the allocation of resources and labor is not typically designed to perceive the nuances of family negotiations or assess the impact of children's strategies for self-determination. With some exceptions (Selby, Murphy, and Lorenzen 1990; Benería and Roldán 1987), the models are rather mechanical: household "needs" and "limits," along with the prevailing Latin American pattern of male dominance and deference to adult authority, conspire to keep children—particularly female children—at home. Yet as I show in this book, families and households are dynamic, fluid organizations of human affect and resource—perhaps especially in the Mexico of the 1980s and 1990s. Students bring ideas and aspirations forged through peer and school culture into the home, and struggles over family rights and obligations may ensue. Often these struggles occur around decisions to leave or stay in school, as well as to continue professional or vocational training.

Subjects' Perspectives. One final way to avoid imposing foreign frameworks on the experience of secondary school students is to pay closer attention to their own perspectives. Of course, all good ethnography—for me, all good social science, in the *Verstehen* tradition—incorporates these perspectives. As William Corsaro (1997) argues for his research on preschool students, care must be taken not to interpret children's activities from the standpoint of traditional socialization theory, which attempts to project these activities into the future—measuring them as developmental benchmarks of one sort or another. This is certainly one of the risks I run in exploring identities and aspirations. Such concerns necessarily beg the question of future trajectories. Yet most students gave little thought to their futures aside from occasions when family, teachers, or the curious anthropologist drew specific attention to them. In reflecting back on her secondary schooling at the age of twenty-two, Leticia provided perhaps the most telling account of this orientation:

For me, the secundaria was a very happy time . . . because it's a time in your life when you don't have so many commitments, you don't have too many responsibilities, and yet you do have freedom to do things. When you're in the primaria, you don't have freedom even though you don't have responsibilities, either, and now, even though you have the freedom, you also have a lot of responsibilities, and it's like the way that you live doesn't permit you to be so natural or to do things as openly as you might like to. When you're in the secundaria, you don't think so much about that; rather, you just live in the moment and enjoy things without getting frustrated about what's past or what might be in the future.

To be sure, Leticia's personal history embodied specific class and gender elements that made her time in the secundaria perhaps especially carefree. Still, most students would have agreed with the radically presentist and relatively unselfconscious moment Leticia evoked. Newfound freedoms and the intensity of peer life in the secundaria create for most a uniquely absorbing experience. How could I honor such experience if my theoretical interests extended well beyond the immediate interactional environment to the temporal and spatial horizons of aspiration and political economy? How might I accommodate the radically subjective, context-bound dimensions of experience to extralocal influences and determinations, all within an ethnographic analysis? I have come to an appreciation of the bind created by counterpoising the local with the extralocal, the micro with the macro. It is a false dualism, to be sure. The macrostructural horizon already informs the rather local and immediate meanings that student activities have for the students themselves (Carspecken 1995; Giddens 1984, 294–307). Many of these meanings are emotionally and bodily based, not necessarily cognitive in the way language-based theories presuppose.[24] I believe a modified phenomenological approach to ethnographic interpretation (Jackson 1996) can capture the vitality of student meanings and perspectives—of subjectivity and "lived experience" (Ellis and Flaherty 1992)—in both local and extralocal terms.[25]

CONCEPTS FOR A CRITICAL ANALYSIS OF STUDENT CULTURE

SELF AND SOCIETY: AGENCY, STRUCTURE, PRACTICE

In developing my account of student culture and identity formation, I have had to join a discussion that remains at the heart of the human sciences: how to conceptualize the dynamic relation between the self and society, between individual agency, on the one hand, and the conditioning structures of social life. To put it most simply, how is it possible to allow for the creativity and self-determination of each person, while also acknowledging the social limits and determinants of such creativity?

In inaugurating a critical materialist tradition, it was Marx who perhaps most poignantly evoked this dynamic with his memorable phrase, "Men [*sic*] make their own history, but they do not make it just as they please" (Marx 1852, in Tucker 1978, 595). Feminist theorists, by forcefully drawing attention to the recurring struggles of women to forge spaces and identities for themselves within the confines of existing institutional and cultural arrangements (Butler and Scott 1992; Smith 1987), have also been among the most astute theorists of self and society. Most recently, this discussion has tended to be phrased in terms of agency and structure—that is, the individual's capacity for thinking and acting in the context of a historically and socially given, indeed a patterned and relatively enduring, set of resources and constraints.[26]

Since the rise of modernity some two to three centuries ago, Western philosophers and social scientists have considered the question of how individual human beings relate to themselves and others (Giddens 1991; Haraway 1991; Taylor 1989; Rose 1996). This perhaps uniquely Western preoccupation was given special impetus by René Descartes's monumental attempt to theorize individual subjectivity as the only certainty in a world of complex beliefs and sensory perceptions. Descartes's radical cognitive individualism split the self off from society, thus forming the basis for a liberal political philosophy. Ever since, many have been trying to bring the self and society back together. Because of the misleading mutual autonomy implied by the terms *individual* and *society*, here I choose to formulate this enduring sociological problematic in terms of *subjectivity* and *structure*. These terms, to be sure, have also developed out of a Western sociological discourse given to binary rationalism. Some have therefore called for abandoning the language of structure as inadequate or misleading for the analysis of social life (Agger 1998). Structure is thought to connote a solidity not conducive to processual analysis. It easily succumbs to the dualism of the Cartesian tradition, which sets the individual within or against society as separable units of analysis. Yet through a reflexive consideration of the very events and forms giving rise to Western social science categories, a renovated sense of structure has emerged. This concept tries to account for what Zygmunt Bauman (1973, 109) calls the "irreducible duality of human existence" without succumbing to a "spurious dualism" (Abrams 1982, 262).[27] The sociologist Norbert Elias, writing mainly from the 1920s through the 1940s but only translated into English after the 1960s, has been a key figure in this development, using terms like *figuration* and *interweaving* to evoke the fundamental interconnectedness of historically emergent social structures and their corresponding forms of subjectivity.[28] Structure has been reconceptualized as an inherently shifting and dynamic set of social forces and arrangements comprising "society"; more acutely, as Anthony Giddens (1979, 63–64) puts it, "structure exists, as time-space presence, only in its instantiations in . . . practices and as memory traces orienting the conduct of knowledgeable human agents." Agency has been reconceptualized as the inherent dynamism of the human being given expression in the multiple and shifting subjectivities that both fashion and are fashioned by the structures s/he incorporates.

How does this fashioning take place? In and through practice. The idea of practice has emerged as a way of accounting for how structure and agency together perform the work of social and cultural reproduction— that is, the emerging and ongoing flow of social life. Practice has been articulated as a powerful heuristic corrective to the structuralisms (which accorded little agency to individual actors and little power to historical emergence) and voluntarisms (which accorded little power to patterned social forces in constraining or enabling individual action) dominating the social sciences of the twentieth century. An emphasis on practice— what Giddens (1984, 288) calls "strategic conduct"—has challenged the reductive tendencies of both materialism and idealism.[29] The reader will forgive the hubris in my hopeful declaration that the concepts of cultural production and practice have helped drive the most promising and far-reaching theoretical synthesis in the history of the human sciences. Finally, the endemic dualism of Western "ordinary language" is giving way to a more thoroughly "relational conception of the social" (Wacquant 1992, 15). In my vision, striking theoretical developments across a range of fields owe much to the deceptively simple concept of situated practice. In scholarly endeavors as seemingly disparate as developmental psychology and cognitive anthropology, the sociology of childhood and adolescence, studies in communications and popular culture, the study of literacy and language, and social history, the more dynamic conception of human personality and society enabled by the concept of practice has led to a simultaneously more humble and powerful understanding.[30] Not coincidentally, a concept of practice as mediating structure and agency also brings into clearer focus the varied sites and modalities of power in human life—a key component of any critical analysis of modernity.

One of my goals in this study is thus to clarify the different levels and domains of structuration as these reciprocally condition and are conditioned by student subjectivities and practice. I wish to account for a range of mutual influences and specify the situated logics of practice without privileging any single instance. Such work is not without precedent, of course. A number of qualitative educational researchers of secondary schooling have explicitly located their studies in the sociological problematic of structure and agency, especially with reference to the formation of identities and aspirations. For instance, Jane Gaskell's (1992) study of course and career choices among female Canadian high school students conceptualizes structure in terms of the course offerings and counseling discourses that channeled students' decisions in crucial ways. Such school practices, in turn, are structured by the political-economic imperatives of a capitalist patriarchal order. Other educational researchers have been less explicit about the relation between structure and agency, but nevertheless wish to elucidate the influences on the forms of secondary student action that emerge in and around schools. These studies range from the micro-ethnographic, including the symbolic interactionist focus on roles and strategies in context (Woods 1990) as well as the sociolinguistic focus on rules and constraints of discourse use (Mehan 1979; Hicks 1996), to the midlevel, many of which I have already cited, that attempt to link student beliefs and practices to a broader social order (Page and Valli 1990; Weis 1990; Wexler 1992).

Practice theorists like Bourdieu, Giddens, and Elias have tried to portray the mutual imbrication of agency and structure, but few empirical researchers have successfully developed case studies showing how these different elements interpenetrate.[31] For instance, the sociologist William Corsaro (1992, 1997) has developed the ingenious concept of "interpretive reproduction" to show how preschool children's creative practice can both draw from and alter the "structures" of the adult social world, yet his examples remain limited to the immediate organizational context of action. The structure that appears most to change is the set of rules and responses that adults have created in the preschool setting. Anthropologists like George Marcus (1986, 1998), Robert Foster (1991), and Ulf Hannerz (1996) have urged a new kind of multisite ethnography as a way of accounting for how diverse and globally scoped forces of the modern world system get taken up in local practice. Here there has been more success, though still there is typically inadequate attention given to the localized and embedded meanings making up local life worlds. While expanding the interpretive frame, there seems a compensatory enthusiasm to exaggerate or privilege the structures of the world system, thereby overlooking the richness of locally contextual frames and determinations—what Corsaro, for one, does so well.

The proof is in the pudding, as they say, and the reader should form her or his own judgment about my attempt to write a practice-based ethnography that does justice to both structure and agency. Ultimately, in formulating the relation between structure and subjectivity, it is necessary to avoid the perennial hubris of the predictive social sciences—that is, the dream of total explanation. The radical contingency, the fundamental indeterminacy, of social action must be understood. This is where I part company with Bourdieu's ambitious "general science of practices" and join the postmodernist skepticism toward "grand narratives"—but not so far as to "give up on data collection" (Clough 1992) altogether. I do this not to reject or vilify social science but to take just consolation in a good-enough interpretive and theoretical practice. Social science does indeed seem condemned to remain at least a step behind the flow of social life; the best that might be done is to develop an interpretive method and style of writing that approximates the flow, capturing it most accurately, most fully, most tellingly. This is where the social sciences shade into hermeneutics and narrative, the telling of a story that "rings true."[32] And this is how it must be, because in the end there remains a fundamental mystery at the heart of human subjectivities (Ellis and Flaherty 1992, 5). Sure, the structures that create the conditions for certain kinds of subjectivity and action can be specified. The tools of, say, psychoanalysis can be used to examine the impact of early childhood object relations on later emotional development; the tools of, say, Marxist political economy can be used to theorize the growth of worker alienation as a precursor to the vilification of new immigrant arrivals. In other words, it is possible to identify material and symbolic trends, and then theorize their effects on human activity. Interventions and new practices to reduce suffering and promote the just expansion of human potential can even be proposed. But the limitations inherent in the social scientific analysis of human action should always be kept in mind. In a late modern world, only such humility breeds practical insight.

In the social science and cultural studies literature, these three terms have received heavy play. I have already discussed the general idea of agency as that expansive capacity of the human subject. The notion of identity, of course, has a long history in the field of psychology, especially since Erik Erikson's (1968) landmark study of youth development. In psychology, the concept of identity typically refers to the more or less stable and enduring sense of self developed over the individual life course. Yet identity has also become an important concept in anthropology and sociology, where it has generally been used to refer to social and cultural identities—that is, the sense of self that the subject shares with other members of some collective group or organization.

The sociologist Erving Goffman (1961) conducted brilliant studies of hospitals and other "total institutions" to explore how each organization served as a

> place for generating assumptions about identity. In crossing the threshold of the establishment, the individual takes on the obligation to be alive to the situation, to be properly oriented and aligned in it . . . to accept being a particular kind of person. (186)

Though he never studied schools as such, Goffman's framework nicely suggests the kind of school identification and schooled identity I present in chapter 5. Goffman also provides the elements to understand institutional resistance. When ESF students engaged in "unprescribed activities" such as fighting or cheating they could be seen as "dodging identity." The "prescribed being" of organizational socialization—the collectively oriented and cooperative adolescent-cum-Mexican citizen—sometimes generated a form of "spiritual leave-taking," a "special kind of absenteeism, a defaulting not from prescribed activity but from prescribed being" (187–88). Indeed, the cultural form of echando relajo (goofing off) often enabled students to coordinate their "spiritual leave-taking." Goffman also highlighted the personal agency that kept institutional actors from ever becoming fully identified with their prescribed roles and activities in organizations. As he put it, "We always find the individual employing methods to keep some distance, some elbow room, between himself [sic]" and the social role prescribed for that person. This led Goffman to define the individual as a

> stance-taking entity, a something that takes up a position somewhere between identification with an organization and opposition to it, and

is ready at the slightest pressure to regain its balance by shifting its involvement in either direction. . . . Our sense of being a person can come from being drawn into a wider social unit; our sense of selfhood can arise through the little ways in which we resist the pull. (319–20)

Goffman used a different language of "person" and "selfhood," one that retained the distinction between a relational identity (person) and some core essence of self. Still, he was describing what I call the ongoing play of structure and subjectivity within modern institutions.

With the anthropologist Roger Rouse (1995), I share a concern about the risks of projecting Western conceptions of identity onto the experiences and cultural categories of all human groups. The concept appears to presuppose that people everywhere will conceive of themselves as bounded individuals with their own "aspirations" and relevant "collectivity" in terms of a Western identity politics. The term still retains a normative sense of unity and stability, as well as a wholly psychological interiority. Unlike Rouse, however, I believe it possible to work from an expanded notion of identity (and aspiration) that both escapes the logic of bourgeois individualism and acknowledges the social realm. The term can be reconstructed to give it a greater valence of shifting, contextual dynamism, even if it carries associations of greater permanence. Although I occasionally describe emergent and situational identities, I prefer to use the term *identity* to refer primarily to the relatively more enduring, culturally derived "imaginings of self in worlds of action" produced in practice (Holland et al. 1998, 5). In this view, the self takes on identities but is not wholly constituted by them (Cohen 1994; Hoffman 1998). In the educational context I studied, moreover, this sense of identity has great currency. For while the Mexican youth I came to know were profoundly involved with the family and community in a relational sense, they were also learning through their schooling precisely to construct and project an autonomous sense of self. Global models of schooling and career preparation had already implanted deep desires to "become someone" in life.

The term *subjectivity* has a long history in Western thought, especially in the disciplines of philosophy and sociology, where it has been used to denote the individual's meaningful apprehension and construction of the so-called objective world. More recently, it has become prominent in poststructuralist writing that, in an attempt to distance itself from the unitary connotations of the term *identity,* has emphasized the multiple and shifting "subject-positions" interpellated by social discourse (Smith

1988). Strains of psychoanalytic thought have also drawn attention to the unconscious as a crucial part of subjectivity. Such analyses sometimes overstate the fragmented nature of awareness, but they do spotlight significant contradictions in social and linguistic influences on subjectivity.

In the analysis presented here, I use subjectivity as a middle term between agency and identity. Agency is the most expansive of the three, denoting the very ground of human intention and creativity, yet precisely its inclusiveness renders it too imprecise for my use in any other but this broad grounding sense. If, on the other hand, identity implies an imagining of self that can be articulated, the concept of subjectivity suggests a rather more diffuse and mostly nondiscursive form of awareness. Indeed, even Bourdieu refers to his habitus as a "socialized subjectivity" (Bourdieu and Wacquant 1992, 126), "an *open system of dispositions* that is constantly subjected to experiences, and therefore constantly affected by them" (133). I stress this "open" quality of habitus in defining *subjectivities* as:

> those forms of awareness, mostly but not exclusively embodied and sensual, that are given by personal and social history yet transmutable by context and contingency.

Finally, Stuart Hall (1986; 1990; 1996, 2) also proposes the useful term *identification* as an alternative or complement to subjectivity. Through "processes of subjectification" members of global contemporary society develop shifting identifications with different groups and projects (Hall 1996, 2). Such identifications, perhaps less enduring and socially grounded than identities, are most liable to be articulated into a hegemonic political formation.

IDEOLOGY AND HEGEMONY

> In our intellectual way, we think that the world will collapse as the result of a logical contradiction: this is the illusion of the intellectual—that ideology must be coherent, every bit of it fitting together, like a philosophical investigation. When, in fact, the whole purpose of what Gramsci called an organic (i.e., historically effective) ideology is that it articulates into a configuration different subjects, different identities, different projects, different aspirations. It does not reflect, it constructs a "unity" out of difference. (Hall 1991, 166)

When Raymond Williams (1977, 128–35) discussed hegemony as constituting a "structure of feeling," he was indexing the affective component of subjectivity. Just what is this notion of hegemony, and why is it central to contemporary critical scholarship? In the passage above, Stuart Hall is actually discussing hegemony. As Hall suggests, the Italian marxist theorist Antonio Gramsci developed the notion of hegemony to describe an "organic ideology" that symbolically "constructs a unity out of difference." Yet to understand hegemony, it is helpful to first have a short introduction to the concept of ideology.

Most neutrally and descriptively, ideology refers to a more or less coherent set of ideas used to justify or explain the purpose of a social organization. Thus, the ideology of the Democratic Party might be reasonably summed up in its electoral platform, while that of a religious cult may be disseminated through flyers and the speeches of a prophet. Yet at least since the time of Marx, ideology developed "negative" meanings. Marx is famous for suggesting that the ruling ideologies of a capitalist epoch produce forms of false consciousness, in effect masking the exploitation inherent to the system. These meanings of ideology have prevailed in critical scholarship, albeit in modified form. For instance, more recent work (Thompson 1990; Eagleton 1991) contends that ideology often lacks the coherence and impositional quality it was once thought to have. In John Thompson's (1990, 56) critical survey

> the analysis of ideology . . . is primarily concerned with the ways in which symbolic forms intersect with relations of power. It is concerned with the ways in which meaning is mobilized in the social world and serves thereby to bolster up individuals and groups who occupy positions of power. . . . *To study ideology is to study the ways in which meaning serves to establish and sustain relations of domination.* (emphasis added)

Thompson goes on to describe five "modes" by which ideology operates in modern societies: legitimation, dissimulation, unification, fragmentation, and reification (naturalization) (60). Each of these modes describes common "ideological strategies" (Eagleton 1991) used to sustain relations of domination.[33]

Like other theorists of ideology, Antonio Gramsci wanted to understand how and why human beings could give their support to economic and political systems so manifestly opposed to their own material interests. Marx had explained this with reference to the "dull compulsion of economic relations" or "false consciousness" wrought by dominant ideology. Gramsci understood that human beings were more complex than this. He saw that what Hall (above) calls an "effective" ideology could appeal to other elements of their subjectivities—perhaps religious, ethnic, or even "political"—and thus render their class oppression less vital or visible. Being made to feel part of a "configuration" of unity, subordinate groups were less likely to perceive their economic condition as one of manifest exploitation. Most important, hegemony was a *process* of political construction. For Gramsci, hegemony referred both to the process by which political groups formed coalitions, or "blocs," to gain power, as well as the process by which they created and diffused ideas about the social order. It is this second meaning that has received the greatest emphasis in critical scholarship. In contemporary interpretations, the "effective ideology" created by dominant groups filters through all levels of society, "articulating" the subjectivities of otherwise antagonistic classes and ratifying the "common sense" of the status quo. *Hegemony*, then, can be defined as:

> a cultural process of domination in which ideas and symbols—in short, practical ideologies—are used to link dominant and subordinate forms of awareness into a legitimated social order.

Since Gramsci, the idea of hegemony has been elaborated and appropriated by a variety of authors (Williams 1977; Hall 1988).[34] While the paradigm case for thinking of hegemony as process was one of class relation and exploitation within the nation-state, feminists (Holland and Eisenhart 1990; Connell 1987, 1995; Grewal and Kaplan 1994), critical race theorists (Gilroy 1987), and postcolonial theorists (Hall 1986, 1991) have extended the concept to the analysis of gender, race, and colonialism, respectively. Hegemony in this broader usage has lost some of its specificity, but still refers to a symbolic process of domination through symbols and meanings. In Mexico, as elsewhere, the process of schooling plays a large role in hegemony, in "constructing unity out of difference." The question is what kind of unity, and in whose interests?

A critical analysis of modernity must avail itself of these two terms. They provide a way of conceptualizing the dynamics of power, domination, and resistance endemic to different levels and sites of the contemporary global order. They offer a means of ascertaining how power is constructed and exercised culturally, thereby pointing to the possibilities of strategic intervention.

One of anthropology's distinctive contributions to the human sciences has been its development of the culture concept, yet there are now calls from many quarters, including anthropology itself (Abu-Lughod 1991), to abandon it. Most critiques of the culture concept have stressed its tendency to reify—that is, make into a singular "thing" what are in reality diverse processes—the complexity of social life (Rosaldo 1989). Anthropology has been vulnerable to this critique because, historically, it has associated the idea of culture with distinct, geographically (or nationally) defined social groups. It has described the "shared" values and meanings, the coherent lifeways, of groups like the Samoans, Nuer, or Mexicans, without probing internal differences or theorizing change and reproduction. Such an orientation gave birth to the emerging fields of "culture and personality" (Wallace 1970) and educational anthropology, which I discussed above (see also Levinson and Holland 1996).

At least since the 1950s, such unitary conceptions of culture have been difficult to sustain. A variety of analytic approaches soon ramified within North American cultural anthropology to challenge the prevailing structural-functionalism and provide contrastive emphases on the ecological, symbolic, or cognitive dimensions of culture. Around the same time, powerful social movements for national independence, women's liberation, and civil rights spawned new critiques of social scientific knowledge. Anthropology was not immune, and developed a growing awareness of its own complicity in projects of colonization and domination. The imperative of recovering the views and experiences of subordinated groups—members of colonized societies, women, and racialized minorities—cast doubts on the extent of "shared" meanings within traditionally defined cultures, and proposed new perspectives from which to view culture. The "recovery" of a world systems perspective (Wolf 1982; Roseberry 1989) and recognition of new transnational diasporas (Rouse 1995; Basch, Glick-Schiller, and Szanton-Blanc 1994) also called into question the tendency to identify culture with a single place (Borofsky 1994; Gupta and Ferguson 1997b; Clifford 1988). If conventional portrayals had underscored cultural consensus within a group, new studies brought conflict, divergence, and hybridity to the fore. Anthropologists were now seeing multiple and partially overlapping microcultures, constituted by diverse interests, identities, and structural locations (for example, women's, children's, or shaman's "culture").[35]

The expansion of multinational capital and the political upheavals of late modernity also forced anthropologists into a growing recognition of cultural complexity (Hannerz 1992). Yet it was not just the new diasporic or postmodern "communities" that were scrutinized in refined cultural terms: the more sophisticated concept was projected back to earlier times and places, with the understanding that cultural processes had always been more complicated and dynamic than previously depicted. This, in turn, led to an increased emphasis on cultural production and reproduction—that is, the ongoing creation and communication of values and meanings within and across "cultures," the continual negotiation of material and symbolic interests that leads to more or less "shared," more or less contested meanings.

As I have said, one response to this theoretical ferment was to eliminate the terms of cultural analysis altogether. Certainly, the rise of practice theory in anthropology (Ortner 1984) was a significant expression of this will to overcome the reification of culture. Ethnographic studies shifted to explore what people were *doing* in practice rather than what their culture "told" them to do. At the same time, the linguistic turn in the social sciences conspired with the rise of postmodernist influences in anthropology (Marcus and Fischer 1986; Rosaldo 1989) and cultural studies (Brantlinger 1990) to elevate the prominence of "discourse" in ethnographic interpretation. It was the French intellectual Michel Foucault (1977) who perhaps more than any other scholar pushed the notion of discourse into the scholarly limelight. Foucault discussed discourses as relatively coherent thematic ensembles, related clusters of terms and judgments along with their associated practices. The language of scientific and administrative classification, for Foucault, had produced discourses that formed the subjects of modernity. Drawing on Foucault, other scholars examined the "effects of truth" contained in everyday discourses (Alonso 1988; Stallybrass and White 1986), and further questioned the fiction of shared culture. Subsequently, anthropologists were more likely than ever to study social life as a play of antagonistic discourses organized around key material interests rather than any sort of shared cultural commitment.

Despite these trends, I believe that the culture concept has been rescued and sufficiently reformed, and so employ it here in a more dynamic formulation. I prefer a working definition of culture that admits the distributive complexity and partially overlapping nature of "shared knowledges and meanings" (Hannerz 1992). This definition must leave culture open to historical and situational contingencies, capturing the active agency, blending, and mobility involved in contemporary meaning production. It must acknowledge the workings of power as well as the uneven representation of interests and perspectives in cultural codes. It should recognize the subjective force of linguistic "discourses" (Hanks 1996) without reducing itself to language (Chartier 1997). Finally, a concept of culture need enable a conceptualization of the linkages, the modes of articulation, between and among variously defined microcultures and the cultures of region, nation, State, and globe.

A reformulated concept of culture should also be accountable to studies of self and the cognitive organization of experience. Cognitive anthropologists like Jean Lave (1988) and Bradd Shore (1996) have drawn attention to how persons think and thereby constitute their practice in relation to specific cultural contexts ("arenas" and "settings," in Lave's terms). In reconciling practice theory with cognitive science, Shore (1996, 372) offers an account of how the individual "creative mind" works out its relation to culture:

> Analogical schematization introduces a gap, a crucial lifegiving contingency, between the conventional forms of cultural life and their inner representations in consciousness. This gap guarantees the ongoing regeneration of conventions through practice just as it makes possible intersubjective meaning.

In Shore's view, cognitive cultural models are "distributed" unevenly across the individual members of a community because the public "instituted models" (the "conventional forms"; see also Geertz 1973) are appropriated and therefore internalized in different ways by such individuals. This accounts for both the partially "shared" nature of cultural knowledge and institutional roles as well as the significant patterns of divergence and variation.

In describing the dynamics of Mexican student culture, I think of cultural production in one moment—the moment of interaction in and around ESF's spaces—as a game, a strategic practice of meaning creation in the school. Yet the emergent student culture in the school's institutional space relates to other orders of culture, including a broader urban youth culture, a national culture, and the class/ethnic intimate cultures of family, neighborhood, and region (Lomnitz-Adler 1992). In all these orders of culture, it is best not to think in terms of "shared meanings" but rather mutually intelligible communicative frames and resources—the discourses organizing social life. As Steve Stern (1995) puts it in his fine study of gender relations in late colonial Mexico, culture can be described as an argument—or at least the codes that enable an argument to take place. Similarly, the sociologist Charles Lemert (1995, 174) defines culture as "the well-organized, if not well-advertised, code of practical instructions whereby members are given permission to talk meaningfully about some things while ignoring others." In sum, culture provides the rules and guidelines for the game of strategic practice.

Focal Student Profiles

In the body of the text, I highlight eight of the twenty-two focal students in 1990, so here I develop short profiles of the remaining ones. These can then be compared with the profiles and table in chapter 7, showing their changes from 1991 to 1998.

GRUPO 3C

ALEJANDRA

Along with her younger sister, Alejandra lived in a large house with her grandmother and some uncles instead of her own parents. She had never "gotten along" with her father, as she put it. She didn't even know about his former job, only that for several years he had been immobilized by a bad spinal injury. Her two younger brothers (four and fourteen) still lived with their parents in a modest neighborhood, where they ran a small grocery store out of the house. Every day, Alejandra would bring the main meal from her grandmother's house to her parents' home and wait to greet her mother on her return from her work as a union officer with the National Electricity Commission. Alejandra had lost two school years along the way, once because of a head injury that forced her out and once more because she was switched from a public primaria to a colegio for grades two through six. Ever since her injury, Alejandra had tended to tire easily. She had been taking a strong medication to prevent epileptic attacks, but she didn't know if her exhaustion was due to the medicine or the injury itself.

Like so many others, Alejandra's physical education teacher drew attention to her age and maturity by commenting that she "has a slightly more advanced mentality, because of her age, she is already thinking more like a young adult than an adolescent." Meanwhile, Alejandra did not have well-defined future plans. Her doctors had instructed her parents to let Alejandra study only to the point she felt comfortable; to push her beyond her limits would risk more attacks. So Alejandra thought she should stay in school to become someone and "defend herself" in life, but she wasn't sure where or what to study. Only toward the end of the year did she express an interest in the secretarial or tourism tracks at the CBTIS. Still, her mother would insist on enrolling Alejandra in the comercio program at the colegio, where she would get more personalized attention from her teachers.

DALIA

Dalia was in many ways quite the opposite of Alejandra. She was among the youngest in 3C, the only child of two schoolteachers who lived in a modest cement home. In our first interview in 1989, Dalia complained about a few classmates from the upper class (*clase rica*) that called her names and ridiculed her friendship group. Apparently by October 1990, when we spoke at length, things had smoothed themselves out, in part because one of the offending girls had transferred out of ESF. Nevertheless, Dalia never felt fully at ease in the grupo. She moved and talked slowly, and had a tendency to withdraw into herself. This was not a recipe for integration into the heady brew of secundaria life.

Dalia had received a lot of attention as an only child. Her mother was clearly dominant in the home, and Dalia admitted that her grandparents kept a close eye on her. Her grandmother had even suggested she quit school when her grades went down in first grade because of her mother's illness. In second grade, her marks dropped even more precipitously because, as she put it, her grandmother would prefer her to drop out than become a doctor or nurse, which was Dalia's greatest desire. So Dalia had become discouraged (*desanimada*). Meanwhile, Dalia's parents kept modest expectations, and they wondered if she would be able to pursue advanced study. Dalia's mother, eventually to become a rural school principal herself, reiterated her support but also encouraged Dalia to consider cosmetology or some other nonacademic career. Yet Dalia rebounded from her poor second-year showing and resolved to "become someone" through advanced study. By the time we spoke in 1990, she had decided on the career of early childhood educator (*educadora*), and her parents were actively supporting her.

VICENTE

The son of a poor welder and ironworker, Vicente always warded me away from his modest home. One afternoon, I went to visit him at his daily job in an auto body shop, where he seemed at ease among the older, rougher men. I started walking him to his house when he got off work, but he manufactured an excuse to go his own way. He seemed ashamed for me to meet his family, and I never learned much about his mother, other than her occupation as a housewife (*ama de casa*). Vicente did say he had an older brother who had never finished secundaria, and two younger siblings still in school. His parents had never studied beyond primaria. There was clearly little active encouragement of further schooling in the household. Instead, Vicente had started contributing to the household at an early age. He was already nailing crates together at a sawmill at age ten. None of his friends and playmates in the neighborhood had stayed in school through their final year of secundaria. Vicente was quite frank about his distaste for studying. He was bored in class and spent little time out of school doing homework. Rather, he enjoyed himself more at work, which he found fun and challenging. Vicente was pretty sure that he had no ambitions beyond secundaria. He wanted to get his certificate, he said, because that would give him a chance at a job in a better "institution," like a government agency.

GRUPO 3B

IVONNE

When I discovered her house on one of my many jaunts through outlying neighborhoods, Ivonne seemed to shrink in the doorway. The sidewalk was soiled with grease, and littered with tree limbs and truck tires. When I glanced in, I could see a simple cement floor in the front room and, beyond that, a dirt courtyard. Ivonne never invited me inside, and I only chatted with her mother briefly a few times outside the house or on chance meetings elsewhere in town. Ivonne's father cut timber and trucked it to a local lumberyard; he worked long hours and spent little time at home. Her oldest brother, now in his first year at the CBTIS, had gone to live with their grandparents near the municipal market at the age of three. Another older brother had barely finished his secundaria at ESF and now worked with her father as a timber cutter (*machetero*). Two younger sisters would soon finish primaria, and a much younger brother would shortly begin primaria.

Ivonne was a fine storyteller. Drawing on a rich colloquial lexicon, she filled our chats and interviews with colorful accounts of important events and activities in her life. She told me about a fall in an animal shed at the age of six that left her right arm permanently deformed. The event forced her to repeat a school year, and thereafter the injury periodically flared up and required several days of rest. Ivonne also lived rather enclosed in a woman's world. Her father, she said, was quite strict and liked to keep the women in the house doing chores. Resentful of this, Ivonne only half joked that she would have preferred to be a man. Yet she had also developed typically female tastes and aspirations. She loved children, and every Saturday spent several hours in a nearby chapel imparting catechism to the young. Moreover, because of her own experience at the hands of careless doctors and nurses, Ivonne would only consider nursing for a future career. She wanted to give children the care they deserved.

In a fascinating portrayal, Ivonne also told me of her experiences with spiritualism. Because she alone of her family had "sweet blood" ("*sangre dulce*"), the curses directed at her relatives invariably attacked her instead. She especially remembered the time a young girl down the street had "bewitched" her ("*me embrujaron*") with a swollen foot. An age-mate of hers next door claimed to have figured out the source of Ivonne's bewitchment and wanted to try out her healing powers. With permission from her parents, the girl used eggs and chants to embody a foreign spirit and "cure" Ivonne. Afterward, the girl became a respected *espiritual* in the neighborhood, healing children and young adults in particular. Ivonne became a believer. When I asked Ivonne what her ESF classmates thought of these experiences, she said they had made fun of her and her beliefs, so now she kept them to herself. In Ivonne's mind, the medical knowledge of nursing and the esoteric knowledge of spiritualist healing were not incompatible. They simply represented separate spheres of Ivonne's daily life. As she herself explained it, "What's from here [the school], stays here, and what's from there [the neighborhood], there" ["*Lo que es de aquí aquí, y lo que es de allá pues allá*"]. I wondered if these spheres would ever collide.

ANTONIA

Antonia always impressed me with her theatrics, her ability to mimic student and teacher mannerisms. Gradually, she incorporated me into her repertoire of tricks and, on occasion, even wielded an imaginary tape recorder to "interview" her fellow students. Antonia's classmates called her the chispa (spark; in other words, class clown) of the grupo, and I wondered if she would ever be straight with me. I was surprised, then, when she took our first interview so seriously, and I discovered in her a verbally precocious and psychologically insightful youth. Many called Antonia by her easily pronounced last name because she belonged to one of the better-known extended families in San Pablo. Her grandfather had built up a ranch and sawmill, and many of her uncles were now professionals and businessmen. Still, Antonia was sensitive to any suggestion that she belonged to the "upper" class ("*la alta*"). She often felt the need to convince her teachers and friends that she did not have as much money as they supposed. This was because her own father had dropped out of the secundaria to start earning his own spending money. Eschewing his father's economic support, he started modestly enough, driving and then finally owning an interstate passenger bus. By 1990, he had assumed the position of chief administrator for the San Pablo office of the region's largest passenger service. He went to work every day at the central bus station. Antonia's mother, a secundaria graduate herself, now took care of the home and her younger children, a son (nine) and daughter (four). Antonia said that her family was extremely "united." She rarely went out to visit friends in the afternoons because she could play with her cousins in the neighborhood and her father often brought home videos for the family to watch.

Among her teachers, Antonia had a reputation as being cheerful and competent although restless (alegre, *pero inquieta*). Mrs. Garfias called her a "parrot" in class, and her weaving shop teacher said she spent too much time shouting and playing, rarely turning in good work. As she prepared herself for the move to the prepa, Antonia recognized she would have to straighten out her act. When we spoke in October, she seemed most interested in studying to be an early childhood educator. In March, before she graduated, Antonia's father would be killed in a tragic automobile accident, and her life would change forever.

PACO

Paco came from one of the larger island villages that relied on a fishing and hatmaking economy, and still preserved much of its indigenous cultural heritage. Like most of the village's adults, Paco's abandoned mother continued speaking the local language in the community, and Paco himself understood it well enough, though he claimed to be inept at speaking. Economically and culturally, the village was obviously undergoing a crisis. As the lake waters dried up, turning shallows into mud beaches and pasture, the fishing economy dried up as well. Many village families had traditionally worked with natural straw and leaf materials to produce handicrafts such as mats, baskets, and principally hats. Yet this cottage industry was not enough to sustain most families. By the late 1980s, young males, and in some cases entire families, began to emigrate. Many, like Paco's older brother, made it to the fields and migrant ghettos of California and Arizona. Others migrated seasonally to pick fruits and vegetables on the coastal plain of Sinaloa, Mexico's most abundant agricultural region. Paco himself still helped his grandfather make straw hats most afternoons, and he almost never missed the 5 P.M. basketball game in the village center.

In our first interview, Paco said he wanted to be a doctor, but his mother preferred that he study law. As an obedient son, he was willing to make an effort (*echarle ganas*) to do whatever his mother wanted. His older brother had barely made it beyond the prepa and was certified as a primary school bilingual teacher, but he still went to the United States to work. His younger sister was planning to follow her mother's directives as well and study to become a secretary. By the end of the school year, though, Paco was thinking about taking a year off from school. He wanted to "clear his head" ("*despejarse*") from the boredom of study, maybe travel with some friends to sell straw hats in Mexico City or near the beach. He worried about the difficulty of making new friends at the prepa as well. It had taken him until his third year at ESF to feel comfortable in the grupo. His older brother, however, warned him to enroll the next year; when he came for a visit in December, he said, he had better find Paco in school.

Over the course of the year, I went to Paco's village twice to meet his family. I also visited his mother on occasion at her fish stall in the San Pablo market. She struck me as a powerful presence, unashamed of her indigenous heritage and practical about the economic demands of the moment. Paco's mother had never gone to school herself. As the oldest of twelve children, she had stayed at home to care for the younger children while her mother traveled to San Pablo to sell fish. All her brothers and sisters managed at least a few years of primaria, some much further. Paco's mother was married "by force" at the age of seventeen and her second child, a girl, was sick for many years before eventually dying. Not long after her youngest daughter's birth, she was abandoned by her husband and forced to fend for herself. Thus, Paco's mother kept a rather sober outlook on life. She wanted her children to "defend" themselves well through a formal education.

ABEL

The youngest child in his family, with four older sisters, Abel was the only boy. His father was a prominent local dentist from a wealthy family, while his mother attended to the home and made plans to open a small store or restaurant at the front of the house. Abel's oldest sister (twenty-six) had already obtained a professional degree in tourist administration, while another (twenty-four) had worked several years as a rural schoolteacher before getting married. Two other sisters (seventeen and twenty) were still completing their studies (law and dentistry). Abel, on the other hand, had always had difficulty in school. He got bad reports from teachers, was said to lack discipline and motivation, and failed nearly half his courses. Abel's mother spent much of her time visiting the school and trying to learn the details of his behavior. Most of Abel's teachers attributed his poor academic performance to indifference or complacency; Abel's mother, they said, overprotected and spoiled him, and anyway, Abel knew that he stood to inherit his father's modest fortune. Since everything had always been given him on a gold platter, they said, why shouldn't he expect it in school, too?

Abel was painfully aware of his teachers' and parents' judgments, and he persisted in his plans to continue studying. During the interview I conducted with his mother, Abel fidgeted and scowled so much when he sat listening in to his mother's laments about his behavior that he eventually slammed the door and left. His parents expected nothing less than a professional career, he explained, though they also threatened to put him to work if he did not bring his grades up. In October 1990, law and computer programming were his top career choices, but he didn't seem to know much about them other than that law was no longer paying well ("*no deja mucho capital*"). He also got animated when describing his dream of becoming an airline pilot—his brother-in-law's job. He realized this career was unlikely, although he knew it paid quite well. By the end of the school year, Abel knew he was in trouble. He had failed a few courses and could not receive his certificate until he had paid for the exams. He still talked about studying law, but he also thought it was time to take a summer job in a mechanic's shop and clean up his act for prepa.

While he did not cause many problems in class, Fidel also seemed rather indifferent to his future. Teachers and classmates alike had noted the change after the sudden death of his father in 1989. Never an excellent student, now Fidel just drifted through each school day, barely completing his assignments. His social studies teacher, Mr. Carrizo, was also his cousin, and they had both grown up in a mestizo village known for its specialty in carving masks. Mr. Carrizo tried in vain to encourage Fidel in school. Fidel had two older brothers, one who had finished secundaria and was looking to join the army, and another who had dropped out of secundaria and crafted wood in their home village. From very young, he claimed to have frequently told his mother that he wanted to become a lawyer ("*Mamá, quiero ser licenciado*") because he had a much older cousin who practiced law in Mexico City. Yet more recently, Fidel had begun to question further studies altogether. Every afternoon he spent at his uncle's workshop, apprenticing for the trade in wood carving and masks. This came to seem more and more attractive. He was getting tired of studying, and even though his mom did try to encourage him, neither of his older brothers offered much help.

GRUPO 3F

LIDIA

I met Lidia in 1988 when she was still in her first year at ESF. She worked evenings in the ticket booth at the main theater, and I stopped to chat with her there on occasion. At any given time, Lidia was likely to have a boyfriend in tow. Yet she would not consider ESF boys as novios. She preferred young men. Of course, Lidia's father did not approve much of her romantic ambitions, but as a traveling kitchenware salesman he spent much of his time on the road. Lidia's parents had married young (twenty-two and fifteen), and neither had gone beyond the secundaria. Her mother had worked briefly as a preschool teacher some years ago, and now spent afternoons helping a sister in her downtown boutique. They had high hopes for their three children—Lidia was the oldest, with a younger sister (eleven) and brother (eight) enrolled in a colegio. Lidia thought she would go on to the prepa, but her aspirations were not yet clearly defined. She liked English in school because she wanted to be a flight attendant (*aeromosa*), yet she also thought about following her aunt's example and studying psychology. By the end of the year, she was pretty sure she would enter the CBTIS to study tourism.

SOCORRO

I felt really dumb when Mrs. Garfias had to inform me, as late as November, that Socorro was missing a hand. He had been so effective at hiding the stump that even after an interview and repeated observations I had failed to notice. Socorro was older (sixteen) than most of his class-mates and frequently missed school. According to his teachers, the loss of his hand in an accident had given Socorro a "complex" that lowered his achievement in class. Most teachers also drew attention to Socorro's poverty, saying that his domestic situation gave him little opportunity to complete his homework.

Socorro had always welcomed our interactions, yet he never invited me to meet his parents. I knew he lived in a poor house in one of the peripheral colonias because we had greeted each other in the area before. In our first extended interview, Socorro confessed that his father had often left the house abruptly for periods lasting a week to three years. He had supported the family by running cockfights, sometimes clandestine, at fairs and festivals around the country. Socorro had grown up learning the trade and really liked it, especially the prospect of quick fortunes. Yet his father now dissuaded him, saying it was a shameful "vice" that Socorro should eschew for a shot at a professional career. Frequent threats and scoldings had reinforced this message, and Socorro's siblings had gotten it, too. Two older brothers (twenty-four and twenty-one) worked delivering pharmaceutical supplies in Mexico City. They had only finished secundaria, but they kept pressure on their younger siblings to go further. Socorro also had an older sister in the CBTIS, a younger brother in his second year at a técnica, and yet another younger sister in primary school. He said they all agreed that school was a "bother" ("*enfadosa*"), but one ought to continue as far as possible. For a negative example, Socorro could always turn to the many neighborhood boys who had dropped out much earlier and taken up drugs. Socorro claimed to spend much of his free time with such boys as they smoked marijuana and sniffed glue, even though he never took the stuff himself. He always got home by 9 P.M., saying his father would scold him until the end of the world, maybe even beat him, if he ever tried drugs. Toward the end of our first talk, Socorro insisted that he wanted to be a profesionista, perhaps even a social studies teacher, yet he also considered cockfighting a legitimate "profession." I wondered how Socorro would resolve the tension between these two models of professional development pulling him in different directions.

ISIDRO

A small and quiet boy, Isidro approached me one day on the basketball court at recess. His father had been working for some years in an Oregon cannery, and he wanted to know more about life in the United States. Isidro was trying to decide whether or not to go there himself. An older brother and sister had already been living there for some time with his father. Two other brothers drove taxis, another drove a logging truck, and another older sister was married in town with a child. Isidro was the youngest of all seven children. Both his parents had grown up in nearby farming villages, children of campesinos, before moving to their modest house in a poor colonia of San Pablo. Neither parent had any formal schooling. His mother, especially, liked to say she knew nothing; her eyes were "closed" because she had never learned to read and never traveled outside the region. Only one of Isidro's older siblings had ever studied beyond the secundaria (one brother completed a year of prepa, and then left to work and get married; one sister had finished at a técnica; and a couple had never gotten beyond their fourth year of primaria). I got the chance to meet his father on one of his rare visits from Oregon when Isidro took me to their house for the first time. Over a hurried lunch before his departure to the United States, Isidro's father told me about how important it was for him to help his children avoid the kind of backbreaking work that he had done his whole life.

In school, Isidro only had a few friends, all in 3F. He rarely saw these friends outside ESF, spending time instead with other boys in his neighborhood who for the most part worked instead of studying. Isidro had often worked himself; only last month had he quit his afternoon job tacking wooden crates together in the sawmill near his house. He wondered whether he would work there again after he graduated from the secundaria. The thought of going to the United States did not thrill him. His mother had always resisted her husband's invitations to join him, using Isidro's dependency as a pretext. Still, Isidro had no clear plans or ambitions. He said his parents encouraged him to finish secundaria, but did not demand it. Isidro himself was motivated to get his certificate in order to obtain a better-paying job. If he continued on to the prepa, it would be to move up from the sawmill job. He liked the idea of studying more about animals, yet he did not know how to go about it.

GRUPO 3A

FIDENCIO

Fidencio struck me early on as one of the most immature boys in the third year. He would make silly jokes in class that found no resonance with his mates, indeed, he would often annoy them to the point of distraction. It was hard to get beyond Fidencio's games. Despite my frequent requests, he never took me to meet his family. I managed to find him in front of his family's furniture business on a few occasions, but he did not invite me inside. Fidencio did claim to help his father in the business some after-noons, accompanying the drivers who would make deliveries. On the other hand, I could learn little else about Fidencio and his family. I knew he had attended a private church colegio for primaria and often stayed with a grandmother in a distant colonia, only occasionally living with his mother and younger siblings in the house behind the furniture store. When asked about his future aspirations, Fidencio typically drew a blank, yet he would always verbally affirm the value of further study. Was this a convenient formula spoken for the anthropologist or did Fidencio really want to study his way out of the furniture business?

JOSÉ

José was a very different sort of case. The oldest of three sons in a modest working-class family, José had developed strong study habits and a resolve to continue his schooling as long as he could. José's mother called herself a housewife, while his father had worked as a store clerk for many years until he was able to purchase his own minivan to drive in the urban transport system. This was his occupation in 1990. Meanwhile, the family had purchased a lot in a peripheral colonia and begun to construct a simple cinder block house room by room. Like Fidencio, José had at-tended a private colegio for primaria, but he had remained quite shy. His parents were pleased to see José open up and communicate more (*desen-volverse*) in the less restricted environment at ESF. At the same time, one of José's brothers was in fifth grade of primaria, while the other was just beginning kindergarten. José emphasized the importance of school for preparing himself, for becoming someone who would make his parents proud. The latter was especially crucial, as José recognized the sacrifices his parents had made to keep him in school. José thought he might like to study law or accounting, but he also mentioned his dream of becoming a highway patrolman.

ANDREA

Tagging along with a clique led by Gisela (chapters five and six), Andrea seemed to participate only marginally in the life of grupo 3A. Yet she often found herself alone or in the company of María, another marginal girl who traveled a long distance each day from her indigenous village. Like María, Andrea was failing many of her subjects by the middle of the school year. Nor had she passed the extraordinary exam for several subjects she had failed in previous years. Andrea clearly lacked energy or direction in completing school assignments. Most of my observations captured her daydreaming, reading magazines, or chatting quietly when classmates were engaged in some project. Teachers speculated that her indifference to school stemmed from her father's frequent travels or her mother's vicious scoldings.

Andrea was among the poorest students at ESF. Her parents made small wooden crafts items, selling them at several kiosks in and around San Pablo, where I could find Andrea some afternoons. When she was still a young child, her family had lived for a few years in Mexico City and Ciudad Juárez as her father worked in small factories and then learned the artisan trade. Andrea's mother was briefly a rural schoolteacher; at her husband's family's insistence, she had long since given up her profession. Like many of her female schoolmates, Andrea insisted that she wanted to become an early childhood educator because she loved children. Nevertheless, she vacillated a great deal about staying in school altogether. Her greatest nemesis was the secretarial shop teacher (taquimecanografía). When it looked as though she would never catch up on her typing assignments, Andrea actually transferred to another secundaria in March. Only after a few weeks did ESF's social worker prevail on her to return.

NOTES

PREFACE

1   See Anderson 1989; McLaren and Giarelli 1995; Carspecken 1995; Lather 1991, 1997; Levinson, Foley, and Holland 1996; Quantz 1992; Simon and Dippo 1986. Some stress the dialogic and radically democratic means by which knowledge is produced, as well as the immediately transformative ends to which that knowledge is directed (for example, Gitlin 1994; Lather 1991); in this sense, only a kind of collaborative action research designed to raise awareness and empower can truly be called critical ethnography. Others place emphasis on the conceptual framework guiding the research and the production of knowledge; critical ethnography is work that seeks to situate and understand local events in the context of broader structural relations of power, and to direct such understanding toward more expansive efforts at structural change, including cultural critique (Carspecken 1995; Levinson, Foley, and Holland 1996). From this perspective, the oft-cited goals of "empowerment" and "liberation" must themselves be subject to scrutiny (Lankshear 1995; LeCompte 1995).

2   My vision of critical theory goes well beyond marxism and the Frankfurt school to include feminist, critical race, practice, and postcolonial theories, among others. For discussions of this broadened vision of a critical social theory, see Calhoun 1995; and Agger 1998. For applications of critical theory to educational studies, see Morrow and Torres 1995.

3   Such an approach engages the postmodernist critique of normative discourse and unitary subjects, while still opting for a critical and "tactical" humanism (Abu-Lughod 1993; Knauft 1996), akin to what Charles Taylor (1989, 515) calls "anthropologies of situated freedom." It seeks a more modest "truth" and "objectivity" through a methodological reflexivity and close attention to "situated knowledge" (Bourdieu and Wacquant 1992; Haraway 1991; Harding 1992). Finally, it anchors theoretical discourse, as much as possible, in the phenomenological life worlds of ethnographers and research subjects (Jackson 1996).

INTRODUCTION

1   Other linguistic and nonlinguistic "signifying practices" (Comaroff 1985; Hebdige 1979)—such as music and dress preferences, church attendance, friendship affiliation, and school ritual—entered into this strategic game, enabling students to weave a complex tapestry of hope and desire, of sameness and difference.

2   "The image of the game without rules emphasizes [the involvement of individuals in the social]. That is to say, if we can envisage a game in which both the objects of play and the rules of play, the number and disposition of players, the very sense of what the game is about are all alterable within the framework of the rule that

everyone is a player and must go on playing, we shall approach a more balanced sense of the part played by individuals in the historical production of social figurations" (Abrams 1988, 234, commenting on Norbert Elias's [1978] concepts of games and figurations).

3 Bourdieu and Wacquant use the game analogy to illustrate what they mean by a "field" of social practice. This is an important difference from Ortner's use of the metaphor to describe "culture" or "practice" per se. According to Bourdieu and Wacquant, the field is *like* a game, but it is "not the product of a deliberate act of creation, and it follows rules or, better, regularities, that are not explicit and codified. Thus we have *stakes* . . . we have an *investment in the game, illusio.* . . . [P]layers are taken in by the game . . . only to the extent that they concur in their belief (*doxa*) in the game and its stakes. . . . Players agree, by the mere fact of playing . . . that the game is worth playing . . . and this *collusion* is the very basis of their competition" (1992, 98).

4 Actually, in 1993, the Mexican government officially declared the secundaria a part of the basic compulsory school system. Until that time, only the six years of *primaria* had been compulsory.

1. HISTORICAL CONTEXTS

1 See, for instance, recent collections by William Roseberry (1989) and George Marcus (1998). See also Elsie Rockwell's (1995, 1999) efforts to account for the presence of history in the "everyday" life of schools.

2 Claudia Saucedo Ramos (1995) discusses the transition from secundaria to the next educational level in her study of a Mexican CONALEP (vocational high school). She describes the concept of responsibility as crucial in this transition, where students, like Iván and Héctor here, chafe against secundaria-like rules and identify themselves with a newfound maturity. Still, Saucedo Ramos provides little evidence that the CONALEP students continue to think of themselves as adolescents. She characterizes the term herself as a socially and institutionally defined identity given to those postprimary youth that continue formal studies (25).

3 See Prawda 1987; Santos del Real 1996a, 1996b.

4 As early as 1937, when the secundaria was still in its infancy, the great reformist president, Lázaro Cárdenas, considered declaring it obligatory. See Meneses Morales 1988, 122.

5 In 1993, some 60 percent of secondary students were enrolled in "general" secundarias, 28 percent were enrolled in "technical" secundarias, and another 12 percent were enrolled in *telesecundarias,* a form of distance education offered to smaller rural communities. See Secretaría de Educación Pública 1993.

6 In fact, from 1989 to 1992, the secundaria cycle experienced a net decrease in enrollments for the first time in many years. See Fuentes 1996, 61.

7 See Foweraker 1993; Cook 1996; Street 1997.

8 For a perspective on this popular rejection of the neoliberal project through the

resurgence of images from the regime of Mexican President Lázaro Cárdenas (1934–1940), see Spenser and Levinson 1999.

9 Work by Noel McGinn and Susan Street (1982, 1984) and Daniel Morales-Gómez and Carlos Torres (1990) would suggest that even these two contradictory emphases aren't really what drives policy formation. This political sociology of policy formation in Mexico during the 1970s and 1980s provides evidence that the building of so-called political capital by educational bureaucrats, and the concern with state legitimation, really motivate the development of educational policy.

10 See also Larissa Adler Lomnitz, Ilya Adler, and Claudio Lomnitz-Adler (1993, 343–71). According to these authors, Richard Morse (1982) was one of the first historians to underscore the hierarchical holism of the Spanish colonial tradition, using the term *patrimonialism.*

11 Larissa Adler Lomnitz, Ilya Adler, and Claudio Lomnitz-Adler (1993) suggest that the postrevolutionary period has, in fact, been characterized by a "series of accommodations" between hierarchical holism and liberalism, but I prefer, at the risk of reification, to call revolutionary nationalism a distinct, albeit hybrid, tradition.

12 Charles Hale, in two separate books (1972, 1989), has authored perhaps the definitive account of Mexican Liberalism in the nineteenth century. He emphasizes the particularities of the Mexican case, especially the rise of scientific positivism and avoidance of the "Indian" question, which was not fully addressed until after the revolution.

13 In 1993, some eighteen million children were enrolled in primary and secondary schools alone—more than 20 percent of Mexico's total estimated population of eighty-five million.

14 See Taboada 1985, 45–46. Charles Hale (1989, 223–34), with Mary Kay Vaughan (1982), argues that the themes of Vasconcelista thought were importantly prefigured by Liberal "scientific positivists" like Gabino Barreda and Justo Sierra. Carlos Newland (1994) situates this Mexican development in the context of Latin America at that time, where the "liberal hegemony" gave to nation-states the charge of centralizing education for the goal of "homogenizing" a diverse population.

15 This is my translation of sections from page 129 of the *Ley Orgánica de la Educación Pública* from 1941, as reproduced in Campos de García 1973, 42–43. This law is an elaboration of the third constitutional article of 1917, which stipulates that education in Mexico will be secular, gratis, and compulsory through primary school. Hammered out even before revolutionary hostilities had ceased, and still the operative national law in Mexico, the 1917 Constitution retained much of the original Liberal Constitution of 1857.

16 The debate over education versus instruction in Mexico apparently dates from the late nineteenth century (Hale 1989, 162). In Spanish, *educación* implies a broad formation of character, manners, and morals, while *instrucción* implies the transmission of specialized knowledge. The church, along with the family, had traditionally held a monopoly over the *educación* of children. Liberals at the end of the

nineteenth century argued among themselves over whether the displacement of church power should include the State's assumption of an educative role. Many contended that education should remain a family affair, with instruction the domain of the State. But by 1890, the Mexican State had begun to provide primary schooling with important educational functions. After the revolution, the State expanded this formative quality of public education and, modeling the German system, extended it to the secundaria (Mejía Zuñiga 1981, 223). Interestingly, in their exhortations to parents to discipline children in the home, ESF teachers in 1990 tended to maintain a distinction between educación and instrucción, emphasizing that educación begins (and for some, ends) in the family.

17 In 1928, there were only seven federal secundarias in the whole country, all of them concentrated in Mexico City. In addition, there were some thirty-two secundarias operated by the states and another thirty-six private secundarias throughout the national territory (Meneses Morales 1986).

18 See Meneses Morales 1986, 479, 603; Santos del Real 1996a, 3; and Gómez 1997, 47–49. The latter quotes Sáenz as explicitly claiming that the secundaria should be "an institution destined for adolescents."

19 Sixty-one percent for the period 1934–1940 (Muñoz Izquierdo 1981, 112).

20 This quote is based on the writings of Juan B. Salazár, Cárdenas's head of secondary education.

21 The quote is from Article 60 of the regulative law of the third constitutional article, published in the *Diario Oficial,* 30 December 1939.

22 See Oikión Solano 1995, 290–306. In 1946, Education Secretary Torres Bodet was also influenced by the internationalist themes of the newly created United Nations, with its call for an education in global solidarity. See Moctezuma Barragán 1994, 52.

23 Others characterize and periodize these policy developments differently, of course. In a recent volume, for instance, Pablo Latapí Sarre (1998) distinguishes five "overlapping educational projects" of the postrevolutionary State: the Vasconcelos project, socialist education, technological education, national unity, and modernization. By the 1990s, elements of all these projects could be observed in educational policy and discourse.

24 Much of this increase was due to the growing participation of female students, who came to form half the student body in most secundarias by the late 1970s.

25 For an analysis of the new secundaria curriculum proposed and enacted in 1993 by the Program for Educational Modernization, and a discussion of its possible consequences, see Levinson 1999.

26 See Carrasco 1976; Becker 1995; Gledhill 1991; Meyer 1976.

27 Mújica tried to break the power of the remaining large landowners almost overnight, passing legislation in favor of peasant and worker rights. He also devoted nearly half the state's budget to education (Vaughan 1982, 155–56).

28 Marjorie Becker's (1995) more recent study highlights the gendered imagery involved in this political struggle.

29 Most of these accounts were gathered under my direction by my research assistant, Ofelia Hernández, in April 1998.

30 My own research into the male/female ratio at ESF, done by five-year increments, revealed a slow, though uneven, rise in the proportion of girls to boys until the late 1970s, when the proportion seemed to even out. My figures for 1955 and 1960 show a proportion of close to 2:1 for boys.

31 The telesecundaria—designed to provide a secondary education to more isolated, rural communities—was first instituted in the late 1960s. All telesecundarias are linked to a national communications network, which broadcasts lessons and programs through televisions in place at each of the schools. Typically, one teacher serves as facilitator and interpreter of these lessons, which cover all subject areas in the normal secundaria curriculum. The telesecundaria graduate obtains a fully valid secundaria certificate. By the 1980s, most villages and towns in the San Pablo region with a population of one thousand or more had their own telesecundarias. Nevertheless, those families that could negotiate it economically and logistically still tended to enroll their children in one of the San Pablo secundarias.

2. ETHNOGRAPHIC BEGINNINGS

1 All proper names, of course, have been changed to protect the anonymity of my research participants. In Mexico, as in most of the Spanish-speaking world, married couples still preserve the use of each of their fathers' surnames. The woman takes her husband's first surname as her new *second* surname—for example, Mrs. Ramírez Solana.

2 In Mexican Spanish, the term *pueblo* is multivalent. Most frequently used to denote a village or small town, it can also refer to a broader national category, as in *el pueblo mexicano* (the Mexican people). Most San Pabloans referred to life *aquí en el pueblo* (here in town), rather than the term for city, *ciudad,* though they also used a condescending diminutive to call the smaller surrounding towns and villages *pueblitos.* The reader will note here that I must sacrifice some detail in this account of San Pablo in order to protect the anonymity of my research participants.

3 While this kind of crafts production was once oriented to regional circuits of barter and trade, it has become increasingly geared toward a tourist market within capitalist relations of production (García Canclini 1981, 1990; Novelo 1976; Dinerman 1974).

4 Anthropologists have problematized the notion of tradition in recent years, especially its connotation within the modernization paradigm as a transhistorical, fixed body of allegedly backward beliefs and practices. Tradition is now used by anthropologists as a relational term denoting the embedded practices and beliefs

constructed locally and historically in opposition to contemporary cultural and economic developments (Hobsbawm and Ranger 1983; Clifford 1988). It is in this sense that I refer to indigenous tradition here and Spanish Catholic tradition below.

5   Robert van Kemper (1987, 73) has discussed how local elites have allied themselves with state bureaucrats to support a regressive development policy encouraging tourism and crafts production—activities that aim to conserve the region's supposedly traditional customs and relations of power—at the expense of more substantial industrial or agricultural projects.

6   I could do little to verify such allegations, of course, but the San Pablo region is a notorious crossroads for the growing traffic in marijuana and heroin. Highway checkpoints and drug busts were common during my stay in the field.

7   I have glossed local categories (see the next section) with terms more familiar to a U.S. and European readership. Care must be taken not to conflate economic or occupational categories with cultural categories of class, however. For instance, Lourdes Arizpe's (1989) otherwise interesting study of "beliefs" in a nearby Mexican city begs the question of local categories by defining various class fractions in terms of their present occupations, such as *grandes empresarios industriales, proveedores de servicios,* or *ejidatarios* (large-scale growers/landowners, owners of stores and services, or communal farmers).

8   In his subtle treatment of Mexican regional class and ethnicity, Lomnitz-Adler (1992) proposes the term "intimate cultures" to replace the more abstract "class culture." Intimate cultures are the "real, regionally differentiated manifestations of class culture. . . . The forms of interaction between intimate cultures constitute the culture of social relations" (28).

9   I have not been able to trace the origins of this term in Mexico, though it is obviously borrowed from English. Similar terms used to describe the children of privileged families, or those who develop pretenses to act like them, are *fresa, popi,* and *niño bien.*

10 In the mid-1980s, a demographic study commissioned by the state put the total municipal population at over 53,000, with 33,000 in San Pablo proper. This same study calculates San Pablo's recent growth rate at over 8 percent, among the highest in the state. It also notes that in 1980, the absolute number of urban residents in the municipality overtook the figure for rural residents for the first time, thus achieving rather late the urban predominance well established in other parts of Mexico. Moreover, the tentative 1990 census, which was published while I was still in the field, gave the municipality of San Pablo over 66,000 inhabitants. Yet numerous city residents, including those in municipal government, claimed this number was perhaps viable as an estimate of the city's population, but not that of the entire municipality. Especially those sympathetic to the national opposition party that had managed to win the mayoralty in 1988 (Partido de la

Revolución Democrática, or PRD) accused the government of underreporting census figures in order to justify fewer funds and services.

11 This mirrors a documented national downturn in secundaria enrollments in the late 1980s, which began to recover by 1992 (Fuentes 1996).

12 The principal actually seemed content that class sizes had become more manageable. Because of its more central location and historical prestige, the principal thought ESF could afford these reduced enrollments. Now ESF just didn't have to turn students away to the other secundarias. The other two public secundarias were at greater risk of losing teaching positions, which had to be justified by sufficient enrollment (Citlali Aguilar Hernández [1991] reports a minimum of thirty to thirty-five students necessary for a primary school position; ESF's vice principal informed me that forty was the corresponding number for secundarias.) In 1990, one of the other public secundarias was aggressively advertising itself with banners and public announcements. For perhaps the first time, a clear market logic had begun to penetrate public school selection.

13 For excellent analyses of teachers' union politics in Mexico, see Cook 1996; Foweraker 1993; Hernández 1986. The well-known "corporatist" structure of the Mexican State permits a carefully controlled representation of sectional interests through formalized and highly bureaucratized connections to labor (Brachet-Márquez 1994; Camp 1993). The SNTE, the largest union in Latin America at over 200,000 strong, had maintained rather strict loyalty to the State's agenda until the more recent challenges by the CNTE.

14 My own sympathies fell with the democráticos. This was partly due to my lifelong democratic socialist politics and partly to the friendship networks I had cultivated on previous trips. Most determining of all, I was residing in the home of two stalwart democráticos, Mr. Solana and Mrs. Ramírez, and from their point of view, I had better learn to develop my democratic sympathies! Through the Solanas and their closest associates, I was privy to some of the inner workings of the democratic movement. But Mrs. Ramírez, especially, understood my need to secure the trust of all teachers. I still recall her many tender exhortations to remain on the margins of the conflict. When Mr. Solana or other democráticos scolded me for time spent with the so-called charros or pressured me to join them on a march to the state capital, Mrs. Ramírez would defend my neutrality. With all this said, my relations with the oficiales were generally more guarded yet still cordial. They knew I lived and partied with the democráticos, but I gradually won the trust of many with persistent goodwill and confidentiality. I observed their classrooms and developed friendships with some.

15 Mexican teachers typically perform a year of service in a rural area immediately after their formal training. As recently as fifteen years ago, such training might have consisted of nothing beyond the equivalent of high school (bachillerato); some ESF teachers had begun their service after completing only secundaria, at the

age of fifteen, more than forty years ago. Stories of rural service constitute an important part of the lore of teaching (Rockwell and Mercado 1986).

16 Perhaps most remarkable of all about the teacher conflict was its failure to significantly affect classroom relations or student aspirations. Except for suspended classes and the occasional public outburst by teachers or parents, students remained strangely insulated from the dispute. Contrary to my initial expectations, and despite their desire to sway students' parents to their side, the democratic teachers did not encourage much open discussion of the matter. (Susan Street's [2001] analysis of the ongoing democratic teachers' movement in this part of Mexico suggests that the democráticos more recently have begun to address classroom practice and community relations). As I mention later, most students, in fact, could not easily distinguish teachers' political sympathies. When discussing teachers, students argued or commiserated about their personal traits or teaching styles—their youth or old age, funny or good looks, friendly or distant styles, fair or unjust grading and assignments. Such traits, of course, did not easily correlate with the teachers' positions within the union conflict.

17 Because federal law mandates free public schooling, the collection of registration fees—like the enforcement of a rule requiring students to wear uniforms (federal law also says students cannot be obligated to don uniforms)—must be negotiated through informal mechanisms. That is why the fee, which at private schools is called a *colegiatura* or *cuota de inscripción*, takes on the voluntary tone of "cooperation." The cooperación is less than fully voluntary, though, and that's why I translate it as a fee. In fact, in 1990, the fee had been elevated to fifty thousand pesos, twice as much as any other public school in town, and beyond the reach of the poorest families. Many teachers attributed the 1990 decline in enrollments to this higher fee, which pushed some students over to the other public schools or kept them from studying altogether.

3. INSTITUTIONAL CONTEXTS

1 Etelvina Sandoval (1998b, 215–17) rightly calls attention to the connection between such rules and the discourse of adolescence.

2 In 1990, ESF had a total enrollment of some 1,400 students, almost 750 in the morning shift and over 600 in the evening. Each of the three years was divided into six groups. In the first year, the average class size was about forty-five, while third-year classes, because of attrition, tended to average around thirty-six students each.

3 It must be noted here that certain modifications to cohort selection were in fact made later. Occasionally, the composition of a grupo escolar had to be altered in order to correct a coincidental concentration of boys or girls, or students from the outlying towns and villages. As well, more powerful parents sometimes intervened to assure their child's placement in a grupo of their preference.

4 For a discussion of how grouping practices have evolved historically in the Mexi-

can secundaria, see Meneses Morales 1986, 483, 603. The national directorate of secondary instruction does not specifically endorse either heterogeneous or homogeneous groupings (which might be considered a form of tracking or ability grouping). It distributes an advisory circular to secundaria administrators that discusses the pros and cons of these different forms of grouping, and provides guidelines for creating the groups. Interestingly, and against the prevailing wisdom among ESF teachers, the circular suggested that homogeneous grouping had clear advantages from the "psychotechnical pedagogical point of view." Unfortunately, no national data exist on rates of different forms of secundaria grouping.

5   Etelvina Sandoval (1996) provides powerful evidence that secundaria principals, especially, spend much of their time searching for funds and polishing the school's external image.

6   As suggested by Larissa Adler Lomnitz, Ilya Adler, and Claudio Lomnitz-Adler (1993) as well as Roger Rouse (1995), this national identity would seem to share elements of both hierarchical holism (corporatism) and liberal individualism. How so? Bruce Kapferer (1988, 14) provides a helpful distinction between the egalitarian individualism of Australian nationalism and the hierarchical conception of Sri Lankan nationalism. He draws on Louis Dumont (1977, 4–5; 1980), for whom the defining feature of modern egalitarian cultural systems, first articulated by Alexis de Tocqueville, is that the "concept of the equality of men [sic] entails that of their similarity" (Dumont 1980, 15; see also 346–47, where Dumont traces Tocqueville's ideas to C. Bouglé's notion of equality as similarity). Mexican educational homogenization attempts to create an equality of similarity *and* identity.

7   When I asked the principal why the grupos stayed together all three years of their secundaria education, he expounded: "In accordance with secondary education, we maintain the principle of solidarity and assistance, of conviviality, to create the most rounded citizens for the fatherland, for Mexico. . . . Our intention is that there be better relations among classmates, so that in the future they can form support groups among themselves. We know that activities turn out better if they're done in a group—experience has told us that—and our objective is precisely that the kids get to know one another better in these three years."

8   Compare Martin Schoenhals's (1993, 109–10) description of the Chinese middle school "ban," an organizational device like the grupo escolar conceived of as a "use of the collective to educate and discipline students. . . . Pride in one's class [ban] . . . is supposed to teach students pride in the national collective."

9   After a new classroom construction project had been completed in the middle of the school year, the principal mandated an experiment: grupos escolares would each be assigned a permanent classroom, and the subject teachers would now rotate to meet them. Teachers generally disliked this arrangement, though they acknowledged it might help cut down on mischief between class periods and create a greater sense of responsibility among students. As far as I know, the experiment did not last beyond the school year.

371   Notes to Chapter Three

10 In general, teachers and administrators frequently intoned the need for constancy in work. The term *trabajo* (work) circulated freely in tones of admonishment or exhortation; student rights (*derechos*) to free time and recreation were often conditioned on work. This was undoubtedly related to the discourse on adolescence. In one interesting example, Mr. Guillén linked trabajo to democracy, saying the school in Mexico was "democratic by law," but required more than the mere presence of students. A democratic school, he said, required dedication and work. I wondered along with the students about just who set the terms of this participation.

11 Compare Nancy Lesko's (1988, 37) study of a private Catholic school in the United States that "unites two fundamentally opposing sets of principles, one a Christian commitment to community and the equal worth of each member of society, and the other a private secondary school commitment to promoting individual achievement." According to Lesko, some occasions such as prayer services and administrator remarks emphasized caring and the collective welfare (54–56). The school was envisioned as a "kin group . . . in which the welfare of individuals and that of the group are inextricably linked" (60). Meanwhile, other teachers and school rites promoted contest and individual competition (54–55). There was little collaborative work in classrooms because learning was assumed to be an "individual endeavor" (56). Like the secundaria, Lesko's Catholic school attempted to reconcile a relational identity-in-solidarity (a common faith, a common nation) with the individualistic and competitive tenets of liberal capitalism.

12 Public speaking (*oratorio*) and dramatic poetry recitation (*declamación,* usually with a nationalistic theme) are highly prized skills in Mexico. Regional and national competitions are frequently held.

13 Because of the prevailing Mexican custom of eating the main meal—the *comida*—around 2 or 3 p.m., no lunch period was provided.

14 Literally the "presiding table," the Mesa Directiva consisted of school administrators, key subject area teachers, and elected parent representatives from each grupo escolar.

15 Less prominent but still celebrated in modest fashion was Friendship Day, corresponding to our Valentine's Day on February 14.

16 For a fuller description and analysis of the curriculum, as well as a discussion of the new curriculum implemented with the Program for Educational Modernization in 1993, see Levinson 1999.

17 The rainy season in this part of Mexico typically begins in late May or early June and ends in early September. Until the recent extension of the school year (1993), the summer vacation period closely corresponded to the rainy season, and thus poor weather rarely interfered with school activities.

18 This has significant consequences for the allotment of teachers' limited time. Because secundaria teachers are hired according to the number of classroom hours they cover, some teachers must attend to some sixteen to eighteen groups in

order to fill out the equivalent of a full-time schedule. In 1990, natural and social science teachers typically attended to four to six groups of thirty-five to forty-five students for seven hours a week. Physical and art education teachers covered as many as seventeen groups. Imagine the task involved in testing and grading some seven hundred students every two and a half months. Consider also that because of low teaching salaries, most teachers must supplement their incomes with other work and thus complete all schoolwork—preparation and grading included—within the confines of their allotted hours.

19 For a discussion of persisting "authoritarian" practices in Mexican classrooms, see García Salord and Vanella 1992.

20 This kind of attribution followed the logic of kinship discourses that are quite generalized in Mexico. The individual person is conceived of as an extension of the family, sharing key qualities and habits. Such symbolic logic figures in the teachers' frequent references to students' parents and, especially, older siblings, many of whom they have taught in prior years. The teachers' experiences with students' older siblings typically lay down a grid of expectations; for example, "I've had these Bautista kids before, [and] they're all aggressive because their father teaches them to fight cocks from an early age." The logic also enters into the even more common and pervasive Mexican practice of greeting and departing with salutations for the interlocutor's parents and children.

21 Erwin Epstein (1985, 59), writing in the early 1980s, notes that levels of female enrollment in Mexican primary and secondary education are above the world average, outpacing levels for comparable "developing" countries and nearly approaching the levels of some "developed" ones. See also Howell 1997, 252; Stromquist 1992.

22 For Mexico, see Delgado 1994, 1995. For Spain, see Subirats and Brullet 1988. For the United States, see Thorne 1993; Orenstein 1994; Eder 1995.

23 Connell includes both official school practices and the unofficial domain of student culture in defining a school's gender regime, yet I believe it is important to highlight the contradictions that emerge both among teachers and students themselves as well as between teachers and students as often-antagonistic groups. By characterizing the regime as "hegemonic" (as Connell does), and thus contested, some of its value as a useful heuristic device can be recuperated.

24 Muñoz Izquierdo and Casillas (1982, 42) maintain that, in general, as the rate of return on postprimary education diminishes for certain sectors, women experience this devaluing of schooling more acutely than men. For a discussion of women teachers' exclusion from the masculine spaces of union and administrative politics, see Aguilar Hernández and Sandoval 1995.

25 Actually, the percentage was higher in the morning shift (45 percent) than in the afternoon.

26 The cultural production of new gender strategies and responsibilities in Latin American social movements has become an important new field of inquiry. For

commentary on women's involvement in Mexican teacher politics, see Foweraker 1993, 24. For broader studies, see Jelin 1991; Gutmann 1996; Radcliffe and Westwood 1993; Escobar and Alvarez 1992.

27 Some work on female secondary students in the United States indicates that a greater facility with written and spoken language provides girls with an important source of power (Finders 1997, 24; Shuman 1986).

28 Unless they made a special petition later, students had to spend all three years in the taller into which they had been initially placed.

29 The vice principal of the morning shift later wrote me to say that girls occasionally requested participation in the corps, but were turned down because the school lacked "proper" instruments. By 1995, when I visited, this former vice principal, now principal of ESF, took great pride in pointing to the several girls who had now joined the corps as drummers.

30 On a couple of occasions, in fact, the color guard was mixed: one or two girls escorted the flag itself in the front part of the formation while boys brought up the rear.

4. SOMOS MUY UNIDOS

1 I also participated in the girls' burgeoning world of romance not only as an object of desire or romantic prospect, but also as confidant, counselor, and intermediary. In this way, I learned about gender and romance from the perspective of an outsider sympathetic to the concerns of the girls. Many came to confide in me some of their deepest conflicts and most secret desires. My ambiguous status in the school allowed me to develop a relation of trust and empathy few girls could expect from other men in their lives.

2 See Matthew Speier's (1976) discussion of the risks of succumbing to the "adult ideological viewpoint," which privileges a teleological notion of maturity.

3 Indeed, overall grade patterns tended to reflect these claims. By and large, second-grade grupos were always among the lowest rankings.

4 See the introduction for a fuller exposition of my fieldwork methods and the selection of focal students. The twenty focal students originally selected expanded to twenty-two when Fidencio and Vicente proved somewhat recalcitrant, and José and Fidel presented themselves in the meantime as willing participants.

5 Though most private colegios had long since been officially incorporated into the federal education system, some families still believed their children could not enroll at a federal secundaria with a private primaria education. Still others knew such enrollment was legally permissible, but nevertheless sought to ease the transition with a year at a public primaria.

6 Drawing on the philosopher Richard Rorty's (1989, 190) notion of solidarity, I understand the teachers and State as encouraging students to expand their "we" intentions beyond their immediate class-ethnic-gender groups. Ideally, the idiom of national unity provides the conceptual basis for an expanding solidarity. Yet the students base this solidarity as much on their "we-ness" as students, per se, than as

Mexicans, so their strategic intentions could be said to run up against those of the teachers and State.

7   In 1997, some six years after graduating from ESF, Rosita recounted this episode as one of the most memorable in her school career, and Benito still fondly recalled Rosita's stance.

8   It should be clear that the subsequent analysis owes a great deal to Paul Willis's (1981b) study of working-class lads' cultural forms, such as "having a laff." While Willis restricts his discussion to the lads' specific counterschool peer culture, however, here I describe cultural forms developed or encouraged by most students at ESF.

9   This observation dovetails with many ethnographic considerations of learning in context. As Hugh Mehan (1979), Jean Lave and Etienne Wenger (1991), and others have shown in different ways, the development of competence and expertise is largely a result of successfully grasping, and participating in, the rules by which a functioning "community" operates.

10 José Macías (1990) and Henry Trueba and Concha Delgado-Gaitán (1985) discuss the dilemmas faced by Mexican schoolchildren in the United States whose tendency to collaborate in this manner is viewed by their teachers there as "copying" or "cheating."

11 I must admit that I sometimes occupied a similar position myself and so felt a strong sympathy for the teachers. It became clear to me at some point that my group interviews were invariably appropriated as an occasion for relajo. The boys tended to be more disruptive than the girls, but it seemed none of them could take my questions seriously before converting them into springboards for humorous banter or physical horseplay. My own proposed value—to hear students seriously reflect on their lives and their experience in school—was thus "suspended" by students' relajo.

12 Douglas Foley's (1990, 101–34) account of "making out games" in Texas high school classrooms also portrays coordinated student action in disrupting—and hence enlivening—the tedious school routine. Yet Foley draws more attention to class and ethnic differences in the manner of "performing" such games, claiming that such differential expressions of classroom behavior help prefigure students' insertion into "capitalist culture." Erving Goffman's (1961, 171–320) account of the "secondary adjustments" made by social selves within organizations sounds remarkably similar to Portilla's relajo and might be considered a more generalized expression of this unique Mexican variant. According to Goffman, a secondary adjustment is "any habitual arrangement by which a member of an organization employs unauthorized means, or obtains unauthorized ends, or both, thus getting around the organization's assumptions as to what he [sic] should do and get and whence what he should be" (189).

13 Normally, a speaker would have emphasized "feeling" better in the environment, but here the student referred also to the theater's cushy seats.

14 In this case, the girls who took the lead in the relajo were among the best students, so the teacher would not have suspected bad intentions. In other instances, though, girls who regularly disrupted class would be scolded or cited for their part in an attempted relajo. Thus, my findings only partly confirm Claudia Saucedo Ramos's (1995, 105) suggestion that because they are quite able in projecting an image of order, girls who are "in reality violating classroom norms" receive the better end of teachers' "differential evaluation" of bad and good conduct.

15 By calling attention to the impulse toward freedom and resistant creativity in much popular culture, Johannes Fabian elaborates a theory of cultural production as communicative praxis. In the case of echando relajo, students were reinventing a genre of cultural action (Fabian 1998, 41, 61) that met the power of the institution with its own kind of power. The link to Robert Everhart's (1983) account of U.S. junior high school students' goofing off as the communication of "regenerative" knowledge should be apparent.

16 I am indebted to Jan Nespor for making this point clear to me.

5. SITES OF SOCIAL DIFFERENCE AND THE PRODUCTION OF SCHOOLED IDENTITY

1 Mexican historians and anthropologists have paid special attention to the evolution of ethnic relations and categories throughout the colonial and independence periods (Arizpe and de Gortari 1990; Frye 1996; Mallon 1995; Hill 1991; Lomnitz-Adler 1992). From the earliest colonial times in Mexico, racial miscegenation was common. Claudio Lomnitz-Adler (1992, 261–81) has illuminated the complex and unstable nature of the Spanish colonial "caste" system, in which the dominant ideology rewarded whiteness, but contradictorily recognized Indian communities as "hierarchical societies in their own right" (274). After independence, there emerged in practice a tripartite conception of racial status, comprised of indios or indígenas (native peoples who still spoke an indigenous language and lived in their own "hierarchical" communities), mestizos (the "mixed" general masses previously referred to as castes, and now primarily the Hispanicized offspring of Indians and Spanish), and criollos or blancos (direct descendants of Spanish colonists). By the middle of the nineteenth century, the liberal ideology of the emerging Mexican State sought to abolish independent Indian communities and reconstitute Indians as allegedly equal national subjects. The effect of this, as Lomnitz-Adler notes, was that the "term 'Indian' became synonymous with a combination of material poverty and cultural 'backwardness'" (276). The dominant value of whiteness was preserved under the Liberal system, while Indians became the object of intense "civilizing" efforts. Notions of ethnicity in Mexico have also been constructed through cultural discourses equating Indianness with rural or agricultural life. Since the colonial period, urbanity in the dominant imaginary has been conversely signified as "civilization," "reason," and "whiteness." Lomnitz-Adler (276) observes that class distinctions during the nineteenth

century had already begun to be posed in racial terms. Yet as the Mexican State has moved more recently toward a multiethnic model of citizenship, official State discourse has largely discarded the notion of an Indian race for the concept of *etnias,* or ethnic groups. Defined primarily by language use, most recent estimates place the number of indigenous people in Mexico at around eight million, or from 8 to 10 percent of the country's population, though Mexico's foremost expert, the late Guillermo Bonfil Batalla, claimed they were closer to twelve to fifteen million in 1992 (García 1992).

2 It is important not to collapse the analytic distinctions between terms like *kinship, family,* and *household.* Henry Selby, Arthur Murphy, and Stephen Lorenzen (1990, 51) define the household as a "coresident group of persons who share most aspects of consumption, drawing on and allocating a common pool of resources to ensure their material reproduction." According to these authors, family is a cultural category not necessarily coextensive with the household, though in San Pablo most people use the term *familia* when referring to this residential unit. Terms such as *parientes* or *familiares* are used when referring to wider kin relations.

3 See Levine 1993; for a contrasting view, see Gutmann 1996.

4 See, for instance, Stephen 1992; J. Martin 1990, 1994; Alonso 1988, 1992a, 1992b.

5 See, for instance, Chaney 1979; Nash and Safa 1986; Jelin 1990; Chant 1991; de Barbieri and de Oliveira 1986; Fernández-Kelly 1983; Massolo 1992a, 1992b; Benería and Roldán 1987.

6 See Behar 1990; Vaughan 1994; Alonso 1995; Fowler-Salamini and Vaughan 1994; Stern 1995; Becker 1995; and Arrom 1985.

7 In Connell's terms, the gender order in Mexico continues to reflect patterns of strong male dominance even if women have begun to successfully challenge specific inequalities in gender regimes within such institutions as the family/household and workplace. The cultural production of new, counterhegemonic gender ideologies has not accompanied the significant gains women have made in localized gender regimes.

8 Matthew Gutmann's (1996) recent study on the "meanings of macho" in a Mexico City neighborhood provides further evidence that strictly separated gender roles have relaxed more in larger urban areas. Gutmann develops a cogent critique of stereotypical notions of the Mexican macho, and suggests that such depictions have little explanatory value even for poorer, provincial regions like San Pablo.

9 My research into ESF's enrollment figures revealed that the proportion of boys and girls did not reach parity until the late 1970s. In 1943, the school's first San Pablo generation, boys outnumbered girls by more than three to one. By 1960, first-year enrollments had approached a two to one ratio, but second- and third-year grupos showed a ratio of three or even four to one, indicating a proportionately heavy attrition rate for girls. By 1970, when class sizes were averaging about sixty students, first-year enrollment figures remained around two to one, but the attrition rate had reversed dramatically: girls now constituted more than 40 percent of

the third-year grupos. It was not until 1979 that a virtually even enrollment pattern emerged, with girls outnumbering boys in many of the grupos. From this time, too, attrition rates apparently evened out, with boys showing a slightly lower chance of completing their secundaria certificate than girls.

10   In 1990, these laudatory gestures became even more poignant as many were beginning to doubt ESF's historical claim to being the best school in the region. Strikes and dissension among teachers had hit ESF hard the year before. Classes had been suspended for various periods, once for as long as a month. Parents began to charge the school with corruption, alleging that many teachers were faltistas (chronic absentees). This process made 1990 a year of recuperation, though the threat of strike and dissension still hung very realistically in the air. Many teachers lamented the recent decline in academic quality, and this may have made their exhortations to students even more forceful. Certainly, the principal made clear appeals to the school's reputation in his statements to both teachers and students. In helping construct a positive school identity, the principal exploited every opportunity to threaten, cajole, exhort, and scold in the name of excellence (compare Sandoval 1996, 1998a for other secundarias). Meanwhile, when I asked parents why their children attended ESF, most tended to preface their response with qualified approbation: "Well, they used to say that ESF was the best around, but I'm not so sure anymore."

11   In 1990, registration at one typical colegio at the secundaria level cost 80,000 pesos, with additional payments of 40,000 pesos distributed over ten months. At 3,000 pesos to the dollar this constituted an expense of nearly $200 for the year. The ESF Sociedad de Padres de Familia collected an initial cooperación of 50,000 pesos, or $17, in August 1990. Yet parents were fond of noting that school officials managed to squeeze a lot more out of them for projects and events throughout the school year. Some even wondered if these payments together approximated the cost of a year at the colegio.

12   The quality of private instruction in a provincial town such as San Pablo differs considerably from that found in larger metropolitan centers. In general, private education is highly uneven across Mexico and quite varied in socioeconomic terms (Muñoz Izquierdo 1981). In places like Mexico City, private schools certainly rank among the best, and local elites send their children there not only for its distinctive morality or status but also a quality education that might gain them entrance into the best schools and universities. Many of these schools hire foreigners and university graduates, and pay them well to teach. Tuition rates are often exorbitant. In San Pablo, by contrast, private schools pay teachers less than (the already miserable) public school salaries. Many of these teachers may be high school graduates with little pedagogical training or nuns of the parish sponsoring the school. Consequently, tuition may even be within the reach of workers' families.

13   Because the San Pablo region had no major industry, most high school and college

graduates would have to find work elsewhere. For instance, the specialized tracks at the local CBTIS included tourism and instrumentation. The tourism specialty had obviously been implemented to train San Pablo residents for the local tourist industry. Yet this industry never developed much beyond small-scale family operations. Consequently, tourism students typically completed a six-month practicum in the coastal resorts of Ixtapa or Acapulco, where they often stayed on to work. Similarly, instrumentation graduates had to travel rather far for jobs in mines, hydroelectric plants, and the like.

14 Actually, I learned that San Pabloans occasionally employed these terms to denote the rural dwellers who came to the city on market days and had begun populating San Pablo's peripheral colonias in greater numbers. The terms themselves were derived from indigenous languages. They could be said with a tone of disgust or paternalistic affection.

15 This was perhaps not unusual, given the fleeting nature of such bonds. According to my calculations, most relationships (*noviazgos*) at ESF lasted some two to three weeks, regardless of whether they were between students both attending ESF. Those that lasted longer generated a great deal of comment among the students and sometimes even the teachers.

16 In San Pablo, a career (*carrera*) did not necessarily carry all the middle-class meanings of self-fulfillment and emotional reward that it does, say, in the United States. Carrera referred to employment that required some kind of professional training, whether at the more modest high school level (*carrera corta,* or "short career," like secretary, assistant accountant, nurse, technician, and the like) or university.

6. FRIENDSHIP GROUPS, YOUTH CULTURE, AND THE LIMITS OF SOLIDARITY

1 Most of the data presented in this chapter were taken from informal group interviews, which not only afforded students an opportunity to reflect on their practice but to censor their responses for the anthropologist as well. While this context must be noted, I should also mention that the questions I posed often followed on observation of students' behavior in other specific contexts. This enabled me to assess the veracity of their accounts and provided a different angle on student practice.

2 The cultural center, it bears mention, was my own sociological abstraction, a relational etic category constructed from prolonged familiarity with the informal groupings that students created. Few students could be securely and continually placed within or without the cultural center. I estimated the composition of the cultural center for third graders at about fifty students, or approximately 20 percent.

3 See Mary Douglas and Baron Isherwood's ([1979] 1996, 37) cultural theory of consumption, which depicts "consumer choices," broadly construed, as a key ma-

trix for "expressing and generating culture." Moral judgments are apt to be made about types of people based on their styles of consumption—in this case, music and other cultural commodities.

4   Among the most popular so-called modern musicians at ESF in 1990 were those with the broadest commercial sound, like Alejandra Guzmán, Garibaldi, Gloria Trevi, Caifanes, Timbiriche, Luís Miguel, Menudo, New Kids on the Block, Milli Vanilli, Madonna, Technotronics, Vanilla Ice, and MC Hammer.

5   For further discussion of the Juanitos, see Levinson 1998a. There I indicate how talk about girls—like talk about indios and machines—was one more way the Juanitos demarcated their friendship group from other students in their respective grupos escolares and the school at large. Maintaining a sharp and invidious gender distinction was therefore also one of the conditions of acceptance into the Juanitos. It was one more way in which they could keep Antonio, never quite ready for flirtation or sexist girl talk, at comfortable arm's length.

6   It bears mentioning here that most of the quoted terms in this section come directly from local speech. As if taking a cue from the script of modernization theory, San Pabloans across most ages and classes used terms like "traditional" to indicate authoritarian, adult-centered, or family-centered practices that had reigned in the past, reserving the terms "modern" or "liberal" for those practices licensing individual freedom and determination.

7   Peter Woods (1990, 191–223) gives an excellent overview of the kinds of social uses to which humor may be put among students. He highlights the role humor plays in "experimenting with identities" and forming friendship groups. Although his ethnographic data come mostly from Britain, many of Woods's observations would hold true for ESF as well.

8   Parents, teachers, and students alike agreed that girls were far more prone to romantic distraction. It was not uncommon to hear teachers lament the tendency for girls to "spend the whole time yearning for her boyfriend" ("*pasársela suspirando por su novio*").

9   Just as Gabriela Delgado (1995, 225, 230) has also described in her research on a private preparatoria, young women at ESF were more apt than men to provide responses to difficult teacher prompts, distribute completed homework for copying, and act otherwise to "protect" their classmates from teachers' efforts at discipline (see chapter 4).

10   Throughout the year, I noted significant gender differences in book cover adornments. Boys used decals and magazine cutouts of sexy women and tough machines (typically race cars or motorcycles), while girls affixed images of handsome celebrities (Luís Miguel, Pedro Armendáriz), animals (such as horses), flowers and hearts, and the like. Both sexes trafficked heavily in stickers, magazine photos, and other minor cultural commodities, but they "performed" their gender subjectivities through rather different images.

11 For an interesting account of the contradictions encoded in the "liberalizing" tendencies of the Mexican "sexual revolution," see Monsiváis 1990, 169–74.

12 One phrase frequently used by some girls to describe others that had gone too far with their flirtation was *se pasan*, or "they cross over" the line. Metaphorically, then, this phrase entailed a sense of proper limits and boundaries.

13 Such was the case for Rosita, as we have seen. While most "jealous" fathers played the part of sexual conservative, I knew several cases in which the mother took more interest in restricting the daughter.

14 Leslie Roman (1988, 180) makes a similar point in her study of young women in a punk subculture in the United States. According to Roman, the young women's varying experiences with intimacy, sexuality, and sexual violence in different "family forms" (female-headed single-parent, traditional nuclear, and dual wage-earning households) determined, far more than "social class" itself, patterns of friendship affiliation.

7. POLITICAL ECONOMIC CHANGE, LIFE TRAJECTORIES, AND IDENTITY FORMATION, 1988–1998

1 Most parents of ESF students had never studied beyond secundaria themselves. Students and their parents thus saw the secundaria as a springboard to pursue the elusive goal of membership in the middle class, of not having to work hard with their hands. Enrollment in secondary education typically signified a commitment to urban culture and advanced study for prestige and status (Loaeza 1988). Even though the economic rationality of advanced study had been compromised by the ongoing fiscal crisis in Mexico, the possession and exercise of cultura—that is, forms of knowledge that can be converted to other forms of capital—still had great value. Soledad Loaeza (1988, 33) also suggests that by the 1980s, the secundaria had become the best place to look at these evolving questions of sorting and status. On the other hand, a recent study by Humberto Muñoz García (1996, 117–40), conducted in the aftermath of severe economic crisis, shows growing distrust among Mexicans in the ability of education to provide a means of socioeconomic mobility. While they might still value the school for its discipline and practical knowledge, more and more Mexicans doubt that the "culture" of schooling can be "later revalued in the labor market" (ibid., 117; see also Rothstein 1996). The persistent and positive discourse of the State around the value of education contrasts with recent "lived and perceived realities" of most Mexicans, and thereby provokes "cognitive dissonance" (Muñoz García 1996, 141). According to Muñoz García and his associates, the lowest social classes, especially those in small and medium cities (for instance, San Pablo), are now most likely to remain skeptical of schooling's benefits.

2 The indigenous language teacher informed me that about ten of his thirty-four students had substantial prior knowledge of the language. Some of the indigenous

students would still not speak clearly in class, even though the teacher had heard them shouting the language to each other in their home communities. They explained to him that his own "purer" form of the language inhibited them from speaking their Hispanicized version. Still, the teacher wondered if this reticence was also due to the symbolic weight of Spanish in the school and city.

3 Due to their frequent mobility, lack of telephone communication, and the like, some former students were particularly difficult to contact and interview. A female research assistant helped me fill in some of the following details by tracking down and interviewing a few students in early 1998.

4 Socorro's father peppered his discourse with affirmative statements like, "*Yo lo sé porque lo viví*" ("I know this because I lived it"). He reminded me that he had attended a special school for socialist workers and continued to believe that capitalism was just full of tricks (*mañas*). I also observed in the father's talk a symbolic opposition frequently expressed by adults across the social classes I knew: the distinction between trabajo (work) and *flojera* (laziness) as a kind of primordial moral axis of judgment. Just as most Mexicans made global judgments about people as *buena gente* or *mala gente,* they also assessed each other as *trabajador* or flojo. This man's judgment was rooted in the teachings of Karl Marx, whom he cited as saying that man had been born to work (*el hombre nació para trabajar*).

5 The practice of "robbing" a bride (*robar la novia*) as a kind of elopement is still fairly common, especially in rural areas of Mexico. In my experience, San Pabloans used the verb *robar* to describe both forced marriages, where the groom and his family circumvented the wishes of the bride and authority of her parents, as well as more consensual elopements.

6 Though his specialty at the CBTIS was accounting, few opportunities existed for social service in that area. The Centro de Salud and an adult literacy program (INEA) provided the greatest number of volunteer positions. CBTIS students had to perform twelve hundred hours of social service in little more than a year, a requirement that translated into full days of summer work and most afternoons of the following school year.

7 Iván also noted for me that he recently learned that of the fifty-three students who had entered CBTIS with his electricity cohort, only eighteen had eventually graduated.

8 Iván liked to claim that he had "jumped ahead" of four older siblings by getting married first. Two older sisters and one older brother had recently married. They all had one or two young children and lived with stable, working-class spouses (a carpenter, meat vendor, and drug supply truck driver). The oldest brother and sister had not yet married. Iván informed me that a terminal accounting degree at the CBTIS was as far as any of his siblings (one brother and one sister) had ever gotten in their studies. His younger sister was currently in the same program herself. Iván didn't think his parents at their age could sustain his sister's studies in the capital, so she would also remain in town.

9   An exception would be JoEllen Fisherkeller (1997), who found that for the U.S. teenagers she studied, "home cultures" still provided them with a powerful "filter," a primary context for the meanings generated in peer- and school-based appropriations of popular culture. This would be true of ESF students as well.

10   Perhaps most of the former ESF students hovered between a relational identity rooted in family and community (like the migrants that Roger Rouse [1991, 1995] studied), and a sense of self as possessive individual.

8. GAMES ARE SERIOUS

1   As David Swartz (1997), Richard Harker, Cheleen Mahar, and Chris Wilkes (1990), and others have pointed out, Bourdieu's concept of habitus cannot be understood apart from his later one concerning social fields, which provide the "context" for the action of the habitus in struggles over various forms of "capital." I believe the concept of fields is necessary, but not sufficient for understanding student culture and identity formation; it allows an appreciation of the struggles over scarce resources in broader educational and social domains without accounting for the emergent and idiosyncratic qualities of particular institutions like ESF.

2   Sometimes this spark can literally explode, as it did recently at Columbine High School in Littleton, Colorado, where two student members of a subculture called "the trenchcoat mafia" went on a killing spree at their own school. In the aftermath of this tragedy, it has become clear that the school athletes, or "jocks," comprised a dominant student group that belittled and intimidated groups like the trenchcoat mafia (see Aronson 2000).

3   Starting with George Foster's (1967) conception of "the image of limited good," Mexicanist students of the countryside have consistently noted the salience of egalitarian ideologies that attempt to downplay or mask community stratification (see also Greenberg 1989, 154, 203–4; Schryer 1990, 317; Nader 1995). Though I cannot say how such community rhetoric might enter into the students' game at ESF, certainly such notions of equality comprise part of what Lomnitz-Adler (1992) would call San Pablo's regional culture of social relations.

4   These observations confirm a long line of ethnographic research in British schools concerned with the phenomenon of "differentiation" and "polarization" in secondary schools (see, for example, Lacey 1970; Abraham 1995).

5   Roger Chartier (1997, 119) also provides a powerful statement about the centrality of "individual aspirations" in liberal democratic societies.

APPENDIX A

1   For some examples of such work, see Hollingshead 1949; Schwartz and Merten 1967; Cusick 1973; Brake 1980; Canaan 1987, 1990; Varenne 1982; Eckert 1989; Walker 1988; Larkin 1979; Foley 1990; MacLeod 1987; Aggleton 1987; Hall and Jefferson [1975] 1993; Jenkins 1983; Lesko 1988; Delamont 1984; Coleman 1961; Stinchcombe 1964; Lacey 1970; Ball 1981; Connell et al. 1982; Page 1991; Brown 1987;

Abraham 1995. I employ the term *cultures* to denote a variety of social and/or status groups that, in the literature, are not always referred to as student cultures per se. Here, I attempt to use the term *student cultures* more inclusively, to highlight the constructed values, meanings, and symbolic identities that appear to be the hallmark of these emergent groups.

2   Some authors prefer to use the terms *developed* or *industrialized* countries to describe what I am calling advanced capitalist or liberal democratic societies. Likewise, they may use the terms *developing* or *industrializing* to portray what I will tend to refer to as former colonial or dependent capitalist societies. Following world-systems theory (Wallerstein 1974), the terms I use question the evolutionary endpoint implied by development, and more accurately name the historical and contemporary relations of power between these different regions and societies.

3   Many identify Louis Althusser's (1971) influential essay, "Ideology and Ideological State Apparatuses," as the paradigmatic effort in this burgeoning critical literature. There Althusser argued that in the presently ascendant period of monopoly capitalism, schooling serves as the dominant ideological state apparatus (ISA). Schools ensure social reproduction by inculcating both the techniques—the basic skills—of different social classes, and the attitudes and behaviors that guarantee the legitimation of the status quo (132). In other words, schools effectively reproduce labor power and the ideology that legitimates the existing relations of production. Importantly, ideology operates through the ISAs to "interpellate" subjects that will take their appropriate place in a structure of dominance. For an excellent early overview of this literature, see Karabel and Halsey 1977.

4   For overviews, see Holland and Eisenhart 1990; Morrow and Torres 1995; Levinson, Foley, and Holland 1996.

5   There is a danger that institutions like schools may still appear as relatively bounded entities vis-à-vis a broader social order. How can patterns of student action and thought within the school be understood in a way that incorporates the effects of broader cultural and political-economic structures and powers? This is one of the crucial mandates of any critical ethnography (Carspecken 1995). The critical social theorist Anthony Giddens (1984), in discussing Paul Willis's classic study of British high school lads, provides yet another way to consider this dynamic as the "duality of structure":

> The practices followed in a given range of contexts are embedded in wider reaches of time and space. . . . How far do the lads, in developing an oppositional culture within the school, draw upon rules and resources more broadly involved than in the immediate contexts of their action? (297–304)

More recently, Jan Nespor (1997) has shown how the spatial flow of bodies, signs, and practices gets "tangled up" in one U.S. elementary school. The cultures within the school can only be fully understood by tracing the historical-spatial flow of meanings and practices back out into neighborhoods, homes, and sites of political-economic decision making.

6   Reba Page and Linda Valli's (1990) work on curriculum differentiation in U.S. secondary schools suggests another way that schools as organizations mediate broader structural forces. While academic tracks and other forms of curricular differentiation represent organizational "transformations" of broader social structures, they do not "cause" people to behave in particular ways. Rather, such structures are resources that people use to situate themselves and interpret their place in the world. Even as Page and Valli acknowledge "macrolevel aspects of social reality" and "macrocontexts of communities" as important structural sources of difference, they assert the value of midlevel interpretive studies, and the need for "institutional analyses which consider the limited autonomy of the school and the curriculum" (10–11). Similarly, the British author Phillip Brown (1987, 27) offers a framework that "allows us to do justice both to the complexity of meanings generated within the school and their relation to wider societal processes." For Brown, students' "frames of reference" are drawn from a "stock of commonly available cultural resources which people in the same class location use in different ways to order their social conduct and make sense of their changing life histories and social situations" (32).

7   Moreover, the symbolic resources for such meaning making did not issue from the school or family alone. On the prompting of Philip Wexler (1987) and others, critical ethnographers began to look more closely at the ways students drew on the media in and out of school to form their identities and cultures.

8   In truth, the symbolic interactionist tradition in the United States produced many fine sociological studies of U.S. student culture prior to or contemporaneous with the emergence of reproduction theory. Authors such as August Hollingshead (1949), Arthur Stinchcombe (1964), James Coleman (1961), Philip Cusick (1973), and Gary Schwartz and Donald Merten (1967) examined the social class structure of peer groups and activities around the high school, seeking to elucidate the impact of student meaning making. Meanwhile, a robust British stream of school ethnography also used interactionist frameworks to interpret the meanings that students ascribed to their experience and the strategies they developed to "cope" with school sorting mechanisms (Hargreaves 1967; Lacey 1970; Ball 1981; Woods 1979). For a fine overview of the British literature on "pupil" cultures, see Woods 1990; Lacey 1982. More recent work has continued to explore secondary student culture within a broadly revised cultural reproduction framework (Eckert 1989; Weis 1990; Wexler 1992; Foley 1990; Raissiguier 1994; Proweller 1998; Fordham 1996; Davidson 1996; Solomon 1992).

9   As the renowned historical sociologist Norbert Elias makes clear in the statement that opens this appendix, individual aspirations and identities ultimately form through the prism of social relations. Elias, like his later French counterpart Pierre

Bourdieu, used the notion of habitus to describe the deeply habituated, embodied sense of the social world—habitus as the "manners and morals" of the social made concrete in the individual. The concept has since been elegantly developed by Bourdieu (1977, 1990) to give a relational rather than dualistic account of the way persons and societies interpenetrate (for important and helpful critical exegeses of Bourdieu's work, especially the concept of habitus, see Calhoun 1993; Harker, Mahar, and Wilkes 1990; Swartz 1997, 95–116). "Social reality exists both inside and outside of individuals, *both* in our minds and in things" (Swartz 1997, 96), and habitus gives expression to this. As a "system of durable, transposable dispositions which . . . generate and organize practices and representations" (Bourdieu 1990, 53), the habitus conditions life chances through its deep internalization of historically evolved social structures. Habitus, then, represents a kind of baseline of student aspirations—that structural-cultural *sense* that students inherit and then adapt to new circumstances. Yet how does this adaptation take place, and what of the habitus changes or stays the same in the process? However adept at analyzing the dispositions of the social subject, Bourdieu provides less insight into the more personal, emergent qualities of identity formation.

David Swartz (1997) develops an especially acute, albeit sympathetic reading of Bourdieu's entire body of work. He notes, along with other critics, the problem Bourdieu has in accounting for change. The role of the habitus in sociocultural reproduction lends it a deterministic cast, but Swartz points out that in Bourdieu's extended (and more recently developed) theory, habitus cannot be understood in isolation from the different social "fields" in which it operates (213). Change occurs precisely in the dynamic interaction, often the "disjuncture," between habitus and field. Swartz also proposes a key distinction between aspirations and *expectations* (105–14). While Bourdieu tends to use the corresponding French terms interchangeably, Swartz believes an analytic distinction might help to understand known instances in which student aspirations seem to outreach their expectations—the latter being more easily understood in terms of the internalization of objective structural conditions.

10 Jay MacLeod (1987) offers an accessible, cogent discussion of structure and agency in the formation of aspirations. He draws on the work of Bourdieu.

11 The team of John Meyer and his students have produced a series of cogent arguments about the consequences of so-called modern school expansion in the postwar period: see Boli and Ramírez 1992; Meyer et al. 1992; Kamens et al. 1996. For a discussion of this work, see Levinson 1999.

12 For discussions of this splintering, which in Britain has been called the "differentiation-polarisation" process, see Abraham 1995; Page and Valli 1990; Natriello 1994; Eckert 1989; Shimahara 1983.

13 Feminist authors have argued that the more flamboyant, public, deviant style of the male subcultures studied by CCCS researchers drew attention away from women's subcultures, where private leisure activities offered a different kind of

resistance, grossly circumscribed by "subordinated institutions" such as the family and home (see Lave et al. 1992, 270; McRobbie 1992; Brunsdon 1996; Proweller 1998). Later feminist critiques began to explore the way sexism, and distinct gender ideologies, were constitutive of the very means by which subcultures constructed identity (Lave et al. 1992, 275). This was a long way from Willis's earliest writings, which tended to portray the lads' sexism as only peripheral to their class-based resistance in school. The various critiques, in turn, led to a questioning of the focus on subcultures—a focus that was said to implicitly valorize the more visible, distinct, often hierarchical cultural formations among (primarily male) youth, while downplaying more quotidian social processes. Dorothy Holland and Margaret Eisenhart (1990, 45–54) and Sue Lees (1986) have given persuasive illustrations of how the cultural reproduction of oppressive gender relations occurs primarily in and through more inclusive, mixed student cultures.

14 Many commentaries on Willis's work now exist. Within the educational literature, for an especially insightful critique and original formulation of disparate appropriations of working-class cultural "resources," see Brown 1987. See also Levinson and Holland 1996, 9–12; Holland and Eisenhart 1990, 44–47. Anthropologists and sociologists outside of education have commented on the value and importance of Willis's study, often using it to exemplify a method of critical analysis (Marcus 1986; Giddens 1984).

15 Much of the recent work, especially by political scientists, has examined how the State influences the form that social movements may take, just as it shows how the State is in turn continually shaped and reshaped by these movements (see, for instance, most of the essays in Foweraker and Craig 1990; Montalvo 1985; Eckstein 1988; Rubin 1996). In other words, the work focuses on specific social movements that emerge in political struggle and analyzes how the State apparatus takes shape in response to them. The question of broader cultural forms, of identity and consciousness, often recedes into the background.

16 For instance, *telenovelas,* Latin American soap operas that draw on so-called popular forms, but are produced by a dominant, urban culture industry, may be "capable of transmitting popular memories" or even providing models of family-based resistance to the commodification of everyday life (Rowe and Schelling 1991, 232–33). Felicitously, scholars working in Latin America have been particularly insightful in analyzing the complexity of popular culture as a field of cultural struggle (García Canclini 1990; Rowe and Schelling 1991; Monsiváis 1981). Pierre Bourdieu's (1984) work on class "distinction," though not usually placed in the cultural studies rubric, advances a similarly relational notion of popular culture.

17 Ulf Hannerz (1996, 69) offers a useful typology of "organizational frames" for the production and circulation of culture. Each frame entails different tendencies in the way that meanings and meaningful forms are produced and circulated in social relationships. The "form of life" frame denotes the characteristic kind of circulation of meaning in households, workplaces, and neighborhoods; such

meanings are often routinized because they result from practical adaptations to enduring circumstances. The "State" frame defines a "flow of meaning" between the State apparatus and the people defined as subjects/citizens. Finally, the "market" frame represents meanings as commodities that pass from buyer to seller.

18 In anthropology, the impact of cultural studies has occasioned the formulation of theories of global and transnational cultural processes. Arjun Appadurai (1990) and his colleagues have elaborated the term "public culture" to describe the emerging formation of transnational circuits of meaning and representation. Their work, along with others (see, for instance, Hannerz 1996; Gupta and Ferguson 1997b), has extended the discussion of popular culture beyond the national domain in which it had been frequently situated (Foster 1991; Alonso 1994).

19 It is also partly due to the fact that secondary education is less well developed and attended than in the compulsory systems of the United States and Europe (Boli and Ramírez 1992; Martin 1994b, 131–32).

20 Renato Rosaldo (1989), Ulf Hannerz (1996), and Eric Wolf (1982) describe why a bounded view of culture is no longer tenable. Margaret Mead's *Coming of Age in Samoa* (1928) is, of course, a classic in this regard. For other examples, see Wax, Diamond, and Gearing 1971; Levinson 2000. For Mexico, see Modiano 1970; Hunt and Hunt 1972.

21 See Bledsoe 1992; Keyes 1991; Reed-Danahay 1996; Rival 1996; Watson-Gegeo and Gegeo 1992.

22 See Biraimah [1982] 1989; Scudder and Colson 1980; Masemann 1974.

23 Juan Carlos Tedesco (1987), Germán Rama (1984), Juan Prawda (1987), Carlos Ornelas (1995), and Olac Molinar Fuentes (1982, 1983) have all called attention to the continuing inequalities in the distribution and accessibility of high-quality education to marginalized groups in Latin America. For these Latin American authors, the question of educational access is central to a more thoroughgoing democratization of political structures. Latin American States have typically built more schools in recent decades without accompanying this expansion with scholarships and other proactive incentives designed to equalize educational offerings. Thus, the gap between the well educated and barely educated has remained severe.

24 See Lesko 1988; Corsaro 1997. Compare Maurice Bloch's (1992) "connectionist" conception of culture and Paul Willis's (1990) concept of "grounded aesthetics," which both highlight the sensuous components of knowing and acting.

25 In this sense, I differ slightly from Pierre Bourdieu, who roundly criticizes the phenomenological approach. Like Jürgen Habermas (1984), who indexes the agency/structure problematic with the terms *lifeworld* and *system,* I believe it possible to analyze the phenomenological dimension of experience as structured both by immediate, context-dependent goals and interests as well as more experience-distant, systemic processes. In Bourdieu's view, the phenomenological experience of the habitus is always already structured by the "objective structures" of social

"fields" (1984). Yet there is little scrutiny of the specifically institutional level as a context for structured "interests" and awareness.

26 Until recently, structure had been conceived of more in terms of limits and constraints on social and individual action. Anthony Giddens's (1979, 1984) genius was to reconceive of structure as simultaneously enabling and constraining, both providing resources and rules for behavior.

27 Bauman (1973, 57) phrases this duality in terms of "creativity" and "dependence," and sketches a concept of praxis to overcome the social scientific reification of the duality with terms like "culture" and "structure."

28 He also used metaphors of game and dance prominently; see Goudsblom and Mennell 1998.

29 Among the most prominent practice theorists have been the sociologists Pierre Bourdieu (1977, 1990, Bourdieu and Wacquant 1992), Anthony Giddens (1979, 1984), and Robert W. Connell (1983, 1987). Bourdieu is the scholar who has most self-consciously undertaken to construct a general "theory of practices," and who uses the term most frequently. Similar and perhaps equally important theorists of practice for me would include Philip Abrams (1982), Norbert Elias (1978, 1991; Goudsblom and Mennell 1998), Marshall Sahlins (1981, 1985), Mary Douglas (1975), Sherry Ortner (1984, 1996), Stuart Hall (1990; Grossberg 1996, 155–57), Michel de Certeau (1984), and Zygmunt Bauman (1973, 1992). Bourdieu, Connell, and Ortner provide the most helpful and explicit discussions of the methodological options entailed by practice theory.

Perhaps more controversially still, I read the Gramsci (1971) of the *Prison Notebooks* as a kind of practice theorist for his sustained attempts to mediate marxian economism and philosophical idealism with a "pragmatological" notion of praxis. As Walter Adamson (1980, 141) puts it, "Gramsci's starting point was the concrete subject situated in a particular historical environment. This formulation implied a complex interaction of 'subjective' and 'objective' historical factors."

30 For developmental psychology and cognitive anthropology, see Rogoff 1990; Chaiklin and Lave 1996; Lave 1988; Lave and Wenger 1991; Shore 1996; Bruner 1996; Serpell 1993; Holland et al. 1998; Cole 1996. For the sociology of childhood and adolescence, see Corsaro 1992, 1997; James and Prout 1990; Griffin 1993. For studies in communications and popular culture, see Kellner 1995; Hall 1981; McRobbie 1992; Slack 1996. For the study of literacy and language, see Hanks 1996 (on language as communicative practice); Woolard 1985; Hill 1991; Street 1993. On social history, see Chartier 1997; Ginzburg 1980.

31 Social historians seem to have been the most successful in this regard. See Chartier 1997; Braudel 1973.

32 See Richard Rorty's (1979) pragmatic "edifying" philosophy, which opts for a hermeneutic "conversation" over the vain attempt to "mirror" an objective world.

33 Jorge Larrain (1994, 14) criticizes Thompson for his failure to highlight the nega-

tive features of ideology, but I side with Thompson's implicit suggestion that power and domination are endemic to human society. For the best critical introduction to the history and definition of ideology, see Eagleton 1991. As Terry Eagleton (1991, 58, 156–57) and others point out, Bourdieu's concept of "misrecognition" is remarkably similar to marxist views of ideology. Bourdieu contends that symbolic violence functions to create a seemingly "natural" world—"*doxa*"—in which the person "misrecognizes" the interests governing actions and relations.

34 It bears mentioning in this regard that Bourdieu's notions of "symbolic power" and "symbolic violence," developed through his analysis of the French educational system, display remarkable similarity to these recent extensions of Gramsci's concept of hegemony (Swartz 1997, 82, 89).

35 Sociologists and historians (see above) had been developing similarly nuanced usages of the culture concept. Tending to deal more with complex, stratified societies and intergroup relations, such scholars began referring to class and organizational cultures—working-class culture, shop-floor culture, corporate culture, and the like. The explosive growth of a field like cultural studies testifies to the enduring power of a sufficiently reworked culture concept.

WORKS CITED

Abraham, John. 1995. *Divide and school: Gender and class dynamics in comprehensive education.* London: Falmer Press.

Abrams, Philip. 1982. *Historical sociology.* London: Routledge.

———. 1988. Notes on the difficulty of studying the state. *Journal of Historical Sociology* 1, no. 1:58–89.

Abu-Lughod, Lila. 1991. Writing against culture. In *Recapturing anthropology: Working in the present,* edited by Richard G. Fox. Santa Fe, N. Mex.: School of American Research.

———. 1993. *Writing women's worlds: Bedouin stories.* Berkeley: University of California Press.

Adamson, Walter L. 1980. *Hegemony and revolution: A study of Antonio Gramsci's political and cultural theory.* Berkeley: University of California Press.

Agger, Ben. 1998. *Critical social theories: An introduction.* Boulder, Colo.: Westview Press.

Aggleton, Peter J. 1987. *Rebels without a cause.* London: Falmer Press.

Aguilar Camín, Héctor. 1993. La invención de México. *Nexos* 187 (July): 49–61.

Aguilar Hernández, Citlali. 1991. El trabajo de los maestros: Una construcción cotidiana. Master's thesis, Departamento de Investigaciones Educativas, Mexico City.

Aguilar Hernández, Citlali, and Etelvina Sandoval. 1995. Ser mujer–ser maestra: Autovaloración profesional y participación sindical. In *Textos y pre-textos:*

Once estudios sobre la mujer. Mexico City: El Colegio de México.

Aguirre Beltrán, Gonzalo. 1967. *Regiones de refugio.* Mexico: Instituto Indígena Interamericano.

Alonso, Ana María. 1988. The effects of truth: Re-presentations of the past and the imagining of community. *Journal of Historical Sociology* 1, no. 1:33–57.

———. 1992a. Gender, power, and historical memory: Discourses of Serrano resistance. In *Feminists theorize the political,* edited by Judith Butler and Joan Scott. New York: Routledge.

———. 1992b. Work and gusto: Gender and re-creation in a north Mexican pueblo. In *Worker's expressions: Beyond accommodation and resistance,* edited by Joseph Calagione, Doris Francis, and Daniel Nugent. Albany: State University of New York Press.

———. 1994. The politics of space, time, and substance: State formation, nationalism, and ethnicity. *Annual Reviews in Anthropology* 23:379–405.

———. 1995. *Thread of blood: Colonialism, revolution, and gender on Mexico's northern frontier.* Tucson: University of Arizona Press.

Althusser, Louis. 1971. Ideology and ideological state apparatuses. In *Lenin and philosophy and other essays.* New York: Monthly Review Press.

Anderson, Benedict. 1983. *Imagined communities: Reflections on the origins of nationalism.* London: Verso.

Anderson, Gary. 1989. Critical ethnography in education: Origins, current sta-

tus, and new directions. *Review of Educational Research* 59:249–70.

Anyon, Jean. 1981. Social class and school
knowledge. *Curriculum Inquiry* 11, no.
1:3–42.

Appadurai, Arjun. 1990. Disjuncture and
difference in the global cultural economy. *Public Culture* 2, no. 2:1–24.

———. 1991. Global ethnoscapes: Notes and
queries for a transnational anthropol-
ogy. In *Recapturing anthropology:
Working in the present,* edited by
Richard G. Fox. Santa Fe, N. Mex.:
School of American Research.

Apple, Michael W. 1979. *Ideology and curriculum.* London: Routledge and
Kegan Paul.

———, ed. 1982. *Cultural and economic reproduction in American education: Essays in class, ideology, and the state.*
Boston: Routledge and Kegan Paul.

Apple, Michael W., and Lois Weis, eds.
1983. *Ideology and practice in schooling.*
Philadelphia, Pa.: Temple University
Press.

Ariès, Philippe. 1962. *Centuries of childhood: A social history of family life.* New
York: Vintage Books.

Arizpe, Lourdes. 1978. *Migración, et-
nicismo, y cambio económico.* Mexico
City: El Colegio de México.

———. 1989. *Cultura y desarrollo: Una etnografía de las creencias de una comunidad mexicana.* Mexico City:
Porrua/El Colegio de México.

Arizpe, Lourdes, and Ludka de Gortari,
eds. 1990. *Repensar la nación: Fron-
teras, etnias y soberanía.* Tlalpan, Mexico: Centro de Investigaciones y
Estudios Superiores en Antropología
Social–Cuadernos de la Casa Chata.

Arnot, Madeline. 1982. Male hegemony,

social class, and women's education.
Journal of Education 164, no. 1:64–89.

Aronson, Elliot. 2000. *Nobody left to hate:
Teaching compassion after Columbine.*
New York: W. H. Freeman.

Arrom, Silvia Marina. 1985. *The women of
Mexico City, 1790–1857.* Stanford,
Calif.: Stanford University Press.

Bakhtin, Mikhail. 1981. Discourse in the
novel. In *The dialogic imagination:
Four essays by M. M. Bakhtin,* edited by
Michael Holquist. Austin: University
of Texas Press.

Ball, Stephen J. 1981. *Beachside comprehensive.* Cambridge, U.K.: Cambridge University Press.

Barkin, David. 1975. Education and class
structure: The dynamics of social control in Mexico. *Politics and Society* 5,
no. 2:185–99.

Bartra, Roger. 1987. *La jaula de la melan-
colía: Identidad y metamórfosis del
mexicano.* Mexico City: Grijalbo.

———. 1993. La crisis del nacionalismo.
In *Oficio mexicano.* Mexico City:
Grijalbo.

Basch, Linda, Nina Glick-Schiller, and
Cristina Szanton-Blanc. 1994. *Nations
unbound: Transnational projects, postcolonial predicaments, and deterrito-
rialized nation-states.* Langhorne, Pa.:
Gordon and Breach Publishers.

Baudelot, Christian, and Roger Establet.
1975. *La escuela capitalista.* Madrid:
Siglo Veintiuno Editores.

Bauman, Zygmunt. 1973. *Culture as
praxis.* London: Routledge and Kegan
Paul.

———. 1992. *Intimations of postmodernity.*
London: Routledge.

Becker, Marjorie. 1987. Black and white
and color: Cardenismo and the search

for a campesino ideology. *Comparative Studies in Society and History* 29, no. 3:453–65.

———. 1989. Lázaro Cárdenas and the counter-revolution: The struggle over culture in Michoacán, 1934–1940. Ph.D. diss., Yale University.

———. 1995. *Setting the virgin on fire: Lázaro Cárdenas, Michoacán peasants, and the redemption of the Mexican revolution.* Berkeley: University of California Press.

Beezley, William H., et al., eds. 1994. *Rituals of rule, rituals of resistance: Public celebrations and popular culture in Mexico.* Wilmington, Del.: Scholarly Resources.

Behar, Ruth. 1990. Rage and redemption: Reading the life story of a Mexican market woman. *Feminist Studies* 16, no. 2:223–58.

Benería, Lourdes, and Martha Roldán. 1987. *The crossroads of class and gender: Industrial homework, subcontracting, and household dynamics in Mexico City.* Chicago: University of Chicago Press.

Berg, Charles Ramírez. 1992. *Cinema of solitude: A critical study of Mexican film, 1967–1983.* Austin: University of Texas Press.

Biraimah, Karen. [1982] 1989. Different knowledge for different folks: Knowledge distribution in a Togolese secondary school. In *Comparative education,* edited by Phillip Altbach, Robert F. Arnove, and Gail P. Kelly. New York: Advent Books.

Bledsoe, Caroline. 1992. The cultural transformation of Western education in Sierra Leone. *Africa* 62, no. 2:182–202.

Bloch, Maurice. 1992. What goes without saying: The conceptualization of Zafimaniry society. In *Conceptualizing society,* edited by Adam Kuper. London: Routledge.

Boli, John, and Francisco O. Ramírez. 1992. Compulsory schooling in the Western cultural context. In *Emergent issues in education: Comparative perspectives,* edited by Robert F. Arnove, Phillip Altbach, and Gail P. Kelly. Albany: State University of New York Press.

Borofsky, Robert, ed. 1994. *Assessing cultural anthropology.* New York: McGraw-Hill.

Bourdieu, Pierre. 1977. *Outline of a theory of practice.* Cambridge, U.K.: Cambridge University Press.

———. 1984. *Distinction: A social critique of the judgment of taste.* Cambridge, Mass.: Harvard University Press.

———. 1989. *Language and symbolic power.* Stanford, Calif.: Stanford University Press.

———. 1990. *The logic of practice.* Stanford, Calif.: Stanford University Press.

Bourdieu, Pierre, and Jean-Claude Passeron. 1977. *Reproduction: In education, society, culture.* Beverly Hills, Calif.: Sage Publications.

Bourdieu, Pierre, and Loïc Wacquant. 1992. The purpose of reflexive sociology (the Chicago workshop). In *An invitation to reflexive sociology,* edited by Pierre Bourdieu and Loïc Wacquant. Cambridge, U.K.: Polity Press.

Bowles, Samuel, and Herbert Gintis. 1976. *Schooling in capitalist America: Educational reform and the contradictions of economic life.* New York: Basic Books.

Brachet-Márquez, Viviane. 1994. *The dynamics of domination: State, class, and*

393   Works Cited

social reform in Mexico, 1910–1990. Pittsburgh, Pa.: University of Pittsburgh Press.

Brake, Michael. 1980. *The sociology of youth culture and youth subcultures: Sex and drugs and rock 'n' roll.* London: Routledge and Kegan Paul.

Brandes, Stanley. 1988. *Power and persuasion: Fiestas and social control in rural Mexico.* Philadelphia: University of Pennsylvania Press.

Brantlinger, Patrick. 1990. *Crusoe's footprints: Cultural studies in Britain and America.* New York: Routledge.

Braudel, Fernand. 1973. *The Mediterranean and the Mediterranean world in the age of Philip II.* New York: Harper and Row.

Brown, Philip. 1987. *Schooling ordinary kids.* London: Routledge and Kegan Paul.

Bruner, Jerome. 1996. *The culture of education.* Cambridge, Mass.: Harvard University Press.

Brunsdon, Charlotte. 1996. A thief in the night: Stories of feminism in the 1970s at cccs. In *Stuart Hall: Critical dialogues in cultural studies,* edited by David Morley and Kuan-Hsing Chen. London: Routledge.

Butler, Judith, and Joan W. Scott, eds. 1992. *Feminists theorize the political.* New York: Routledge.

Calhoun, Craig. 1993. Habitus, field, and capital: The question of historical specificity. In *Bourdieu: Critical perspectives,* edited by Craig Calhoun, Edward LiPuma, and Moishe Poistone. Chicago: University of Chicago Press.

——. 1995. *Critical social theory: Culture, history, and the challenge of difference.* Oxford, U.K.: Blackwell Publishers.

Calvo Pontón, Beatriz. 1989. *Educación normal y control político.* Mexico City: Ediciones De La Casa Chata.

Camp, Roderic Ai. 1993. *Politics in Mexico.* Oxford: Oxford University Press.

Campos de García, Margarita. 1973. *Escuela y comunidad en Tepetlaoxtoc.* Mexico City: Sepsetentas.

Canaan, Joyce. 1987. A comparative analysis of American suburban middle class, middle school, and high school teenage cliques. In *Interpretive ethnography of education: At home and abroad,* edited by George and Louise Spindler. Hillsdale, N.J.: Lawrence Erlbaum.

——. 1990. Passing notes and telling jokes: Gendered strategies among American middle school teenagers. In *Uncertain terms: Negotiating gender in American culture,* edited by Faye Ginsburg and Anna Lowenhaupt Tsing. Boston: Beacon Press.

Carlson, Dennis. 1987. Teachers as political actors: From reproductive theory to the crisis of schooling. *Harvard Educational Review* 57:283–307.

Carrasco, Pedro. 1976. *El catolicismo popular de los tarascos.* Mexico City: Sepsetentas.

Carspecken, Phil Francis. 1995. *Critical ethnography in educational research: A theoretical and practical guide.* New York: Routledge.

Certeau, Michel de. 1984. *The practice of everyday life.* Berkeley: University of California Press.

Chaiklin, Seth, and Jean Lave, eds. 1996. *Understanding practice: Perspectives on activity and context.* Cambridge, U.K.: Cambridge University Press.

Chaney, Elsa. 1979. *Supermadre: Women*

in politics in Latin America. Austin: University of Texas Press.

Chant, Sylvia. 1991. *Women and survival in Mexican cities: Perspectives on gender, labour, and low-income households.* Manchester, U.K.: Manchester University Press.

Chartier, Roger. 1997. *On the edge of the cliff: History, language, and practices.* Translated by Lydia G. Cochrane. Baltimore, Md.: Johns Hopkins University Press.

Chávez, Leo R. 1992. *Shadowed lives: Undocumented immigrants in American society.* New York: Harcourt Brace Jovanovich.

Christian-Smith, Linda. 1997. Foreword to *Just girls: Hidden literacies and life in junior high,* by Margaret Finders. New York: Teachers College Press.

Clifford, James. 1988. *The predicament of culture: Twentieth-century ethnography, literature, and art.* Cambridge, Mass.: Harvard University Press.

Clough, Patricia T. 1992. *The end(s) of ethnography.* Newbury Park, Calif.: Sage Publications.

Cohen, Anthony P. 1994. *Self consciousness: An alternative anthropology of identity.* New York: Routledge.

Cole, Michael. 1996. *Cultural psychology: A once and future discipline.* Cambridge, Mass.: Belknap Press of Harvard University Press.

Coleman, James. 1961. *The adolescent society: The social life of the teenager and its impact on education.* New York: Free Press.

Comaroff, Jean. 1985. *Body of power, spirit of resistance: The culture and history of a South African people.* Chicago: University of Chicago Press.

Connell, Robert W. 1983. *Which way is up? Essays on class, sex, and culture.* London: Allen and Unwin.

———. 1987. *Gender and power: Society, the person, and sexual politics.* Stanford, Calif.: Stanford University Press.

———. 1995. *Masculinities.* Berkeley: University of California Press.

Connell, Robert W., D. J. Ashenden, S. Kessler, and G. W. Dowsett. 1982. *Making the difference: Schools, families, and social division.* Sydney: George Allen and Unwin.

Cook, María Lorena. 1996. *Organizing dissent: Unions, the state, and the democratic teachers' movement in Mexico.* University Park: Penn State Press.

Córdova, Arnoldo. 1974. *La ideología de la revolución mexicana.* Mexico City: Era.

———. 1984. El populismo en la educación nacional, 1920–1940. In *Ideología educativa de la revolución mexicana,* edited by Graciela Lechuga. Mexico City: Universidad Autónoma Metropolitana.

Corona Vázquez, Rodolfo. 1988. Migración y retorno y migraciones sucesivas. In *Migración en el occidente de México,* edited by Gustavo López Castro and Sergio Pardo Galván. Zamora, Mexico: El Colegio de Michoacán.

Corrigan, Philip, and Derek Sayer. 1985. *The great arch: English state formation as cultural revolution.* Oxford: Blackwell Publishers.

Corsaro, William A. 1992. Interpretive reproduction in children's peer cultures. *Social Psychology Quarterly* 55, no. 2:160–77.

———. 1997. *The sociology of childhood.* Thousand Oaks, Calif.: Pine Forge Press.

Cortina, Regina. 1989. Women as leaders

in Mexican education. *Comparative Education Review* 33, no. 3:357–76.

Cusick, Philip. 1973. *Inside high school: The student's world.* New York: Holt, Rinehart and Winston.

Danesi, Marcel. 1994. *Cool: The signs and meanings of adolescence.* Toronto, Canada: University of Toronto Press.

Davidson, Anne Locke. 1996. *Making and molding identity in schools: Student narratives on race, gender, and academic engagement.* Albany: State University of New York Press.

de Barbieri, Teresita, and Orlandina de Oliveira. 1986. Nuevos sujetos sociales: La presencia política de las mujeres en América Latina. *Nueva Antropología* 8, no. 30:5–29.

de Ibarrola, María, and Elsie Rockwell, eds. 1985. *Educación y clases populares en América Latina.* Mexico City: Departamento de Investigaciones Educativas.

Delamont, Sara. 1984. Debs, dollies, swots, and weeds: Classroom styles at St. Lukes. In *British public schools: Policy and practice,* edited by Geoffrey Walford. London: Falmer Press.

Delgado, Gabriela. 1994. La importancia de la etnografía en los estudios de género. In *La etnografía en educación: Panorama, prácticas, y problemas,* edited by Mario Rueda, Gabriela Delgado, and Zardel Jacobo. Mexico City: Universidad Nacional Autónoma de México.

———. 1995. Influencias del género en las relaciones dentro del aula. In *Estudios de género y feminismo,* edited by Patricia Bedolla. Vol. 2. Mexico City: Universidad Nacional Autónoma de México.

Demerath, Peter. 1999. The cultural production of educational utility in Pere village, Papua New Guinea. *Comparative Education Review* 43, no. 2:162–92.

Díaz Pontones, Mónica, 1998. Estrategias de enseñanza en la escuela secundaria: Un estudio etnográfico. In *Nuevos paradigmas, compromisos renovados: Experiencias de investigación cualitativa en educación,* edited by Beatriz Calvo Pontón, Gabriela Delgado, and Mario Rueda. Ciudad Juárez, Chihuahua: Universidad Autónoma de Ciudad Juárez.

Dinerman, Ina R. 1974. *Los tarascos: Campesinos y artesanos de Michoacán.* Mexico City: Sepsetentas.

Douglas, Mary. 1975. *Implicit meanings.* London: Routledge.

Douglas, Mary, and Baron Isherwood. [1979] 1996. *The world of goods: Towards an anthropology of consumption.* London: Routledge.

Dumont, Louis. 1977. *From Mandeville to Marx.* Chicago: University of Chicago Press.

———. 1980. *Homo hierarchicus.* Chicago: University of Chicago Press.

Eagleton, Terry. 1991. *Ideology: An introduction.* London: Verso.

Eckert, Penelope. 1989. *Jocks and burnouts: Social categories and identity in the high school.* New York: Teachers College Press.

Eckstein, Susan. 1988. *The poverty of revolution: The state and the urban poor in Mexico.* Princeton, N.J.: Princeton University Press.

Eder, Donna. 1995. *School talk: Gender and adolescent culture.* New Brunswick, N.J.: Rutgers University Press.

Edwards, Verónica. 1985. *Los sujetos y la*

construcción social del conocimiento escolar en primaria: Un estudio etnográfico. Master's thesis, Departamento de Investigaciones Educativas, Mexico City.

———. 1995. Las formas del conocimiento en el aula. In *La escuela cotidiana,* edited by Elsie Rockwell. Mexico City: Fondo de Cultura Económica.

Eisenhart, Margaret, and Elizabeth Graue. 1993. Constructing cultural differences and educational achievement in schools. In *Minority education: Anthropological perspectives,* edited by Evelyn Jacob and Cathie Jordan. Norwood, N.J.: Ablex.

Eley, Geoff, and Ronald Grigor Suny, eds. 1996. *Becoming national: A reader.* New York: Oxford University Press.

Elias, Norbert. 1978. *The history of manners.* Vol. 1 of *The civilizing process.* New York: Urizen Books.

———. 1991. *The society of individuals.* Oxford: Basil Blackwell.

Ellis, Carolyn, and Michael G. Flaherty, eds. 1992. *Investigating subjectivity: Research on lived experience.* Newbury Park, Calif.: Sage Publications.

Epstein, Erwin. 1985. National consciousness and education in Mexico. In *Education in Latin America,* edited by Colin Brock and Hugh Lawlor. London: Croom Helm.

Erikson, Erik H. 1968. *Identity: Youth and crisis.* New York: W. W. Norton and Company.

Escobar, Arturo, and Sonia E. Alvarez, eds. 1992. *The making of social movements in Latin America: Identity, strategy, and democracy.* Boulder, Colo.: Westview Press.

Everhart, Robert. 1983. *Reading, writing,* and resistance: Adolescence and labor in a junior high school. London: Routledge and Kegan Paul.

Ezpeleta, Justa. 1989. *Escuelas y maestros: Condiciones del trabajo docente en Argentina.* Santiago, Chile: United Nations Education, Scientific, and Cultural Organization.

Ezpeleta, Justa, and Elsie Rockwell. 1985. Escuela y clases subalternas. In *Educación y clases populares en América Latina,* edited by María de Ibarrola and Elsie Rockwell. Mexico City: Departamento de Investigaciones Educativas.

Fabian, Johannes. 1998. *Moments of freedom: Anthropology and popular culture.* Charlottesville: University of Virginia Press.

Farrell, Joseph P. 1992. Conceptualizing education and the drive for social equality. In *Emergent issues in education: Comparative perspectives,* edited by Robert F. Arnove, Phillip Altbach, and Gail P. Kelly. Albany: State University of New York Press.

Fernández, Celestino. 1988. Migración hacia los Estados Unidos: Caso Santa Inés, Michoacán. In *Migración en el occidente de México,* edited by Gustavo López Castro and Sergio Pardo Galván. Zamora, Mexico: Colegio de Michoacán.

Fernández-Kelly, María Patricia. 1983. *For we are sold, I and my people: Women and industry on Mexico's frontier.* Albany: State University of New York Press.

Finders, Margaret. 1997. *Just girls: Hidden literacies and life in junior high.* New York: Teachers College Press.

Fine, Gary Alan. 1987. *With the boys: Little league baseball and preadolescent cul-*

ture. Chicago: University of Chicago Press.

Fine, Michelle. 1991. *Framing dropouts: Notes on the politics of an urban public high school.* Albany: State University of New York Press.

Fischer, Janice. 1975. *The social life of the upper sector girl in a Mexican town.* Greeley: University of Northern Colorado.

Fisherkeller, JoEllen. 1997. Everyday learning about identities among young adolescents in television culture. *Anthropology and Education Quarterly* 28, no. 4:467–92.

Foley, Douglas E. 1977. Anthropological studies of schooling in developing countries: Some recent findings and trends. *Comparative Education Review* (June/October): 311–28.

———. 1990. *Learning capitalist culture: Deep in the heart of Tejas.* Philadelphia: University of Pennsylvania Press.

———. 1998. On writing reflexive realist narratives. In *Being reflexive in critical educational and social research,* edited by Geoffrey Shacklock and John Smyth. London: Falmer Press.

Fordham, Signithia. 1988. Racelessness as a factor in black students' school success: Pragmatic strategy or Pyrrhic victory. *Harvard Educational Review* 58, no. 1:54–84.

———. 1991. Peer-proofing academic competition among black adolescents: "Acting white" black American style. In *Empowerment through multicultural education,* edited by Christine E. Sleeter. Albany: State University of New York Press.

———. 1993. "Those loud black girls": (Black) women, silence, and gender

"passing" in the academy. *Anthropology and Education Quarterly* 24, no. 1:3–32.

———. 1996. *Blacked out: Dilemmas of race, identity, and success at Capital High.* Chicago: University of Chicago Press.

Foster, George. 1967. *Tzintzuntzan: Mexican peasants in a changing world.* Boston: Little, Brown and Company.

Foster, Robert. 1991. Making national cultures in the global ecumene. *Annual Reviews in Anthropology* 20:235–60.

Foucault, Michel. 1977. *Language, counter-memory, practice,* edited by Donald F. Bouchard. Ithaca, N.Y.: Cornell University Press.

Foweraker, Joe. 1993. *Popular mobilization in Mexico: The teachers' movement, 1977–1987.* Cambridge, U.K.: Cambridge University Press.

Foweraker, Joe, and Ann L. Craig, eds. 1990. *Popular movements and political change in Mexico.* Boulder, Colo.: Lynne Rienner.

Fowler-Salamini, Heather, and Mary Kay Vaughan, eds. 1994. *Women of the Mexican countryside, 1856–1990.* Tucson: University of Arizona Press.

Franco, Jean. 1988. Beyond ethnocentrism: Gender, power, and the third-world intelligentsia. In *Marxism and the interpretation of culture,* edited by Lawrence Grossberg and Cary Nelson. Champaign-Urbana: University of Illinois Press.

Friedlander, Judith. 1975. *Being Indian in Hueyapan: A study of forced identity in contemporary Mexico.* New York: St. Martin's Press.

Friedrich, Paul. 1970. *Agrarian revolt in a Mexican village.* Chicago: University of Chicago Press.

———. 1986. *The princes of Naranja: An essay in anthrohistorical method.* Austin: University of Texas Press.

Frye, David. 1996. *Indians into Mexicans: History and identity in a Mexican town.* Austin: University of Texas Press.

Fuentes, Olac Molinar. 1978. Enseñanza media básica en México, 1970–1976. *Cuadernos Políticos* 15:90–104.

———. 1982. Educación pública y sociedad. In *México hoy,* edited by Pablo González Casanova and Enrique Florescano. Mexico City: Siglo Vientiuno.

———. 1983. *Educación y política en México.* Mexico City: Nueva Imagen.

———. 1996. La educación secundaria: Cambios y perspectivas [versión estenográfica]. In *La educación secundaria: Cambios y perspectivas,* edited by Instituto Estatal de Educación Pública de Oaxaca. Oaxaca, Mexico: Instituto de Educación Pública de Oaxaca.

Gamoran, Adam, and Martha Berends. 1987. The effects of stratification in secondary schools: Synthesis of survey and ethnographic research. *Review of Educational Research* 57:415–35.

García, Manuel. 1992. La identidad, en su hora cero. *Unomásuno* 745:1–3.

García Canclini, Nestor. 1981. *Las culturas populares en el capitalismo.* Mexico City: Nueva Imagen.

———. 1990. *Culturas híbridas: Estrategias para entrar y salir de la modernidad.* Mexico City: Grijalbo.

García Salord, Susana, and Liliana Vanella. 1992. *Normas y valores en el salón de clases.* Mexico City: Siglo Veintiuno.

Gaskell, Jane. 1992. *Gender matters from school to work.* Philadelphia, Pa.: Open University Press.

Geertz, Clifford. 1973. *The interpretation of cultures: Selected essays.* New York: Basic Books.

Giddens, Anthony. 1979. *Central problems in social theory: Action, structure, and contradiction in social analysis.* Berkeley: University of California Press.

———. 1984. *The constitution of society.* Berkeley: University of California Press.

———. 1991. *Modernity and self-identity: Self and society in the late modern age.* Stanford, Calif.: Stanford University Press.

Gillborn, Paul. 1990. *Race, ethnicity, and education.* London: Unwin Hyman.

Gilly, Adolfo. 1971. *La revolución interrumpida.* Mexico City: El Caballito.

Gilroy, Paul. 1987. *"Ain't no black in the Union Jack": The cultural politics of race and nation.* London: Hutchinson.

Ginzburg, Carlo. 1980. *The cheese and the worms: The cosmos of a sixteenth-century miller.* Baltimore, Md.: Johns Hopkins University Press.

Giroux, Henry. 1983. *Theory and resistance in education: A pedagogy for the opposition.* South Hadley, Mass.: Bergin and Garvey.

Gitlin, Andrew, ed. 1994. *Power and method: Political activism and educational research.* New York: Routledge.

Gledhill, John. 1991. *Casi nada: A study of agrarian reform in the homeland of cardenismo.* Austin: University of Texas Press.

———. 1995. *Neoliberalism, transnationalization, and rural poverty: A case study of Michoacán, Mexico.* Boulder, Colo.: Westview Press.

Goffman, Erving. 1961. *Asylums: Essays on the social situation of mental patients and other inmates.* Garden City, N.Y.: Doubleday Anchor.

Gómez, Nashiki A. 1997. Historia de la educación: La creación de la escuela secundaria. *Educación 2001* 22:47–49.

Goudsblom, Johan, and Stephen Mennell, eds. 1998. *The Norbert Elias reader.* Oxford, U.K.: Blackwell Publishers.

Gramsci, Antonio. 1971. *Selections from the prison notebooks.* Edited by Quentin Hoare and Geoffrey Nowell Smith. New York: International Publishers.

Greenberg, James B. 1989. *Blood ties: Life and violence in rural Mexico.* Tucson: University of Arizona Press.

Grewal, Inderpal, and Caren Kaplan, eds. 1994. *Scattered hegemonies: Postmodernity and transnational feminist practices.* Minneapolis: University of Minnesota Press.

Griffin, Christine. 1993. *Representations of youth: The study of youth and adolescence in Britain and America.* Cambridge, U.K.: Polity Press.

Grossberg, Lawrence. 1996. History, politics, and postmodernism: Stuart Hall and cultural studies. In *Stuart Hall: Critical dialogues in cultural studies,* edited by David Morley and Kuan-Hsing Chen. London: Routledge.

Grossberg, Lawrence, Cary Nelson, and Paula Treichler, eds. 1992. *Cultural studies.* New York: Routledge.

Guevara Niebla, Gilberto, and Néstor García Canclini, eds. 1992. *La educación y la cultura ante el tratado de libre comercio.* Mexico City: Nueva Imagen.

Gupta, Akhil, and James Ferguson. 1992. Beyond "culture": Space, identity, and the politics of difference. *Cultural Anthropology* 7, no. 1:6–23.

——, eds. 1997. *Culture, power, place: Explorations in critical anthropology.* Durham, N.C.: Duke University Press.

Gutmann, Matthew C. 1996. *The meanings of macho: Being a man in Mexico City.* Berkeley: University of California Press.

Habermas, Jürgen. 1984. *The theory of communicative action: Volume 1, Reason and the rationalization of society.* Boston: Beacon Press.

Hale, Charles A. 1972. *El liberalismo mexicano en la época de Mora, 1821–1853.* Mexico City: Siglo XXI (Veintiuno).

——. 1989. *The transformation of liberalism in late-nineteenth-century Mexico.* Princeton, N.J.: Princeton University Press.

Hall, Stuart. 1981. Notes on deconstructing the "popular." In *People's history and socialist theory,* edited by Ralph Samuel. London: Routledge.

——. 1986. Gramsci's relevance for the study of race and ethnicity. *Journal of Communication Inquiry* 10, no. 2:5–27.

——. 1988. The toad in the garden: Thatcherism among the theorists. In *Marxism and the interpretation of culture,* edited by Cary Nelson and Lawrence Grossberg. Urbana: University of Illinois Press.

——. 1990. Cultural identity and diaspora. In *Identity, community, culture, difference,* edited by John Rutherford. London: Lawrence and Wishart.

——. 1991. Old and new identities, old and new ethnicities. In *Culture, globalization, and the world-system: Contemporary conditions for the representation of identity,* edited by Anthony D. King. Binghamton: State University of New York Press.

——. 1996. Introduction: Who needs "identity"? In *Questions of cultural* identity, edited by Stuart Hall and Paul du Gay. London: Sage Publications.

Hall, Stuart, and Tony Jefferson, eds. [1975] 1993. *Resistance through rituals: Youth subcultures in post-war Britain.* London: Routledge.

Hamilton, Nora. 1982. *The limits of state autonomy: Post-revolutionary Mexico.* Princeton, N.J.: Princeton University Press.

Hanks, William F. 1996. *Language and communicative practice: Critical essays in anthropology.* Boulder, Colo.: Westview Press.

Hannerz, Ulf. 1992. *Cultural complexity: Studies in the social organization of meaning.* New York: Columbia University Press.

———. 1996. *Transnational connections: Culture, people, places.* London: Routledge.

Haraway, Donna J. 1991. *Simians, cyborgs, and women: The reinvention of nature.* New York: Routledge.

Harding, Sandra. 1992. After the neutrality ideal: Science, politics, and "strong objectivity." *Social Research* 59, no. 3:567–87.

Hargreaves, David. 1967. *Social relations in a secondary school.* London: Routledge and Kegan Paul.

Harker, Richard, Cheleen Mahar, and Chris Wilkes, eds. 1990. *An introduction to the work of Pierre Bourdieu: The practice of theory.* London: Macmillan Publishers Ltd.

Hebdige, Dick. 1979. *Subculture: The meaning of style.* London: Methuen.

Heller, Agnes. 1984. *Everyday life.* Boston: Routledge and Kegan Paul.

Hernández, Luis. 1986. The SNTE and the teachers' movement, 1982–1984. In *The Mexican left, popular movements, and the politics of austerity,* edited by Barry Carr and Ricardo Anzaldúa Montoya. Vol. 18. La Jolla: Center for U.S.-Mexican Studies, University of California, San Diego.

Herrnstein-Smith, Barbara. 1981. Narrative versions, narrative theories. In *On Narrative,* edited by W. J. T. Mitchell. Chicago: University of Chicago Press.

Herzfeld, Michael. 1997. *Cultural intimacy: Social poetics in the nation-state.* New York: Routledge.

Hewitt de Alcántara, Cynthia. 1988. *Imágenes del campo: La interpretación antropológica del México rural.* Mexico City: El Colegio de México.

Hicks, Deborah, ed. 1996. *Discourse, learning, and schooling.* New York: Cambridge University Press.

Higgins, Michael. 1990. Martyrs and virgins: Popular religion in Mexico and Nicaragua. In *Class, politics, and popular religion in Mexico and Central America,* edited by Lynn Stephen and James Dow. Vol. 10. Washington, D.C.: Society for Latin American Anthropology Publication Series.

Hill, Jane H. 1991. In Neca gobierno de Puebla: Mexicano penetrations of the Mexican state. In *Nation-states and Indians in Latin America,* edited by Greg Urban and Joel Sherzer. Austin: University of Texas Press.

Hobsbawm, Eric, and Terence Ranger, eds. 1983. *The invention of tradition.* Cambridge, U.K.: Cambridge University Press.

Hoffman, Diane. 1998. A therapeutic moment? Identity, self, and culture in the anthropology of education. *Anthropology and Education Quarterly* 29, no. 3:324–46.

Holland, Dorothy. 1992. How cultural systems become desire: A case study of American romance. In *Cultural models and motivation,* edited by Roy D'Andrade and Claudia Strauss. Cambridge, U.K.: Cambridge University Press.

Holland, Dorothy, and Margaret Eisenhart. 1990. *Educated in romance: Women, achievement, and college culture.* Chicago: University of Chicago Press.

Holland, Dorothy, William Lachicotte Jr., Debra Skinner, and Carole Cain. 1998. *Identity and agency in cultural worlds.* Cambridge, Mass.: Harvard University Press.

Hollingshead, August B. 1949. *Elmtown's youth.* New York: Wiley and Sons.

Hondagneu-Sotelo, Pierrette. 1994. *Gendered transitions: Mexican experiences of immigration.* Berkeley: University of California Press.

Howell, Jayne. 1997. "This job is harder than it looks": Rural Oaxacan women explain why they became teachers. *Anthropology and Education Quarterly* 28, no. 2:251–79.

Hunt, Robert, and Eva Hunt. 1972. Education as an interface institution in rural Mexico and the American inner city. In *Language and cultural diversity in American education,* edited by Roger Abrahams and Rudolph Troike. Englewood Cliffs, N.J.: Prentice-Hall.

Hurtig, Janise. 1997. Gender lessons: Benign neglect and the reproduction of patriarchy at a Venezuelan high school. Ph.D. diss., University of Michigan.

Ibargüengoitia, Jorge. [1969] 1990. *Instrucciones para vivir en México.* Mexico City: Joaquín Mortiz.

Ingham, John. 1986. *Mary, Michael, and Lucifer: Folk Catholicism in central Mexico.* Austin: University of Texas Press.

Jackson, Michael, ed. 1996. *Things as they are: New directions in phenomenological anthropology.* Bloomington: Indiana University Press.

James, Allison, and Alan Prout, eds. 1990. *Constructing and reconstructing childhood: Contemporary issues in the sociological study of childhood.* London: Falmer Press.

Jelin, Elizabeth, ed. 1990. *Women and social change in Latin America.* London: Zed Books.

———, ed. 1991. *Family, household, and gender relations in Latin America.* London: Kegan Paul International.

Jenkins, Richard P. 1983. *Lads, citizens, and ordinary kids: Working-class youth lifestyles in Belfast.* London: Routledge and Kegan Paul.

Johnson, Richard. 1986–1987. What is cultural studies anyway? *Social Text* 6, no. 1:38–80.

Joseph, Gilbert M., and Daniel Nugent, eds. 1994. *Everyday forms of state formation: Revolution and the negotiation of rule in modern Mexico.* Durham, N.C.: Duke University Press.

Kamens, David H., et al. 1996. Worldwide patterns in academic secondary education curricula. *Comparative Education Review* 40, no. 2:116–38.

Kapferer, Bruce. 1988. *Legends of people, myths of state: Violence, intolerance, and political culture in Sri Lanka and Australia.* Washington, D.C.: Smithsonian Institution Press.

Karabel, Jerome, and A. H. Halsey, eds. 1977. *Power and ideology in education.* New York: Oxford University Press.

Kellner, Douglas. 1995. *Media culture.* London: Routledge.

Kemper, Robert van. 1987. Urbanización y desarrollo en la región tarasca a partir de 1940. In *Antropología social de la región Purépecha,* edited by Guillermo de la Peña. Zamora, Mexico: El Colegio de Michoacán.

Keyes, Charles, ed. 1991. *Reshaping local worlds: Formal education and cultural change in rural Southeast Asia.* Monograph no. 36. New Haven, Conn.: Yale Southeast Asian Studies.

King, Linda. 1994. *Roots of identity: Language and literacy in Mexico.* Stanford, Calif.: Stanford University Press.

King, Richard. 1967. *The school at Mopass: A problem of identity.* New York: Holt, Rinehart and Winston.

Knauft, Bruce. 1996. *Genealogies for the present in cultural anthropology.* New York: Routledge.

Knight, Alan. 1986. *The Mexican revolution.* Vol. 2. Cambridge, U.K.: Cambridge University Press.

Lacey, Colin. 1970. *Hightown grammar: The school as a social system.* Manchester, U.K.: Manchester University Press.

———. 1982. Freedom and constraints in British education. In *Custom and conflict in British society,* edited by Ronald Frankenberg. Manchester, U.K.: Manchester University Press.

Lankshear, Colin. 1995. Afterword: Some reflections on "empowerment." In *Critical theory and educational research,* edited by Peter L. McLaren and James M. Giarelli. Albany: State University of New York Press.

Lareau, Annette. 1989. *Home advantage: Social class and parental intervention in elementary education.* New York: Falmer Press.

Lareau, Annette, and Jeffrey Schultz, eds. 1996. *Journeys through ethnography: Realistic accounts of fieldwork.* Boulder, Colo.: Westview Press.

Larkin, Ralph. 1979. *Suburban youth in cultural crisis.* New York: Oxford University Press.

Larrain, Jorge. 1994. *Ideology and cultural identity: Modernity and the third world presence.* London: Blackwell Publishers.

Latapí Sarre, Pablo. 1998. Un siglo de educación nacional: Una sistematización. In *Un siglo de educación en México,* edited by Pablo Latapí Sarre. Vol. 1. Mexico City: Fondo de Cultura Económica.

Lather, Patti. 1991. *Getting smart: Feminist research and pedagogy with/in the postmodern.* New York: Routledge.

———. 1997. Drawing the line at angels: Working the ruins of feminist ethnography. *Qualitative Studies in Education* 10, no. 3:285–304.

Lave, Jean. 1988. *Cognition in practice.* Cambridge, U.K.: Cambridge University Press.

Lave, Jean, Paul Duguid, Nadine Fernández, and Erik Axel. 1992. Coming of age in Birmingham: Cultural studies and conceptions of subjectivity. *Annual Reviews in Anthropology* 21:257–82.

Lave, Jean, and Etienne Wenger. 1991. *Situated learning: Legitimate peripheral participation.* Cambridge, U.K.: Cambridge University Press.

LeCompte, Margaret D. 1995. Some notes on power, agenda, and voice: A researcher's personal evolution toward critical collaborative research. In *Critical theory and educational research,* edited by Peter L. McLaren and James M. Giarelli. Albany: State University of New York Press.

Lees, Sue. 1986. *Losing out: Sexuality and adolescent girls.* London: Hutchinson.

Lemert, Charles. 1995. *Sociology after the crisis.* Boulder, Colo.: Westview Press.

Lesko, Nancy. 1988. *Symbolizing society: Stories, rites, and structure in a Catholic high school.* New York: Falmer Press.

———. 1996. Past, present, and future conceptions of adolescence. *Educational Theory* 46, no. 4:453–72.

Levine, Robert A., and Merry I. White. 1986. *Human conditions: The cultural basis of educational development.* London: Routledge and Kegan Paul.

Levine, Sarah. 1993. *Dolor y alegría: Women and social change in urban Mexico.* Madison: University of Wisconsin Press.

Levinson, Bradley A. U. 1993. Todos somos iguales: Cultural production and social difference at a Mexican secondary school. Ph.D. diss., University of North Carolina–Chapel Hill.

———. 1996. Social difference and schooled identity at a Mexican secundaria. In *The cultural production of the educated person: Critical ethnographies of schooling and local practice,* edited by Bradley A. U. Levinson, Douglas Foley, and Dorothy Holland. Albany: State University of New York Press.

———. 1998a. (How) can a man do feminist ethnography of education? *Qualitative Inquiry* 4, no. 3:335–67.

———. 1998b. The moral construction of student rights: Discourse and judgment among Mexican secondary

school students. *Journal of Contemporary Ethnography* 27, no. 1:45–84.

———. 1998c. The social commitment of the educational ethnographer: Notes on fieldwork in Mexico and the field of work in the United States. In *Being reflexive in critical educational and social research,* edited by Geoffrey Shacklock and John Smyth. London: Falmer Press.

———. 1999. "Una etapa siempre difícil": Concepts of adolescence and secondary education in Mexico. *Comparative Education Review* 43, no. 2:129–61.

———, ed. 2000. *Schooling the symbolic animal: Social and cultural dimensions of education.* Lanham, Md.: Rowman and Littlefield.

Levinson, Bradley A. U., Douglas Foley, and Dorothy Holland, eds. 1996. *The cultural production of the educated person: Critical ethnographies of schooling and local practice.* Albany: State University of New York Press.

Levinson, Bradley A. U., and Dorothy C. Holland. 1996. The cultural production of the educated person: An introduction. In *The cultural production of the educated person: Critical ethnographies of schooling and local practice,* edited by Bradley A. U. Levinson, Douglas Foley, and Dorothy Holland. Albany: State University of New York Press.

Liechty, Mark. 1995. Media, markets, and modernization: Youth identities and the experience of modernity in Kathmandu, Nepal. In *Youth cultures,* edited by Vered Amit-Talai and Helen Wulff. London: Routledge.

Liston, Daniel. 1988. *Capitalist schools: Explanation and ethics in radical studies in schooling*. London: Routledge and Kegan Paul.

Loaeza, Soledad. 1988. *Clases medias y política en México: La querella escolar, 1959–1963*. Mexico City: El Colegio de México.

——. 1997. México en 1994: Los síntomas de una crisis moral. In *Los valores humanos en México*, edited by Jorge González and Josué Landa. Mexico City: Siglo XXI (Veintiuno).

Lomnitz, Larissa Adler. 1975. *Como sobreviven los marginados*. Mexico City: Siglo XXI.

Lomnitz, Larissa Adler, Ilya Adler, and Claudio Lomnitz-Adler. 1993. The function of the form: Power play and ritual in the 1988 Mexican presidential campaign. In *Constructing culture and power in Latin America*, edited by Daniel H. Levine. Ann Arbor: University of Michigan Press.

Lomnitz, Larissa Adler, and Marisol Pérez-Lizaur. 1984. Dynastic growth and survival strategies: The solidarity of Mexican grand-families. In *Kinship ideology and practice in Latin America*, edited by Raymond T. Smith. Chapel Hill: University of North Carolina Press.

——. 1987. *A Mexican elite family, 1820–1980: Kinship, class, and culture*. Princeton, N.J.: Princeton University Press.

Lomnitz-Adler, Claudio. 1992. *Exits from the labyrinth: Culture and ideology in the Mexican national space*. Berkeley: University of California Press.

López Castro, Gustavo. 1986. *La casa dividida: Un estudio de caso sobre la migración a Estados Unidos en un pueblo michoacano*. Zamora, Mexico: El Colegio de Michoacán.

López Castro, Gustavo, and Sergio Pardo Galván, eds. 1988. *Migración en el occidente de México*. Zamora, Mexico: El Colegio de Michoacán.

Luykx, Aurolyn. 1999. *The citizen factory: Schooling and cultural production in Bolivia*. Albany: State University of New York Press.

Mabry, Donald J. 1985. Twentieth-century Mexican education: A review. *History of Education Quarterly* 25:221–25.

Macías, Anna. 1982. *Against all odds: The feminist movement in Mexico to 1940*. Westport, Conn.: Greenwood Press.

Macías, José. 1990. Scholastic antecedents of immigrant students: Schooling in a Mexican immigrant-sending community. *Anthropology and Education Quarterly* 21:291–318.

MacLeod, Jay. 1987. *Ain't no makin' it: Leveled aspirations in a low-income neighborhood*. Boulder, Colo.: Westview Press.

Madeira, Felicia, and Guiomar Namo, eds. 1985. *Educao na América Latina, os modelos teóricos e a realidade social*. Sao Paulo, Brazil: Cortez Editores.

Mallon, Florencia E. 1994. Exploring the origins of democratic patriarchy in Mexico: Gender and popular resistance in the Puebla highlands, 1850–1876. In *Women of the Mexican countryside, 1850–1990*, edited by Heather Fowler-Salamini and Mary Kay Vaughan. Tucson: University of Arizona Press.

——. 1995. *Peasant and nation: The making of postcolonial Mexico and Peru*. Berkeley: University of California Press.

Marcus, George. 1986. Contemporary problems of ethnography in the modern world system. In *Writing culture: The poetics and politics of ethnography,* edited by James Clifford and George Marcus. Berkeley: University of California Press.

———. 1998. *Ethnography through thick and thin.* Princeton, N.J.: Princeton University Press.

Marcus, George, and Michael Fischer. 1986. *Anthropology as cultural critique: An experimental moment in the human sciences.* Chicago: University of Chicago Press.

Margolies, Barbara Luise. 1975. *Princes of the earth: Subcultural diversity in a Mexican municipality.* Washington, D.C.: Special Publications of the American Anthropological Association.

Martin, Christopher James. 1990. "To hold one's own in the world": Issues in the educational culture of working class families in west Mexico. *Compare* 20:115–39.

———. 1994a. "Let the young birds fly": Schooling, work, and emancipation in rural west Mexico. *Compare* 24, no. 3:259–77.

———. 1994b. *Schooling in Mexico: Staying in or dropping out.* Aldershot, U.K.: Avebury Press.

Martin, JoAnn. 1990. Motherhood and power: The production of a women's culture of politics in a Mexican community. *American Ethnologist* 17, no. 3:470–90.

———. 1994. Antagonisms of gender and class in Morelos. In *Women of the Mexican countryside, 1850–1990,* edited by Heather Fowler-Salamini and Mary Kay Vaughan. Tucson: University of Arizona Press.

Marx, Karl. [1852] 1978. The eighteenth brumaire of Louis Bonaparte. Reprinted in *The Marx-Engels reader,* 2d ed., edited by Robert C. Tucker. New York: W. W. Norton.

Masemann, Vandra. 1974. The hidden curriculum of a West African boarding school. *Canadian Journal of African Studies* 8, no. 3:479–94.

Massey, Douglas, Rafael Alarcón, Jorge Durand, and Humberto González. 1987. *Return to Aztlán: The social process of international migration from western Mexico.* Berkeley: University of California Press.

Massolo, Alejandra. 1992a. *Por amor y coraje: Mujeres en movimientos urbanos de la ciudad de México.* Mexico City: El Colegio de México.

———, ed. 1992b. *Mujeres y ciudades: Participación social, vivienda, y vida cotidiana.* Mexico City: El Colegio de México.

Mathews, Holly F. 1985. We are *mayordomo:* A reinterpretation of women's roles in the Mexican cargo system. *American Ethnologist* 17:285–301.

———. 1987. Intracultural variation in beliefs about gender in a Mexican community. *American Behavioral Scientist* 31, no. 2:219–33.

McCall, Leslie. 1992. Does gender fit? Bourdieu, feminism, and conceptions of social order. *Theory and Society* 21, no. 6:837–67.

McGinn Noel, and Susan Street. 1982. Has Mexican education generated human or political capital? *Comparative Education* 20, no. 3:323–38.

———. 1984. The political rationality of resource allocation in Mexican public education. *Comparative Education Review* 10:178–98.

McLaren, Peter L. 1986. *Schooling as a ritual performance.* London: Routledge.

McLaren, Peter L., and James M. Giarelli, eds. 1995. *Critical theory and educational research.* Albany: State University of New York Press.

McNeil, Linda. 1986. *Contradictions of control.* London: Routledge and Kegan Paul.

McQuillan, Patrick James. 1998. *Educational opportunity in an urban American high school: A cultural analysis.* Albany: State University of New York Press.

McRobbie, Angela. 1992. *Feminism and youth culture.* London: Unwin Hyman.

Mead, Margaret. 1928. *Coming of age in Samoa.* New York: Morrow.

Mehan, Hugh. 1979. *Learning lessons: Social organization in the classroom.* Cambridge, Mass.: Harvard University Press.

———. 1992. Understanding inequality in schools: The contribution of interpretive studies. *Sociology of Education* 65, no. 1:1–20.

Mehan, Hugh, Alma J. Hertweck, and J. Lee Meihls. 1986. *Handicapping the handicapped: Decision making in students' careers.* Stanford, Calif.: Stanford University Press.

Mehan, Hugh, Lea Hubbard, and Irene Villanueva. 1996. *Constructing school success.* Cambridge, U.K.: Cambridge University Press.

Mejía Zuñiga, Raúl. 1981. La escuela que surge de la revolución. In *Historia de la educación pública en México,* edited by Fernando Solana, Raúl Cardiel Reyes, and Raúl Bolaños Martínez. Mexico City: Fondo de Cultura Económica.

Meneses Morales, Ernesto. 1986. *Tendencias educativas oficiales en México, 1911–1934.* Mexico City: Centro de Estudios Educativos.

———. 1988. *Tendencias educativas oficiales en México, 1934–1964.* Mexico City: Centro de Estudios Educativos.

Mercado, Ruth. 1985. La educación primaria gratuita: Una lucha popular cotidiana. *Cuadernos de investigación.* Vol. 17. Mexico City: Departamento de Investigaciones Educativas.

———. 1994. *Saberes* and social voices in teaching. In *Education as cultural construction,* edited by Antonio Alvarez and Pablo del Río. Madrid: Infancia y Aprendizaje.

Meyer, Jean. 1976. *The Cristero rebellion: The Mexican people between church and state.* Cambridge, U.K.: Cambridge University Press.

———. 1991. Revolution and reconstruction in the 1920s. In *Mexico since Independence,* edited by Leslie Bethell. Cambridge, U.K.: Cambridge University Press.

Meyer, John, David H. Kamens, and Aaron Benavot, with Yun-Kyung Cha and Suk-Ying Wong. 1992. *School knowledge for the masses: World models and national primary curricular categories in the twentieth century.* Washington, D.C.: Falmer Press.

Mir, Adolfo. 1979. Orígenes socioeconómicos, status de la escuela, y aspiraciones y expectativas educativas y ocupacionales de estudiantes de secundaria. In *La educación y desarrollo dependiente en América Latina,* edited by Daniel Morales-Gómez. Mexico City: Centro de Estudios Educativos.

Moctezuma Barragán, Esteban. 1994. *La educación pública frente a las nuevas re-*

alidades. Mexico City: Fondo de Cultura Económica.

Modiano, Nancy. 1970. The relevancy of schooling in a Mexican peasant village. In *Education and culture,* edited by George Spindler. Rev. ed. New York: Holt, Rinehart and Winston.

Molina, Silvia. 1989. El paraíso perdido. In *Dicen que me case yo.* Mexico City: Cal y Arena.

Monsiváis, Carlos. 1981. Notas sobre el estado, la cultura nacional, y las culturas populares en Mexico. *Cuadernos Políticos* 30:33–45.

———. 1990. Entre condones: Notas sobre la revolución sexual en México. In *El nuevo arte de amar: Usos y costumbres sexuales en México,* edited by Hermann Bellinghausen. Mexico City: Cal y Arena.

———. 1992. Muerte y resurreción del nacionalismo mexicano. In *El nacionalismo Mexicano,* edited by Carlos Noriega Elio. Zamora, Mexico: El Colegio de Michoacán.

Montalvo, Enrique. 1985. *El nacionalismo contra la nación.* Mexico City: Grijalbo.

Morales-Gómez, Daniel A., and Carlos A. Torres. 1990. *The state, corporatist politics, and educational policy-making in Mexico, 1970–1988.* New York: Praeger.

Morley, David, and Kuan-Hsing Chen, eds. 1996. *Stuart Hall: Critical dialogues in cultural studies.* London: Routledge.

Morrow, Raymond Allen, and Carlos Alberto Torres. 1995. *Social theory and education: A critique of theories of social and cultural reproduction.* Albany: State University of New York Press.

Morse, Richard. 1982. *El espejo de Próspero: Dialéctica del Nuevo Mundo.* Mexico City: Siglo Veintiuno.

Muñoz García, Humberto. 1996. *Los valores educativos y el empleo en México.* Mexico City: Universidad Nacional Autónoma de México.

Muñoz Izquierdo, Carlos. 1981. Socioeconomía de la educación privada y pública: El caso de México. *Revista latinoamericana de estudios educativos* 11, no. 1:111–32.

Muñoz Izquierdo, Carlos, and María de Lourdes Casillas. 1982. Educación secundaria, desarrollo regional, tecnologías de producción, y mercados de trabajo. *Revista latinoamericana de estudios educativos* 12, no. 2:9–44.

Muñoz Izquierdo, Carlos, and Manuel I. Ulloa. 1992. Cuatro tesis sobre el origen de las desigualdades educativas: Una reflexión apoyada en el caso de México. *Revista latinoamericana de estudios educativos* 22, no. 2:11–58.

Nader, Laura. 1995. *Harmony ideology.* Berkeley: University of California Press.

Nash, June, and Helen Safa, eds. 1986. *Women and change in Latin America: New directions in sex and class.* South Hadley, Mass.: Bergin and Garvey.

Natriello, Gary. 1994. Coming together and breaking apart: Unifying and differentiating processes in schools and classrooms. In *Research in sociology of education and socialization,* edited by Aaron M. Pallas. Greenwich, Conn.: JAI Press.

Navarro, Yolanda. 1996. La secundaria general. In *La educación secundaria: Cambios y perspectivas,* edited by Instituto Estatal de Educación Pública de Oaxaca. Oaxaca, Mexico: Instituto Estatal de Educación Pública de Oaxaca.

Nespor, Jan. 1997. *Tangled up in school:*

Politics, space, bodies, and signs in the educational process. Mahwah, N.J.: Lawrence Erlbaum Associates.

Neubauer, John. 1992. *The fin-de-siècle culture of adolescence.* New Haven, Conn.: Yale University Press.

Newland, Carlos. 1994. The estado docente and its expansion: Spanish American elementary education, 1900–1950. *Journal of Latin American Studies* 26, no. 2:449–67.

Novelo, Victoria. 1976. *Artesanías y capitalismo en México.* Mexico City: Secretaría de Educación Pública–Instituto Nacional de Antropología e Historia.

Nugent, Daniel. 1993. *Spent cartridges of revolution: An anthropological history of Namiquipa, Chihuahua.* Chicago: University of Chicago Press.

Nutini, Hugo G., et al. 1976. *Essays on Mexican kinship.* Pittsburgh, Pa.: University of Pittsburgh Press.

Oikión Solano, Verónica. 1995. *Michoacán en la vía de la unidad nacional, 1940–1944.* Mexico City: Instituto Nacional de Estudios Históricos de la Revolución Mexicana.

O'Malley, Irene V. 1986. *The myth of the revolution: Hero cults and the institutionalization of the Mexican state, 1920–1940.* New York: Greenwood Press.

Orenstein, Peggy. 1994. *Schoolgirls: Young women, self-esteem, and the confidence gap.* New York: Anchor Books.

Ornelas, Carlos. 1984. La educación técnica y la ideología de la revolución Mexicana. In *La ideología educativa de la revolución mexicana,* edited by Graciela Lechuga. Mexico City: Universidad Autónoma Metropolitana.

——. 1995. *El sistema educativo mexicano.*

Mexico City: Secretaría de Educación Pública.

Ortner, Sherry B. 1984. Theory in anthropology since the sixties. *Comparative Studies in Society and History* 26:126–66.

——. 1996. *Making gender: The politics and erotics of culture.* Boston: Beacon Press.

Page, Reba. 1987. Teachers' perceptions of students: A link between classrooms, school cultures, and the social order. *Anthropology and Education Quarterly* 18, no. 1:77–99.

——. 1991. *Lower track classrooms: A curricular and cultural perspective.* New York: Teachers College Press.

Page, Reba, and Linda Valli, eds. 1990. *Curriculum differentiation: Interpretive studies in U.S. secondary schools.* Albany: State University of New York Press.

Popkewitz, Thomas S. 1987. Ideology and social formation in teacher education. In *Critical studies in teacher education,* edited by Thomas S. Popkewitz. London: Falmer Press.

Portilla, Jorge. [1966] 1984. *Fenomenología del relajo.* Mexico City: Fondo de Cultura Económica.

Prawda, Juan. 1987. *Logros, inequidades y retos del futuro del sistema educativo mexicano.* Mexico City: Grijalbo.

Proweller, Amanda. 1998. *Constructing female identities: Meaning making in an upper middle class youth culture.* Albany: State University of New York Press.

Quantz, Richard. 1992. On critical ethnography. In *The handbook of qualitative research in education,* edited by Margaret D. LeCompte, Wendy L.

Millroy, and Judith Preissle. San Diego, Calif.: Academic Press.

Quintanilla, Susana. 1996. Los principios de la reforma educativa socialista: Imposición, consenso y negociación. *Revista mexicana de investigación educativa* 1, no. 1:137–52.

Quiroz, Rafael. 1987. *El maestro y el saber especializado.* Mexico City: Departamento de Investigaciones Educativas.

———. 1991. Obstáculos para la apropiación de los contenidos académicos en la escuela secundaria. *Infancia y Aprendizaje* 55:45–58.

———. 1992. El tiempo cotidiano en la escuela secundaria. *Nueva Antropología* 12, no. 42:89–100.

———. 1993. La reforma curricular de la escuela secundaria en México. In *Educación, ciencia y tecnología: Los nuevos desafíos para América Latina,* edited by Julio Labastida Martín, Giovanna Valenti, and Lorenzo Villa Lever. Mexico City: Universidad Nacional Autónoma de México.

Raby, David. 1974. *La educación socialista en México: 1920–1940.* Mexico City: Sepsetentas.

———. 1987. Ideología y construcción del estado: La función política de la educación rural en México, 1921–1935. *Revista mexicana de sociología* 2:305–20.

Radcliffe, Sarah A., and Sallie Westwood, eds. 1993. *"Viva": Women and popular protest in Latin America.* New York: Routledge.

Raissiguier, Catherine. 1994. *Becoming women/becoming workers: Identity formation in a French vocational school.* Albany: State University of New York Press.

Rama, Germán. 1984. *Educación, participación, y estilos de desarrollo en América Latina.* Santiago: Comisión Económica para América Latina.

Reed-Danahay, Deborah. 1987. Farm children at school: Educational strategies in rural France. *Anthropological Quarterly* (April):83–89.

———. 1996. *Education and identity in rural France: The politics of schooling.* Cambridge, U.K.: Cambridge University Press.

Reichert, Joshua. 1982. A town divided: Economic stratification and social relations in a Mexican migrant community. *Social Problems* 29:411–23.

Reyes Rocha, José. 1986. Educación secundaria. In *Acciones educativas en el estado de Michoacán, 1980–1986,* edited by José Reyes Rocha. Morelia, Mexico: Secretaría de Educación Pública.

Rist, Ray C. 1970. Student social class and teacher expectations: The self-fulfilling prophecy in ghetto education. *Harvard Educational Review* 40 (August):411–50.

Rival, Laura. 1996. Formal schooling and the production of modern citizens in the Ecuadorian Amazon. In *The cultural production of the educated person,* edited by Bradley A. U. Levinson, Douglas Foley, and Dorothy C. Holland. Albany, N.Y.: State University of New York Press.

Rockwell, Elsie. 1987. *Desde la perspectiva del trabajo docente.* Mexico City: Departamento de Investigaciones Educativas.

———. 1991. Ethnography and critical knowledge of education in Latin America. *Prospects* 21, no. 2:156–67.

———. 1994. Schools of the revolution: Enacting and contesting state forms in Tlaxcala (1910–1930). In *Everyday* forms of state formation: Revolution and the negotiation of rule in modern Mexico, edited by Gilbert M. Joseph and Daniel Nugent. Durham, N.C.: Duke University Press.

——. 1995. De huellas, bardas, y veredas: Una historia cotidiana en la escuela. In La escuela cotidiana, edited by Elsie Rockwell. Mexico City: Fondo de Cultura Económica.

——. 1996. Keys to appropriation: Rural schooling in Mexico. In The cultural production of the educated person: Critical ethnographies of schooling and local practice, edited by Bradley A. U. Levinson, Douglas Foley, and Dorothy Holland. Albany: State University of New York Press.

——. 1999. Recovering history in the study of schooling: From the longue durée to everyday co-construction. Human Development 42:113–28.

Rockwell, Elsie, and Ruth Mercado. 1986. La escuela, lugar del trabajo docente. Mexico City: Departamento de Investigaciones Educativas.

Rodríguez, Richard. 1982. Hunger of memory: The education of Richard Rodríguez. New York: Bantam Books.

Rogoff, Barbara. 1990. Apprenticeship in thinking. New York: Oxford University Press.

Roman, Leslie. 1988. Intimacy, labor, and class: Ideologies of feminine sexuality in the punk slam dance. In Becoming feminine: The politics of popular culture, edited by Leslie Roman and Linda K. Christian-Smith. New York: Falmer Press.

Rorty, Richard. 1979. Philosophy and the mirror of nature. Princeton, N.J.: Princeton University Press.

——. 1989. Contingency, irony, solidarity. Cambridge, U.K.: Cambridge University Press.

Rosaldo, Renato. 1989. Culture and truth: The remaking of social analysis. Boston: Beacon Press.

Rose, Nikolas. 1996. Identity, genealogy, history. In Questions of cultural identity, edited by Stuart Hall and Paul du Gay. London: Sage Publications.

Roseberry, William. 1989. Anthropologies and histories. New Brunswick, N.J.: Rutgers University Press.

Rosenbaum, James. 1976. Making inequality. New York: Wiley and Sons.

Rothstein, Frances Abrahamer. 1996. Flexible accumulation, youth labor, and schooling in a rural community in Mexico. Critique of Anthropology 16, no. 4:361–79.

Rouse, Roger. 1991. Mexican migration and the social space of postmodernism. Diaspora 1, no. 1:8–23.

——. 1992. Making sense of settlement: Class transformation, cultural struggle, and transnationalism among Mexican migrants in the United States. In Towards a transnational perspective on migration: Race, class, ethnicity, and nationalism reconsidered, edited by Nina Glick Schiller, Linda Basch, and Cristina Szanton-Blanc. New York: Annals of the New York Academy of Sciences.

——. 1995. Questions of identity: Personhood and collectivity in transnational migration to the United States. Critique of Anthropology 15, no. 4:351–80.

Rowe, William, and Vivian Schelling. 1991. Memory and modernity: Popular culture in Latin America. London: Verso.

Rubin, Jeffrey W. 1996. Decentering the regime: Culture and regional politics in Mexico. *Latin American Research Review* 31, no. 3:85–126.

Sáenz, Moisés. [1936] 1992. *Carapán*. 3d ed. Pátzcuaro, Michoacán: Centro Regional de Educación Funcional para América Latina.

Sahlins, Marshall. 1981. *Historical metaphors and mythical realities: Structure in the early history of the Sandwich Islands kingdom*. Ann Arbor: University of Michigan Press.

———. 1985. *Islands of history*. Chicago: University of Chicago Press.

Sandoval, Etelvina. 1992. Condición femenina, valoración social, y autovaloración del trabajo docente. *Nueva Antropología* 12, no. 42:57–72.

———. 1996. La secundaria: Elementos para debatir (y pensar el cambio de) su organización y gestión. In *La educación secundaria: Cambios y perspectivas,* edited by Instituto Estatal de Educación Pública de Oaxaca. Oaxaca, Mexico: Instituto Estatal de Educación Pública de Oaxaca.

———. 1997. *Quienes son los maestros de escuela secundaria?* Paper presented at the annual conference of the Comparative and International Education Society, 21 March, Mexico City.

———. 1998a. *Escuela secundaria: Institución, relaciones, y saberes*. Ph.D. diss., Universidad Nacional Autónoma de México, Mexico City.

———. 1998b. Los estudiantes en la escuela secundaria. In *Nuevos paradigmas, compromisos renovados: Experiencias de investigación cualitativa en educación,* edited by Beatriz Calvo Pontón, Gabriela Delgado, and Mario Rueda.

Ciudad Juárez, Chihuahua: Universidad Autónoma de Ciudad Juárez.

Santos del Real, Annette. 1996a. *La educación secundaria en México (1923–1993).* Unpublished manuscript. Mexico City: Centro de Estudios Educativos.

———. 1996b. La secundaria: Modalidades y tendencias. In *La educación secundaria: Cambios y perspectivas,* edited by Instituto Estatal de Educación Pública de Oaxaca. Oaxaca, Mexico: Instituto Estatal de Educación Pública de Oaxaca.

Saucedo Ramos, Claudia. 1995. Expresiones genéricas de los adolescentes en el contexto sociocultural de un CON-ALEP. Master's thesis, Departamento de Investigaciones Educativas, Mexico City.

Sault, Nicole L. 1985. Baptismal sponsorship as a source of power for Zapotec women in Oaxaca, Mexico. *Journal of Latin American Lore* 11, no. 2:225–43.

Sayer, Derek. 1994. Everyday forms of state formation: Some dissident remarks on "hegemony." In *Everyday forms of state formation: Revolution and the negotiation of rule in modern Mexico,* edited by Gilbert M. Joseph and Daniel Nugent. Durham, N.C.: Duke University Press.

Schoenhals, Martin. 1993. *The paradox of power in a People's Republic of China middle school*. Armonk, N.Y.: M. E. Sharpe.

Schryer, Frans J. 1990. *Ethnicity and class conflict in rural Mexico*. Princeton, N.J.: Princeton University Press.

Schwartz, Gary, and Donald Merten. 1967. The language of adolescence: An anthropological approach to the youth culture. *American Journal of Sociology* 72:435–68.

Scott, James C. 1990. *Domination and the arts of resistance.* New Haven, Conn.: Yale University Press.

Scudder, Thayer, and Elizabeth Colson. 1980. *Secondary education and the formation of an elite: The impact of education on Gwembe district, Zambia.* London: Academic Press.

Selby, Henry A., Arthur P. Murphy, and Stephen A. Lorenzen. 1990. *The Mexican urban household: Organizing for self-defense.* Austin: University of Texas Press.

Sennett, Richard, and Jonathan Cobb. 1972. *The hidden injuries of class.* New York: Vintage.

Serpell, Robert. 1993. *The significance of schooling: Life journeys in African society.* New York: Cambridge University Press.

Secretaría de Educación Pública. (SEP). 1993. *Educación básica secundaria: Plan y programas de estudio.* Mexico City: Secretaría de Educación Pública.

Shacklock, Geoffrey, and John Smyth, eds. 1998. *Being reflexive in critical educational and social research.* London: Falmer Press.

Shapiro, Svi. 1990. *Between capitalism and democracy.* New York: Bergin and Garvey.

Shaw, Thomas A. 1991. Schooling for success in a non-Western culture: A case from Taiwan. *International Journal of Qualitative Studies in Education* 4, no. 2:109–20.

———. 1994. The semiotic mediation of identity. *Ethos* 22, no. 1:83–119.

———. 1996. Taiwanese schools against themselves: School culture versus the subjectivity of youth. In *The cultural production of the educated person: Crit-* *ical ethnographies of schooling and local practice,* edited by Bradley A. U. Levinson, Douglas Foley, and Dorothy Holland. Albany: State University of New York Press.

Shimahara, Nobuo K. 1983. Polarized socialization in an urban high school. *Anthropology and Education Quarterly* 14:109–30.

Shore, Bradd. 1996. *Culture in mind: Cognition, culture, and the problem of meaning.* Oxford: Oxford University Press.

Shuman, Amy. 1986. *Storytelling rights: The uses of oral and written texts by urban adolescents.* New York: Cambridge University Press.

Shweder, Richard A. 1996. True ethnography: The lore, the law, and the lure. In *Ethnography and human development: Context and meaning in social inquiry,* edited by Richard Jessor, Anne Colby, and Richard A. Shweder. Chicago: University of Chicago Press.

Simon, Roger, and Donald Dippo. 1986. On critical ethnographic work. *Anthropology and Education Quarterly* 17, no. 3:195–202.

Slack, Jennifer D. 1996. The theory and method of articulation in cultural studies. In *Stuart Hall: Critical dialogues in cultural studies,* edited by David Morley and Kuan-Hsing Chen. London: Routledge.

Smith, Dorothy E. 1987. *The everyday world as problematic: A feminist sociology.* Toronto, Canada: University of Toronto Press.

Smith, Paul. 1988. *Discerning the subject.* Minneapolis: University of Minnesota Press.

Smith, Peter H. 1991. Mexico since 1946:

Dynamics of an authoritarian regime. In *Mexico since Independence,* edited by Leslie Bethell. Cambridge, U.K.: Cambridge University Press.

Smith, Raymond T., ed. 1984. *Kinship ideology and practice in Latin America.* Chapel Hill: University of North Carolina Press.

Solana, Fernando, Raúl Cardiel Reyes, and Raúl Bolaños Martínez, eds. 1981. *Historia de la educación pública en México.* Mexico City: Fondo de Cultura Económica.

Solomon, R. Patrick. 1992. *Black resistance in high school: Forging a separatist culture.* Albany: State University of New York Press.

Spenser, Daniela, and Bradley A. U. Levinson. 1999. Linking state and society in discourse and action: Political and cultural studies of the Cárdenas era in Mexico. *Latin American Research Review* 34, no. 2:227–45.

Spindler, George, and Louise Spindler. 1973. *Burbach: Urbanization and identity in a German village.* New York: Holt, Rinehart and Winston.

Stallybrass, Peter, and Allon White. 1986. *The politics and poetics of transgression.* Ithaca, N.Y.: Cornell University Press.

Speier, Matthew. 1976. The adult ideological viewpoint. In *Rethinking childhood,* edited by Arlene Skolnick. Boston: Little, Brown.

Stambach, Amy. 1996. "Seeded" in the market economy: Schooling and social transformations on Mount Kilimanjaro. *Anthropology and Education Quarterly* 27, no. 4:545–67.

———. 2000. *Lessons from Mount Kilimanjaro: Schooling, community, and culture in East Africa.* New York: Routledge.

Steele, Cynthia. 1992. *Politics, gender, and the Mexican novel, 1968–1988: Beyond the pyramid.* Austin: University of Texas Press.

Stephen, Lynn. 1992. *Zapotec women.* Austin: University of Texas Press.

Stephen, Lynn, and James Dow, eds. 1990. *Class, politics, and popular religion in Mexico and Central America.* Vol. 10. Washington, D.C.: Society for Latin American Anthropology Publication Series.

Stern, Steve J. 1995. *The secret history of gender: Women, men, and power in late colonial Mexico.* Chapel Hill: University of North Carolina Press.

Stinchcombe, Arthur. 1964. *Rebellion in a high school.* Chicago: Quadrangle.

Street, Brian, ed. 1993. *Cross-cultural approaches to literacy.* Cambridge, U.K.: Cambridge University Press.

Street, Susan. 2001. When politics becomes pedagogy: Oppositional discourse as policy in Mexican teachers' struggles for union democracy. In *Policy as practice: Toward a comparative sociocultural analysis of educational policy,* edited by Margaret Sutton and Bradley A. U. Levinson. Stamford, Conn.: Ablex.

Stromquist, Nelly P., ed. 1992. *Women and education in Latin America: Knowledge, power, and change.* Boulder, Colo.: Lynne Rienner.

Subirats, Marina, and Cristina Brullet. 1988. *Rosa y azul: La transmisión de los géneros en la escuela mixta.* Madrid: Ministerio de la Cultura.

Swartz, David. 1997. *Culture and power: The sociology of Pierre Bourdieu.* Chicago: University of Chicago Press.

Taboada, Eva. 1985. Educación y lucha

ideológica en el México postrevolu-
cionario. In *Educación y clases populares en América Latina,* edited by
María de Ibarrola and Elsie Rockwell.
Mexico City: Departamento de Investigaciones Educativas.

Taylor, Charles. 1989. *Sources of the self:
The making of modern identity.* Cam-
bridge, Mass.: Harvard University
Press.

Tedesco, Juan Carlos. 1983. Crítica al re-
productivismo educativo. *Cuadernos
Políticos* 37.

———. 1987. Paradigms of socioeducational
research in Latin America. *Comparative Education Review* 31, no. 4:509–32.

Thompson, John B. 1990. *Ideology and
modern culture.* Stanford, Calif.: Stanford University Press.

Thorne, Barrie. 1993. *Gender play: Girls
and boys in school.* New Brunswick,
N.J.: Rutgers University Press.

Trueba, Henry T., and Concha Delgado-
Gaitán. 1985. Dilema en la socializa-
ción de niños mexicanos: Para la cooperación, o para la competencia?
compartir o copiar? *Revista latinoamericana de estudios educativos* 15, no.
4:69–84.

Tuñón Pablos, Julia. 1987. *Mujeres en
México: Una historia olvidada.* Mexico
City: Planeta.

Valenzuela Arce, José Manuel, ed. 1992.
*Decadencia y auge de las identidades:
Cultura nacional, identidad cultural y
modernización.* Tijuana, Mexico: El
Colegio de la Frontera Norte.

Valli, Linda. 1986. *Becoming clerical
workers.* London: Routledge and Kegan
Paul.

Varenne, Hervé. 1982. Jocks and freaks. In
Doing the ethnography of schooling, ed-
ited by George Spindler. New York:
Holt, Rinehart and Winston.

Varenne, Hervé, and Ray McDermott.
1998. *Successful failure: The school
America builds.* Boulder, Colo.: Westview Press.

Vaughan, Mary Kay. 1982. *The state, education, and social class in Mexico, 1880–
1928.* Dekalb: Northern Illinois University Press.

———. 1990. Women schoolteachers in the
Mexican revolution: The story of Reyna's braids. *Journal of Women's History*
2, no. 1:143–68.

———. 1994. Rural women's literacy and
education during the Mexican revolution: Subverting a patriarchal event? In
*Women of the Mexican countryside,
1850–1990,* edited by Heather Fowler-
Salamini and Mary Kay Vaughan. Tucson: University of Arizona Press.

———. 1997. *Cultural politics in revolution:
Teachers, peasants, and schools in Mex-
ico, 1930–1940.* Tucson: University of
Arizona Press.

Wacquant, Loïc. 1992. Toward a social
praxeology: The structure and logic of
Bourdieu's sociology. In *An invitation
to reflexive sociology,* edited by Pierre
Bourdieu and Loïc Wacquant. Cambridge, U.K.: Polity Press.

Walker, J. C. 1988. *Louts and legends: Male
youth culture in an inner city school.*
Sydney: Allen and Unwin.

Wallace, Anthony. 1970. *Culture and personality.* 2d ed. New York: Random
House.

Wallerstein, Immanuel. 1974. *The modern
world-system: Capitalist agriculture and
the origins of the European world-
economy in the sixteenth century.* New
York: Academic Press.

Watson-Gegeo, Karen Ann, and David Welchman Gegeo. 1992. Schooling, knowledge, and power: Social transformation in the Solomon Islands. *Anthropology and Education Quarterly* 23, no. 1:10–29.

Wax, Murray L., Stanley Diamond, and Frederick O. Gearing, eds. 1971. *Anthropological perspectives on education*. New York: Basic Books.

Weis, Lois. 1990. *Working class without work: High school students in a deindustrializing economy*. New York: Routledge.

Wexler, Philip. 1987. *Social analysis of education*. London: Routledge and Kegan Paul.

——. 1992. *Becoming somebody: Toward a social psychology of school*. London: Falmer Press.

White, Merry. 1993. *The material child: Coming of age in Japan and America*. Berkeley: University of California Press.

Williams, Raymond. 1977. *Marxism and literature*. New York: Oxford University Press.

Willis, Paul. 1981a. Cultural production is different from cultural reproduction is different from social reproduction is different from reproduction. *Interchange* 12, nos. 2–3:48–67.

——. 1981b. *Learning to labor: How working class kids get working class jobs*. New York: Columbia University Press.

——. 1983. Cultural production and theories of reproduction. In *Race, class, and education*, edited by Len Barton and Stephanie Walker. London: Croom Helm.

Willis, Paul, with Simon Jones, Joyce Canaan, and Geoff Hurd. 1990. *Common culture: Symbolic work and play in the everyday cultures of the young*. Boulder, Colo.: Westview Press.

Wolf, Eric. 1956. Aspects of group relations in a complex society: Mexico. *American Anthropologist* 58:1065–78.

——. 1982. *Europe and the people without history*. Berkeley: University of California Press.

Woods, Peter. 1979. *The divided school*. London: Routledge and Kegan Paul.

——. 1990. *The happiest days? How pupils cope with school*. London: Falmer Press.

——, ed. 1980. *Teacher strategies*. London: Croom Helm.

Woolard, Kathryn A. 1985. Language variation and cultural hegemony: Toward an integration of sociolinguistic and social theory. *American Ethnologist*: 738–48.

Wulff, Helen. 1988. *Twenty girls: Growing up, ethnicity, and excitement in a south London microculture*. Stockholm: University of Stockholm.

Young, Michael F. D., ed. 1971. *Knowledge and control*. London: Collier-Macmillan.

Zizumbo Villareal, Lilia. 1986. Zurumútaro: La expansión del capitalismo. In *Estudios michoacanos*, edited by Carlos Herrejón Peredo. Vol. 2. Zamora, Mexico: El Colegio de Michoacán.

INDEX

Abel (focal ESF student): academic failure of, 233; aspirations of, 316; family background of, 102, 314, 357–58; friendship group of, 196; identification and, 308; on music, 195; postsecondary experiences, 244, 248–49, 296; on social class, 178, 200

Abrams, Philip, 332, 389 n. 29

Academic failure, 78–79, 81–82, 233, 234. *See also* Extraordinary exams

Acta de Matrimonio, 216–17, 218, 225

Acto y Fiesta de Clasura, 71, 73, 142, 233, 234

Adamson, Walter, 389 n. 29

Adler, Ilya, 18, 365 nn. 10 and 11 , 371 n. 6

Admission exam: at Escuela Secundaria Federal, 55–56

Adolescence: adults on meaning of, 14–15, 16; identity formation and, 7, 96–97, 306–11, 313–14, 318; meanings of, 14–15; parents on, 14; puberty and, 100; role of education in, 20, 25, 26; secundaria creation and, 16–18, 20, 25, 26; students on meaning of, 15–16; subcultural identification and, 7; teachers on, 14, 15, 80–81; violence and, 383 n. 2

Agapitos Lopis Casta, 197

Age: friendship groups and, 203, 226–27

Agency: concept and implications of, 339, 340, 344. *See also* Structure

Agosín, Mr. (teacher), 79–80, 98

Aguirre Beltrán, Gonzalo, 39

Alberto (focal ESF student): class elections and, 127; family background of, 103, 117–19, 196; identification and, 308, 309; masculine identity of, 91; postsecondary experiences, 244, 271–74, 314, 316; on social class, 178–79, 199, 200

Alejandra (focal ESF student), 108, 229, 247, 295, 351–52

Alonso, Mr. (teacher), 80, 98, 119–20

Althusser, Louis, 384 n. 3

Álvarez, Mr. (teacher), 40, 239, 240

Anderson, Benedict, 330

Andrea (focal ESF student): academic failure of, 234; aspirations of, 295; family background of, 107, 314, 362; friendship group of, 220, 221, 308; heterosexual romantic relations and, 222, 223; migration of, 296; postsecondary experiences, 243, 247, 261–63; schooled identity and, 316

Andrés (ESF student), 202, 204

Angélica (ESF student), 125, 126

Anniversary notes, 67

Antonia (focal ESF student): aspirations of, 296; cultural center opinion of, 205–6; family background of, 106, 315, 355; occupation of, 297; postsecondary experiences, 243, 246, 256–58; schooled identity and, 316; sexuality jokes and, 208

Antonio (ESF student), 198–201, 238, 380 n. 5

Appadurai, Arjun, 316–17, 388 n. 18

Apple, Michael, 325

Arizpe, Lourdes, 148–49, 152, 368 n. 7

Aspirations: definition of, 326; focal student, 294–301, 314–20, 386 n. 9; identity and, 326–27, 343; modernization theory and, 333

Athletic competitions, 71

Auto-aprendizaje, 79–80

Ávila Camacho, Manuel, 26, 32

Banda de guerra, male, 89

Barreda, Gabino, 365 n. 14

theory and, 389 n. 29; on structure of cathexis, 299; on student groups, 327

Consejo Técnico, 239

Conservatives, 18

Constantín (ESF student), 178, 197, 271, 316

Cooperación, 52–53, 370 n. 17, 378 n. 11

Coordinadora Nacional de Trabajdores de Educación (CNTE), 49, 369 n. 13

Corrigan, Philip, 331

Corsaro, William, 138, 336, 340

Cortina, Regina, 84–85

Cristero War, 30–31

Critical ethnography, xv-xvi, 325, 363 nn. 1 and 3 (Preface)

Critical social theory, 363 n. 2 (Preface)

Cultural center, at Escuela Secundaria Federal: definition of, 193, 379 n. 2; equality and, 204, 205–6, 209, 226, 308–9; influence of, 193–96; members of, 194, 377 n. 2; morality and, 231; music and, 194–95, 196, 210; sexuality and, 208, 228–31; teachers and, 193–94, 204

Cultural media: bookbags and, 70; book covers, 380 n. 10; echando relajo as form of, 142–43; effect on academic success, 82; moral judgments and choice of, 380 n. 3; resistance and, 376 n. 15; as site of youth identity formation, 159–63, 318, 319, 385 n. 7; telenovelas as, 387 n. 16

Cultural missions, 21–22

Cultural reproduction, 37, 318, 326, 339, 348. *See also* Social reproduction theory

Culture: changing concepts of, 347–50, 388 n. 20; definition of, 384 n. 1, 390 n. 35; indigenous (*see* Indigenous cultures); institutional, 305–6, 311–14; intimate (*see* Intimate cultures); merchant, 296–97; public, 388 n. 18; student (*see* Student culture)

Curriculum: of secundarias, 24, 25, 73–74

Cusick, Philip, 385 n. 8

Dalia (focal ESF student), 106, 243, 246, 259–61, 296, 297, 315, 316, 352–53

Dances, 72, 160–61, 195–96

Davidson, Anne Locke, 329

Delgado, Gabriela, 380 n. 9

Delgado-Gaitán, Concha, 375 n. 10

Democráticos, 49–50, 51, 233, 369 n. 14

Democratic Teachers' Movement (MDM), 50–51

Departamento de Investigaciones Educativas (DIE), 334–35

Descartes, René, 338

Developing countries: terminology for, 384 n. 2

Dewey, John, 21

Día de los Muertos celebrations, 72

Díaz, Mr. (teacher), 78–79

Díaz Pontones, Mónica, 76

DIE (Departamento de Investigaciones Educativas), 334–35

Difference. *See* Otherness

Discrimination: against girls, 130–31 (*see also* Gender); tracking as, 60, 311, 371 n. 4

Domestic sphere, 154–55, 158

Douglas, Mary, 389 n. 29

Drop-out rates, 7, 183–85, 209

Drug trafficking, 238, 368 n. 6

Drum and bugle corps, male, 67, 88, 374 n. 29

Dualism, 338–39. *See also* Structure

Dumont, Louis, 371 n. 6

Eagleton, Terry, 390n. 33

Easter celebrations, 72

Echando relajo ("goofing off"), 5, 139–44, 342, 375 n. 12, 376 n. 14

Eckert, Penelope, 316, 327

gender-specific practices at, 87–89; grading procedures at, 74–75, 374 n. 3; graduation ceremonies of, 71, 73, 142, 233, 234; grupos escolares at (*see* Grupos escolares); holiday celebrations of, 64, 71–73, 90, 161, 163, 196, 372 n. 15; identification of students with, 163–69; indigenous students at, 149–50; institutional culture and equality, 305–6, 311–14; lack of resources at, 80; layout and ground plan of, 56–57; location of, 39; lunch period, 372 n. 13; male/female ratio at, 32, 34, 367 n. 30, 377–78 n. 9; methodology for study of, 8–10; morning shift routines of, 65–66, 239; negative student attitudes at, 240–41; noviazgos at, 379 n. 15; parents' preference for, 165–66, 378 n. 10; principals of, 32–33, 53, 62, 64, 66, 67–68, 127, 163, 369 n. 12, 371 n. 7; reasons for selection as study site, 6–7, 37–38; recess at, 70; registration "fees," 52–53; school identification and, 5; second-year students, 59, 100; sexual division of labor at, 85–86; sexuality at, 208, 222, 223, 228–31; socioeconomic status of students at, 42–43, 47–48, 226; socioeconomic survey of student population of, 10; student population of, 7; subcultures in, 306; surveys of, 46–47; talleres at, 88; tardiness at, 66; teachers at (*see* Teachers); teaching methods used at, 75–80; theory of student dynamics in, 3–4; third-year students (*see* Grupos escolares); vice principals of, 59–60, 64, 66, 374 n. 29; weekly civic ceremony routines of, 66–68

Escuela Secundaria Federal (Turno Vespertino) (ESF-TV), 47, 48

ESF. *See* Escuela Secundaria Federal (ESF)

ESF-TV (Escuela Secundaria Federal (Turno Vesperino), 47, 48

Establet, Roger, 325

Ethnicity. *See* Indigenous cultures

Etilio, Mr. (teacher), 64–65

Everhart, Robert, 141, 376 n. 15

Extraordinary exams, 74–75, 234, 254. *See also* Academic failure

Ezpeleta, Justa, 331

Fabian, Johannes, 376 n. 15

Falta de interés, 81–82

Family: academic failure and shaming of, 78–79; academic success and, 81, 82; focal student aspirations and, 314–15; gender regimes in, 154–56; grupos escolares and, 315; household and, 377 n. 2; identification and, 150–51, 298–99; kinship relations and, 150–51, 373 n. 20, 377 n. 2; nuclear, 151; as organizational frame, 387–88 n. 17; as primary context for cultural meanings, 383 nn. 9 and 10. *See also* Intimate cultures; *names of individual focal students*

Fathers: daughters and, 157, 158–59; focal students' (*see names of individual focal students*); occupations of, 47–48

Fátima (ESF student), 223

Faviola (ESF student), 206–7, 208

Favoritism, 129

Female students. *See* Gender

Feminist authors, 155, 338, 386–87 n. 13

Fenomenología del relajo (Portilla), 139, 140–41

Ferguson, James, 162

Fernando (ESF student), 203–4

Fidel (focal ESF student), 105, 172, 210, 212–13, 246, 263–64, 295, 316, 358, 374 n. 4

Fidencio (focal ESF student), 103, 243, 245, 250–51, 295, 296, 316, 361, 374 n. 4

Figuration, 339

Finders, Margaret, 16

Fine, Gary Alan, 138

First-year students, 55–56, 99–100

Fisherkeller, JoEllen, 383 n. 9

Focal students: on adolescence, 15–16; aspirations of, 294–301, 314–20, 386 n. 9; background summary tabulations of, 102–8; as cultural center, 194; identification and, 308, 309; identity and (*see* Identity); lessons learned from study of, 293–301; life trajectories tabulations of, 241–47; migration to United States by, 46, 224, 249–50, 295–96, 316, 317; nationalism and, 320–21; religion and, 271, 274, 282, 283, 288–89, 320; selection of, 9–10, 374 n. 4. *See also entries under "Grupo"; names of individual students*

Foley, Douglas, 327, 328, 375 n. 12

Foster, George, 383 n. 3

Foster, Robert, 340

Foucault, Michel, 331, 348

Franco (focal ESF student), 15, 102, 115–16, 171–72, 244, 265–68, 314, 316

Friedlander, Judith, 148

Friendship Day celebrations, 372 n. 15

Friendship groups: age and, 203, 226–27; basis for formation of, 207–8, 212–13, 221–22, 315–16, 381 n. 14; cultural center and, 193–96, 226; differences between female, 226–27; elites and, 196–201; equality in, 192; exclusive, 62, 132; female, 220–31; gender and, 380 n. 5; humor in, 214–16, 380 n. 7; impact on aspirations of focal students, 315–16; intimate cultures and, 189; Juanitos, 196–201, 214, 316, 380 n. 5; male versus female, 216–17; Potrillos, 201–4, 316; social distinctions and grupos escolares, 196–204; use of *todos somos iguales* by, 2

Functionalism, 325

Games: of equality (*see* Equality: game

of); institutional demands and, 304–5, 311–14; as metaphor for practice, 4, 303–4, 364 n. 3 (*see also* Practice); "serious," 3–4

Gamoran, Adam, 311

Garfias, Mrs. (teacher), 214

Gaskell, Jane, 340

Gastélum, Bernardo, 23

Gender: ambiguous practices, 89–91; analysis of, 6; banda de guerra and, 89; book covers and, 380 n. 10; class differences and, 173–79, 191; color guard and, 67, 89–90, 374 n. 30; division of labor, 85–86, 152, 154–57, 215–16; drum and bugle corps and, 67, 88, 374 n. 29; elites and female, 191; enrollments and, 373 n. 21; equality and, 84–85, 214–15; equality contradictions and, 129–34; family and, 154–56; female friendship groups and, 216–17, 220–31; female identity, 298; females and schooling, 130, 157; female students' response to teachers, 380 n. 9; freedom and, 158–59, 381 n. 13; humor and meanings of, 214–15, 232; ideologies, 213–17, 297–98, 387 n. 13; leadership and, 87–88, 217–20, 232; machismo and, 156, 167, 377 n. 8; male dominance and, 377 n. 7; male/female ratio of ESF, 32, 34, 367 n. 30, 377–78 n. 9; male friendship groups and, 196–204, 380 n. 5; male identity and, 91, 298–99; marriage roles and, 216–17; Mexican literature on, 154–55; patriarchy and, 328, 340; peer-based relations of, 232; plazas and, 173–79; practice and, 87–91; promotional presentations and, 89; regimes, 82–84, 153, 154–56, 373 n. 23, 377 n. 7; relational theory of, 153; relations, 82–84; religion and, 151–53, 230; research in Mexico on, 154; romantic relationships and, 95, 179–83, 220–31,

Hidden injuries: of class, 43–44

Hierarchical holism: versus liberalism, 365 n. 11, 371 n. 6; pre-Hispanic polities and, 18; secundaria policies and, 28; Spanish colonial tradition and, 365 n. 10, 376 n. 1

Hill, Jane, 310

Hinojosa, Ms. (teacher), 79, 119

History: formation of identity and, 334; in grupos escolares narratives, 97–100; historical-spatial flow in schools, 384–85 n. 5; Latin American societies and awareness of, 13–14; of Mexican secundarias, 20–28, 366 n. 17; Mexican secundarias use of, 67, 72, 318; of San Pablo, 28–30

Holiday celebrations: religious, 72–73; secular, 64, 71–72, 90, 161, 163, 196

Holland, Dorothy, 328, 387 n. 13

Hollingshead, August, 385 n. 8

Household: definition of, 377 n. 2

Household maids, 158

Huaraches: as signal of ethnicity, 175

Humor, 213–16, 232, 380 n. 7

Hurtig, Janise, 334

Ibargüengoitia, Jorge, 145

Identification: adolescence subcultural, 7; of elites with private schools, 166–67, 168; focal students and, 308, 309; group, 312, 316; school, 5, 163–69; subjectivity and, 344; teachers and grupos escolares, 61–64, 123–24

Identity: aspirations and, 326–27, 343; class, 43–45, 167–68, 178–79; class and ethnicity, 328; concept of, 342–43, 344; critique of currents works on, 312–13; cultural media as site of youth, 159–63, 318, 319, 385 n. 7; family and, 150–51, 298–99; female, 298; formation and adolescence, 7, 96–97, 306–11, 313–14, 318; formation sites of, 318 (see also

Family); grupos escolares and, 61–64; historical-cultural shifts and formation of, 334; history and, 334; indigenous cultures and, 147–50, 309–10; male, 298–99; middle class, 42–43, 153, 158; music and, 160–61, 194–95, 196, 210; national, 22, 60–61, 63–64, 137, 310, 320–21, 330–33; place and, 294–95; practices and formation of, 329; religion and, 151–53; reproduction theory and student, 3; resistant, 329; romantic relationships and women's, 328; schooled (see Schooled identity); situated and enduring nested, 188–89; situational identity groups, 192; student subcultures and, 327; todos somos iguales and, 2; uniforms as projection of, 163; vocabulary of, 178–79, 198–99, 214; women and, 328, 338

Ideological state apparatus, 384 n. 3

Ideology: gender, 213–17, 297–98, 387 n. 13; hegemony and, 344–46; meanings of, 345

"Ideology and Ideological State Apparatuses" (Althusser), 384 n. 3

Idioculture, 138

Imagined communities, 330

Immigration: into San Pablo, 45

Independence Day celebrations, 64, 72, 163

Indigenous cultures: attitudes toward, 198–201, 202, 205–6; elites from, 149; huaraches as symbol of, 175; identity and, 147–50, 309–10; indios and, 174, 175, 376 n. 1; language knowledge and, 381–82 n. 2; liberalism and, 376–77 n. 1; linguistic condescension and, 197–98; plazas and, 173–79, 277; population of, 377 n. 1; in San Pablo, 147–50; social symbolism of, 376 n. 1; State and, 30, 331, 332, 376–77 n. 1; students at ESF, 149–50; teachers and, 310; versus urban culture (*see* Rural/urban divide). *See also* Mestización

Mexican State and, 23, 24, 30–31; in San Pablo, 29, 51

Romantic gender relationships. *See* Gender: romantic relationships and

Rorty, Richard, 374 n. 6, 389 n. 32

Rosaldo, Renato, 388 n. 20

Rosita (focal ESF student): on adolescence, 15; on elitism of private schools, 166–67; family background of, 101, 106, 109–11; freedom and father's role, 158–59, 381 n. 13; friendship group of, 220, 225, 226, 229, 315; on grupo solidarity, 125–26, 375 n. 7; postsecondary experiences, 243, 246, 277–83; university studies of, 242

Rouse, Roger, 312–13, 343, 371 n. 6

Rural schools, 21, 31

Rural/urban divide, 147–50, 205–7, 209–13, 227, 379 n. 14

Saénz, Moisés, 21, 24, 30, 366 n. 18

Sahlins, Marshall, 389 n. 29

Salaries: of teachers, 17, 50, 373 n. 18

Salinas de Gortari, Carlos, 236, 237

Sandoval, Etelvina, 76, 370 n. 1, 371 n. 5

San Pablo: class, culture, and economy of, 38–40; demographic structure in, 46; effect of globalization on, 238–41; government of, 29–30; historical background of, 28–30; indigenous cultures in, 147–50; migration from, 45–46, 224, 249–50, 295–96, 316, 317; occupations in, 41, 157, 158, 297, 379 n. 16; place and identity formation, 294–95; political economy of, 40–42; population in, 45–46, 368 n. 10; as power region, 147; religion in, 29, 51; tourism in, 41, 367 n. 3, 368 n. 5; weather in, 372 n. 17

Santos del Real, Annette, 18

Saucedo Ramos, Claudia, 141, 143, 364 n. 2, 376 n. 14

Saúl (ESF student), 184, 185

Sayer, Derek, 331, 332

Schedules, 7, 75, 372–73 n. 18

Schoenhal, Martin, 371 n. 8

Schooled identity: absence of formation of, 316; ambivalence toward, 181–82, 296; challenges to, 179–83; dropping out of school and, 7, 183–85, 209; gender differences in, 183–89; marriage and, 185–87; migration and, 317; otherness and, 173–79, 207; una persona educada and, 169, 334; resistance to, 306–11, 316, 329, 376 n. 15; secundarias and, 169–70, 306–11; social worth and schooling in, 170–73

Schools: attrition factors in, 335–36; difference and, 334, 385 n. 6; historical-spatial flow in, 384–85 n. 5; history of Mexican, 20–28, 366 n. 17; major options and paths in Mexican, 8; primarias, 17, 26, 85, 366 n. 16, 374 n. 5; private (*see* Private schools); public, 164–65; reproduction theory and, 3, 324–30; role in formation of national identity (*see* Nationality and identity, schooling role in formation of); rural, 21, 31; secundarias (*see* Secundarias); as state institution, 332. *See also* Education; Escuela Secundaria Federal (ESF)

Schwartz, Gary, 385 n. 8

Second-year students, 59, 100, 374 n. 3

Secretariat of Public Education, 17, 21, 23, 73

Secundarias: adolescence and creation of, 16–18, 20, 25, 26; age segregation of, 143; characteristics of, 7–8; characteristics of graduates of, 25; class differences between, 47, 165; compulsory schooling at, 17, 28, 364 n. 4; cultural practice patterns of, 305–6; curriculum of, 24, 25, 73–74; drop out rates of, 7, 183–85, 209; educational philosophy and policy

Secundarias *cont.*

of Mexican, 18–20; enrollments in, 27, 33–34, 364 nn. 5 and 6, 366 nn. 19 and 24, 369 nn. 11 and 12, 373 n. 21; first-year students, 55–56, 99–100; goals of, 23–24; as habitus, 303–4; history of Mexican, 20–28, 366 n. 17; identity and (*see* Identity); oppositional subcultures in, 306; origin of idea of, 23; reasons for research on, 7–8; schooled identity and, 169–70, 306–11; second-year students, 59, 100, 374 n. 3; as site of identity formation, 162; socioeconomic mobility and, 26–27; teachers at (*see* Teachers); técnicas, 27, 34, 165; telesecundarias, 211, 367 n. 31; use of history, 67, 72, 318; vocational education and, 17, 25; women students in, 366 n. 24. *See also* Escuela Secundaria Federal (ESF)

Selby, Henry, 377 n. 2

Self-learning, 79–80

Sencillez: concept of, 167–69

Sexuality: cultural center and, 208, 228–31; girls on, 222, 223, 381 n. 12; male friendship groups and, 203–4; sexist wordplay and, 227; teachers on heterosexual romance and, 231, 380 n. 8; women and, 226, 228–31

Shaming, 78–79

Shaw, Thomas, 334

Shore, Bradd, 349

Shweder, Richard, 138

Sierra, Justo, 365 n. 14

Silvia (ESF student), 229

Sindicato Nacional de Trabajadores de Educación (SNTE), 49, 77, 237, 369 n. 13

Singing, 67

Situational identity groups, 192

Slogans, 64

SNTE (Sindicato Nacional de Trabaja-

dores de Educación), 49, 77, 237, 369 n. 13

Social class. *See* Class

Socialist education, 25–26, 29–30, 31, 33

Socialization theory, 336

Social reproduction theory: cultural production and, 37, 318, 326, 339, 348; in education, 2–3, 324–30; methodology for (*see entries under* Levinson, Bradley A.); parents and, 325; Plan for Educational Modernization, 51; studies prior to emergence of, 385 n. 8; teachers and, 325; for unique Mexican case, 6, 307–8; use by Mexican scholars, 334–35; women and, 326

Social sciences: narrative and, 340

Social service requirement, 382 n. 6

Sociedad de Alumnos (Students' Society), 126–28, 190

Sociedad de Padres de Familia (Parents' Association), 52, 71, 378 n. 11

The Society of Individuals (Elias), 323

Socioeconomic status: of ESF students, 42–43, 47–48, 226; secundarias and increase in, 26–27; survey of ESF students, 10

Socorro (focal ESF student), 105, 234, 245, 254–56, 295, 296, 359–60, 382 n. 4

Solana, Mr. (teacher), 36, 37, 68, 69, 110, 119, 124, 234–35, 369 n. 14

Solana Ramírez family, 37

Solidarity, collective: among grupos escolares, 64–65, 122, 123–28, 130, 135–39, 212, 312, 371 n. 7, 375 n. 7; of emerging communities, 161–62; identity-in-, 372 n. 11; national unity and, 374–75 n. 6; parents and grupo, 137; practices inhibiting, 311–12

Sonidos, 160–61

Stambach, Amy, 334

State: formation of, 61, 63–64, 76, 312;

guidelines for education, 73; ideological state apparatus and, 384 n. 3; indigenous cultures and, 30, 331, 332, 376–77 n. 1; as organizational frame, 388 n. 17; role in education, 17, 20–28, 30, 61; Roman Catholic Church and Mexican, 23, 24, 30–31; social movements and, 387 n. 15. *See also* Nationality and identity, schooling role in formation of

Stern, Steve, 349–50

Stinchcombe, Arthur, 385 n. 8

Street, Susan, 365 n. 9, 370 n. 16

Strikes: teacher, 49–50, 51, 52, 233, 369 n. 14, 370 n. 16, 378 n. 10

Structure: concept and implications of, 338–39, 340, 341, 384 n. 5, 389 n. 26. *See also* Agency

Student culture: agency and subjectivity, 342–44; culture and discourse, 346–50; European and U.S. scholarly perspectives on, 333–34; ideology and hegemony, 344–46; influence on school attendance, 336; Mexican scholarly perspectives on, 334–36; self and society, 337–41; subjects' perspectives on, 336–37. *See also* Grupos escolares

Student subcultures: formation of, 2, 306, 327, 383 n. 2

Student teachers (*prefectos*), 67

Subaltern discourse, 43

Subcultures: formation of student, 2, 306, 327, 383 n. 2

Subjectivity: concept and implications of, 147, 338, 341, 343–44

Substantive equality, 129

Surveys: of Escuela Secundaria Federal students, 10, 46–47

Susana (ESF student), 129

Swartz, David, 383 n. 1, 386 n. 9

Symbolic violence: of schooling, 43–44, 145–46, 390 n. 34

Tactic of consumption, 143–44

Talleres: gender and, 88–89; secretarial, 90–91; students and, 374 n. 28

Taylor, Charles, 363 n. 3

Teachers: absenteeism of, 37; on adolescence, 14, 15, 80–81; classroom competition and, 64–65; cultural center and, 193–94, 204; on cultural media, 162; differences between secundaria and primaria, 77; discrimination against students by, 60; echando relajo and, 141, 142, 375 n. 12; on falta de interés, 81–82; female students' response to, 380 n. 9; gender and, 83, 84–86, 380 n. 9; grupos escolares identification and, 61–64, 123–24; on heterosexual romance, 231, 380 n. 8; humor and, 213–14; indigenous cultures and, 310; logic of evaluation use by, 77–79, 134; memorization and formula use by, 79; moral community and, 138; morning lineup and, 239; narratives on grupos escolares, 98–99, 190–91, 205; numbers at ESF, 57; opinions of focal students, 101; on relation between schooling and social worth, 170–71; role in state formation, 61, 63–64, 76; rural, 21; salaries of, 17, 50, 373 n. 18; schedules of, 372–73 n. 18; self-learning and, 79–80; siblings of students and, 373 n. 20; socialist education and, 31; social reproduction theory and, 325; strikes of, 49–50, 51, 52, 233, 369 n. 14, 370 n. 16, 378 n. 10; student, 67; student identification with school and, 164; students on idiosyncrasies of, 68–69, 370 n. 17; teaching practices of, 75–80; training of, 77, 80; on uniforms, 64; unions of, 49–52, 86, 237; values stressed by, 33; year of service, 369–70 n. 15. *See also names of individual teachers*

proper behavior for, 230; percentage of teaching faculty, 85, 373 n. 25; post-primary return on schooling and, 373 n. 24; romantic relationships and identity, 328; sexuality and, 226, 228–31; social reproduction theory and, 326; as students in secundarias, 366 n. 24

Women's rights, 82–83

Woods, Peter, 380 n. 7

Young, Michael, 325

Zapata, Emiliano, 20

Much of chapter 1 was previously published as " 'Una Etapa Siempre Difícil': Concepts of Adolescence and Secondary Education in Mexico," *Comparative Education Review* 43, no. 2 (1998): 129–61. Reprinted by permission of University of Chicago Press. Portions of chapters 3, 4, and 8 were previously published in "Student Culture and the Contradictions of Equality at a Mexican Secondary School," *Anthropology and Education Quarterly* 29, no. 3 (1998): 267–96. Reprinted by permission of the American Anthropological Association. Portions of chapter 6 were previously published as "The Balance of Power: Gender Relations and Women's Action at a Mexican Secondary School," in *Nuevos Paradigmas, Compromisos Renovados: Estudios Cualitativos de la Educación*, ed. Beatriz Calvo, Gabriela Delgado, and Mario Rueda (Ciudad Juárez, México: Universidad Autónoma de Ciudad Juárez, 1999).

BRADLEY A. U. LEVINSON is Assistant Professor in the Department of Educational Leadership and Policy Studies and Adjunct Assistant Professor in the Department of Anthropology at Indiana University.

Library of Congress Cataloging-in-Publication Data
Levinson, Bradley A. U.
We are all equal : student culture
and identity at a Mexican secondary school, 1988–1998 /
Bradley A. U. Levinson.
p. cm.   Includes bibliographical references and index.
ISBN 0-8223-2700-7 (cloth : alk. paper)
ISBN 0-8223-2699-X (pbk. : alk. paper)
1. Educational anthropology—Mexico—Longitudinal studies.
2. Education, Secondary—Social aspects—Mexico—
Longitudinal studies. I. Title.
LB45.L48 2001   306.43—dc21   2001018941